CRYPTOGRAPHY AND NETWORK SECURITY

CRYPTOGRAPHY AND NETWORK SECURITY

Yemi Adeleke
Fatou Ndiaye

Kruger Brentt
Publishers
2026

Kruger Brentt Publishers UK. LTD.
Company Number 9728962

Regd. Office: 68 St Margarets Road, Edgware, Middlesex HA8 9UU

ISBN: 978-1-78715-638-8

For information on all our publications visit our website at http://krugerbrentt.com/

PREFACE

The rapid expansion of digital communication has made information security a foundational requirement across all sectors of society. As data travels through increasingly interconnected networks, protecting it from unauthorized access, tampering, and misuse has become essential for ensuring trust, privacy, and operational stability. Cryptography and network security together form the cornerstone of secure information exchange, enabling confidentiality, integrity, authentication, and resilience in both traditional and emerging technological environments.

Cryptography and Network Security provides a comprehensive and systematic introduction to the principles, algorithms, protocols, and practices that safeguard modern communication systems. The text examines classical and contemporary cryptographic techniques, network security architectures, security protocols, and the threat landscape shaped by evolving cyberattacks. Emerging topics such as post-quantum cryptography, blockchain security, intrusion detection, and zero-trust models are also addressed to reflect current advancements in the field.

The book is structured to serve students, researchers, and professionals in computer science, information technology, and cybersecurity. By combining theoretical underpinnings with practical insights, the text aims to develop a thorough understanding of secure system design, implementation challenges, and best practices essential to protecting digital infrastructures in an increasingly complex cyber environment.

Yemi Adeleke

Fatou Ndiaye

CONTENTS

Chapter-0

Concepts and Notation: An Review

The material in this section is meant as a review. Despite that, many students report that they find this review useful for the rest of the book.

0.1 Logs & Exponents

You probably learned (and then forgot) these identities in middle school or high school:

$$\begin{aligned}(x^a)(x^b) &= x^{a+b}\\ (x^a)^b &= x^{ab}\\ \log_x(ab) &= \log_x a + \log_x b\\ a\log_x b &= \log_x(b^a)\end{aligned}$$

Well, it's time to get reacquainted with them again.

In particular, never ever write $(x^a)(x^b) = x^{ab}$. If you write this, your cryptography instructor will realize that life is too short, immediately resign from teaching, and join a traveling circus. But not before changing your grade in the course to a zero.

0.2 Modular Arithmetic

We write the set of integers as:

$$\mathbb{Z} \stackrel{\text{def}}{=} \{\dots, -2, -1, 0, 1, 2, \dots\}$$

and the set of natural numbers (nonnegative integers) as:

$$\mathbb{N} \stackrel{\text{def}}{=} \{0, 1, 2, \dots\}$$

Note that 0 is considered a natural number.

Definition 0.1 For $x, n \in \mathbb{Z}$, we say that n divides x (or x is a multiple of n), and write $n \mid x$, if there exists an integer k such that $x = kn$.

Remember that the definitions apply to both positive and negative numbers (and to zero). We generally only care about this definition in the case where n is positive, but it is common to consider both positive and negative values of x.

Example 7 divides 84 because we can write $84 = 12 \cdot 7$.

7 divides 0 because we can write $0 = 0 \cdot 7$.

7 divides -77 because we can write $-77 = (-11) \cdot 7$.

-7 divides 42 because we can write $42 = (-6) \cdot (-7)$.

1 divides every integer (so does - 1). The only integer that 0 divides is itself.

Definition 0.2 Let n be a positive integer, and let a be any integer. The expression a $\%n$ (usually read as "a (% operator) **mod**n") represents the remainder after dividing a by n. More formally, $a\%n$ is the unique $r \in \{0, \dots, n-1\}$ such that $n \mid (a-r)$.[1]

Pay special attention to the fact that $a\%n$ is always a nonnegative number, even if a is negative. A good way to remember how this works is:

$$a \text{ is } (\ a\%n\ ) \text{ more than a multiple of } n.$$

Example $21\%7 = 0$ because $21 = 3 \cdot 7 + \underline{0}$.

$20\%7 = 6$ because $20 = 2 \cdot 7 + \underline{6}$.

$-20\%7 = 1$ because $-20 = (-3) \cdot 7 + \underline{1}$. (-20 is one more than a multiple of 7 .)

$-1\%7 = 6$ because $-1 = (-1) \cdot 7 + \underline{6}$.

Unfortunately, some programming languages define % for negative numbers as $(\ -a\ )\ \%\ n = -(a\%n)$, so they would define $-20\%7$ to be $-(20\%7) = -6$. This is madness, and it's about time we stood up to these programming language designers and smashed them over the head with some mathematical truth! For now, if you are using some programming environment to play around with the concepts in the class, be sure to check whether it defines % in the correct way.

Definition 0.3 For positive n, we write $\mathbb{Z}_n \overset{\text{def}}{=} \{0, \dots, n-1\}$ to denote the set of integers modulo n. These $(\mathbb{Z}_n)$ are the possible remainders one obtains by dividing by n^2

Definition 0.4 For positive n, we say that integers a and b are congruent modulo n, and write $a \equiv_n b$, if $(\equiv_n)\ n \mid (a-b)$. An alternative definition is that $a \equiv_n b$ if and only if $a\%n = b\%n$.

You'll be in a better position to succeed in this class if you can understand the (subtle) distinction between $a \equiv_n b$ and $a = b\%n$:

$a \equiv_n b$: In this expression, a and b can be integers of any size, and any sign. The left and right side have a certain relationship modulo n.

$a = b\%n$: This expression says that two integers are equal. The " $=$ " rather than " $\equiv$ " is your clue that the expression refers to equality over the integers. " $b\%n$ " on the right-hand side is an operation performed on two integers that returns an integer result. The result of $b\%n$ is an integer in the range $\{0, \ldots, n-1\}$.

Example " $99 \equiv_{10} 19$ " is true. Applying the definition, you can see that 10 divides $99 - 19$.

On the other hand, " $99 = 19\%10$ " is false. The right-hand side evaluates to the integer 9, but 99 and 9 are different integers.

In short, expressions like $a \equiv_n b$ make sense for any a, b (including negative!), but expressions like $a = b\%n$ make sense only if $a \in \mathbb{Z}_n$.

Most other textbooks will use notation " $a \equiv b(\text{mod} n)$ " instead of " $a \equiv_n b$." I dislike this notation because " $(\text{mod} n)$ " is easily mistaken for an operation or action that only affects the right-hand side, when in reality it is like an adverb that modifies the entire expression $a \equiv b$. Even though $\equiv_n$ is a bit weird, I think the weirdness is worth it.

If $d \mid x$ and $d \mid y$, then d is a common divisor of x and y. The largest possible such d is called the greatest common divisor (GCD), denoted $\gcd(x, y)$. If $\gcd(x, y) = 1$, then we say that x and y are relatively prime. The oldest "algorithm" is the recursive process that Euclid described for computing GCDs (ca. 300 bce):

$$
\begin{aligned}
&\text{GCD}(x, y)\text{:// Euclid's algorithm}\\
&\text{if } y = 0 \text{ then return } x\\
&\text{else return GCD}(y, x\%y)
\end{aligned}
$$

Tips & Tricks

You may often be faced with some complicated expression and asked to find the value of that expression mod$n$. This usually means: find the unique value in $\mathbb{Z}_n$ that is congruent to the result. The straightforward way to do this is to first compute the result over the integers, and then reduce the answer mod$n$ (i.e., with the $\%n$ operator).

While this approach gives the correct answer (and is a good anchor for your understanding), it's usually advisable to simplify intermediate values mod n. Doing so will result in the same answer, but will usually be easier or faster to compute:

Example We can evaluate the expression $6 \cdot 7 \cdot 8 \cdot 9 \cdot 10 \% 11$ without ever calculating that product over the integers, by using the following reasoning:

$$\begin{aligned} 6 \cdot 7 \cdot 8 \cdot 9 \cdot 10 &= (42) \cdot 8 \cdot 9 \cdot 10 \\ &\equiv_{11} 9 \cdot 8 \cdot 9 \cdot 10 \\ &= (72) \cdot 9 \cdot 10 \\ &\equiv_{11} 6 \cdot 9 \cdot 10 \\ &= (54) \cdot 10 \\ &\equiv_{11} 10 \cdot 10 \\ &= 100 \\ &\equiv_{11} 1 \end{aligned}$$

In the steps that only work mod 11, we write " $\equiv_{11}$ ". We can write " $=$ " when the step holds over the integers, although it wouldn't be wrong to write " $\equiv_{11}$ " in those cases too. If two expressions represent the same integer, then they surely represent values that are congruent mod11.

My advice is to simplify intermediate values mod$n$, but "simplify" doesn't always mean "reduce mod$n$ with the $\%n$ operation." Sometimes an expression can by "simplified" by substituting a value with something congruent, but not in the range $\{0, \dots, n-1\}$:

Example I can compute $7^{500} \% 8$ in my head, by noticing that $7 \equiv_8 -1$ and simplifying thusly:

$$7^{500} \equiv_8 (-1)^{500} = 1$$

Similarly, I can compute $89^2 \% 99$ in my head, although I have not memorized the integer 89^2. All I need to do is notice that $89 \equiv_{99} -10$ and compute this way:

$$89^2 \equiv_{99} (-10)^2 = 100 \equiv_{99} 1$$

You can compute either of these examples the "hard way" to verify that these shortcuts lead to the correct answer.

Since addition, subtraction, and multiplication are defined over the integers (i.e., adding/subtracting/multiplying integers always results in an integer), these kinds of tricks can be helpful.

On the other hand, dividing integers doesn't always result in an integer. Does it make sense to use division when working mod$n$, where the result always has to lie in $\mathbb{Z}_n$? We will answer this question later in the book.

0.3 Strings

We write $\{0,1\}^n$ to denote the set of n-bit binary strings, and $\{0,1\}^*$ to denote the set of all (finite-length) binary strings. When x is a string of bits, we write $|x|$ to denote the length (in bits) of that string, and we write $\bar{x}$ to denote the result of flipping every bit in x. When it's clear from context that we're talking about strings instead of numbers, we write 0^n and 1^n to denote strings of n zeroes and n ones, respectively (rather than the result of raising the integers 0 or 1 to the n power). As you might have noticed, I also try to use a different font and color for characters (including bits, anything that could be used to build a string through concatenation) vs. integers.

Definition 0.5 When x and y are strings of the same length, we write $x \oplus y$ to denote the bitwise exclusive-or ($\oplus$, XOR) (XOR) of the two strings. The expression $x \oplus y$ is generally not defined when the strings are different lengths, but in rare occasions it is useful to consider the shorter string being padded with 0s. When that's the case, we must have an explicit convention about whether the shorter string is padded with leading 0s or trailing 0s.

For example, $0011 \oplus 0101 = 0110$. The following facts about the xor operation are frequently useful:

$x \oplus x = 000\cdots$	XOR'ing a string with itself results in zeroes.
$x \oplus 000\cdots = x$	XOR'ing with zeroes has no effect.
$x \oplus 111\cdots = \bar{x}$	XOR'ing with ones flips every bit.
$x \oplus y = y \oplus x$	XOR is symmetric.
$(x \oplus y) \oplus z = x \oplus (y \oplus z)$	XOR is associative.

See if you can use these properties to derive the very useful fact below:

$$a = b \oplus c \Leftrightarrow b = a \oplus c \Leftrightarrow c = a \oplus b.$$

There are a few ways to think about xor that may help you in this class:

- Bit-flipping: Note that xor'ing a bit with 0 has no effect, while xor'ing with 1 flips that bit. You can think of $x \oplus y$ as: "starting with x, flip the bits at all the positions where y has a 1 ." So if y is all 1 's, then $x \oplus y$ gives the bitwise-complement of x. If $y = 1010\cdots$ then $x \oplus y$ means "(the result of) flipping every other bit in x."

- Many concepts in this course can be understood in terms of bit-flipping. For example, we might ask "what happens when I flip the first bit of x and send it into the algorithm?" This kind of question could also be phrased as "what happens when I send $x \oplus 1000 \cdots$ into the algorithm?" Usually there is nothing special about flipping just the first bit of a string, so it will often be quite reasonable to generalize the question as "what happens when I send $x \oplus y$ into the algorithm, for an arbitrary (not-all-zeroes) string y ?"

- Addition mod-2: xor is just addition mod2 in every bit. This way of thinking about xor helps to explain why "algebraic" things like $(x \oplus y) \oplus z = x \oplus (y \oplus z)$ are true. They are true for addition, so they are true for xor.

- This also might help you remember why $x \oplus x$ is all zeroes. If instead of xor we used addition, we would surely write $x + x = 2x$. Since $2 \equiv_2 0$, we get that $2x$ is congruent to $0x = 0$.

Definition 0.6 We write $x \| y$ to denote the result of concatenating x and y. (II, concatenation)

0.4 Functions

Let X and Y be finite sets. A function $f: X \rightarrow Y$ is:

injective (1-to-1) if it maps distinct inputs to distinct outputs. Formally: $x \neq x' \Rightarrow f(x) \neq f(x')$. If there is an injective function from X to Y, then we must have $|Y| \geqslant |X|$.

surjective (onto) if every element in Y is a possible output of f. Formally: for all $y \in Y$ there exists an $x \in X$ with $f(x) = y$. If there is a surjective function from X to Y, then we must have $|Y| \leqslant |X|$.

bijective (1 -to- 1 correspondence) if f is both injective and surjective. If there is a bijective function from X to Y, then we must have $|X| = |Y|$.

0.5 Probability

Definition 0.7 A (discrete) probability distribution over a set X of outcomes is usually written as a (Distribution) function " Pr " that associates each outcome $x \in X$ with a probability $\Pr[x]$. We often say that the distribution assigns probability $\Pr[x]$ to outcome x.

For each outcome $x \in X$, the probability distribution must satisfy the condition $0 \leqslant \Pr[x] \leqslant 1$. Additionally, the sum of all probabilities $\sum_{x \in X} \Pr[x]$ must equal 1.

Definition 0.8 A special distribution is the uniform distribution over a finite set X, in which every $x \in X$ (Uniform) is assigned probability $\Pr[x] = 1/|X|$.

We also extend the notation Pr to events, which are collections of outcomes. If you want to be formal, an event A is any subset of the possible outcomes, and its probability is defined to be $\Pr[A] = \sum_{x \in A} \Pr[x]$. We always simplify the notation slightly, so instead of writing $\Pr[\{x \mid x$ satisfies some condition $\}]$, we write Pr [condition].

Example A 6-sided die has faces numbered $\{1,2, \ldots, 6\}$. Tossing the die (at least for a mathematician) induces a uniform distribution over the choice of face. Then Pr[3 is rolled] = 1/6, and Pr[an odd number is rolled] = 1/2 and Pr[a prime is rolled] = 1/2.

Tips & Tricks

Knowing one of the probabilities $\Pr[A]$ and $\Pr[\neg A]$ (which is "the probability that A doesn't happen") tells you exactly what the other probability is, via the relationship

$$\Pr[A] = 1 - \Pr[\neg A].$$

This is one of the most basic facts about probability, but it can be surprisingly useful since one of $\Pr[A]$ and $\Pr[\neg A]$ is often much easier to calculate than the other. If you get stuck trying to come up with an expression for $\Pr[A]$, try working out an expression for $\Pr[\neg A]$ instead.

Example I roll a six-sided die, six times. What is the probability that there is some repeated value? Let's think about all the ways of getting a repeated value. Well, two of the rolls could be 1 , or three of rolls could be 1 , or all of them could be 1 , two of them could be 1 and the rest could be 2, etc. Oh no, am I double-counting repeated $2s$ and repeated 1s? Uhh. . .

An easier way to attack the problem is to realize that the probability we care about is actually $1 - \Pr[$ all 6 rolls are distinct$]$. This complementary event (all 6 rolls distinct) happens exactly when the sequence of dice rolls spell out a permutation of $\{1, \ldots, 6\}$. There are $6! = 720$ such permutations, out of $6^6 = 46656$ total possible outcomes. Hence, the answer to the question is

$$1 - \frac{6!}{6^6} = 1 - \frac{720}{46656} = \frac{45936}{46656} \approx 0.9846$$

Another trick is one I like to call setting breakpoints on the universe. Imagine stopping the universe at a point where some random choices have happened, and others have not yet happened. This is best illustrated by example:

Example *A* classic question asks: when rolling two 6 -sided dice what is the probability that the dice match? Here is a standard (and totally correct way) to answer the question:

When rolling two 6 -sided dice, there are $6^2 = 36$ total outcomes (a pair of numbers), so each has probability $1/36$ under a uniform distribution. There are 6 outcomes that make the dice match: both dice 1 , both dice 2 , both dice 3, and so on. Therefore, the probability of rolling matching dice is $6/36 = 1/6$.

A different way to arrive at the answer goes like this:

> *Imagine I roll the dice one after another, and I pause the universe (set a breakpoint) after rolling the first die but before rolling the second one. The universe has already decided the result of the first die, so let's call that value d. The dice will match only if the second roll comes up d. Rolling d on the second die (indeed, rolling any particular value) happens with probability* $1/6$.

This technique of setting breakpoints is simple but powerful and frequently useful. Some other closely related tricks are: (1) postponing a random choice until the last possible moment, just before its result is used for the first time, and (2) switching the relative order of independent random choices.

Precise Terminology

It is tempting in this course to say things like " x is a random string." But a statement like this is sloppy on several accounts.

First, is 42 a random number? Is "heads" a random coin? What is even being asked by these questions? Being "random" is not a property of an outcome (like a number or a side of a coin) but a property of the process that generates an outcome. [3] Instead of saying " x is a random string," it's much more precise to say " x was chosen randomly."

Second, usually when we use the word "random," we don't mean any old probability distribution. We usually mean to refer to the uniform distribution. Instead of saying " x was chosen randomly," it's much more precise to say " x was chosen uniformly" (assuming that really is what you mean).

Every cryptographer I know (yes, even your dear author) says things like " is a random string" all the time to mean " x was chosen uniformly [from some set of strings]." Usually the meaning is clear from context, at least to the other cryptographers in the room. But all of us could benefit by having better habits about this sloppy language. Students especially will benefit by internalizing the fact that randomness is a property of the process, not of the individual outcome.

0.6 Notation in Pseudocode

We'll often describe algorithms/processes using pseudocode. In doing so, we will use several different operators whose meanings might be easily confused:

$\leftarrow$ When $\mathcal{D}$ is a probability distribution, we write " $x \leftarrow \mathcal{D}$ " to mean "sample x according to the distribution $\mathcal{D}$."

If $\mathcal{A}$ is an algorithm that takes input and also makes some internal random choices, then it is natural to think of its output $\mathcal{A}(y)$ as a distribution - possibly a different distribution for each input y. Then we write " $x \leftarrow \mathcal{A}(y)$ " to mean the natural thing: "run $\mathcal{A}$ on input y and assign the output to x."

We overload the "$\leftarrow$" notation slightly, writing " $x \leftarrow X$ " when X is a finite set to mean that x is sampled from the uniform distribution over X.

$:=$ We write $x := y$ for assignments to variables: "take the value of expression y and assign it to variable x."

$\stackrel{?}{=}$ We write comparisons as $\stackrel{?}{=}$ (analogous to "==" in your favorite programming language). So $x \stackrel{?}{=} y$ doesn't modify x (or y), but rather it is an expression which returns true if x and y are equal.

You will often see this notation in the conditional part of an if-statement, but also in return statements as well. The following two snippets are equivalent:

return $x \stackrel{?}{=} y$	$\Leftrightarrow$	if $x \stackrel{?}{=} y$:
		  return `true`
		else:
		  return `false`

In a similar way, we write $x \stackrel{?}{\in} S$ as an expression that evaluates to true if x is in the set S.

Subroutine conventions

We'll use mathematical notation to define the types of subroutine arguments:

$$\frac{\text{FOO } (x \in \{0,1\}^*):}{\cdots} \quad \text{means "void foo(string } x\text{)}\{\ldots\}\text{"}$$

0.7 Asymptotics (Big-O)

Let $f : \mathbb{N} \to \mathbb{N}$ be a function. We characterize the asymptotic growth of f in the following ways:

$$f(n) \text{ is } O(g(n)) \overset{\text{def}}{\Leftrightarrow} \lim_{n\to\infty} \frac{f(n)}{g(n)} < \infty$$
$$\Leftrightarrow \exists c > 0\text{: for all but finitely many } n\text{: } f(n) < c \cdot g(n)$$
$$f(n) \text{ is } \Omega(g(n)) \overset{\text{def}}{\Leftrightarrow} \lim_{n\to\infty} \frac{f(n)}{g(n)} > 0$$
$$\Leftrightarrow \exists c > 0\text{: for all but finitely many } n\text{: } f(n) > c \cdot g(n)$$
$$f(n) \text{ is } \Theta(g(n)) \overset{\text{def}}{\Leftrightarrow} f(n) \text{ is } O(g(n)) \text{ and } f(n) \text{ is } \Omega(g(n))$$
$$\Leftrightarrow 0 < \lim_{n\to\infty} \frac{f(n)}{g(n)} < \infty$$
$$\Leftrightarrow \exists c_1, c_2 > 0\text{: for all but finitely many } n\text{:}$$
$$c_1 \cdot g(n) < f(n) < c_2 \cdot g(n)$$

Exercises

0.1 Rewrite each of these expressions as something of the form 2^x.

(a) $(2^n)^n =??$

(b) $2^n + 2^n = ??$

(c) $(2^n)(2^n) = ??$

(d) $(2^n)/2 =??$

(e) $\sqrt{2^n} = ??$

(f) $(2^n)^2 = ??$

0.2. (a) What is $0 + 1 + 2 + \cdots + (n-2) + (n-1)\%n$, when n is an odd integer? Prove your answer!

(b) What is $0 + 1 + 2 + \cdots + (n-2) + (n-1) \% n$, when n is even? Prove your answer!

0.3 . What is $(-99) \% 10$?

0.4. Without using a calculator, what are the last two digits of 357998^6 ?

0.5 . Without using a calculator, what is $1000! \% 427$? (That's not me being excited about the number one thousand, it's one thousand factorial!)

0.6. Which values $x \in \mathbb{Z}_{11}$ satisfy $x^2 \equiv_{11} 5$? Which satisfy $x^2 \equiv_{11} 6$?

0.7. What is the result of xor'ing every n bit string? For example, the expression below is the xor of every 5-bit string:

$$00000 \oplus 00001 \oplus 00010 \oplus 00011 \oplus \cdots \oplus 11110 \oplus 11111$$

Give a convincing justification of your answer.

0.8. Consider rolling several d-sided dice, where the sides are labeled $\{0, \ldots, d-1\}$.

(a) When rolling two of these dice, what is the probability of rolling snake-eyes (a pair of 1 s) ?

(b) When rolling two of these dice, what is the probability that they don't match?

(c) When rolling three of these dice, what is the probability that they all match?

(d) When rolling three of these dice, what is the probability that they don't all match (including the case where two match)?

(e) When rolling three of these dice, what is the probability that at least two of them match (including the case where all three match)?

(f) When rolling three of these dice, what is the probability of seeing at least one 0 ?

0.9 When rolling two 6 -sided dice, there is some probability of rolling snake-eyes (two 1 s). You determined this probability in the previous problem. In some game, I roll both dice each time it is my turn. What is the smallest value t such that:

$$\Pr[I \text{ have rolled snake-eyes in at least one of my first } t \text{ turns }] \geqslant 0.5?$$

In other words, how many turns until my probability of getting snake-eyes exceeds 50% ?

Chapter-1

One-Time Pad & Kerckhoffs' Principle

You can't learn about cryptography without meeting Alice, Bob, and Eve. This chapter is about the classic problem of private communication, in which Alice has a message that she wants to convey to Bob, while also keeping the contents of the message hidden from an eavesdropper [1] Eve. You'll soon learn that there is more to cryptography than just private communication, but it is the logical place to start.

1.1 What Is [Not] Cryptography?

> *"To define is to limit."*
>
> *-Oscar Wilde*

Cryptography is not a magic spell that solves all security problems. Cryptography can provide solutions to cleanly defined problems that often abstract away important but messy real-world concerns. Cryptography can give guarantees about what happens in the presence of certain well-defined classes of attacks. These guarantees may not apply if real-world attackers "don't follow the rules" of a cryptographic security model.

Always keep this in mind as we define (i.e., limit) the problems that we solve in this course.

Encryption Basics & Terminology

Let's begin to formalize our scenario involving Alice, Bob, and Eve. Alice has a message m that she wants to send (privately) to Bob. We call m the plaintext. We assume she will somehow transform that plaintext into a value c (called the ciphertext) that she will actually send to Bob. The process of transforming m into c is called encryption, and we will use Enc to refer to the encryption algorithm. When Bob receives c, he runs a corresponding decryption algorithm Dec to recover the original plaintext m.

We assume that the ciphertext may be observed by the eavesdropper Eve, so the (informal) goal is for the ciphertext to be meaningful to Bob but meaningless to Eve.

Secrets & Kerckhoffs' Principle

Something important is missing from this picture. If we want Bob to be able to decrypt c, but Eve to not be able to decrypt c, then Bob must have some information that Eve doesn't have (do you see why?). Something has to be kept secret from Eve.

You might suggest to make the details of the Enc and Dec algorithms secret. This is how cryptography was done throughout most of the last 2000 years, but it has major drawbacks. If the attacker does eventually learn the details of Enc and Dec, then the only way to recover security is to invent new algorithms. If you have a system with many users, then the only way to prevent everyone from reading everyone else's messages is to invent new algorithms for each pair of users. Inventing even one good encryption method is already hard enough!

The first person to articulate this problem was Auguste Kerckhoffs. In 1883 he formulated a set of cryptographic design principles. Item #2 on his list is now known as Kerckhoffs' principle:

Kerckhoffs' Principle:
"Il faut qu'il n'exige pas le secret, et qu'il puisse sans inconvénient tomber entre les mains de l'ennemi."

Literal translation: [The method] must not be required to be secret, and it must be able to fall into the enemy's hands without causing inconvenience.

Bottom line: Design your system to be secure even if the attacker has complete knowledge of all its algorithms.

If the algorithms themselves are not secret, then there must be some other secret information in the system. That information is called the (secret) key. The key is just an extra piece of information given to both the Enc and Dec algorithms. Another way to interpret Kerckhoffs' principle is that all of the security of the system should be concentrated in the secrecy of the key, not the secrecy of the algorithms. If a secret key gets compromised, you only need to choose a new one, not reinvent an entirely new encryption algorithm. Multiple users can all safely use the same encryption algorithm but with independently chosen secret keys.

The process of choosing a secret key is called key generation, and we write KeyGen to refer to the (randomized) key generation algorithm. We call the collection of three algorithms (Enc, Dec, KeyGen) an encryption scheme. Remember that Kerckhoffs' principle says that we should assume that an attacker knows the details of the KeyGen algorithm. But also remember that knowing the details (i.e., source code) of a randomized algorithm doesn't mean you know the specific output it gave when the algorithm was executed.

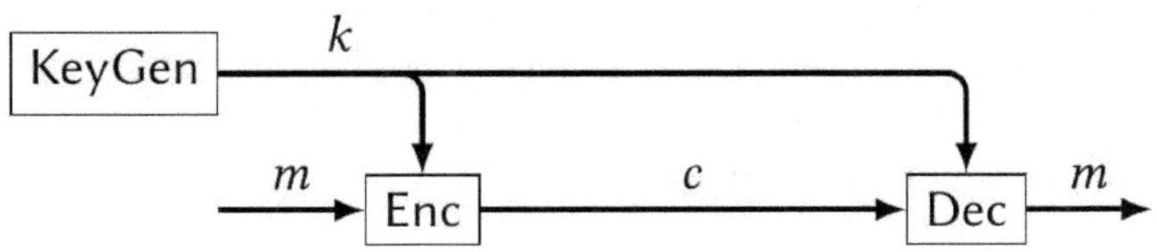

Excuses, Excuses

Let's practice some humility. Here is just a partial list of issues that are clearly important for the problem of private communication, but which are not addressed by our definition of the problem.

- We are not trying to hide the fact that Alice is sending something to Bob, we only want to hide the contents of that message. Hiding the existence of a communication channel is called steganography.
- We won't consider the question of how c reliably gets from Alice to Bob. We'll just take this issue for granted.
- For now, we are assuming that Eve just passively observes the communication between Alice & Bob. We aren't considering an attacker that tampers with c (causing Bob to receive and decrypt a different value), although we will consider such attacks later in the book.
- We won't discuss how Alice and Bob actually obtain a common secret key in the real world. This problem (known as key distribution) is clearly incredibly important, and we will discuss some clever approaches to it much later in the book.
- In my defense, the problem we are solving is already rather non-trivial: once two users have established a shared secret key, how can they use that key to communicate privately?
- We won't discuss how Alice and Bob keep their key secret, even after they have established it. One of my favorite descriptions of cryptography is due to Lea Kissner (former principal security engineer at Google): "cryptography is a tool for turning lots of different problems into key management problems."
- Throughout this course we simply assume that the users have the ability to uniformly sample random strings. Indeed, without randomness there is no cryptography. In the real world, obtaining uniformly random bits from

deterministic computers is extremely non-trivial. John von Neumann famously said, "Any one who considers arithmetical methods of producing random digits is, of course, in a state of sin." Again, even when we take uniform randomness for granted, we still face the non-trivial question of how to use that randomness for private communication (and other applications), and also how to use only a manageable amount of randomness.

Not Cryptography

People use many techniques to try to hide information, but many are "non-cryptographic" since they don't follow Kerckhoffs' principle:

- Encoding/decoding methods like base64...
- joy of cryptography ↔ b25seSBuZXJkcyB3aWxsIHJLYWQgdGhpcw==
- . . . are useful for incorporating arbitrary binary data into a structured file format that supports limited kinds of characters. But since base64 encoding/decoding involves no secret information, it adds nothing in terms of security.
- Sometimes the simplest way to describe an encryption scheme is with operations on binary strings (i.e., 0s and 1s) data. As we will see, one-time pad is defined in terms of plaintexts represented as strings of bits. (Future schemes will require inputs to be represented as a bitstring of a specific length, or as an element of $\mathbb{Z}_n$, etc.)

In order to make sense of some algorithms in this course, it may be necessary to think about data being converted into binary representation. Just like with base64, representing things in binary has no effect on security since it does not involve any secret information. Writing something in binary is not a security measure!

1.2 Specifics of One-Time Pad

People have been trying to send secret messages for roughly 2000 years, but there are really only 2 useful ideas from before 1900 that have any relevance to modern cryptography. The first idea is Kerckhoffs' principle, which you have already seen. The other idea is one-time pad (OTP), which illustrates several important concepts, and can even still be found hiding deep inside many modern encryption schemes.

One-time pad is sometimes called "Vernam's cipher" after Gilbert Vernam, a telegraph engineer who patented the scheme in 1919. However, an earlier description of one-time pad was rather recently discovered in an 1882 text by Frank Miller on telegraph encryption. [2]

In most of this book, secret keys will be strings of bits. We generally use the variable λ to refer to the length (# of bits) of the secret key in a scheme, so that keys are elements of the set $\{0,1\}^\lambda$. In the case of one-time pad, the choice of λ doesn't affect security ($\lambda = 10$ is "just as secure" as $\lambda = 1000$); however, the length of the keys and plaintexts must be compatible. In future chapters, increasing λ has the effect of making the scheme harder to break. For that reason, λ is often called the security parameter of the scheme.

In one-time pad, not only are the keys λ-bit strings, but plaintexts and ciphertexts are too. You should consider this to be just a simple coincidence, because we will soon encounter schemes in which keys, plaintexts, and ciphertexts are strings of different sizes.

The specific KeyGen, Enc, and Dec algorithms for one-time pad are given below:

Construction 1.1

(One-time pad)

KeyGen:	$\underline{\text{Enc}(k, m \in \{0,1\}^\lambda)}$:	$\underline{\text{Dec}(k, c \in \{0,1\}^\lambda)}$:
$k \leftarrow \{0,1\}^\lambda$	return $k \oplus m$	return $k \oplus c$
return k		

Recall that " $k \leftarrow \{0,1\}^\lambda$ " means to sample k uniformly from the set of λ-bit strings. This uniform choice of key is the only randomness in all of the one-time pad algorithms. As we will see, all of its security stems from this choice of using the uniform distribution; keys that are chosen differently do not provide equivalent security.

Example Encrypting the following 20-bit plaintext m under the 20-bit key k using OTP results in the ciphertext c below:

$$\begin{array}{rll} & 11101111101111100011 & (m) \\ \oplus & 00011001110000111101 & (k) \\ \hline & 11110110011111011110 & (c = \text{Enc}(k, m)) \end{array}$$

Decrypting the following ciphertext c using the key k results in the plaintext m below:

$$\begin{array}{rll} & \texttt{00001001011110010000} & (c) \\ \oplus & \texttt{10010011101011100010} & (k) \\ \hline & \texttt{10011010110101110010} & (m = \text{Dec}(k, c)) \end{array}$$

Note that Enc and Dec are essentially the same algorithm (return the xor of the two arguments). This results in some small level of convenience and symmetry when implementing one-time pad, but it is more of a coincidence than something truly fundamental about encryption (see Exercises 1.12 & 2.5). Later on you'll see encryption schemes whose encryption & decryption algorithms look very different.

Correctness

The first property of one-time pad that we should confirm is that the receiver does indeed recover the intended plaintext when decrypting the ciphertext. Without this property, the thought of using one-time pad for communication seems silly. Written mathematically:

Claim 1.2 For all $k, m \in \{0,1\}^\lambda$, it is true that $\text{Dec}(k, \text{Enc}(k, m)) = m$.

Proof This follows by substituting the definitions of OTP Enc and Dec, then applying the properties of xor listed in Chapter 0.3. For all $k, m \in \{0,1\}^\lambda$, we have:

$$\begin{aligned} \text{Dec}(k, \text{Enc}(k, m)) &= \text{Dec}(k, k \oplus m) \\ &= k \oplus (k \oplus m) \\ &= (k \oplus k) \oplus m \\ &= 0^\lambda \oplus m \\ &= m \end{aligned}$$

Example Encrypting the following plaintext m under the key k results in ciphertext c, as follows:

$$\begin{array}{rll} & \texttt{00110100110110001111} & (m) \\ \oplus & \texttt{11101010011010001101} & (k) \\ \hline & \texttt{11011110101100000010} & (c) \end{array}$$

Decrypting c using the same key k results in the original m :

$$\begin{array}{rll} & \texttt{11011110101100000010} & (c) \\ \oplus & \texttt{11101010011010001101} & (k) \\ \hline & \texttt{00110100110110001111} & (m) \end{array}$$

Security

Suppose Alice and Bob are using one-time pad but are concerned that an attacker sees their ciphertext. They can't presume what an attacker will do after seeing the ciphertext. But they would like to say something like, "because of the specific way the ciphertext was generated, it doesn't reveal any information about the plaintext to the attacker, no matter what the attacker does with the ciphertext."

We must first precisely specify how the ciphertext is generated. The Enc algorithm already describes the process, but it is written from the point of view of Alice and Bob. When talking about security, we have to think about what Alice and Bob do, but from the eavesdropper's point of view! From Eve's point of view, Alice uses a key that was chosen in a specific way (uniformly at random), she encrypts a plaintext with that key using OTP, and finally reveals only the resulting ciphertext (and not the key) to Eve.

More formally, from Eve's perspective, seeing a ciphertext corresponds to receiving an output from the following algorithm:

$$\begin{array}{l} \underline{\text{EAVESDROP}(m \in \{0,1\}^\lambda):} \\ \qquad k \leftarrow \{0,1\}^\lambda \\ c := k \oplus m \\ \text{return } c \end{array}$$

It's crucial that you appreciate what this eavesdrop algorithm represents. It is meant to describe not what the attacker does, but rather the process (carried out by Alice and Bob!) that produces what the attacker sees. We always treat the attacker as some (unspecified) process that receives output from this eavesdrop algorithm. Our goal is to say something like "the output of eavesdrop doesn't reveal the input m."

EAVESDROP is a randomized algorithm - remember that " $k \leftarrow \{0,1\}^\lambda$ " means to sample k from the uniform distribution on λ-bit strings. If you call eavesdrop several times, even on the same input, you are likely to get different outputs. Instead of thinking of "eavesdrop(m)" as a single string, you should think of it as a probability distribution over strings. Each time you call eavesdrop (m), you see a sample from that distribution.

Example: Let's take $\lambda = 3$ and work out by hand the distributions EAVESDROP(010) and EAVESDROP(111). In each case eavesdrop chooses a value of k uniformly in $\{0,1\}^3$ - each of the possible values with probability 1/8. For each possible choice of k, we can compute what the output of eavesdrop (c) will be:

EAVESDROP(010):

Pr	*k*	*output* $c = k \oplus 010$
1/8	000	010
1/8	001	011
1/8	010	000
1/8	011	001
1/8	100	110
1/8	101	111
1/8	110	100
1/8	111	101

EAVESDROP(111):

Pr	*k*	*output* $c = k \oplus 111$
1/8	000	111
1/8	001	110
1/8	010	101
1/8	011	100
1/8	100	011
1/8	101	010
1/8	110	001
1/8	111	000

So the distribution eavesdrop(010) assigns probabilty 1/8 to 010, probability 1/8 to 011, and so on.

In this example, notice how every string in $\{0,1\}^3$ appears exactly once in the c column of eavesdrop(010). This means that eavesdrop assigns probability 1/8 to every string in $\{0,1\}^3$, which is just another way of saying that the distribution is the uniform distribution on $\{0,1\}^3$. The same can be said about the distribution eavesdrop(111), too. Both distributions are just the uniform distribution in disguise!

There is nothing special about 010 or 111 in these examples. For any λ and any $m \in \{0,1\}^\lambda$, the distribution eavesdrop(m) is the uniform distribution over $\{0,1\}^\lambda$.

Claim 1.3: For every $m \in \{0,1\}^\lambda$, the distribution eavesdrop(m) is the uniform distribution on $\{0,1\}^\lambda$. Hence, for all $m, m' \in \{0,1\}^\lambda$, the distributions eavesdrop (m) and eavesdrop (m') are identical.

Proof: Arbitrarily fix $m, c \in \{0,1\}^\lambda$. We will calculate the probability that eavesdrop(m) produces output c. That event happens only when

$$c = k \oplus m \Leftrightarrow k = m \oplus c.$$

The equivalence follows from the properties of xor given in Section 0.3. That is,

$$\Pr[\text{EAVESDROP}(m) = c] = \Pr[k = m \oplus c]$$

where the probability is over uniform choice of $k \leftarrow \{0,1\}^\lambda$.

We are considering a specific choice for m and c, so there is only one value of k that makes $k = m \oplus c$ true (causes m to encrypt to c), and that value is exactly $m \oplus c$. Since k is chosen uniformly from $\{0,1\}^\lambda$, the probability of choosing the particular value $k = m \oplus c$ is $1/2^\lambda$.

In summary, for every m and c, the probability that eavesdrop (m) outputs c is exactly $1/2^\lambda$. This means that the output of eavesdrop(m), for any m, follows the uniform distribution.

> *One way to interpret this statement of security in more down-to-earth terms:*
>
> *If an attacker sees a single ciphertext, encrypted with one-time pad, where the key is chosen uniformly and kept secret from the attacker, then the ciphertext appears uniformly distributed.*

Why is this significant? Taking the eavesdropper's point of view, suppose someone chooses a plaintext m and you get to see the resulting ciphertext - a sample from the distribution eavesdrop(m). But this is a distribution that you can sample from yourself, even if you don't know m ! You could have chosen a totally different m' and run eavesdrop(m') in your imagination, and this would have produced the same distribution as eavesdrop(m). The "real" ciphertext that you see doesn't carry any information about m if it is possible to sample from the same distribution without even knowing m !

Discussion

- **Isn't there a paradox?** Claim 1.2 says that c can always be decrypted to get m, but Claim 1.3 says that c contains no information about m ! The answer to this riddle is that Claim 1.2 talks about what can be done with knowledge of the key k (Alice & Bob's perspective). Claim 1.3 talks about the output distribution of the eavesdrop algorithm, which doesn't include k (Eve's perspective). In short, if you know k, then you can decrypt c to obtain m; if you don't know k, then c carries no information about m (in fact, it looks uniformly distributed). This is because m, c, k are all correlated in a delicate way. [3]

- **Isn't there another paradox?** Claim 1.3 says that the output of eavesdrop(m) doesn't depend on m, but we can see the eavesdrop algorithm literally using its argument m right there in the last line! The answer to this riddle is perhaps best illustrated by the previous illustrations of the eavesdrop(010) and eavesdrop(111) distributions. The two tables of values are indeed different (so the choice of $m \in \{010,111\}$ clearly has some effect), but they represent the same probability distribution (since order doesn't matter). Claim 1.3 considers only the resulting probability distribution.

- You probably think about security in terms of a concrete "goal" for the attacker: recover the key, recover the plaintext, etc. Claim 1.3 doesn't really refer to attackers in that way, and it certainly doesn't specify a goal. Rather, we are thinking about security by comparing to some hypothetical "ideal" world. I would be satisfied if the attacker sees only a source of uniform bits, because in this hypothetical world there are no keys and no plaintexts to recover! Claim 1.3 says that when we actually use OTP, it looks just like this hypothetical world, from the attacker's point of view. If we imagine any "goal" at all for the attacker in this kind of reasoning, it's to detect that ciphertexts don't follow a uniform distribution. By showing that the attacker can't even achieve this modest goal, it shows that the attacker couldn't possibly achieve other, more natural, goals like key recovery and plaintext recovery.

Limitations

One-time pad is incredibly limited in practice. Most notably:

- Its keys are as long as the plaintexts they encrypt. This is basically unavoidable (see Exercise 2.11) and leads to a kind of chicken-and-egg dilemma in practice: If two users want to privately convey a λ-bit message, they first need to privately agree on a λ-bit string.
- A key can be used to encrypt only one plaintext (hence, "one-time" pad); see Exercise 1.6. Indeed, we can see that the eavesdrop subroutine in Claim 1.3 provides no way for a caller to guarantee that two plaintexts are encrypted with the same key, so it is not clear how to use Claim 1.3 to argue about what happens in one-time pad when keys are intentionally reused in this way.

Despite these limitations, one-time pad illustrates fundamental ideas that appear in most forms of encryption in this course.

Exercises

1.1. The one-time pad encryption of plaintext mario (when converted from AscII to binary in the standard way) under key k is:

$$1000010000000111010101000001110000011101.$$

What is the one-time pad encryption of luigi under the same key?

1.2. Alice is using one-time pad and notices that when her key is the all-zeroes string $k = 0^\lambda$, then $\text{Enc}(k, m) = m$ and her message is sent in the clear! To avoid this problem, she decides to modify KeyGen to exclude the all-zeroes key. She modifies KeyGen to choose a key uniformly from $\{0,1\}^\lambda \setminus \{0^\lambda\}$, the set of all λ-bit strings except 0^λ. In this way, she guarantees that her plaintext is never sent in the clear.

Is it still true that the eavesdropper's ciphertext distribution is uniformly distributed on $\{0,1\}^\lambda$? Justify your answer.

1.3 When Alice encrypts the key k itself using one-time pad, the ciphertext will always be the all-zeroes string! So if an eavesdropper sees the all-zeroes ciphertext, she learns that Alice encrypted the key itself. Does this contradict Claim 1.3? Why or why not?

1.4. What is so special about defining OTP using the xor operation? Suppose we use the bitwise-And operation (which we will write as '&') and define a variant of OTP as follows:

KeyGen:	$\text{Enc}(k, m \in \{0,1\}^\lambda)$:
$k \leftarrow \{0,1\}^\lambda$ return k	return $k \,\&\, m$

Is this still a good choice for encryption? Why / why not?

1.5. Describe the flaw in this argument: Consider the following attack against one-time pad: upon seeing a ciphertext c, the eavesdropper tries every candidate key $k \in \{0,1\}^\lambda$ until she has found the one that was used, at which point she outputs the plaintext m. This contradicts the argument in Section 1.2 that the eavesdropper can obtain no information about m by seeing the ciphertext.

1.6. Suppose Alice encrypts two plaintexts m and m' using one-time pad with the same key k. What information about m and m' is leaked to an eavesdropper by doing this (assume the eavesdropper knows that Alice has reused k)? Be as specific as you can!

1.7. You (Eve) have intercepted two ciphertexts:

$$c_1 = 1111100101111001110011000001011110000110$$

$$c_2 = 1111101001100111110111010000100110001000$$

You know that both are OTP ciphertexts, encrypted with the same key. You know that either c_1 is an encryption of alpha and c_2 is an encryption of bravo or c_1 is an encryption of delta and c_2 is an encryption of gamma (all converted to binary from ASCII in the standard way).

Which of these two possibilities is correct, and why? What was the key k ?

1.8. A known-plaintext attack refers to a situation where an eavesdropper sees a ciphertext $c = \text{Enc}(k, m)$ and also learns/knows what plaintext m was used to generate c.

(a) Show that a known-plaintext attack on OTP results in the attacker learning the key k.

(b) Can OTP be secure if it allows an attacker to recover the encryption key? Is this a contradiction to the security we showed for OTP? Explain.

1.9. Suppose we modify the subroutine discussed in Claim 1.3 so that it also returns k :

$$\begin{array}{l} \text{EAVESDROP}'(m \in \{0,1\}^\lambda): \\ k \leftarrow \{0,1\}^\lambda \\ c := k \oplus m \\ \text{return } (k, c) \end{array}$$

Is it still true that for every m, the output of eavesdrop' (m) is distributed uniformly in $(\{0,1\}^\lambda)^2$? Or is the output distribution different for different choice of m ?

1.10. In this problem we discuss the security of performing one-time pad encryption twice:

(a) Consider the following subroutine that models the result of applying one-time pad encryption with two independent keys:

$$\begin{array}{l} \text{EAVESDROP}'(m \in \{0,1\}^\lambda): \\ k_1 \leftarrow \{0,1\}^\lambda \\ k_2 \leftarrow \{0,1\}^\lambda \\ c := k_2 \oplus (k_1 \oplus m) \\ \text{return } c \end{array}$$

Show that the output of this subroutine is uniformly distributed in $\{0,1\}^\lambda$.

(b) What security is provided by performing one-time pad encryption twice with the same key?

1.11. We mentioned that one-time pad keys can be used to encrypt only one plaintext, and how this was reflected in the eavesdrop subroutine of Claim 1.3. Is there a similar restriction about re-using plaintexts in OTP (but with independently random keys for different ciphertexts)? If an eavesdropper knows that the same plaintext is encrypted twice (but doesn't know what the plaintext is), can she learn anything? Does Claim 1.3 have anything to say about a situation where the same plaintext is encrypted more than once?

1.12. There is nothing exclusively special about strings and XOR in OTP. We can get the same properties using integers mod$n$ and addition mod$n$.

This problem considers a variant of one-time pad, in which the keys, plaintexts, and ciphertexts are all elements of $\mathbb{Z}_n$ instead of $\{0,1\}^\lambda$.

(a) What is the decryption algorithm that corresponds to the following encryption algorithm?

$$\frac{\text{Enc}(k, m \in \mathbb{Z}_n):}{\text{return}(k+m)\%n}.$$

(b) Show that the output of the following subroutine is uniformly distributed in $\mathbb{Z}_n$:

$$\begin{array}{l} \text{EAVESDROP}'(m \in \mathbb{Z}_n): \\ k \leftarrow \mathbb{Z}_n \\ c := (k+m)\%n \\ \text{return } c \end{array}$$

(c) It's not just the distribution of keys that is important. The way that the key is combined with the plaintext is also important. Show that the output of the following subroutine is not necessarily uniformly distributed in $\mathbb{Z}_n$:

$\textbf{EAVESDROP}'(m \in \mathbb{Z}_n)$:
$k \leftarrow \mathbb{Z}_n$
$c := (k \cdot m)\%n$
return c

Chapter 2

Provable Security: The Basic

Edgar Allan Poe was not only an author, but also a cryptography enthusiast. He once wrote, in a discussion on the state of the art in cryptography: [1]

"Human ingenuity cannot concoct a cipher which human ingenuity cannot resolve."

This was an accurate assessment of the cryptography that existed in 1841 . Whenever someone would come up with an encryption method, someone else would inevitably find a way to break it, and the cat-and-mouse game would repeat again and again.

Modern 21st-century cryptography, however, is different. This book will introduce you to many schemes whose security we can prove in a very specific sense. The codemakers can win against the code-breakers.

It's only possible to prove things about security by having formal definitions of what it means to be "secure." This chapter is about the fundamental skills that revolve around security definitions: how to write them, how to understand & interpret them, how to prove security using the hybrid technique, and how to demonstrate insecurity using attacks against the security definition.

2.1 Security Definition

So far the only form of cryptography we've seen is one-time pad, so our discussion of security has been rather specific to one-time pad. It would be preferable to have a vocabulary to talk about security in a more general sense, so that we can ask whether any encryption scheme is secure.

In this section, we'll develop two security definitions for encryption.

What Doesn't Go Into a Security Definition

A security definition should give guarantees about what can happen to a system in the presence of an attacker. But not all important properties of a system refer to an attacker. For encryption specifically:

- We don't reference any attacker when we say that the Enc algorithm takes two arguments (a key and a plaintext), or that the KeyGen algorithm takes no arguments. Specifying the types of inputs/outputs (i.e., the "function signature") of the various algorithms is therefore not a statement about security. We call these properties the syntax of the scheme.
- Even if there is no attacker, it's still important that decryption is an inverse of encryption. This is not a security property of the encryption scheme. Instead, we call it a correctness property.

Below are the generic definitions for syntax and correctness of symmetric-key encryption:

Definition 2.1 (Encryption syntax)

A symmetric-key encryption (SKE) scheme consists of the following algorithms:

- KeyGen: a randomized algorithm that outputs a key $k \in \mathcal{K}$.
- Enc: a (possibly randomized) algorithm that takes a key $k \in \mathcal{K}$ and plaintext $m \in \mathcal{M}$ as input, and outputs a ciphertext $c \in C$.
- Dec: a deterministic algorithm that takes a key $k \in \mathcal{K}$ and ciphertext $c \in C$ as input, and outputs a plaintext $m \in \mathcal{M}$.

We call $\mathcal{K}$ the key space, $\mathcal{M}$ the message space, and C the ciphertext space of the scheme. Sometimes we refer to the entire scheme (the collection of all three algorithms) by a single variable Σ. When we do so, we write Σ.KeyGen, Σ.Enc, Σ.Dec, $\Sigma.\mathcal{K}, \Sigma.\mathcal{M}$, and $\Sigma.C$ to refer to its components.

Definition 2.2 (SKE correctness)

An encryption scheme Σ satisfies correctness if for all $k \in \Sigma.\mathcal{K}$ and all $m \in \Sigma.\mathcal{M}$,

$$\Pr[\Sigma \cdot \mathrm{Dec}(k, \Sigma \cdot \mathrm{Enc}(k, m)) = m] = 1.$$

The definition is written in terms of a probability because Enc is allowed to be a randomized algorithm. In other words, decrypting a ciphertext with the same key that was used for encryption must always result in the original plaintext.

Example

An encryption scheme can have the appropriate syntax but still have degenerate behavior like $\mathrm{Enc}(k, m) = 0^\lambda$ (i.e., every plaintext is "encrypted" to 0^λ). Such a scheme would not satisfy the correctness property.

A different scheme defined by $\text{Enc}(k, m) = m$ (i.e., the "ciphertext" is always equal to the plaintext itself) and $\text{Dec}(k, c) = c$ does satisfy the correctness property, but would not satisfy any reasonable security property.

"Real-vs-Random" Style of Security Definition

Let's try to make a security definition that formalizes the following intuitive idea:

"an encryption scheme is a good one if its ciphertexts look like random junk to an attacker."

Security definitions always consider the attacker's view of the system. What is the "interface" that Alice & Bob expose to the attacker by their use of the cryptography, and does that particular interface benefit the attacker?

In this example, we're considering a scenario where the attacker gets to observe ciphertexts. How exactly are these ciphertexts generated? What are the inputs to Enc (key and plaintext), and how are they chosen?

- Key: It's hard to imagine any kind of useful security if the attacker knows the key. Hence, we consider that the key is kept secret from the attacker. Of course, the key is generated according to the KeyGen algorithm of the scheme.
- At this point in the course, we consider encryption schemes where the key is used to encrypt only one plaintext. Somehow this restriction must be captured in our security definition. Later, we will consider security definitions that consider a key that is used to encrypt many things.
- Plaintext: It turns out to be useful to consider that the attacker actually chooses the plaintexts. This a "pessimistic" choice, since it gives much power to the attacker. However, if the encryption scheme is indeed secure when the attacker chooses the plaintexts, then it's also secure in more realistic scenarios where the attacker has some uncertainty about the plaintexts.

These clarifications allow us to fill in more specifics about our informal idea of security:

"an encryption scheme is a good one if its ciphertexts look like random junk to an attacker . . . when each key is secret and used to encrypt only one plaintext, even when the attacker chooses the plaintexts."

A concise way to express all of these details is to consider the attacker as a calling program to the following subroutine:

$$\begin{array}{l} \underline{\text{CTXT}(m \in \Sigma.\mathcal{M}):} \\ k \leftarrow \Sigma.\text{KeyGen} \\ c := \Sigma.\text{Enc}(k, m) \\ \text{return } c \end{array}$$

A calling program can choose the argument to the subroutine (in this case, a plaintext), and see only the resulting return value (in this case, a ciphertext). The calling program can't see values of privately-scoped variables (like k in this case). If the calling program makes many calls to the subroutine, a fresh key k is chosen each time.

The interaction between an attacker (calling program) and this CTXT subroutine appears to capture the relevant scenario. We would like to say that the outputs from the CTXT subroutine are uniformly distributed. A convenient way of expressing this property is to say that this ctxt subroutine should have the same effect on every calling program as a ctxt subroutine that (explicitly) samples its output uniformly.

$$\boxed{\begin{array}{l} \underline{\text{cTxt}(m \in \Sigma.\mathcal{M}):} \\ k \leftarrow \Sigma.\text{KeyGen} \\ c := \Sigma.\text{Enc}(k, m) \\ \text{return } c \end{array}} \quad \text{vs.} \quad \begin{array}{l} \underline{\text{cTxt}(m \in \Sigma.\mathcal{M}):} \\ c \leftarrow \Sigma.C \\ \text{return } c \end{array}.$$

Intuitively, no calling program should have any way of determining which of these two implementations is answering subroutine calls. As an analogy, one way of saying that "Foo is a correct sorting algorithm" is to say that "no calling program would behave differently if FOO were replaced by an implementation of mergesort."

In summary, we can define security for encryption in the following way:

> *"an encryption scheme is a good one if, when you plug its KeyGen and Enc algorithms into the template of the CTXT subroutine above, the two implementations of ctxt induce identical behavior in every calling program."*

In a few pages, we introduce formal notation and definitions for the concepts introduced here. In particular, both the calling program and subroutine can be randomized algorithms, so we should be careful about what we mean by "identical behavior."

Example One-time pad is defined with KeyGen sampling k uniformly from $\{0,1\}^\lambda$ and $\text{Enc}(k, m) = k \oplus m$. It satisfies our new security property since, when we plug in this algorithms into the above template, we get the following two subroutine implementations:

```
CTXT(m):                                          CTXT(m):
  k ← {0,1}^λ   // KeyGen of OTP        vs.         c ← {0,1}^λ   // C of OTP
  c := k ⊕ m    // Enc of OTP                       return c
  return c
```

and these two implementations have the same effect on all calling programs.

"Left-vs-Right" Style of Security Definition

Here's a different intuitive idea of security:

> *"an encryption scheme is a good one if encryptions of m_L look like encryptions of m_R to an attacker (for all possible m_L, m_R)"*

As above, we are considering a scenario where the attacker sees some ciphertext(s). These ciphertexts are generated with some key; where does that key come from? These ciphertexts encrypt either some m_L or some m_R; where do m_L and m_R come from? We can answer these questions in a similar way as the previous example. Plaintexts m_L and m_R can be chosen by the attacker. The key is chosen according to KeyGen so that it remains secret from the attacker (and is used to generate only one ciphertext).

> *"an encryption scheme is a good one if encryptions of m_L look like encryptions of m_R to an attacker, when each key is secret and used to encrypt only one plaintext, even when the attacker chooses m_L and m_R."*

As before, we formalize this idea by imagining the attacker as a program that calls a particular interface. This time, the attacker will choose two plaintexts m_L and m_R, and get a ciphertext in return. [2] Depending on whether m_L or m_R is actually encrypted, those interfaces are implemented as follows:

```
EAVESDROP(m_L, m_R ∈ Σ.M):          EAVESDROP(m_L, m_R ∈ Σ.M):
  k ← Σ.KeyGen                   ;     k ← Σ.KeyGen
  c := Σ.Enc(k, m_L)                   c := Σ.Enc(k, m_R)
  return c                             return c
```

Now the formal way to say that encryptions of m_L "look like" encryptions of m_R is:

> *"an encryption scheme is a good one if, when you plug its KeyGen and Enc algorithms into the template of the EAVESDROP subroutines above, the two implementations of EAVESDROP induce identical behavior in every calling program."*

Example: *Does one-time pad satisfy this new security property? To find out, we plug in its algorithms to the above template, and obtain the following implementations:*

EAVESDROP(m_L, m_R):
$k \leftarrow \{0,1\}^\lambda$ // KeyGen of OTP
$c := k \oplus m_L$ // Enc of OTP
return c

EAVESDROP(m_L, m_R):
$k \leftarrow \{0,1\}^\lambda$ // KeyGen of OTP
$c := k \oplus m_R$ // Enc of OTP
return c

If these two implementations have the same effect on all calling programs (and indeed they do), then we would say that OTP satisfies this security property.

Is this a better/worse way to define security than the previous way? One security definition considers an attacker whose goal is to distinguish real ciphertexts from random values (real-vs-random paradigm), and the other considers an attacker whose goal is to distinguish real ciphertexts of two different plaintexts (left-vs-right paradigm). Is one "correct" and the other one "incorrect?" We save such discussion until later in the chapter.

2.2 Formalisms for Security Definitions

So far, we've defined security in terms of a single, self-contained subroutine, and imagined the attacker as a program that calls this subroutine. Later in the course we will need to generalize beyond a single subroutine, to a collection of subroutines that share common (private) state information. Staying with the software terminology, we call this collection a library:

Definition 2.3 (Libraries) :A library $\mathcal{L}$ is a collection of subroutines and private/static variables. A library's interface consists of the names, argument types, and output type of all of its subroutines (just like a Fava interface). If a program $\mathcal{A}$ includes calls to subroutines in the interface of $\mathcal{L}$, then we write $\mathcal{A} \diamond \mathcal{L}$ to denote the result of linking $\mathcal{A}$ to $\mathcal{L}$ in the natural way (answering those subroutine calls using the implementation specified in $\mathcal{L}$). We write $\mathcal{A} \diamond \mathcal{L} \Rightarrow z$ to denote the event that program $\mathcal{A} \diamond \mathcal{L}$ outputs the value z.

If $\mathcal{A}$ or $\mathcal{L}$ is a program that makes random choices, then the output of $\mathcal{A} \diamond \mathcal{L}$ is a random variable. It is often useful to consider probabilities like $\Pr[\mathcal{A} \diamond \mathcal{L} \Rightarrow \text{true}]$.

Example Here is a familiar library:

$\mathcal{L}$
CTXT(m):
$k \leftarrow \{0,1\}^\lambda$
$c := k \oplus m$
return c

And here is one possible calling program:

$\mathcal{A}$:
$m \leftarrow \{0,1\}^\lambda$
$c :=$ **cTXT**(m)
return $m \stackrel{?}{=} c$

You can hopefully convince yourself that

$$\Pr[\mathcal{A} \diamond \mathcal{L} \Rightarrow \text{ true }] = 1/2^\lambda.$$

If this $\mathcal{A}$ is linked to a different library, its output probability may be different. If a different calling program is linked to this $\mathcal{L}$, the output probability may be different.

Example: A library can contain several subroutines and private variables that are kept static between subroutine calls. For example, here is a simple library that picks a string s uniformly and allows the calling program to guess s.

$\mathcal{L}$
$s \leftarrow \{0,1\}^\lambda$
RESET():
$s \leftarrow \{0,1\}^\lambda$
GUESs$(x \in \{0,1\}^\lambda)$:
return$x \stackrel{?}{=} s$

Our convention is that code outside of a subroutine (like the first line here) is run once at initialization time. Variables defined at initialization time (likes here) are available in all subroutine scopes (but not to the calling program).

Interchangeability

The idea that "no calling program behaves differently in the presence of these two libraries" still makes sense even for libraries with several subroutines. Since this is such a common concept, we devote new notation to it:

Definition 2.4 (Interchangeable) *Let $\mathcal{L}_{left}$ and $\mathcal{L}_{right}$ be two libraries that have the same interface. We say that $\mathcal{L}_{left}$ and $\mathcal{L}_{right}$ are interchangeable, and write $\mathcal{L}_{left} \equiv \mathcal{L}_{right}$, iffor all programs $\mathcal{A}$ that output a boolean value,*

$$\Pr[\mathcal{A} \diamond \mathcal{L}_{\text{left}} \Rightarrow \text{true}] = \Pr[\mathcal{A} \diamond \mathcal{L}_{\text{right}} \Rightarrow \text{true}].$$

This definition considers calling programs that give boolean output. Imagine a calling program / attacker whose only goal is to distinguish two particular libraries (indeed, we often refer to the calling program as a distinguisher). A boolean output is enough for that task. You can think of the output bit as the calling program's "guess" for which library the calling program thinks it is linked to.

The distinction between "calling program outputs true" and "calling program outputs false" is not significant. If two libraries don't affect the calling program's probability of outputting true, then they also don't affect its probability of outputting false:

$$\begin{aligned} \Pr[\mathcal{A} \diamond \mathcal{L}_{\text{left}} \Rightarrow \text{true}] &= \Pr[\mathcal{A} \diamond \mathcal{L}_{\text{right}} \Rightarrow \text{true}] \\ \Leftrightarrow 1 - \Pr[\mathcal{A} \diamond \mathcal{L}_{\text{left}} \Rightarrow \text{true}] &= 1 - \Pr[\mathcal{A} \diamond \mathcal{L}_{\text{right}} \Rightarrow \text{true}] \\ \Leftrightarrow \Pr[\mathcal{A} \diamond \mathcal{L}_{\text{left}} \Rightarrow \text{false}] &= \Pr[\mathcal{A} \diamond \mathcal{L}_{\text{right}} \Rightarrow \text{false}] \end{aligned}$$

Example: *Here are some very simple and straightforward ways that two libraries may be interchangeable. Hopefully it's clear that each pair of libraries has identical behavior, and therefore identical effect on all calling programs.*

Despite being very simple examples, each of these concepts shows up as a building block in a real security proof in this book.

Their only difference happens in an unreachable block of code.

```
FOO(x):
  if x is even:
    return 0
  else if x is odd:
    return 1
  else:
    return -1
```

≡

```
FOO(x):
  if x is even:
    return 0
  else if x is odd:
    return 1
  else:
    return ∞
```

Their only difference is the value they assign to a variable that is never actually used.

```
FOO(x):
  return BAR(x, x)

BAR(a, b):
  k ← {0,1}^λ
  return k ⊕ a
```

≡

```
FOO(x):
  return BAR(x, 0^λ)

BAR(a, b):
  k ← {0,1}^λ
  return k ⊕ a
```

Their only difference is that one library unrolls a loop that occurs in the other library.

```
FOO(x, n):
  for i = 1 to λ:
    BAR(x, i)
```

≡

```
FOO(x, n):
  for i = 1 to n:
    BAR(x, i)
  for i = n + 1 to λ:
    BAR(x, i)
```

Their only difference is that one library inlines a subroutine call that occurs in the other library.

```
FOO(x):
  k ← {0,1}^λ
  y ← {0,1}^λ
  return k ⊕ y ⊕ x
```

≡

```
FOO(x):
  k ← {0,1}^λ
  return k ⊕ BAR(x)

BAR(x):
  y ← {0,1}^λ
  return y ⊕ x
```

Example Here are more simple examples of interchangeable libraries that involve randomness:

FOO(): $x \leftarrow \{0,1\}^\lambda$ $y \leftarrow \{0,1\}^\lambda$ return $x\|y$	$\equiv$	FOO(): $z \leftarrow \{0,1\}^{2\lambda}$ return z

The uniform distribution over strings acts independently on different characters in the string ("‖" refers to concatenation).

$k \leftarrow \{0,1\}^\lambda$ FOO(x): return $k \oplus x$	$\equiv$	FOO(x): if k not defined: $k \leftarrow \{0,1\}^\lambda$ return $k \oplus x$

Sampling a value "eagerly" (as soon as possible) vs. sampling a value "lazily" (at the last possible moment before the value is needed). We assume that k is static/global across many calls to FOO, and initially undefined.

Formal Restatements of Previous Concepts

We can now re-state our security definitions from the previous section, using this new terminology.

Our "real-vs-random" style of security definition for encryption can be expressed as follows:

Definition 2.5 (Uniform ctxts): An encryption scheme Σ has one-time uniform ciphertexts if:

$\mathcal{L}^{\Sigma}_{\text{ots\$-real}}$ CTXT($m \in \Sigma.\mathcal{M}$): $k \leftarrow \Sigma.\text{KeyGen}$ $c \leftarrow \Sigma.\text{Enc}(k, m)$ return c	$\equiv$	$\mathcal{L}^{\Sigma}_{\text{ots\$-rand}}$ CTXT($m \in \Sigma.\mathcal{M}$): $c \leftarrow \Sigma.\mathcal{C}$ return c

In other words, if you fill in the specifics of Σ (i.e., the behavior of its KeyGen and Enc) into these two library "templates," and you get two libraries that are interchangeable (i.e., have the same effect on all calling programs), we will say that Σ has one-time uniform ciphertexts.

Throughout this course, we will use the "$" symbol to denote randomness (as in real-vs-random). [3]

Our "left-vs-right" style of security definition can be expressed as follows:

Definition 2.6 (One-time secrecy): *An encryption scheme Σ has one-time secrecy if:*

$\mathcal{L}^{\Sigma}_{\text{ots-L}}$
EAVESDROP$(m_L, m_R \in \Sigma.\mathcal{M})$:
$k \leftarrow \Sigma.\mathsf{KeyGen}$
$c \leftarrow \Sigma.\mathsf{Enc}(k, m_L)$
return c

$\equiv$

$\mathcal{L}^{\Sigma}_{\text{ots-R}}$
EAVESDROP$(m_L, m_R \in \Sigma.\mathcal{M})$:
$k \leftarrow \Sigma.\mathsf{KeyGen}$
$c \leftarrow \Sigma.\mathsf{Enc}(k, m_R)$
return c

Previously in Claim 1.3 we argued that one-time-pad ciphertexts follow the uniform distribution. This actually shows that OTP satisfies the uniform ciphertexts definition:

Claim 2.7 (OTP rule): *One-time pad satisfies the one-time uniform ciphertexts property. In other words:*

$\mathcal{L}_{\text{otp-real}}$
EAVESDROP$(m \in \{0,1\}^\lambda)$:
$k \leftarrow \{0,1\}^\lambda$ // OTP.KeyGen
return $k \oplus m$ // OTP.Enc(k, m)

$\equiv$

$\mathcal{L}_{\text{otp-rand}}$
EAVESDROP$(m \in \{0,1\}^\lambda)$:
$c \leftarrow \{0,1\}^\lambda$ // OTP.C
return c

Because this property of OTP is quite useful throughout the course, I've given these two libraries special names (apart from $\mathcal{L}^{\text{OTP}}_{\text{ots \$-real}}$ and $\mathcal{L}^{\text{OTP}}_{\text{ots \$-rand}}$).

Discussion, Pitfalls

It is a common pitfall to imagine the calling program $\mathcal{A}$ being simultaneously linked to both libraries, but this is not what the definition says. The definition of $\mathcal{L}_1 \equiv \mathcal{L}_2$ refers to two different executions: one where $\mathcal{A}$ is linked only to $\mathcal{L}_1$ for its entire lifetime, and one where $\mathcal{A}$ is linked only to $\mathcal{L}_2$ for its entire lifetime. There is never a time where some of $\mathcal{A}$'s subroutine calls are answered by $\mathcal{L}_1$ and others by $\mathcal{L}_2$. This is an especially important distinction when $\mathcal{A}$ makes several subroutine calls in a single execution.

Another common pitfall is confusion about the difference between the algorithms of an encryption scheme (e.g., what is shown in Construction 1.1) and the libraries used in a security definition (e.g., what is shown in Definition 2.6). The big difference is:

- The algorithms of the scheme show a regular user's view of things. For example, the Enc algorithm takes two inputs: a key and a plaintext. Is there any way of describing an algorithm that takes two arguments other than writing something like Construction 1.1?

- The libraries capture the attacker's view of of a particular scenario, where the users use the cryptographic algorithms in a very specific way. For example, when we talk about security of encryption, we don't guarantee security when Alice lets the attacker choose her encryption key! But letting the attacker choose the plaintext is fine; we can guarantee security in that scenario. That's why Definition 2.5 describes a subroutine that calls Enc on a plaintext that is chosen by the calling program, but on a key k chosen by the library.
- A security definition says that some task (e.g., distinguishing ciphertexts from random junk) is impossible, when the attacker is allowed certain influence over the inputs to the algorithms (e.g., full choice of plaintexts, but no influence over the key), and is allowed to see certain outputs from those algorithms (e.g., ciphertexts).

It's wrong to summarize one-time secrecy as: "I'm not allowed to choose what to encrypt, I have to ask the attacker to choose for me." The correct interpretation is: "If I encrypt only one plaintext per key, then I am safe to encrypt things even if the attacker sees the resulting ciphertext and even if she has some influence or partial information on what I'm encrypting, because this is the situation captured in the one-time secrecy library."

Kerckhoffs' Principle, Revisited

Kerckhoffs' Principle says to assume that the attacker has complete knowledge of the algorithms being used. Assume that the choice of keys is the only thing unknown to the attacker. Let's see how Kerckhoffs' Principle is reflected in our formal security definitions.

Suppose I write down the source code of two libraries, and your goal is to write an effective distinguisher. So you study the source code of the two libraries and write the best distinguisher that exists. It would be fair to say that your distinguisher "knows" what algorithms are used in the libraries, because it was designed based on the source code of these libraries. The definition of interchangeability considers literally every calling program, so it must also consider calling programs like yours that "know" what algorithms are being used.

However, there is an important distinction to make. If you know you might be linked to a library that executes the statement " $k \leftarrow \{0,1\}^{\lambda}$ ", that doesn't mean you know the actual value of k that was chosen at runtime. Our convention is that all variables within the library are privately scoped, and the calling program can learn about them only indirectly through subroutine outputs. In the library-distinguishing game, you are not allowed to pick a different calling program based on random choices that the library makes! After we settle on a calling program, we measure its effectiveness in terms of probabilities that take into account all possible outcomes of the random choices in the system.

In summary, the calling program "knows" what algorithms are being used (and how they are being used!) because the choice of the calling program is allowed to depend on the 2 specific libraries that we consider. The calling program "doesn't know" things like secret keys because the choice of calling program isn't allowed to depend on the outcome of random sampling done at runtime.

Kerckhoffs' Principle, applied to our formal terminology:

Assume that the attacker knows every fact in the universe, except for:

1. which of the two possible libraries it is linked to in any particular execution, and
2. the random choices that the library will make during any particular execution (which are usually assigned to privately scoped variables within the library).

2.3 Demonstrate Insecurity with Attacks

We always define security with respect to two libraries - or, if you like, two library templates that describe how to insert the algorithms of a cryptographic scheme into two libraries. If the two libraries that you get (after filling in the specifics of a particular scheme) are interchangeable, then we say that the scheme satisfies the security property. If we want to show that some scheme is insecure, we have to demonstrate just one calling program that behaves differently in the presence of those two libraries.

Let's demonstrate this process with the following encryption scheme, which is like one-time pad but uses bitwise-AND instead of xor:

Construction 2.8

$\mathcal{K}$	$= \{0,1\}^\lambda$	KeyGen:	Enc (k, m):	
$\mathcal{M}$	$= \{0,1\}^\lambda$		$k \leftarrow \{0,1\}^\lambda$	return $k\&m$
$\mathcal{C}$	$= \{0,1\}^\lambda$	return k		

I haven't shown the Dec algorithm, because in fact there is no way to write one that satisfies the correctness requirement. But let's pretend we haven't noticed that yet, and ask whether this encryption scheme satisfies the two security properties defined previously.

Claim 2.9 *Construction 2.8 does not have one-time uniform ciphertexts (Definition 2.5).*

Proof: *To see whether Construction 2.8 satisfies uniform one-time ciphertexts, we have to plug in its algorithms into the two libraries of Definition 2.5 and see whether the resulting libraries are interchangeable. We're considering the following two libraries:*

$\mathcal{L}^{\Sigma}_{\text{ots\$-real}}$
CTXT($m \in \{0,1\}^{\lambda}$):
$k \leftarrow \{0,1\}^{\lambda}$ // Σ.KeyGen
$c := k \,\&\, m$ // Σ.Enc
return c

$\mathcal{L}^{\Sigma}_{\text{ots\$-rand}}$
CTXT($m \in \{0,1\}^{\lambda}$):
$c \leftarrow \{0,1\}^{\lambda}$ // Σ.C
return c

To show that these two libraries are not interchangeable, we need to write a calling program that behaves differently in their presence. The calling program should make one or more calls to the ctxt subroutine. That means it needs to choose the input m that it passes, and it must make some conclusion (about which of the two libraries it is linked to) based on the return value that it gets. What m should the calling program choose as input to ctxt? What should the calling program look for in the return values?

There are many valid ways to write a good calling program, and maybe you can think of several. One good approach is to observe that bitwise-and with k can never "turn a 0 into a 1." So perhaps the calling program should choose m to consist of all 0 s. When $m = 0^{\lambda}$, the $\mathcal{L}_{\text{ots \$-real}}$ library will always return all zeroes, but the $\mathcal{L}_{\text{ots \$-rand}}$ library may return strings with both 0s and 1s.

We can formalize this idea with the following calling program:

$$\begin{gathered}\mathcal{A}: \\ c := \text{CTXT}(0^{\lambda}). \\ \text{return } c \stackrel{?}{=} 0^{\lambda}\end{gathered}$$

Next, let's ensure that this calling program behaves differently when linked to each of these two libraries.

When $\mathcal{A}$ is linked to $\mathcal{L}_{\text{ots \$-real}}$, c is computed as $k\&0^{\lambda}$. No matter what k is, the result is always all-zeroes. Therefore, $\mathcal{A}$ will always return true.

$\mathcal{A}$:		$\mathcal{L}^{\Sigma}_{\text{ots\$-real}}$
$c := \text{CTXT}(0^{\lambda})$ return $c \stackrel{?}{=} 0^{\lambda}$	$\diamond$	$\text{CTXT}(m)$: $\quad k \leftarrow \{0,1\}^{\lambda}$ $\quad c := k \,\&\, m$ $\quad$return c

In other words, $\Pr[\mathcal{A} \diamond \mathcal{L}_{\text{ots\$-real}} \Rightarrow \text{true}] = 1$.

When $\mathcal{A}$ is linked to $\mathcal{L}_{\text{ots \$-rand}}$, c is chosen uniformly from $\{0,1\}^{\lambda}$. The probability that c then happens to be all-zeroes is $1/2^{\lambda}$.

$\mathcal{A}$:		$\mathcal{L}^{\Sigma}_{\text{ots\$-rand}}$
$c := \text{CTXT}(0^{\lambda})$ return $c \stackrel{?}{=} 0^{\lambda}$	$\diamond$	$\text{CTXT}(m)$: $\quad c \leftarrow \{0,1\}^{\lambda}$ $\quad$return c

In other words, $\Pr[\mathcal{A} \diamond \mathcal{L}_{\text{ots \$-rand}} \Rightarrow \text{true}] = 1/2^{\lambda}$.

Since these two probabilities are different, this shows that $\mathcal{L}^{\Sigma}_{\text{ots\$-real}} \not\equiv \mathcal{L}^{\Sigma}_{\text{ots\$-rand}}$. In other words, the scheme does not satisfy this uniform ciphertexts property.

So far we have two security definitions. Does this encryption scheme satisfy one but not the other?

Claim 2.10 *Construction 2.8 does not satisfy one-time secrecy (Definition 2.6).*

Proof: This claim refers to a different security definition, which involves two different libraries. When we plug in the details of Construction 2.8 into the libraries of Definition 2.6, we get the following:

$\mathcal{L}^{\Sigma}_{\text{ots-L}}$	$\mathcal{L}^{\Sigma}_{\text{ots-R}}$
$\text{EAVESDROP}(m_L, m_R)$: $\quad k \leftarrow \{0,1\}^{\lambda}$ // Σ.KeyGen $\quad c := k \,\&\, m_L$ // Σ.Enc(k, m_L) $\quad$return c	$\text{EAVESDROP}(m_L, m_R)$: $\quad k \leftarrow \{0,1\}^{\lambda}$ // Σ.KeyGen $\quad c := k \,\&\, m_R$ // Σ.Enc(k, m_R) $\quad$return c

Now we need to write a calling program that behaves differently in the presence of these two libraries. We can use the same overall idea as last time, but not the same actual calling program, since these libraries provide a different interface. In this example, the calling program needs to call the eavesdrop subroutine which takes t wo arguments m_L and m_R. How should the calling program choose m_L and m_R ? Which two plaintexts have different looking ciphertexts?

A good approach is to choose m_L to be all zeroes and m_R to be all ones. We know from before that an all-zeroes plaintext always encrypts to an all-zeroes ciphertext, so the calling program can check for that condition. More formally, we can define the calling program:

$\mathcal{A}$:
$c := \textbf{Eavesdrop}(0^\lambda, 1^\lambda)$
return $c \stackrel{?}{=} 0^\lambda$

Next, we need to compute its output probabilities in the presence of the two libraries.

When $\mathcal{A}$ is linked to $\mathcal{L}_{\text{ots-L}}$, c is computed as an encryption of $m_L = 0^\lambda$. No matter what k is, the result is always all-zeroes. So,

$\mathcal{A}$:		$\mathcal{L}^{\Sigma}_{\text{ots-L}}$
$c := \text{EAVESDROP}(0^\lambda, 1^\lambda)$ return $c \stackrel{?}{=} 0^\lambda$	$\diamond$	EAVESDROP(m_L, m_R): $k \leftarrow \{0,1\}^\lambda$ $c := k \;\&\; m_L$ return c

$$\Pr\left[\mathcal{A} \diamond \mathcal{L}_{\text{ots-L}} \Rightarrow \text{true}\right] = 1.$$

When $\mathcal{A}$ is linked to $\mathcal{L}_{\text{ots-R}}$, c is computed as an encryption of $m_R = 1^\lambda$. In other words, $c := k\&1^\lambda$. But the bitwise-And of any string k with all 1 s is just k itself. So c is just equal to k, which was chosen uniformly at random. The probability that a uniformly random c happens to be all-zeroes is

$\mathcal{A}$:	$\diamond$	$\mathcal{L}^{\Sigma}_{\text{ots-R}}$
$c := \text{EAVESDROP}(0^\lambda, 1^\lambda)$ return $c \stackrel{?}{=} 0^\lambda$		$\text{EAVESDROP}(m_L, m_R)$: $k \leftarrow \{0,1\}^\lambda$ $c := k \,\&\, m_R$ return c

$$\Pr\left[\mathcal{A} \diamond \mathcal{L}_{\text{ots-R}} \Rightarrow \text{true}\right] = 1/2^\lambda.$$

Since these two probabilities are different, $\mathcal{L}^{\Sigma}_{\text{ots-L}} \not\equiv \mathcal{L}^{\Sigma}_{\text{ots-R}}$ and the scheme does not have one-time secrecy. □

2.4 Prove Security with The Hybrid Technique

We proved that one-time pad satisfies the uniform ciphertexts property (Claim 1.3) by carefully calculating certain probabilities. This will not be a sustainable strategy as things get more complicated later in the course. In this section we will introduce a technique for proving security properties, which usually avoids tedious probability calculations.

Chaining Several Components

Before getting to a security proof, we introduce a convenient lemma. Consider a compound program like $\mathcal{A} \diamond \mathcal{L}_1 \diamond \mathcal{L}_2$. Our convention is that subroutine calls only happen from left to right across the △ symbol, so in this example, $\mathcal{L}_1$ can make calls to subroutines in $\mathcal{L}_2$, but not vice-versa. Depending on the context, it can sometimes be convenient to interpret $\mathcal{A} \diamond \mathcal{L}_1 \diamond \mathcal{L}_2$ as:

- $(\mathcal{A} \diamond \mathcal{L}_1) \diamond \mathcal{L}_2$: a compound calling program linked to $\mathcal{L}_2$. After all, $\mathcal{A} \diamond \mathcal{L}_1$ is a program that makes calls to the interface of $\mathcal{L}_2$.
- or: $\mathcal{A} \diamond (\mathcal{L}_1 \diamond \mathcal{L}_2)$: $\mathcal{A}$ linked to a compound library. After all, $\mathcal{A}$ is a program that makes calls to the interface of ($\mathcal{L}_1 \diamond \mathcal{L}_2$).

The placement of the parentheses does not affect the functionality of the overall program, just like how splitting up a real program into different source files doesn't affect its functionality.

In fact, every security proof in this book will have some intermediate steps that involve compound libraries. We will make heavy use of the following helpful result:

Lemma 2.11 (Chaining) If $\mathcal{L}_{\text{left}} \equiv \mathcal{L}_{\text{right}}$ then, for any library $\mathcal{L}^*$, we have $\mathcal{L}^* \diamond \mathcal{L}_{\text{left}} \equiv \mathcal{L}^* \diamond \mathcal{L}_{\text{right}}$.

Proof Note that we are comparing $\mathcal{L}^* \diamond \mathcal{L}_{\text{left}}$ and $\mathcal{L}^* \diamond \mathcal{L}_{\text{right}}$ as compound libraries. Hence we consider a calling program $\mathcal{A}$ that is linked to either $\mathcal{L}^* \diamond \mathcal{L}_{\text{left}}$ or $\mathcal{L}^* \diamond \mathcal{L}_{\text{right}}$.

Let $\mathcal{A}$ be such an arbitrary calling program. We must show that $\mathcal{A} \diamond (\mathcal{L}^* \diamond \mathcal{L}_{\text{left}})$ and $\mathcal{A} \diamond (\mathcal{L}^* \diamond \mathcal{L}_{\text{right}})$ have identical output distributions. As mentioned above, we can interpret $\mathcal{A} \diamond \mathcal{L}^* \diamond \mathcal{L}_{\text{left}}$ as a calling program $\mathcal{A}$ linked to the library $\mathcal{L}^* \diamond \mathcal{L}_{\text{left}}$, but also as a calling program $\mathcal{A} \diamond \mathcal{L}^*$ linked to the library $\mathcal{L}_{\text{left}}$. Since $\mathcal{L}_{\text{left}} \equiv \mathcal{L}_{\text{right}}$, swapping $\mathcal{L}_{\text{left}}$ for $\mathcal{L}_{\text{right}}$ has no effect on the output of any calling program. In particular, it has no effect when the calling program happens to be the compound program $\mathcal{A} \diamond \mathcal{L}^*$. Hence we have:

$$\begin{aligned}
\Pr[\mathcal{A} \diamond (\mathcal{L}^* \diamond \mathcal{L}_{\text{left}}) \Rightarrow \text{true}] &= \Pr[(\mathcal{A} \diamond \mathcal{L}^*) \diamond \mathcal{L}_{\text{left}} \Rightarrow \text{true}] && \text{(change of perspective)} \\
&= \Pr[(\mathcal{A} \diamond \mathcal{L}^*) \diamond \mathcal{L}_{\text{right}} \Rightarrow \text{true}] && (\text{since } \mathcal{L}_{\text{left}} \equiv \mathcal{L}_{\text{right}}) \\
&= \Pr[\mathcal{A} \diamond (\mathcal{L}^* \diamond \mathcal{L}_{\text{right}}) \Rightarrow \text{true}] && \text{(change of perspective)}
\end{aligned}$$

Since $\mathcal{A}$ was arbitrary, we have proved the lemma.

An Example Hybrid Proof

In this section we will prove something about the following scheme, which encrypts twice with OTP, using independent keys:

Construction 2.12 ("Double OTP")

$\mathcal{K} = (\{0,1\}^\lambda)^2$ $\mathcal{M} = \{0,1\}^\lambda$ $\mathcal{C} = \{0,1\}^\lambda$	KeyGen: $k_1 \leftarrow \{0,1\}^\lambda$ $k_2 \leftarrow \{0,1\}^\lambda$ return (k_1, k_2)	$\text{Enc}((k_1, k_2), m)$: $c_1 := k_1 \oplus m$ $c_2 := k_2 \oplus c_1$ return c_2	$\text{Dec}((k_1, k_2), c_2)$: $c_1 := k_2 \oplus c_2$ $m := k_1 \oplus c_1$ return m

It would not be too hard to directly show that ciphertexts in this scheme are uniformly distributed, as we did for plain OTP. However, the new hybrid technique will allow us to leverage what we already know about OTP in an elegant way, and avoid any probability calculations.

Claim 2.13 *Construction 2.12 has one-time uniform ciphertexts (Definition 2.6).*

Proof In terms of libraries, we must show that:

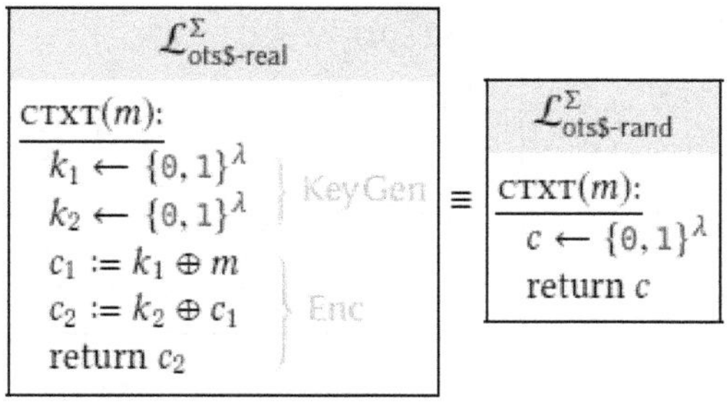

Instead of directly comparing these two libraries, we will introduce some additional libraries $\mathcal{L}_{\text{hyb-1}}$, $\mathcal{L}_{\text{hyb-2}}$, $\mathcal{L}_{\text{hyb-3}}$, and show that:

$$\mathcal{L}^{\Sigma}_{\text{ots \$-real}} \equiv \mathcal{L}_{\text{hyb-1}} \equiv \mathcal{L}_{\text{hyb-2}} \equiv \mathcal{L}_{\text{hyb-3}} \equiv \mathcal{L}^{\Sigma}_{\text{ots \$-rand}}$$

Since the ≡ symbol is transitive, this will achieve our goal.

The intermediate libraries are called hybrids, since they will contain a mix of characteristics from the two "endpoints" of this sequence. These hybrids are chosen so that it is very easy to show that consecutive libraries in this sequence are interchangeable. The particular hybrids we have in mind here are:

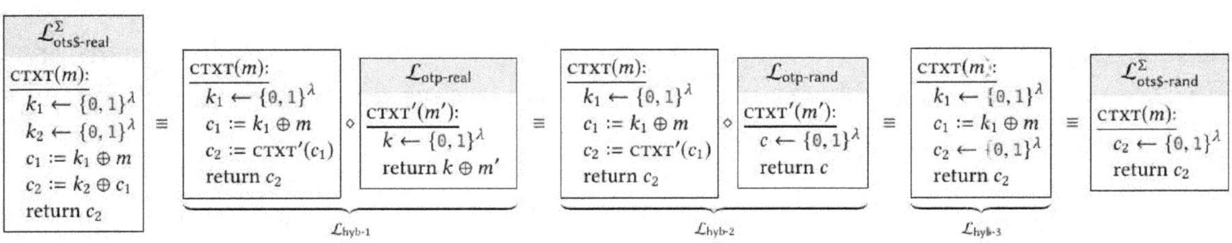

Next, we provide a justification for each " ≡ " in the expression above. For each pair of adjacent libraries, we highlight their differences below:

$\mathcal{L}^{\Sigma}_{\text{ots\$-real}}$

CTXT(m):
 $k_1 \leftarrow \{0,1\}^\lambda$
 $k_2 \leftarrow \{0,1\}^\lambda$
 $c_1 := k_1 \oplus m$
 $c_2 := k_2 \oplus c_1$
 return c_2

$\equiv$

CTXT(m):
 $k_1 \leftarrow \{0,1\}^\lambda$
 $c_1 := k_1 \oplus m$
 $c_2 :=$ CTXT$'(c_1)$
 return c_2

$\diamond$

$\mathcal{L}_{\text{otp-real}}$

CTXT$'(m')$:
 $k \leftarrow \{0,1\}^\lambda$
 return $k \oplus m'$

$\mathcal{L}_{\text{hyb-1}}$

The only difference between these two libraries is that the highlighted expressions have been factored out into a separate subroutine, and some variables have been renamed. In both libraries, c_2 is chosen as the xor of c_1 and a uniformly chosen string. These differences make no effect on the calling program. Importantly, the subroutine that we have factored out is exactly the one in the $\mathcal{L}_{\text{otp-real}}$ library (apart from renaming the subroutine).

CTXT(m):
 $k_1 \leftarrow \{0,1\}^\lambda$
 $c_1 := k_1 \oplus m$
 $c_2 :=$ CTXT$'(c_1)$
 return c_2

$\diamond$

$\mathcal{L}_{\text{otp-real}}$

CTXT$'(m')$:
 $k \leftarrow \{0,1\}^\lambda$
 return $k \oplus m'$

$\mathcal{L}_{\text{hyb-1}}$

$\equiv$

CTXT(m):
 $k_1 \leftarrow \{0,1\}^\lambda$
 $c_1 := k_1 \oplus m$
 $c_2 :=$ CTXT$'(c_1)$
 return c_2

$\diamond$

$\mathcal{L}_{\text{otp-rand}}$

CTXT$'(m')$:
 $c \leftarrow \{0,1\}^\lambda$
 return c

$\mathcal{L}_{\text{hyb-2}}$

Claim 2.7 says that $\mathcal{L}_{\text{otp-real}} \equiv \mathcal{L}_{\text{otp-rand}}$, so Lemma 2.11 says that we can replace an instance of $\mathcal{L}_{\text{otp-real}}$ in a compound library with $\mathcal{L}_{\text{otp-rand}}$, as we have done here. This change will have no effect on the calling program.

CTXT(m):
 $k_1 \leftarrow \{0,1\}^\lambda$
 $c_1 := k_1 \oplus m$
 $c_2 :=$ CTXT$'(c_1)$
 return c_2

$\diamond$

$\mathcal{L}_{\text{otp-rand}}$

CTXT$'(m')$:
 $c \leftarrow \{0,1\}^\lambda$
 return c

$\mathcal{L}_{\text{hyb-2}}$

$\equiv$

CTXT(m):
 $k_1 \leftarrow \{0,1\}^\lambda$
 $c_1 := k_1 \oplus m$
 $c_2 \leftarrow \{0,1\}^\lambda$
 return c_2

$\mathcal{L}_{\text{hyb-3}}$

The only difference between these two libraries is that a subroutine call has been inlined. This difference has no effect on the calling program.

$\mathcal{L}_{\text{hyb-3}}$		$\mathcal{L}^{\Sigma}_{\text{ots\$-rand}}$
$\underline{\text{CTXT}(m):}$ $k_1 \leftarrow \{0,1\}^\lambda$ $c_1 := k_1 \oplus m$ $c_2 \leftarrow \{0,1\}^\lambda$ return c_2	$\equiv$	$\underline{\text{CTXT}(m):}$ $c_2 \leftarrow \{0,1\}^\lambda$ return c_2

The only difference between these two libraries is that the two highlighted lines have been removed. But it should be clear that these lines have no effect: k_1 is used only to compute c_1, which is never used again. Hence, this difference has no effect on the calling program.

The final hybrid is exactly $\mathcal{L}^{\Sigma}_{\text{ots\$-rand}}$ (although with a variable name changed). We have shown that $\mathcal{L}^{\Sigma}_{\text{ots \$-rand}} \equiv \mathcal{L}^{\Sigma}_{\text{ots \$-real}}$, meaning that this encryption scheme has one-time uniform ciphertexts.

Hybrid Technique: Concise Summary

We have now seen our first example of the hybrid technique for security proofs. All security proofs in this book use this technique.

- Proving security means showing that two particular libraries, say $\mathcal{L}_{\text{left}}$ and $\mathcal{L}_{\text{right}}$, are interchangeable.
- Often $\mathcal{L}_{\text{left}}$ and $\mathcal{L}_{\text{right}}$ are significantly different, making them hard to compare directly. To make the comparison more manageable, we can show a sequence of hybrid libraries, beginning with $\mathcal{L}_{\text{left}}$ and ending with $\mathcal{L}_{\text{right}}$. The idea is to break up the large "gap" between $\mathcal{L}_{\text{left}}$ and $\mathcal{L}_{\text{right}}$ into smaller ones that are easier to justify.
- It is helpful to think of "starting" at $\mathcal{L}_{\text{left}}$, and then making a sequence of small modifications to it, with the goal of eventually reaching $\mathcal{L}_{\text{right}}$. You must justify why each modification doesn't affect the calling program (i.e., why the two libraries before/after your modification are interchangeable).
- As discussed in Section 2.2, simple things like inlining/factoring out subroutines, changing unused variables, changing unreachable statements, or unrolling loops are always "allowable" modifications in a hybrid proof since they have no effect on

- the calling program. As we progress in the course, we will see more kinds of useful modifications.

A Contrasting Example

Usually the boundary between secure and insecure is razor thin. Let's make a small change to the previous encryption scheme to illustrate this point. Instead of applying OTP to the plaintext twice, with independent keys, what would happen if we use the same key?

Construction 2.14 ("dOuB ℓ∃ OTP")

	KeyGen:	Enc(k, m):	Dec(k, c_2):
$\mathcal{K} = \{0,1\}^\lambda$	$k \leftarrow \{0,1\}^\lambda$	$c_1 := k \oplus m$	$c_1 := k \oplus c_2$
$\mathcal{M} = \{0,1\}^\lambda$	return k	$c_2 := k \oplus c_1$	$m := k \oplus c_1$
$\mathcal{C} = \{0,1\}^\lambda$		return c_2	return m

You probably noticed that the ciphertext c_2 is computed as $c_2 := k \oplus (k \oplus m)$, which is just a fancy way of saying $c_2 := m$. There is certainly no way this kind of "double-OTP" is secure.

For educational purposes, let's try to repeat the steps of our previous security proof on this (insecure) scheme and see where things break down. If we wanted to show that Construction 2.14 has uniform ciphertexts, we would have to show that the following two libraries are interchangeable:

$\mathcal{L}^{\Sigma}_{\text{ots\$-real}}$		$\mathcal{L}^{\Sigma}_{\text{ots\$-rand}}$
CTXT(m):	$\stackrel{?}{\equiv}$	CTXT(m):
$k \leftarrow \{0,1\}^\lambda$ // KeyGen		$c \leftarrow \{0,1\}^\lambda$
$c_1 := k \oplus m$ } Enc		return c
$c_2 := k \oplus c_1$ } Enc		
return c_2		

In the previous hybrid proof, the first step was to factor out the statements " $k_2 \leftarrow \{0,1\}^\lambda$; $c_2 := k_2 \oplus c_1$ " into a separate subroutine, so we could argue that the result of c_2 was uniformly distributed. If we do something analogous with this example, we get:

$\mathcal{L}^{\Sigma}_{\text{ots\$-real}}$

```
CTXT(m):
  k ← {0,1}^λ
  c1 := k ⊕ m
  c2 := k ⊕ c1
  return c2
```

$\stackrel{?}{\equiv}$

```
CTXT(m):
  c1 := k ⊕ m  // ??
  c2 := CTXT'(c1)
  return c2
```

$\diamond$

$\mathcal{L}_{\text{otp-real}}$

```
CTXT'(m'):
  k ← {0,1}^λ
  return k ⊕ m'
```

$\mathcal{L}_{\text{hyb}}$

Do you see the problem? In " $\mathcal{L}_{\text{hyb}}$ ", we have tried to move the variable k into $\mathcal{L}_{\text{otp-real}}$. Since this scope is private, every operation we want to do with k has to be provided by its container library $\mathcal{L}_{\text{otp-real}}$. But there is a mismatch: $\mathcal{L}_{\text{otp-real}}$ only gives us a way to use k in one xor expression, whereas we need to use the same k in two xor expressions to match the behavior of $\mathcal{L}_{\text{ots \$-real}}$. The compound library $\mathcal{L}_{\text{hyb}}$ has an unresolved reference to k in the line " $c_1 := k \oplus m$ " and therefore doesn't have the same behavior as $\mathcal{L}_{\text{ots \$-real}}$.[4] This is the step of the security proof that breaks down.

Here's a more conceptual way to understand what went wrong here. The important property of OTP is that its ciphertexts look uniform when the key is used to encrypt only one plaintext. This "double OTP" variant uses OTP in a way that doesn't fulfill that condition, and therefore provides no security guarantee. The previous (successful) proof was able to factor out some xor's in terms of $\mathcal{L}_{\text{otp-real}}$ without breaking anything, and that's how we know the scheme was using OTP in a way that is consistent with its security guarantee.

As you can hopefully see, the process of a security proof provides a way to catch these kinds of problems. It is very common in a hybrid proof to factor out some statements in terms of a library from some other security definition. This step can only be done successfully if the underlying cryptography is being used in an appropriate way.

2.5 Compare/Contrast Security Definitions

In math, a definition can't really be "wrong," but it can be "not as useful as you hoped" or it can "fail to adequately capture your intuition" about the concept.

Security definitions are no different. In this chapter we introduced two security definitions: one in the "real-vs-random" style and one in the "left-vs-right" style. In this section we treat the security definitions themselves as objects worth studying. Are both of these security definitions "the same," in some sense? Do they both capture all of our intuitions about security?

One Security Definition Implies Another

One way to compare/contrast two security definitions is to prove that one implies the other. In other words, if an encryption scheme satisfies definition #1, then it also satisfies definition #2.

Theorem 2.15 *If an encryption scheme Σ has one-time uniform ciphertexts (Definition 2.5), then Σ also has one-time secrecy (Definition 2.6). In other words:*

$$\mathcal{L}^{\Sigma}_{\text{ots \$-real}} \equiv \mathcal{L}^{\Sigma}_{\text{ots \$-rand}} \Rightarrow \mathcal{L}^{\Sigma}_{\text{ots-L}} \equiv \mathcal{L}^{\Sigma}_{\text{ots-R}}.$$

If you are comfortable with what all the terminology means, then the meaning of this statement is quite simple and unsurprising. "If all plaintexts m induce a uniform distribution of ciphertexts, then all m induce the same distribution of ciphertexts."

This fairly straight-forward statement can be proven formally, giving us another example of the hybrid proof technique:

Proof We are proving an if-then statement. We want to show that the "then"-part of the statement is true; that is, $\mathcal{L}^{\Sigma}_{\text{ots-L}} \equiv \mathcal{L}^{\Sigma}_{\text{ots-R}}$. We are allowed to use the fact that the "if"-part is true; that is, $\mathcal{L}^{\Sigma}_{\text{ots\$-real}} \equiv \mathcal{L}^{\Sigma}_{\text{ots\$-rand}}$.

The proof uses the hybrid technique. We will start with the library $\mathcal{L}_{\text{ots-L}}$, and make a small sequence of justifiable changes to it, until finally reaching $\mathcal{L}_{\text{ots-r}}$. Along the way, we can use the fact that $\mathcal{L}_{\text{ots \$-real}} \equiv \mathcal{L}_{\text{ots \$-rand}}$. This suggests some "strategy" for the proof: if we can somehow get $\mathcal{L}_{\text{ots \$-real}}$ to appear as a component in one of the hybrid libraries, then we can replace it with $\mathcal{L}_{\text{ots \$-rand}}$ (or vice-versa), in a way that hopefully makes progress towards our goal of transforming $\mathcal{L}_{\text{ots-L}}$ to $\mathcal{L}_{\text{ots-R}}$.

Below we list the sequence of hybrid libraries, and justify why each one is interchangeable with the previous library.

The starting point of our hybrid sequence is $\mathcal{L}^{\Sigma}_{\text{ots-L}}$.

$\mathcal{L}^{\Sigma}_{\text{ots-L}}$
EAVESDROP (m_L, m_R):
$k \leftarrow \Sigma.\textbf{KeyGen}$
$c \leftarrow \Sigma.\textbf{Enc}(k, m_L)$
return$c$

Factoring out a block of statements into a subroutine makes it possible to write the library as a compound one, but does not affect its external behavior. Note that the new subroutine is exactly the $\mathcal{L}^{\Sigma}_{\text{ots\$-real}}$ li brary from Definition 2.5. This was a strategic choice, because of what happens next.

EAVESDROP(m_L, m_R):	$\diamond$	$\mathcal{L}^{\Sigma}_{\text{ots\$-real}}$
$c :=$ CTXT(m_L)		CTXT(m):
return c		$k \leftarrow \Sigma.\mathsf{KeyGen}$
		$c \leftarrow \Sigma.\mathsf{Enc}(k, m)$
		return c

$\mathcal{L}^{\Sigma}_{\text{ots\$-real}}$ has been replaced with $\mathcal{L}^{\Sigma}_{\text{ots \$-rand}}$. The chaining lemma Lemma 2.11 says that this change has no effect on the library's behavior, since the two $\mathcal{L}_{\text{ots\$-}\star}$ libraries are interchangeable.

EAVESDROP(m_L, m_R):	$\diamond$	$\mathcal{L}^{\Sigma}_{\text{ots\$-rand}}$
$c :=$ CTXT(m_L)		CTXT(m):
return c		$c \leftarrow \Sigma.\mathcal{C}$
		return c

The argument to CTXT has been changed from m_L to m_R. This has no effect on the library's behavior since CTXT does not actually use its argument in these hybrids!

EAVESDROP(m_L, m_R):	$\diamond$	$\mathcal{L}^{\Sigma}_{\text{ots\$-rand}}$
$c :=$ CTXT(m_R)		CTXT(m):
return c		$c \leftarrow \Sigma.\mathcal{C}$
		return c

The previous transition is the most important one in the proof, as it gives insight into how we came up with this particular sequence of hybrids. Looking at the desired endpoints of our sequence of hybrids $-\mathcal{L}^{\Sigma}_{\text{ots-L}}$ and $\mathcal{L}^{\Sigma}_{\text{ots-R}}$ - we see that they differ only in swapping m_L for m_R. If we are not comfortable eyeballing things, we'd like a better justification for why it is "safe" to exchange m_L for m_R (i.e., why it has no effect on the calling program). However, the uniform ciphertexts property shows that $\mathcal{L}^{\Sigma}_{\text{ots-L}}$ in fact has the same behavior as a library $\mathcal{L}_{\text{hyb- 2}}$ that doesn't use either of m_L or m_R. In a program that doesn't use m_L or m_R, it is clear that we can switch them!

Having made this crucial change, we can now perform the same sequence of steps, but in reverse.

$\mathcal{L}^{\Sigma}_{\text{ots\$-rand}}$ has been replaced with $\mathcal{L}^{\Sigma}_{\text{ots\$-real}}$. This is another application of the chaining lemma.

```
EAVESDROP(m_L, m_R):        ◇   L^Σ_ots$-real
  c := CTXT(m_R)                CTXT(m):
  return c                        k ← Σ.KeyGen
                                  c ← Σ.Enc(k, m)
                                  return c
```

A subroutine call has been inlined, which has no effect on the library's behavior. The result is exactly $\mathcal{L}^{\Sigma}_{\text{ots-R}}$.

```
L^Σ_ots-R
EAVESDROP(m_L, m_R):
  k ← Σ.KeyGen
  c ← Σ.Enc(k, m_R)
  return c
```

Putting everything together, we showed that $\mathcal{L}^{\Sigma}_{\text{ots-L}} \equiv \mathcal{L}_{\text{hyb-1}} \equiv \cdots \equiv \mathcal{L}_{\text{hyb-4}} \equiv \mathcal{L}^{\Sigma}_{\text{ots-R}}$. This completes the proof, and we conclude that Σ satisfies the definition of one-time secrecy.

One Security Definition Doesn't Imply Another

Another way we might compare security definitions is to identify any schemes that satisfy one definition without satisfying the other. This helps us understand the boundaries and "edge cases" of the definition.

A word of warning: If we have two security definitions that both capture our intuitions rather well, then any scheme which satisfies one definition and not the other is bound to appear unnatural and contrived. The point is to gain more understanding of the security definitions themselves, and unnatural/contrived schemes are just a means to do that.

Theorem 2.16 :There is an encryption scheme that satisfies one-time secrecy (Definition 2.6) but not one-time uniform ciphertexts (Definition 2.5). In other words, one-time secrecy does not necessarily imply one-time uniform ciphertexts.

Proof : One such encryption scheme is given below:

	KeyGen:	$\text{Enc}(k, m \in \{0,1\}^\lambda)$:	$\text{Dec}(k, c \in \{0,1\}^{\lambda+2})$:
$\mathcal{K} = \{0,1\}^\lambda$ $\mathcal{M} = \{0,1\}^\lambda$ $\mathcal{C} = \{0,1\}^{\lambda+2}$	$k \leftarrow \{0,1\}^\lambda$ return k	$c' := k \oplus m$ $c := c' \| 00$ return c	c' := first λ bits of c return $k \oplus c'$

This scheme is just OTP with the bits 00 added to every ciphertext. The following facts about the scheme should be believable (and the exercises encourage you to prove them formally if you would like more practice at that sort of thing):

- This scheme satisfies one-time one-time secrecy, meaning that encryptions of m_L are distributed identically to encryptions of m_R, for any m_L and m_R of the attacker's choice. We can characterize the ciphertext distribution in both cases as " λ uniform
- bits followed by 00." Think about how you might use the hybrid proof technique to formally prove that this scheme satisfies one-time secrecy!
- This scheme does not satisfy the one-time uniform ciphertexts property. Its ciphertexts always end with 00 , whereas uniform strings end with 00 with probability 1/4. Think about how you might formallize this observation as a calling program / distinguisher for the relevant two libraries!

You might be thinking, surely this can be fixed by redefining the ciphertext space as C as the set of $\lambda + 2$-bit strings whose last two bits are 00. This is a clever idea, and indeed it would work. If we change the definition of the ciphertext space C following this suggestion, then the scheme would satisfy the uniform ciphertexts property (this is because the $\mathcal{L}_{\text{ots \$-rand}}$ library samples uniformly from whatever C is specified as part of the encryption scheme).

But this observation raises an interesting point. Isn't it weird that security hinges on how narrowly you define the set C of ciphertexts, when C really has no effect on the functionality of encryption? Again, no one really cares about this contrived "OTP + 00" encryption scheme. The point is to illuminate interesting edge cases in the security definition itself!

Exercises

2.1. Below are two calling programs $\mathcal{A}_1, \mathcal{A}_2$ and two libraries $\mathcal{L}_1, \mathcal{L}_2$ with a common interface:

$\mathcal{A}_1$	$\mathcal{A}_2$	$\mathcal{L}_1$	$\mathcal{L}_2$
r_1 := RAND(6) r_2 := RAND(6) return $r_1 \stackrel{?}{=} r_2$	r := RAND(6) return $r \stackrel{?}{\geqslant} 3$	RAND(n): $r \leftarrow \mathbb{Z}_n$ return r	RAND(n): return 0

(a) What is $\Pr[\mathcal{A}_1 \diamond \mathcal{L}_1 \Rightarrow \text{true}]$?

(b) What is $\Pr[\mathcal{A}_1 \diamond \mathcal{L}_2 \Rightarrow \text{true}]$?

(c) What is $\Pr[\mathcal{A}_2 \diamond \mathcal{L}_1 \Rightarrow \text{true}]$?

(d) What is $\Pr[\mathcal{A}_2 \diamond \mathcal{L}_2 \Rightarrow \text{true}]$?

2.2. In each problem, a pair of libraries are described. State whether or not $\mathcal{L}_{\text{left}} \equiv \mathcal{L}_{\text{right}}$. If so, show how they assign identical probabilities to all outcomes. If not, then describe a successful distinguisher.

Assume that both libraries use the same value of n. Does your answer ever depend on the choice of n ?

In part (a), $\bar{x}$ denotes the bitwise-complement of x. In part (d), $x \& y$ denotes the bitwiseAND of the two strings:

(a)

$\mathcal{L}_{\text{left}}$	$\mathcal{L}_{\text{right}}$
QUERY() : $x \leftarrow \{0,1\}^n$ return x	QUERY() : $x \leftarrow \{0,1\}^n$ $y := \overline{x}$ return y

(b)

$\mathcal{L}_{\text{left}}$	$\mathcal{L}_{\text{right}}$
QUERY() : $x \leftarrow \mathbb{Z}_n$ return x	QUERY() : $x \leftarrow \mathbb{Z}_n$ $y := 2x \,\%\, n$ return y

(c)

$\mathcal{L}_{\text{left}}$	$\mathcal{L}_{\text{right}}$
QUERY($c \in \mathbb{Z}_n$) : if $c = 0$ return null $x \leftarrow \mathbb{Z}_n$ return x	QUERY($c \in \mathbb{Z}_n$) : if $c = 0$ return null $x \leftarrow \mathbb{Z}_n$ $y := cx \,\%\, n$ return y

(d)

$\mathcal{L}_{\text{left}}$	$\mathcal{L}_{\text{right}}$
QUERY() : $x \leftarrow \{0,1\}^n$ $y \leftarrow \{0,1\}^n$ return $x \,\&\, y$	QUERY() : $z \leftarrow \{0,1\}^n$ return z

2.3. Show that the following libraries are interchangeable:

$\mathcal{L}_{\text{left}}$
QUERY($m \in \{0,1\}^\lambda$):
$x \leftarrow \{0,1\}^\lambda$
$y := x \oplus m$
return (x, y)

$\mathcal{L}_{\text{right}}$
QUERY($m \in \{0,1\}^\lambda$):
$y \leftarrow \{0,1\}^\lambda$
$x := y \oplus m$
return (x, y)

Note that x and y are swapped in the first two lines, but not in the return statement.

2.4. Show that the following libraries are not interchangeable. Describe an explicit distinguishing calling program, and compute its output probabilities when linked to both libraries:

$\mathcal{L}_{\text{left}}$
EAVESDROP($m_L, m_R \in \{0,1\}^\lambda$):
$k \leftarrow \{0,1\}^\lambda$
$c := k \oplus m_L$
return (k, c)

$\mathcal{L}_{\text{right}}$
EAVESDROP($m_L, m_R \in \{0,1\}^\lambda$):
$k \leftarrow \{0,1\}^\lambda$
$c := k \oplus m_R$
return (k, c)

★ 2.5. In abstract algebra, a (finite) group is a finite set $\mathbb{G}$ of items together with an operator $\otimes$ satisfying the following axioms:

- Closure: for all $a, b \in \mathbb{G}$, we have $a \otimes b \in \mathbb{G}$.
- Identity: there is a special identity element $e \in \mathbb{G}$ that satisfies $e \otimes a = a \otimes e = a$ for all $a \in \mathbb{G}$. We typically write " 1 " rather than e for the identity element.
- Associativity: for all $a, b, c \in \mathbb{G}$, we have $(a \otimes b) \otimes c = a \otimes (b \otimes c)$.
- Inverses: for all $a \in \mathbb{G}$, there exists an inverse element $b \in \mathbb{G}$ such that $a \otimes b = b \otimes a$ is the identity element of $\mathbb{G}$. We typically write " a^{-1} " for the inverse of a.

Define the following encryption scheme in terms of an arbitrary group ($\mathbb{G}, \otimes$):

$\mathcal{K}$	$= \mathbb{G}$	**KeyGen:** $k \leftarrow \mathbb{G}$	**Enc(k, m):** **return$k$** $\otimes m$	**Dec(k, c):** ??
$\mathcal{M}$	$= \mathbb{G}$			
$\mathcal{C}$	$= \mathbb{G}$	return k		

(a) Prove that $\{0,1\}^\lambda$ is a group with respect to the xor operator. What is the identity element, and what is the inverse of a value $x \in \{0,1\}^\lambda$?

(b) Fill in the details of the Dec algorithm and prove (using the group axioms) that the scheme satisfies correctness.

(c) Prove that the scheme satisfies one-time secrecy.

2.6. In the proof of Claim 2.9 we considered an attacker / calling program that calls $\text{ctxt}(0^\lambda)$.

(a) How does this attacker's effectiveness change if it calls $\text{ctxt}(1^\lambda)$ instead?

(b) How does its effectiveness change if it calls $\text{ctxt}(m)$ for a uniformly chosen m ?

2.7. The following scheme encrypts a plaintext by simply reordering its bits, according to the secret permutation k.

$$\mathcal{K} = \left\{ \begin{array}{c} \text{permutations} \\ \text{of } \{1, \ldots, \lambda\} \end{array} \right\}$$

$\mathcal{M} = \{0,1\}^\lambda$

$\mathcal{C} = \{0,1\}^\lambda$

KeyGen:

Enc(k, m):

for $i := 1$ to λ:

$c_{k(i)} := m_i$

return $c_1 \cdots c_\lambda$

Dec(k, c):

$k \leftarrow \mathcal{K}$

return k

for $i := 1$ to λ:

$m_i := c_{k(i)}$

return $m_1 \cdots m_\lambda$

Show that the scheme does not have one-time secrecy, by constructing a program that distinguishes the two relevant libraries from the one-time secrecy definition.

2.8. Show that the following encryption scheme does not have one-time secrecy, by constructing a program that distinguishes the two relevant libraries from the one-time secrecy definition.

$\mathcal{K}$	$= \{1, \ldots, 9\}$		KeyGen:	Enc(k, m):
$\mathcal{M}$	$= \{1, \ldots, 9\}$		$k \leftarrow \{1, \ldots, 9\}$	
$\mathcal{C}$	$= \mathbb{Z}_{10}$		return k	

2.9. Consider the following encryption scheme. It supports plaintexts from $\mathcal{M} = \{0,1\}^\lambda$ and ciphertexts from $C = \{0,1\}^{2\lambda}$. Its keyspace is:

$$\mathcal{K} = \{k \in \{0,1,-\}^{2\lambda} \mid k \text{ contains exactly } \lambda'' - \text{"characters}\}$$

To encrypt plaintext m under key k, we "fill in" the _ characters in k using the bits of m.

Show that the scheme does not have one-time secrecy, by constructing a program that distinguishes the two relevant libraries from the one-time secrecy definition.

Example: Below is an example encryption of $m = 1101100001$.

$$\begin{aligned} k &= 1\_0\_11010\_1\_0\_0\_ \\ m &= 110100001 \\ \Rightarrow \text{Enc}(k,m) &= 1110011101011000001 \end{aligned}$$

2.10. Suppose we modify the scheme from the previous problem to first permute the bits of m (as in Exercise 2.7) and then use them to fill in the "_" characters in a template string. In other words, the key specifies a random permutation on positions $\{1, \ldots, \lambda\}$ as well as a random template string that is 2λ characters long with λ" " characters.

Show that even with this modification the scheme does not have one-time secrecy.

⋆ 2.11. Prove that if an encryption scheme Σ has $|\Sigma.\mathcal{K}| < |\Sigma.\mathcal{M}|$ then it cannot satisfy onetime secrecy. Try to structure your proof as an explicit attack on such a scheme (i.e., a distinguisher against the appropriate libraries).

The Enc algorithm of one-time pad is deterministic, but our definitions of encryption allow Enc to be randomized (i.e., it may give different outputs when called twice with the same k and m). For full credit, you should prove the statement even for the case of Enc is randomized. However, you may assume that Dec is deterministic.

2.12. Let Σ denote an encryption scheme where $\Sigma.C \subseteq \Sigma.\mathcal{M}$ (so that it is possible to use the scheme to encrypt its own ciphertexts). Define Σ^2 to be the following nested-encryption scheme:

Prove that if Σ satisfies one-time secrecy, then so does Σ^2.

2.13. Let Σ denote an encryption scheme and define Σ^2 to be the following encrypt-twice scheme:

$$\mathcal{K} = (\Sigma.\mathcal{K})^2$$
$$\mathcal{M} = \Sigma.\mathcal{M}$$
$$\mathcal{C} = \Sigma.\mathcal{C}$$

KeyGen:
$k_1 \leftarrow \Sigma.\mathcal{K}$
$k_2 \leftarrow \Sigma.\mathcal{K}$
return (k_1, k_2)

$\text{Enc}((k_1, k_2), m)$:
$c_1 := \Sigma.\text{Enc}(k_1, m)$
$c_2 := \Sigma.\text{Enc}(k_2, m)$
return (c_1, c_2)

$\text{Dec}((k_1, k_2), (c_1, c_2))$:
$m_1 := \Sigma.\text{Dec}(k_1, c_1)$
$m_2 := \Sigma.\text{Dec}(k_2, c_2)$
if $m_1 \neq m_2$ return err
return m_1

Prove that if Σ satisfies one-time secrecy, then so does Σ^2.

2.14. Prove that an encryption scheme Σ satisfies one-time secrecy if and only if the following two libraries are interchangeable:

$\mathcal{L}^{\Sigma}_{\text{left}}$	$\mathcal{L}^{\Sigma}_{\text{right}}$
$\text{FOO}(m \in \Sigma.\mathcal{M})$:	$\text{FOO}(m \in \Sigma.\mathcal{M})$:
$k \leftarrow \Sigma.\text{KeyGen}$	$k \leftarrow \Sigma.\text{KeyGen}$
	$m' \leftarrow \Sigma.\mathcal{M}$
$c \leftarrow \Sigma.\text{Enc}(k, m)$	$c \leftarrow \Sigma.\text{Enc}(k, m')$
return c	return c

Note: you must prove both directions of the if-and-only-if with a hybrid proof.

2.15. Prove that an encryption scheme Σ has one-time secrecy if and only if the following two libraries are interchangeable:

$\mathcal{L}^{\Sigma}_{\text{left}}$	$\mathcal{L}^{\Sigma}_{\text{right}}$
$\text{FOO}(m_L, m_R \in \Sigma.\mathcal{M})$:	$\text{FOO}(m_L, m_R \in \Sigma.\mathcal{M})$:
$k_1 \leftarrow \Sigma.\text{KeyGen}$	$k_1 \leftarrow \Sigma.\text{KeyGen}$
$c_1 := \Sigma.\text{Enc}(k_1, m_L)$	$c_1 := \Sigma.\text{Enc}(k_1, m_R)$
$k_2 \leftarrow \Sigma.\text{KeyGen}$	$k_2 \leftarrow \Sigma.\text{KeyGen}$
$c_2 := \Sigma.\text{Enc}(k_2, m_R)$	$c_2 := \Sigma.\text{Enc}(k_2, m_L)$
return (c_1, c_2)	return (c_1, c_2)

Note: you must prove both directions of the if-and-only-if with a hybrid proof.

2.16. Formally define a variant of the one-time secrecy definition in which the calling program can obtain two ciphertexts (on chosen plaintexts) encrypted under the same key. Call it two-time secrecy.

(a) Suppose someone tries to prove that one-time secrecy implies two-time secrecy. Show where the proof appears to break down.

(b) Describe an attack demonstrating that one-time pad does not satisfy your definition of two-time secrecy.

2.17. In this problem we consider modifying one-time pad so that the key is not chosen uniformly. Let $\mathcal{D}_\lambda$ denote the probability distribution over $\{0,1\}^\lambda$ where we choose each bit of the result to be 0 with probability 0.4 and 1 with probability 0.6 .

Let Σ denote one-time pad encryption scheme but with the key sampled from distribution $\mathcal{D}_\lambda$ rather than the uniform distribution on $\{0,1\}^\lambda$.

(a) Consider the case of $\lambda = 5$. A calling program $\mathcal{A}$ for the $\mathcal{L}^{\Sigma}_{\text{ots-}\star}$ libraries calls EAVESDROP(01011, 10001) and receives the result 01101. What is the probability that this happens, assuming that $\mathcal{A}$ is linked to $\mathcal{L}_{\text{ots-L}}$? What about when $\mathcal{A}$ is linked to $\mathcal{L}_{\text{ots-R}}$?

(b) Turn this observation into an explicit attack on the one-time secrecy of Σ.

2.18. Complete the proof of Theorem 2.16.

(a) Formally prove (using the hybrid technique) that the scheme in that theorem satisfies one-time secrecy.

(b) Give a distinguishing calling program to show that the scheme doesn't satisfy one-time uniform ciphertexts.

Chapter-3

Secret Sharing

DNS is the system that maps human-memorable Internet domains like irs.gov to machine-readable IP addresses like 166.123.218.220. If an attacker can masquerade as the DNS system and convince your computer that irs.gov actually resides at some other IP address, it might result in a bad day for you.

To protect against these kinds of attacks, a replacement called DNSSEC has been proposed. DNSSEC uses cryptography to make it impossible to falsify a domain-name mapping. The cryptography required to authenticate DNS mappings is certainly interesting, but an even more fundamental question remains: Who can be trusted with the master cryptographic keys to the system? The non-profit organization in charge of these kinds of things (ICANN) has chosen the following system. The master key is split into 7 pieces and distributed on smart cards to 7 geographically diverse people, who keep them in safe-deposit boxes.

At least five key-holding members of this fellowship would have to meet at a secure data center in the United States to reboot [DNSSEC] in case of a very unlikely system collapse.

"If you round up five of these guys, they can decrypt [the root key] should the West Coast fall in the water and the East Coast get hit by a nuclear bomb," [said] Richard Lamb, program manager for DNSSEC at ICANN. [1]

How is it possible that any 5 out of the 7 key-holders can reconstruct the master key, but (presumably) 4 out of the 7 cannot? The solution lies in a cryptographic tool called a secret-sharing scheme, the topic of this chapter.

3.1 Definitions

We begin by introducing the syntax of a secret-sharing scheme:

Definition 3.1 (Secret-sharing): *A t-**out-of-** n **threshold secret-sharing scheme (TSSS)** consists of the following algorithms:*

- Share: a randomized algorithm that takes a message $m \in \mathcal{M}$ as input, and outputs a sequence $s = (s_1, \ldots, s_n)$ of shares.

- Reconstruct: a deterministic algorithm that takes a collection of t or more shares as input, and outputs a message.

We call $\mathcal{M}$ the message space of the scheme, and t its threshold. As usual, we refer to the parameters/components of a scheme Σ as $\Sigma.t, \Sigma.n, \Sigma.\mathcal{M}, \Sigma.$ Share, $\Sigma.$ Reconstruct.

In secret-sharing, we number the users as $\{1, \dots, n\}$, with user i receiving share s_i. Let $U \subseteq \{1, \dots, n\}$ be a subset of users. Then $\{s_i \mid i \in U\}$ refers to the set of shares belonging to users U. If $|U| \geqslant t$, we say that U is authorized; otherwise it is unauthorized. The goal of secret sharing is for all authorized sets of users/shares to be able to reconstruct the secret, while all unauthorized sets learn nothing.

Definition 3.2 (TSSS correctness): *At-out-of-n TSSS satisfies correctness if, for all authorized sets* $U \subseteq \{1, \dots, n\}$ *(i.e.,* $|U| \geqslant t$ *) and for all* $\mathbf{s} \leftarrow Share(m)$, *we have* $Reconstruct(\{s_i \mid i \in U\}) = m$.

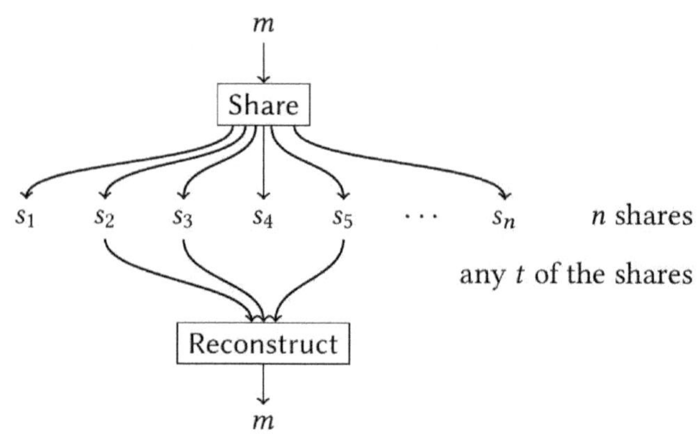

Security Definition

We'd like a security guarantee that says something like:

> *if you know only an unauthorized set of shares, then you learn no information about the choice of secret message.*

To translate this informal statement into a formal security definition, we define two libraries that allow the calling program to learn a set of shares (for an unauthorized set), and that differ only in which secret is shared. If the two libraries are interchangeable, then we conclude that seeing an unauthorized set of shares leaks no information about the choice of secret message. The definition looks like this:

Definition 3.3 (TSSS security):*Let Σ be a threshold secret-sharing scheme. We say that Σ is secure if $\mathcal{L}^{\Sigma}_{tsss-L} \equiv \mathcal{L}^{\Sigma}_{tsss-R}$, where:*

$\mathcal{L}^{\Sigma}_{\text{tsss-L}}$
SHARE($m_L, m_R \in \Sigma.\mathcal{M}, U$):
if $\lvert U\rvert \geqslant \Sigma.t$: return err
$s \leftarrow \Sigma.\text{Share}(m_L)$
return $\{s_i \mid i \in U\}$

$\mathcal{L}^{\Sigma}_{\text{tsss-R}}$
SHARE($m_L, m_R \in \Sigma.\mathcal{M}, U$):
if $\lvert U\rvert \geqslant \Sigma.t$: return err
$s \leftarrow \Sigma.\text{Share}(m_R)$
return $\{s_i \mid i \in U\}$

In an attempt to keep the notation uncluttered, we have not written the type of the argument U, which is $U \subseteq \{1, \dots, \Sigma.n\}$.

Discussion & Pitfalls

- Similar to the definition of one-time secrecy of encryption, we let the calling program choose the two secret messages that will be shared. As before, this models an attack scenario in which the adversary has partial knowledge or influence on the secret m being shared.

- The calling program also chooses the set U of users' shares to obtain. The libraries make it impossible for the calling program to obtain the shares of an authorized set (returning err in that case). This does not mean that a user is never allowed to distribute an authorized number of shares (this would be strange indeed, since it would make any future reconstruction impossible). It just means that we want a security definition that says something about an attacker who sees only an unauthorized set of shares, so we formalize security in terms of libraries with this restriction.

- Consider a 6-out-of-10 threshold secret-sharing scheme. With the libraries above, the calling program can receive the shares of users {1, ... ,5} (an unauthorized set) in one call to SHARE, and then receive the shares of users {6, ... ,10} in another call. It might seem like the calling program can then combine these shares to reconstruct the secret (if the same message was shared in both calls). However, this is not the case because these two sets of shares came from two independent executions of the Share algorithm. Shares generated by one call to Share should not be expected to function with shares generated by another call, even if both calls to Share used the same secret message.

- Recall that in our style of defining security using libraries, it is only the internal differences between the libraries that must be hidden. Anything that is the same between the two libraries need not be hidden. One thing that is the same for the two libraries here is the fact that they output the shares belonging to the same set of users U. This security definition does not require shares to hide which user they belong to. Indeed, you can modify a secret-sharing scheme so that each user's identity is appended to his/her corresponding share, and the result would still satisfy the security definition above.

- Just like the encryption definition does not address the problem of key distribution, the secret-sharing definition does not address the problem of who should run the Share algorithm (if its input m is so secret that it cannot be entrusted to any single person), or how the shares should be delivered to the n different users. Those concerns are considered out of scope by the problem of secret-sharing (although we later discuss clever approaches to the first problem). Rather, the focus is simply on whether it is even possible to encode data in such a way that an unauthorized set of shares gives no information about the secret, while any authorized set completely reveals the secret.

An Insecure Approach

One way to understand the security of secret sharing is to see an example of an "obvious" but insecure approach for secret sharing, and study why it is insecure.

Let's consider a 5 -out-of- 5 secret-sharing scheme. This means we want to split a secret into 5 pieces so that any 4 of the pieces leak nothing. One way you might think to do this is to literally chop up the secret into 5 pieces. For example, if the secret is 500 bits, you might give the first 100 bits to user 1 , the second 100 bits to user 2 , and so on.

Construction 3.4

(Insecure TSSS)

$\mathcal{M} = \{0,1\}^{500}$ $t = 5$ $n = 5$	Share(m): split m into $m = s_1 \| \cdots \| s_5$, where each $\lvert s_i \rvert = 100$ return $(s_1, \ldots, s_5)$	Reconstruct($s_1, \ldots, s_5$): return $s_1 \| \cdots \| s_5$

It is true that the secret can be constructed by concatenating all 5 shares, and so this construction satisfies the correctness property. (The only authorized set is the set of all 5 users, so we write Reconstruct to expect all 5 shares.)

However, the scheme is insecure (as promised). Suppose you have even just 1 share. It is true that you don't know the secret in its entirety, but the security definition (for 5-out-of- 5 secret sharing) demands that a single share reveals nothing about the secret. Of course knowing 100 bits of something is not the same as than knowing nothing about it.

We can leverage this observation to make a more formal attack on the scheme, in the form of a distinguisher between the two $\mathcal{L}_{\text{tsss-}\star}$ libraries. As an extreme case, we can distinguish between shares of an all-0 secret and shares of an all-1 secret:

$$\begin{array}{l}\mathcal{A}\\ s_1 := \text{sHARE}(0^{500}, 1^{500}, \{1\})\\ \text{return } s_1 \stackrel{?}{=} 0^{100}\end{array}$$

Let's link this calling program to both of the $\mathcal{L}_{\text{tsss-}\star}$ libraries and see what happens:

$\mathcal{A}$		$\mathcal{L}_{\text{tsss-L}}$
$s_1 := \text{SHARE}(0^{500}, 1^{500}, \{1\})$ return $s_1 \stackrel{?}{=} 0^{100}$	$\diamond$	SHARE(m_L, m_R, U): if $\lvert U\rvert \geqslant t$: return err $s \leftarrow$ Share(m_L) return $\{s_i \mid i \in U\}$

When $\mathcal{A}$ is linked to $\mathcal{L}_{\text{tsss-L}}$, it receives a share of 0^{500}, which will itself be a string of all zeroes. In this case, $\mathcal{A}$ outputs 1 with probability 1.

$\mathcal{A}$		$\mathcal{L}_{\text{tsss-R}}$
$s_1 := \text{SHARE}(0^{500}, 1^{500}, \{1\})$ return $s_1 \stackrel{?}{=} 0^{100}$	$\diamond$	SHARE(m_L, m_R, U): if $\lvert U\rvert \geqslant t$: return err $s \leftarrow$ Share(m_R) return $\{s_i \mid i \in U\}$

When $\mathcal{A}$ is linked to $\mathcal{L}_{\text{tsss-R}}$, it receives a share of 1^{500} which will be a string of all ones. In this case, $\mathcal{A}$ outputs 1 with probability 0.

We have constructed a calling program which behaves very differently (indeed, as differently as possible) in the presence of the two libraries. Hence, this secret-sharing scheme is not secure.

Hopefully this example demonstrates one of the main challenges (and amazing things) about secret-sharing schemes. It is easy to reveal information about the secret gradually as more shares are obtained, like in this insecure example. However, the security definition of secret sharing is that the shares must leak absolutely no information about the secret, until the number of shares passes the threshold value.

3.2 A Simple 2-out-of-2 Scheme

Believe it or not, we have already seen a simple secret-sharing scheme! In fact, it might even be best to think of one-time pad as the simplest secret-sharing scheme.

Construction 3.5

(2-out-of-2 TSSS)

$\mathcal{M} = \{0,1\}^{500}$ $t = 5$ $n = 5$	Share(m): split m into $m = s_1 \| \cdots \| s_5$, where each $\|s_i\| = 100$ return $(s_1, \ldots, s_5)$	Reconstruct($s_1, \ldots, s_5$): return $s_1 \| \cdots \| s_5$

Since it's a 2 -out-of- 2 scheme, the only authorized set of users is $\{1,2\}$, so Reconstruct is written to expect both shares s_1 and s_2 as its inputs. Correctness follows easily from what we've already learned about the properties of xor.

Example: *If we want to share the string* $m = 1101010001$ *then the Share algorithm might choose*

$$\begin{aligned} s_1 &:= 0110000011 \\ s_2 &:= s_1 \oplus m \\ &= 0110000011 \oplus 1101010001 = 1011010010 \end{aligned}$$

Then the secret can be reconstructed by xoring the two shares together, via:

$$s_1 \oplus s_2 = 0110000011 \oplus 1011010010 = 1101010001 = m.$$

Remember that this example shows just one possible execution of Share(1101010001), but Share is a randomized algorithm and many other values of (s_1, s_2) *are possible.*

Theorem 3.6 Construction 3.5 is a secure 2-out-of-2 threshold secret-sharing scheme.

Proof Let Σ denote Construction 3.5. We will show that $\mathcal{L}^{\Sigma}_{\text{tsss-L}} \equiv \mathcal{L}^{\Sigma}_{\text{tsss-R}}$ using a hybrid proof.

As usual, the starting point is $\mathcal{L}^{\Sigma}_{\text{tsss-L}}$, shown here with the details of the secret-sharing scheme filled in (and the types of the subroutine arguments omitted to reduce clutter).

$\mathcal{L}^{\Sigma}_{\text{tsss-L}}$:

$\mathcal{L}^{\Sigma}_{\text{tsss-L}}$

```
SHARE(m_L, m_R, U):
  if |U| ⩾ 2: return err
  s_1 ← {0,1}^ℓ
  s_2 := s_1 ⊕ m_L
  return {s_i | i ∈ U}
```

It has no effect on the library's behavior if we duplicate the main body of the library into 3 branches of a new if-statement. The reason for doing so is that the scheme generates s_1 and s_2 differently. This means that our proof will eventually handle the 3 different unauthorized sets ($\{1\}, \{2\}$, and $\emptyset$) in fundamentally different ways.

```
SHARE(m_L, m_R, U):
  if |U| ⩾ 2: return err
  if U = {1}:
    s_1 ← {0,1}^ℓ
    s_2 := s_1 ⊕ m_L
    return {s_1}
  elsif U = {2}:
    s_1 ← {0,1}^ℓ
    s_2 := s_1 ⊕ m_L
    return {s_2}
  else return ∅
```

The definition of s_2 has been changed in the first if-branch. This has no effect on the library's behavior since s_2 is never actually used in this branch.

```
SHARE(m_L, m_R, U):
  if |U| ⩾ 2: return err
  if U = {1}:
    s_1 ← {0,1}^ℓ
    s_2 := s_1 ⊕ m_R
    return {s_1}
  elsif U = {2}:
    s_1 ← {0,1}^ℓ
    s_2 := s_1 ⊕ m_L
    return {s_2}
  else return ∅
```

Recognizing the second branch of the if-statement as a one-time pad encryption (of m_L under key s_1), we factor out the generation of s_2 in terms of the library $\mathcal{L}^{\text{OTP}}_{\text{ots-L}}$ from the one-time secrecy definition. This has no effect on the library's behavior. Importantly, the subroutine in $\mathcal{L}^{\text{OTP}}_{\text{ots-L}}$ expects two arguments, so that is what we must pass. We choose to pass m_L and m_R for reasons that should become clear very soon.

```
SHARE(m_L, m_R, U):
  if |U| ⩾ 2: return err
  if U = {1}:
    s_1 ← {0,1}^ℓ
    s_2 := s_1 ⊕ m_R
    return {s_1}
  elsif U = {2}:
    s_2 ← EAVESDROP(m_L, m_R)
    return {s_2}
  else return ∅
```

◇

```
L^OTP_ots-L
EAVESDROP(m_L, m_R):
  k ← {0,1}^ℓ
  c := k ⊕ m_L
  return c
```

We have replaced $\mathcal{L}^{\text{OTP}}_{\text{ots-L}}$ with $\mathcal{L}^{\text{OTP}}_{\text{ots-R}}$. From the one-time secrecy of one-time pad (and the composition lemma), this change has no effect on the library's behavior.

```
SHARE(m_L, m_R, U):
  if |U| ⩾ 2: return err
  if U = {1}:
    s_1 ← {0,1}^ℓ
    s_2 := s_1 ⊕ m_R
    return {s_1}
  elsif U = {2}:
    s_2 ← EAVESDROP(m_L, m_R)
    return {s_2}
  else return ∅
```

◇

```
L^OTP_ots-R
EAVESDROP(m_L, m_R):
  k ← {0,1}^ℓ
  c := k ⊕ m_R
  return c
```

A subroutine has been inlined; no effect on the library's behavior.

```
SHARE(m_L, m_R, U):
  if |U| ≥ 2: return err
  if U = {1}:
    s1 ← {0,1}^ℓ
    s2 := s1 ⊕ m_R
    return {s1}
  elsif U = {2}:
    s1 ← {0,1}^ℓ
    s2 := s1 ⊕ m_R
    return {s2}
  else return ∅
```

The code has been simplified. Specifically, the branches of the if-statement can all be unified, with no effect on the library's behavior. The result is $\mathcal{L}^{\Sigma}_{\text{tsss-R}}$.

$\mathcal{L}^{\Sigma}_{\text{tsss-R}}$:

```
L^Σ_tsss-R
SHARE(m_L, m_R, U):
  if |U| ≥ 2: return err
  s1 ← {0,1}^ℓ
  s2 := s1 ⊕ m_R
  return {s_i | i ∈ U}
```

We showed that $\mathcal{L}^{\Sigma}_{\text{tsss-L}} \equiv \mathcal{L}_{\text{hyb-1}} \equiv \cdots \equiv \mathcal{L}_{\text{hyb-5}} \equiv \mathcal{L}^{\Sigma}_{\text{tsss-R}}$, and so the secret-sharing scheme is secure.

We in fact proved a slightly more general statement. The only property of one-time pad we used was its one-time secrecy. Substituting one-time pad for any other one-time secret encryption scheme would still allow the same proof to go through. So we actually proved the following:

Theorem 3.7 *If Σ is an encryption scheme with one-time secrecy, then the following 2-out-of-2 threshold secret-sharing scheme $\mathcal{S}$ is secure:*

$\mathcal{M} = \Sigma.\mathcal{M}$ $t = 2$ $n = 2$	Share(m): $s_1 \leftarrow \Sigma.$ KeyGen $s_2 \leftarrow \Sigma.\text{Enc}(s_1, m)$ return (s_1, s_2)	Reconstruct(s_1, s_2): return Σ.Dec (s_1, s_2)

3.3 Polynomial Interpolation

You are probably familiar with the fact that two points determine a line (in Euclidean geometry). It is also true that 3 points determine a parabola, and so on. The next secretsharing scheme we discuss is based on the following principle:

$d+1$ points determine a unique degree- d polynomial.

A note on terminology: If f is a polynomial that can be written as $f(x)=\sum_{i=0}^{d} f_i x^i$, then we say that f is a degree- d polynomial. It would be more technically correct to say that the degree of f is at most d since we allow the leading coefficient f_d to be zero. For convenience, we'll stick to saying "degree- d " to mean "degree at most d "

Polynomials Over the Reals

Theorem 3.8 (Poly Interpolation) Let $\{(x_1, y_1), \ldots, (x_{d+1}, y_{d+1})\} \subseteq \mathbb{R}^2$ be a set of points whose x_i values are all distinct. Then there is a unique degree-d polynomial f with real coefficients that satisfies $y_i = f(x_i)$ for all i.

Proof To start, consider the following polynomial:

$$\ell_1(\boldsymbol{x}) = \frac{(\boldsymbol{x}-x_2)(\boldsymbol{x}-x_3)\cdots(\boldsymbol{x}-x_{d+1})}{(x_1-x_2)(x_1-x_3)\cdots(x_1-x_{d+1})}.$$

The notation is potentially confusing. ℓ_1 is a polynomial with formal variable $\boldsymbol{x}$ (written in bold). The non-bold x_i values are just plain numbers (scalars), given in the theorem statement. Therefore the numerator in ℓ_1 is a degree- d polynomial in $\boldsymbol{x}$. The denominator is just a scalar, and since all of the x_i 's are distinct, we are not dividing by zero. Overall, ℓ_1 is a degree- d polynomial.

What happens when we evaluate ℓ_1 at one of the special x_i values?

- Evaluating $\ell_1(x_1)$ makes the numerator and denominator the same, so $\ell_1(x_1)=1$.
- Evaluating $\ell_1(x_i)$ for $i \neq 1$ leads to a term $(x_i - x_i)$ in the numerator, so $\ell_1(x_i) = 0$.

Of course, ℓ_1 can be evaluated at any point (not just the special points $x_1, \ldots, x_{d+1}$), but we don't care about what happens in those cases.

We can similarly define other polynomials ℓ_j :

$$\ell_j(\boldsymbol{x}) = \frac{(\boldsymbol{x}-x_1)\cdots(\boldsymbol{x}-x_{j-1})(\boldsymbol{x}-x_{j+1})\cdots(\boldsymbol{x}-x_{d+1})}{(x_j-x_1)\cdots(x_j-x_{j-1})(x_j-x_{j+1})\cdots(x_j-x_{d+1})}.$$

The pattern is that the numerator is "missing" the term ($\boldsymbol{x} - x_j$) and the denominator is missing the term $(x_j - x_j)$, because we don't want a zero in the denominator. Polynomials of this kind are called LaGrange polynomials. They are each degree- d polynomials, and they satisfy the property:

$$\ell_j(x_i) = \begin{cases} 1 & \text{if } i = j \\ 0 & \text{if } i \neq j \end{cases}$$

Now consider the following polynomial:

$$f(\boldsymbol{x}) = y_1\ell_1(\boldsymbol{x}) + y_2\ell_2(\boldsymbol{x}) + \cdots + y_{d+1}\ell_{d+1}(\boldsymbol{x}).$$

Note that f is a degree- d polynomial since it is the sum of degree- d polynomials (again, the y_i values are just scalars).

What happens when we evaluate f on one of the special x_i values? Since $\ell_i(x_i) = 1$ and $\ell_j(x_i) = 0$ for $j \neq i$, we get:

$$\begin{aligned} f(x_i) &= y_1\ell_1(x_i) + \cdots + y_i\ell_i(x_i) + \cdots + y_{d+1}\ell_{d+1}(x_i) \\ &= y_1 \cdot 0 + \cdots + y_i \cdot 1 + \cdots + y_{d+1} \cdot 0 \\ &= y_i \end{aligned}$$

So $f(x_i) = y_i$ for every x_i, which is what we wanted. This shows that there is some degree- d polynomial with this property.

Now let's argue that this f is unique. Suppose there are two degree- d polynomials f and f' such that $f(x_i) = f'(x_i) = y_i$ for $i \in \{1, \ldots, d+1\}$. Then the polynomial $g(\boldsymbol{x}) = f(\boldsymbol{x}) - f'(\boldsymbol{x})$ also is degree- d, and it satisfies $g(x_i) = 0$ for all i. In other words, each x_i is a root of g, so g has at least $d+1$ roots. But the only degree- d polynomial with $d+1$ roots is the identically-zero polynomial $g(\boldsymbol{x}) = 0$. If $g(\boldsymbol{x}) = 0$ then $f = f'$. In other words, any degree- d polynomial f' that satisfies $f'(x_i) = y_i$ must be equal to f. So f is the unique polynomial with this property. □

Example *Let's figure out the degree-3 polynomial that passes through the points* $(3,1), (4,1), (5,9), (2,6)$ *:*

i	1	2	3	4
x_i	3	4	5	2
y_i	1	1	9	6

First, let's construct the appropriate LaGrange polynomials:

$$\ell_1(\boldsymbol{x}) = \frac{(\boldsymbol{x}-x_2)(\boldsymbol{x}-x_3)(\boldsymbol{x}-x_4)}{(x_1-x_2)(x_1-x_3)(x_1-x_4)} = \frac{(\boldsymbol{x}-4)(\boldsymbol{x}-5)(\boldsymbol{x}-2)}{(3-4)(3-5)(3-2)} = \frac{\boldsymbol{x}^3-11\boldsymbol{x}^2+38\boldsymbol{x}-40}{2}$$
$$\ell_2(\boldsymbol{x}) = \frac{(\boldsymbol{x}-x_1)(\boldsymbol{x}-x_3)(\boldsymbol{x}-x_4)}{(x_2-x_1)(x_2-x_3)(x_2-x_4)} = \frac{(\boldsymbol{x}-3)(\boldsymbol{x}-5)(\boldsymbol{x}-2)}{(4-3)(4-5)(4-2)} = \frac{\boldsymbol{x}^3-10\boldsymbol{x}^2+31\boldsymbol{x}-30}{-2}$$
$$\ell_3(\boldsymbol{x}) = \frac{(\boldsymbol{x}-x_1)(\boldsymbol{x}-x_2)(\boldsymbol{x}-x_4)}{(x_3-x_1)(x_3-x_2)(x_3-x_4)} = \frac{(\boldsymbol{x}-3)(\boldsymbol{x}-4)(\boldsymbol{x}-2)}{(5-3)(5-4)(5-2)} = \frac{\boldsymbol{x}^3-9\boldsymbol{x}^2+26\boldsymbol{x}-24}{6}$$
$$\ell_4(\boldsymbol{x}) = \frac{(\boldsymbol{x}-x_1)(\boldsymbol{x}-x_2)(\boldsymbol{x}-x_3)}{(x_4-x_1)(x_4-x_2)(x_4-x_3)} = \frac{(\boldsymbol{x}-3)(\boldsymbol{x}-4)(\boldsymbol{x}-5)}{(2-3)(2-4)(2-5)} = \frac{\boldsymbol{x}^3-12\boldsymbol{x}^2+47\boldsymbol{x}-60}{-6}$$

As a sanity check, notice how:

$$\ell_1(x_1) = \ell_1(3) = \frac{3^3-11\cdot 3^2+38\cdot 3-40}{2} = \frac{2}{2} = 1$$
$$\ell_1(x_2) = \ell_1(4) = \frac{4^3-11\cdot 4^2+38\cdot 4-40}{2} = \frac{0}{2} = 0$$

It will make the next step easier if we rewrite all LaGrange polynomials to have the same denominator 6 :

$$\ell_1(x) = \frac{3x^3-33x^2+114x-120}{6} \qquad \ell_3(x) = \frac{x^3-9x^2+26x-24}{6}$$
$$\ell_2(x) = \frac{-3x^3+30x^2-93x+90}{6} \qquad \ell_4(x) = \frac{-x^3+12x^2-47x+60}{6}$$

Our desired polynomial is

$$
\begin{aligned}
f(x) &= y_1 \cdot \ell_1(x) + y_2 \cdot \ell_2(x) + y_3 \cdot \ell_3(x) + y_4 \cdot \ell_4(x) \\
&= 1 \cdot \ell_1(x) + 1 \cdot \ell_2(x) + 9 \cdot \ell_3(x) + 6 \cdot \ell_4(x) \\
&= \frac{1}{6}\begin{pmatrix} 1 \cdot (3x^3 - 33x^2 + 114x & & -120) \\ \quad +1 \cdot (-3x^3 + 30x^2 & -93x & +90) \\ +9 \cdot (-x^3 + 9x^2 + 26x & & -24) \\ \quad +6 \cdot (-x^3 + 12x^2 & -47x & +60) \end{pmatrix} \\
&= \frac{1}{6}(3x^3 - 12x^2 - 27x + 114) \\
&= \frac{x^3}{2} - 2x^2 - \frac{9x}{2} + 19
\end{aligned}
$$

And indeed, f gives the correct values:

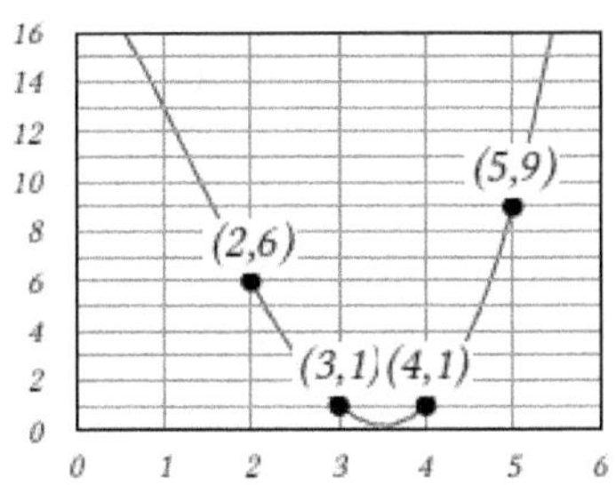

$$f(x_1) = f(3) = \frac{3^3}{2} - 2 \cdot 3^2 - \frac{9 \cdot 3}{2} + 19 = 1 = y_1$$

$$f(x_2) = f(4) = \frac{4^3}{2} - 2 \cdot 4^2 - \frac{9 \cdot 4}{2} + 19 = 1 = y_2$$

$$f(x_3) = f(5) = \frac{5^3}{2} - 2 \cdot 5^2 - \frac{9 \cdot 5}{2} + 19 = 9 = y_3$$

$$f(x_4) = f(2) = \frac{2^3}{2} - 2 \cdot 2^2 - \frac{9 \cdot 2}{2} + 19 = 6 = y_4$$

Polynomials mod$p$

We will see a secret-sharing scheme based on polynomials, whose Share algorithm must choose a polynomial with uniformly random coefficients. Since we cannot have a uniform distribution over the real numbers, we must instead consider polynomials with coefficients in $\mathbb{Z}_p$.

It is still true that $d + 1$ points determine a unique degree- d polynomial when working modulo p, if p is a prime!

Theorem 3.9 (Interp mod$p$): *Let p be a prime, and let $\{(x_1, y_1), \dots, (x_{d+1}, y_{d+1})\} \subseteq (\mathbb{Z}_p)^2$ be a set of points whose x_i values are all distinct. Then there is a unique degree-d polynomial f with coefficients from $\mathbb{Z}_p$ that satisfies $y_i \equiv_p f(x_i)$ for all i.*

The proof is the same as the one for Theorem 3.8, if you interpret all arithmetic modulo p. Addition, subtraction, and multiplication mod$p$ are straight forward; the only nontrivial question is how to interpret "division mod$p$ ", which is necessary in the definition of the ℓ_j polynomials. For now, just accept that you can always "divide" mod$p$ (except by zero) when p is a prime. If you are interested in how division mod$p$ works, look ahead to Chapter 13.

We can also generalize the observation that $d+1$ points uniquely determine a degree- d polynomial. It turns out that:

For any k points, there are exactly p^{d+1-k} polynomials of degree- d that hit those points, mod$p$.

Note how when $k=d+1$, the statement says that there is just a single polynomial hitting the points.

Corollary 3.10 (# of polys): *Let $\mathcal{P}=\{(x_1,y_1),\ldots,(x_k,y_k)\}\subseteq(\mathbb{Z}_p)^2$ be a set of points whose x_i values are distinct. Let d satisfy $k\leqslant d+1$ and $p>d$. Then the number of degree- d polynomials f with coefficients in $\mathbb{Z}_p$ that satisfy the condition $y_i\equiv_p f(x_i)$ for all i is exactly p^{d+1-k}.*

Proof The proof is by induction on the value $d+1-k$. The base case is when $d+1-k=0$. Then we have $k=d+1$ distinct points, and Theorem 3.9 says that there is a unique polynomial satisfying the condition. Since $p^{d+1-k}=p^0=1$, the base case is true.

For the inductive case, we have $k\leqslant d$ points in $\mathcal{P}$. Let $x^*\in\mathbb{Z}_p$ be a value that does not appear as one of the x_i 's. Every polynomial must give some value when evaluated at x^*. So,

[# of degree- d polynomials passing through points in $\mathcal{P}$]

$$
\begin{aligned}
&=\sum_{y^*\in\mathbb{Z}_p}[\#\text{ of degree- }d\text{ polynomials passing through points in }\mathcal{P}\cup\{(x^*,y^*)\}]\\
&\overset{(\star)}{=}\sum_{y^*\in\mathbb{Z}_p}p^{d+1-(k+1)}\\
&=p\cdot(p^{d+1-k-1})=p^{d+1-k}
\end{aligned}
$$

The equality marked (★) follows from the inductive hypothesis, since each of the terms involves a polynomial passing through a specified set of $k+1$ points with distinct x coordinates.

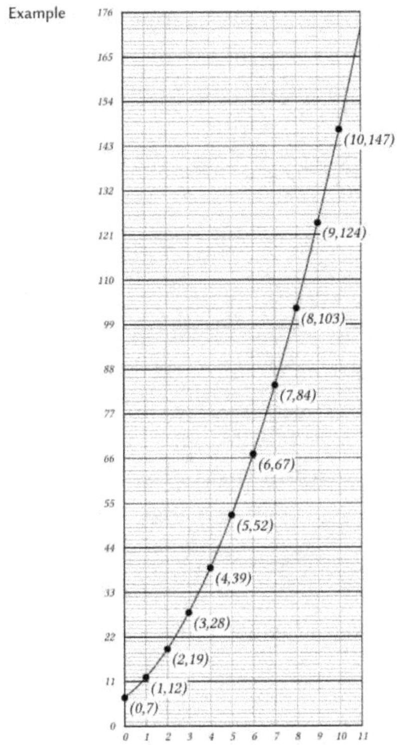

What does a "polynomial mod p" look like? Consider an example degree-2 polynomial:

$$f(x) = x^2 + 4x + 7$$

When we plot this polynomial over the real numbers (the picture on the left), we get a familiar parabola.

Let's see what this polynomial "looks like" modulo 11 (i.e., in $\mathbb{Z}_{11}$). Working mod 11 means to "wrap around" every time the polynomial crosses over a multiple of 11 along the y-axis. This results in the blue plot below:

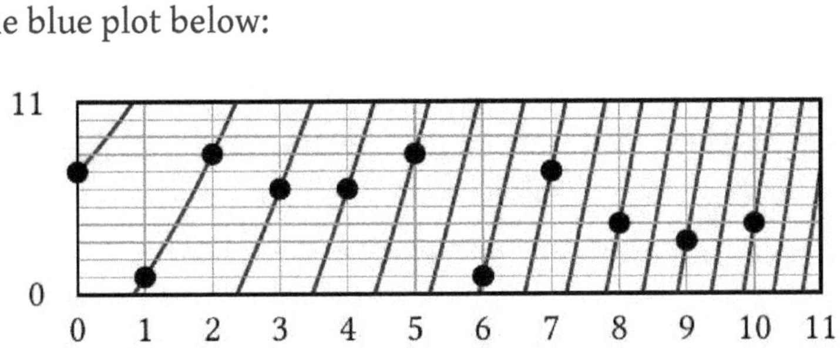

This is a picture of a mod-11 parabola. In fact, since we care only about $\mathbb{Z}_{11}$ inputs to f, you could rightfully say that just the 11 highlighted points alone (not the blue curve) are a picture of a mod-11 parabola.

3.4 Shamir Secret Sharing

Part of the challenge in designing a secret-sharing scheme is making sure that anyauthorized set of users can reconstruct the secret. We have just seen that any $d+1$ points on a degree- d polynomial are enough to uniquely reconstruct the polynomial. So a natural approach for secret sharing is to let each user's share be a point on a polynomial.

That's exactly what Shamir secret sharing does. To share a secret $m \in \mathbb{Z}_p$ with threshold t, first choose a degree- $(t-1)$ polynomial f that satisfies $f(0) \equiv_p m$, with all other coefficients chosen uniformly in $\mathbb{Z}_p$. The i th user receives the point ($i, f(i) \% p$) on the polynomial. The interpolation theorem says that any t of the shares can uniquely determine the polynomial f, and hence recover the secret $f(0)$.

Construction 3.11

(Shamir SSS)

	Share (m):
	$f_1, \ldots, f_{t-1} \leftarrow \mathbb{Z}_p$
	$f(\boldsymbol{x}) := m + \sum_{j=1}^{t-1} f_j \boldsymbol{x}^j$
	for $i = 1$ to n:
$\mathcal{M} = \mathbb{Z}_p$	$s_i := (i, f(i) \% p)$
p: prime	return $\boldsymbol{s} = (s_1, \ldots, s_n)$
$n < p$	
$t \leqslant n$	Reconstruct $(\{s_i \mid i \in U\})$:
	$f(\boldsymbol{x}) :=$ unique degree- $(t-1)$
	polynomial mod$p$ passing
	through points $\{s_i \mid i \in U\}$
	return $f(0)$

Correctness follows from the interpolation theorem.

Example: *Here is an example of 3-out-of-5 secret sharing over* $\mathbb{Z}_{11}$ *(so* $p = 11$ *). Suppose the secret being shared is* $m = 7 \in \mathbb{Z}_{11}$*. The Share algorithm chooses a random degree-2 polynomial with constant coefficient 7 .*

Let's say that the remaining two coefficients are chosen as $f_2 = 1$ *and* $f_1 = 4$*, resulting in the following polynomial:*

$$f(x) = 1x^2 + 4x + 7$$

This is the same polynomial illustrated in the previous example:

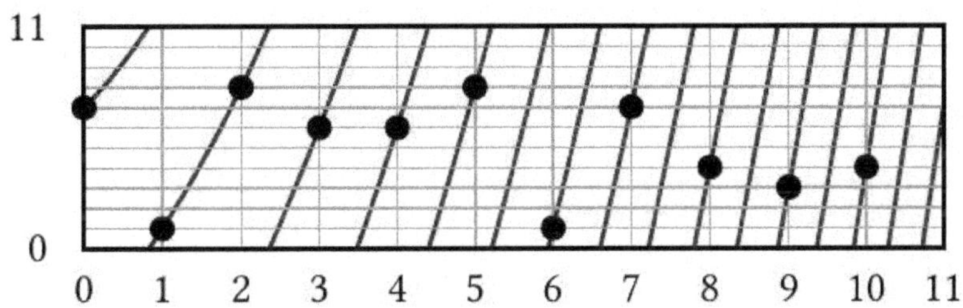

For each user $i \in \{1, \dots, 5\}$*, we distribute the share (* $i, f(i)\%11$ *). These shares correspond to the highlighted points in the mod-11 picture above.*

user (i)	$f(i)$	share ($i, f(i)\%11$)
1	$f(1) = 12$	(1,1)
2	$f(2) = 19$	(2,8)
3	$f(3) = 28$	(3,6)
4	$f(4) = 39$	(4,6)
5	$f(5) = 52$	(5,8)

Remember that this example illustrates just one possible execution of Share. Because Share is a randomized algorithm, there are many valid sharings of the same secret (induced by different choices of the highlighted coefficients in f *).*

Security

To show the security of Shamir secret sharing, we first show a convenient lemma about the distribution of shares in an unauthorized set:

Lemma 3.12 : *Let p be a prime and define the following two libraries:*

$\mathcal{L}_{\text{shamir-real}}$
$\text{POLY}(m, t, U \subseteq \{1, \ldots, p\})$:
if $\lvert U\rvert \geqslant t$: return err
$f_1, \ldots, f_{t-1} \leftarrow \mathbb{Z}_p$
$f(x) := m + \sum_{j=1}^{t-1} f_j x^j$
for $i \in U$:
$s_i := (i, f(i) \% p)$
return $\{s_i \mid i \in U\}$

$\mathcal{L}_{\text{shamir-rand}}$
$\text{POLY}(m, t, U \subseteq \{1, \ldots, p\})$:
if $\lvert U\rvert \geqslant t$: return err
for $i \in U$:
$y_i \leftarrow \mathbb{Z}_p$
$s_i := (i, y_i)$
return $\{s_i \mid i \in U\}$

$\mathcal{L}_{\textit{shamir-real}}$ chooses a random degree- $(t-1)$ polynomial that passes through the point $(0, m)$, then evaluates it at the given x-coordinates (specified by U). $\mathcal{L}_{\textit{shamir-rand}}$ simply gives uniformly chosen points, unrelated to any polynomial.

The claim is that these libraries are interchangeable: $\mathcal{L}_{\textit{shamir-real}} \equiv \mathcal{L}_{\textit{shamir-rand}}$.

Proof Fix a message $m \in \mathbb{Z}_p$, fix set U of users with $|U| < t$, and for each $i \in U$ fix a value $y_i \in \mathbb{Z}_p$. We wish to consider the probability that a call to $\text{poly}(m, t, U)$ outputs $\{(i, y_i) \mid i \in U\}$, in each of the two libraries. [2]

In library $\mathcal{L}_{\text{shamir-real}}$, the subroutine chooses a random degree- $(t-1)$ polynomial f such that $f(0) \equiv_p m$. From Corollary 3.10, we know there are p^{t-1} such polynomials.

In order for poly to output points consistent with our chosen y_i 's, the library must have chosen one of the polynomials that passes through $(0, m)$ and all of the $\{(i, y_i) \mid i \in U\}$ points. The library must have chosen one of the polynomials that passes through a specific choice of $|U| + 1$ points, and Corollary 3.10 tells us that there are $p^{t-(|U|+1)}$ such polynomials.

The only way for poly to give our desired output is for it to choose one of the $p^{t-(|U|+1)}$ "good" polynomials, out of the p^{t-1} possibilities. This happens with probability exactly

$$\frac{p^{t-|U|-1}}{p^{t-1}} = p^{-|U|}$$

Now, in library $\mathcal{L}_{\text{shamir-rand}}$, poly chooses its $|U|$ output values uniformly in $\mathbb{Z}_p$. There are $p^{|U|}$ ways to choose them. But only one of those ways causes poly (m, t, U) to output our specific choice of $\{(i, y_i) \mid i \in U\}$. Hence, the probability of receiving this output is $p^{-|U|}$.

For all possible inputs to poly, both libraries assign the same probability to every possible output. Hence, the libraries are interchangeable. □

Theorem 3.13 *Shamir's secret-sharing scheme (Construction 3.11) is secure according to Definition 3.3.*

Proof Let $\mathcal{S}$ denote the Shamir secret-sharing scheme. We prove that $\mathcal{L}^{\mathcal{S}}_{\text{tsss-L}} \equiv \mathcal{L}^{\mathcal{S}}_{\text{tsss-R}}$ via a hybrid argument.

Our starting point is $\mathcal{L}^{\mathcal{S}}_{\text{tsss-L}}$, shown here with the details of Shamir secret-sharing filled in.

$\mathcal{L}^{\mathcal{S}}_{\text{tsss-L}}$:

```
L^S_tsss-L
SHARE(m_L, m_R, U):
  if |U| ≥ t: return err
  f_1, ..., f_{t-1} ← Z_p
  f(x) := m_L + Σ_{j=1}^{t-1} f_j x^j
  for i ∈ U:
    s_i := (i, f(i) % p)
  return {s_i | i ∈ U}
```

Almost the entire body of the share subroutine has been factored out in terms of the $\mathcal{L}_{\text{shamir-real}}$ library defined above. The only thing remaining is the "choice" of whether to share m_L or m_R. Restructuring the code in this way has no effect on the library's behavior.

```
SHARE(m_L, m_R, U):
  return POLY(m_L, t, U)
```

$\diamond$

```
L_shamir-real
POLY(m, t, U):
  if |U| ≥ t: return err
  f_1, ..., f_{t-1} ← Z_p
  f(x) := m + Σ_{j=1}^{t-1} f_j x^j
  for i ∈ U:
    s_i := (i, f(i) % p)
  return {s_i | i ∈ U}
```

By Lemma 3.12, we can replace $\mathcal{L}_{\text{shamir-real}}$ with $\mathcal{L}_{\text{shamir-rand}}$, having no effect on the library's behavior.

```
SHARE(m_L, m_R, U):
  return POLY(m_L, t, U)
```

◇

```
L_shamir-rand
POLY(m, t, U):
  if |U| ≥ t: return err
  for i ∈ U:
    y_i ← Z_p
    s_i := (i, y_i)
  return {s_i | i ∈ U}
```

The argument to poly has been changed from m_L to m_R. This has no effect on the library's behavior, since poly is actually ignoring its argument in these hybrids.

```
SHARE(m_L, m_R, U):
  return POLY( m_R , t, U)
```

◇

```
L_shamir-rand
POLY(m, t, U):
  if |U| ≥ t: return err
  for i ∈ U:
    y_i ← Z_p
    s_i := (i, y_i)
  return {s_i | i ∈ U}
```

Applying the same steps in reverse, we can replace $\mathcal{L}_{\text{shamir-rand}}$ with $\mathcal{L}_{\text{shamir-real}}$, having no effect on the library's behavior.

```
SHARE(m_L, m_R, U):
  return POLY(m_R, t, U)
```

◇

```
L_shamir-real
POLY(m, t, U):
  if |U| ≥ t: return err
  f_1, ..., f_{t-1} ← Z_p
  f(x) := m + Σ_{j=1}^{t-1} f_j x^j
  for i ∈ U:
    s_i := (i, f(i) % p)
  return {s_i | i ∈ U}
```

A subroutine has been inlined, which has no effect on the library's behavior. The resulting library is $\mathcal{L}^{\mathcal{S}}_{\text{tsss-R}}$.

$\mathcal{L}^S_{\text{tsss-R}}$:

$\mathcal{L}^S_{\text{tsss-R}}$
SHARE(m_L, m_R, U):
if $\lvert U \rvert \geqslant t$: return err
$f_1, \ldots, f_{t-1} \leftarrow \mathbb{Z}_p$
$f(x) := m_R + \sum_{j=1}^{t-1} f_j x^j$
for $i \in U$:
$s_i := (i, f(i) \% p)$
return $\{s_i \mid i \in U\}$

We showed that $\mathcal{L}^S_{\text{tsss-L}} \equiv \mathcal{L}_{\text{hyb-1}} \equiv \cdots \equiv \mathcal{L}_{\text{hyb-4}} \equiv \mathcal{L}^S_{\text{tsss-R}}$, so Shamir's secret sharing scheme is secure. □

3.5 Visual Secret Sharing

Here is a fun variant of 2 -out-of- 2 secret-sharing called visual secret sharing. In this variant, both the secret and the shares are black-and-white images. We require the same security property as traditional secret-sharing - that is, a single share (image) by itself reveals no information about the secret (image). What makes visual secret sharing different is that we require the reconstruction procedure to be done visually.

More specifically, each share should be printed on transparent sheets. When the two shares are stacked on top of each other, the secret image is revealed visually. We will discuss a simple visual secret sharing scheme that is inspired by the following observations:

when  is stacked on top of , the result is 

when  is stacked on top of , the result is 

when  is stacked on top of , the result is 

when  is stacked on top of , the result is 

Importantly, when stacking shares on top of each other in the first two cases, the result is a 2 × 2 block that is half-black, half-white (let's call it "gray"); while in the other cases the result is completely black.

The idea is to process each pixel of the source image independently, and to encode each pixel as a 2 × 2 block of pixels in each of the shares. A white pixel should be shared in a way that the two shares stack to form a "gray" 2 × 2 block, while a black pixel is shared in a way that results in a black 2 × 2 block.

More formally:

Construction 3.14

```
Share(m):
  initialize empty images s1, s2, with dimensions twice that of m
  for each position (i, j) in m:
    randomly choose b1 ← {▚, ▞}
    if m[i, j] is a white pixel: set b2 := b1
    if m[i, j] is a black pixel: set b2 to the "opposite" of b1 (i.e., {▚, ▞} \ {b1})
    add 2 × 2 block b1 to image s1 at position (2i, 2j)
    add 2 × 2 block b2 to image s2 at position (2i, 2j)
  return (s1, s2)
```

It is not hard to see that share s_1 leaks no information about the secret image m, because it consists of uniformly chosen 2 × 2 blocks. In the exercises you are asked to prove that s_2 also individually leaks nothing about the secret image.

Note that whenever the source pixel is white, the two shares have identical 2 × 2 blocks (so that when stacked, they make a "gray" block). Whenever a source pixel is black, the two shares have opposite blocks, so stack to make a black block.

Example

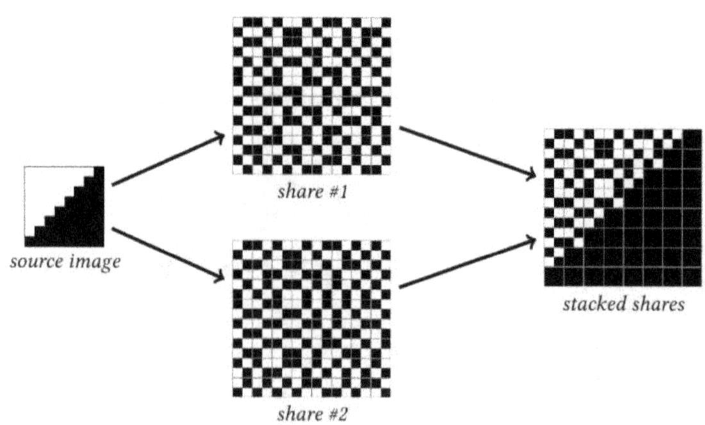

Exercises

3.1. Generalize Construction 3.5 to be an n-out-of- n secret-sharing scheme, and prove that your scheme is correct and secure.

3.2. Prove Theorem 3.7.

3.3. Fill in the details of the following alternative proof of Theorem 3.6: Starting with $\mathcal{L}_{\text{tsss-L}}$, apply the first step of the proof as before, to duplicate the main body into 3 branches of a new if-statement. Then apply Exercise 2.3 to the second branch of the if-statement. Argue that m_L can be replaced with m_R and complete the proof.

3.4. Suppose T is a fixed (publicly known) invertible $n \times n$ matrix over $\mathbb{Z}_p$, where p is a prime.

(a) Show that the following two libraries are interchangeable:

$\mathcal{L}_{\text{left}}$
QUERY():
$r \leftarrow (\mathbb{Z}_p)^n$
return r

;

$\mathcal{L}_{\text{right}}$
QUERY():
$r \leftarrow (\mathbb{Z}_p)^n$
return $T \times r$

.

(b) Show that the following two libraries are interchangeable:

$\mathcal{L}_{\text{left}}$
QUERY($\boldsymbol{v} \in (\mathbb{Z}_p)^n$):
$r \leftarrow (\mathbb{Z}_p)^n$
$z := \boldsymbol{v} + Tr$
return z

;

$\mathcal{L}_{\text{right}}$
QUERY($\boldsymbol{v} \in (\mathbb{Z}_p)^n$):
$z \leftarrow (\mathbb{Z}_p)^n$
return z

.

3.5. Consider a t-out-of- n threshold secret sharing scheme with $\mathcal{M} = \{0,1\}^\ell$, and where each user's share is also a string of bits. Prove that if the scheme is secure, then every user's share must be at least ℓ bits long.

3.6. n users have shared two secrets using Shamir secret sharing. User i has a share $s_i = (i, y_i)$ of the secret m, and a share $s_i' = (i, y_i')$ of the secret m'. Both sets of shares use the same prime modulus p.

Suppose each user i locally computes $z_i = (y_i + y_i')\%p$.

(a) Prove that if the shares of m and shares of m' had the same threshold, then the resulting $\{(i, z_i) \mid i \leqslant n\}$ are a valid secret-sharing of the secret $m + m'$.

(b) Describe what the users get when the shares of m and m' had different thresholds (say, t and t', respectively).

3.7. Suppose there are 5 people on a committee: Alice (president), Bob, Charlie, David, Eve. Suggest how they can securely share a secret so that it can only be opened by:

- Alice and any one other person
- Any three people

Describe in detail how the sharing algorithm works and how the reconstruction works (for all authorized sets of users).

Note: It is fine if different users have shares which are of different sizes (e.g., different number of bits to represent), and it is also fine if the Reconstruct algorithm depends on the identities of the users who are contributing their shares.

3.8. Suppose there are 9 people on an important committee: Alice, Bob, Carol, David, Eve, Frank, Gina, Harold, & Irene. Alice, Bob & Carol form a subcommittee; David, Eve & Frank form another subcommittee; and Gina, Harold & Irene form another subcommittee.

Suggest how a dealer can share a secret so that it can only be opened when a majority of each subcommittee is present. Describe why a 6-out-of-9 threshold secret-sharing scheme does not suffice.

3.9. (a) Generalize the previous exercise. A monotone formula is a boolean function $\phi : \{0,1\}^n \to \{0,1\}$ that when written as a formula uses only and and or operations (no nots). For a set $A \subseteq \{1, \ldots, n\}$, let χ_A be the bitstring where whose i th bit is 1 if and only if $i \in A$.

For every monotone formula $\phi: \{0,1\}^n \to \{0,1\}$, construct a secret-sharing scheme whose authorized sets are $\{A \subseteq \{1, \ldots, n\} \mid \phi(\chi_A) = 1\}$. Prove that your scheme is secure.

(b) Give a construction of a t-out-of- n secret-sharing scheme in which all shares are binary strings, and the only operation required of Share and Reconstruct is xor (so no mod- p operations).

How big are the shares, compared to the Shamir scheme?

3.10. Prove that share s_2 in Construction 3.14 is distributed independently of the secret m.

3.11. Using actual transparencies or with an image editing program, reconstruct the secret shared in these two images:

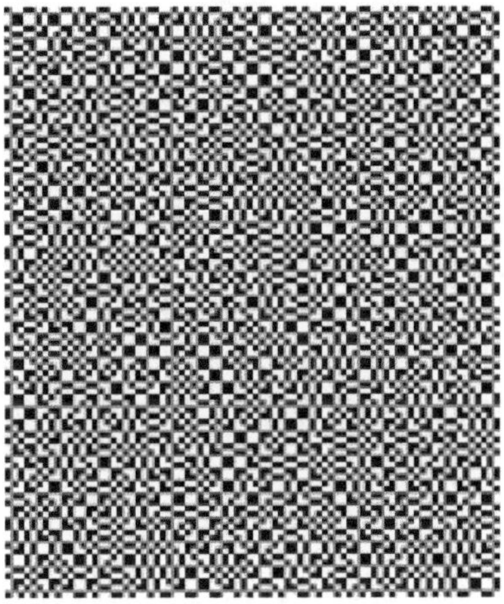

★ 3.12. Construct a 3-out-of-3 visual secret sharing scheme. Any two shares should together reveal nothing about the source image, but any three reveal the source image when stacked together.

Chapter-4

Basing Cryptography on Intractable Computations

John Nash was a mathematician who earned the 1994 Nobel Prize in Economics for his work in game theory. His life story was made into a successful movie, A Beautiful Mind.

In 1955, Nash was in correspondence with the United States National Security Agency (NSA), [1] discussing new methods of encryption that he had devised. In these letters, he also proposes some general principles of cryptography (bold highlighting not in the original):s

> *... in principle the enemy needs very little information to begin to break down the process. Essentially, as soon as λ bits [2] of enciphered message have been transmitted the key is about determined. This is no security, for a practical key should not be too long. But this does not consider how easy or difficult it is for the enemy to make the computation determining the key. If this computation, although possible in principle, were sufficiently long at best then the process could still be secure in a practical sense.*

Nash is saying something quite profound: it doesn't really matter whether attacks are impossible, only whether attacks are computationally infeasible. If his letters hadn't been kept classified until 2012, they might have accelerated the development of "modern" cryptography, in which security is based on intractable computations. As it stands, he was decades ahead of his time in identifying one of the most important concepts in modern cryptography.

4.1 What Qualifies as a "Computationally Infeasible" Attack?

Schemes like one-time pad cannot be broken, even by an attacker that performs a bruteforce attack, trying all possible keys (see Exercise 1.5). However, all future schemes that we will see can indeed be broken by such an attack. Nash is quick to point out that, for a scheme with λ-bit keys:

> *The most direct computation procedure would be for the enemy to try all 2^λ possible keys, one by one. Obviously this is easily made impractical for the enemy by simply choosing λ large enough.*

We call λ the security parameter of the scheme. It is like a knob that allows the user to tune the security to any desired level. Increasing λ makes the difficulty of a bruteforce attack grow exponentially fast. Ideally, when using λ-bit keys, every attack (not just a brute-force attack) will have difficulty roughy 2^λ. However, sometimes faster attacks are inevitable. Later in this chapter, we will see why many schemes with λ-bit keys have attacks that cost only $2^{\lambda/2}$. It is common to see a scheme described as having n-bit security if the best known attack requires 2^n steps.

Just how impractical is a brute-force computation on a 64 -bit key? A 128 -bit key? Huge numbers like 2^{64} and 2^{128} are hard to grasp at an intuitive level.

Example: It can be helpful to think of the cost of a computation in terms of monetary value, and a convenient way to assign such monetary costs is to use the pricing model of a cloud computing provider. Below, I have calculated roughly how much a computation involving 2^λ CPU cycles would cost on Amazon EC2, for various choices of λ. [3]

clock cycles	approx cost	reference
2^{50}	$3.50	cup of coffee
2^{55}	$100	decent tickets to a Portland Trailblazers game
2^{65}	$130,000	median home price in Oshkosh, WI
2^{75}	$130 million	budget of one of the Harry Potter movies
2^{85}	$140 billion	GDP of Hungary
2^{92}	$20 trillion	GDP of the United States
2^{99}	$2 quadrillion	all of human economic activity since 300,000*BC*[4]
2^{128}	really a lot	a billion human civilizations' worth of effort

Remember, this table only shows the cost to perform 2^λ clock cycles. A brute-force attack checking 2^λ keys would take many more cycles than that! But, as a disclaimer, these numbers reflect only the retail cost of performing a computation, on fairly standard general-purpose hardware. A government organization would be capable of manufacturing special-purpose hardware that would *significantly reduce the computation's cost. The exercises explore some of these issues, as well as non-financial ways of conceptualizing the cost of huge computations.*

Example: *In 2017, the first collision in the SHA-1 hash function was found (we will discuss hash functions later in the course). The attack involved evaluating the SHA-1 function* 2^{63} *times on a cluster of GPUs. An article in Ars Technica* [5] *estimates the monetary cost of the attack as follows:*

> *Had the researchers performed their attack on Amazon's Web Services platform, it would have cost $560,000 at normal pricing. Had the researchers been patient and waited to run their attack during off-peak hours, the same collision would have cost $110,000.*

Asymptotic Running Time

It is instructive to think about the monetary cost of an enormous computation, but it doesn't necessarily help us draw the line between "feasible" attacks (which we want to protect against) and "infeasible" ones (which we agreed we don't need to care about). We need to be able to draw such a line in order to make security definitions that say "only feasible attacks are ruled out."

Once again, John Nash thought about this question. He suggested to consider the asymptotic cost of an attack - how does the cost of a computation scale as the security parameter λ goes to infinity?

> *So a logical way to classify enciphering processes is by the way in which the computation length for the computation of the key increases with increasing length of the key. This is at best exponential and at worst probably a relatively small power of* λ, $a \cdot \lambda^2$ *or* $a \cdot \lambda^3$, *as in substitution ciphers.*

Nash highlights the importance of attacks that run in polynomial time:

Definition 4.1: *A program runs in polynomial time if there exists a constant* $c > 0$ *such that for all sufficiently long input strings* x, *the program stops after no more than* $O(|x|^c)$ *steps.*

Polynomial-time algorithms scale reasonably well (especially when the exponent is small), but exponential-time algorithms don't. It is probably no surprise to modern readers to see "polynomial-time" as a synonym for "efficient." However, it's worth pointing out that, again, Nash is years ahead of his time relative to the field of computer science.

In the context of cryptography, our goal will be to ensure that no polynomial-time attack can successfully break security. We will not worry about attacks like brute-force that require exponential time.

Polynomial time is not a perfect match to what we mean when we informally talk about "efficient" algorithms. Algorithms with running time $\Theta(n^{1000})$ are technically polynomialtime, while those with running time $\Theta(n^{\log \log \log n})$ aren't. Despite that, polynomial-time is extremely useful because of the following closure property: repeating a polynomial-time process a polynomial number of times results in a polynomial-time process overall.

Potential Pitfall: Numerical Algorithms

When we study public-key cryptography, we will discuss algorithms that operate on very large numbers (e.g., thousands of bits long). You must remember that representing the number N on a computer requires only $\sim \log_2 N$ bits. This means that $\log_2 N$, rather than N, is our security parameter! We will therefore be interested in whether certain operations on the number N run in polynomial-time as a function of $\log_2 N$, rather than in N. Keep in mind that the difference between running time $O(\log N)$ and $O(N)$ is the difference between writing down a number and counting to the number.

For reference, here are some numerical operations that we will be using later in the class, and their known efficiencies:

Efficient algorithm known:	No known efficient algorithm:
Computing GCDs	Factoring integers
Arithmetic mod$N$	Computing $\phi(N)$ given N
Inverses mod$N$	Discrete logarithm
Exponentiation mod$N$	Square roots mod composite N

Again, "efficient" means polynomial-time. Furthermore, we only consider polynomialtime algorithms that run on standard, classical computers. In fact, all of the problems in the right-hand column do have known polynomial-time algorithms on quantum computers.

4.2 What Qualifies as a "Negligible" Success Probability?

It is not enough to consider only the running time of an attack. For example, consider an attacker who just tries to guess a victim's secret key, making a single guess. This attack is extremely cheap, but it still has a nonzero chance of breaking security!

In addition to an attack's running time, we also need to consider its success probability. We don't want to worry about attacks that are as expensive as a brute-force attack, and we don't want to worry about attacks whose success probability is as low as a blind-guess attack.

An attack with success probability 2^{-128} should not really count as an attack, but an attack with success probability 1/2 should. Somewhere in between 2^{-128} and 2^{-1} we need to find a reasonable place to draw a line.

Example: Now we are dealing with extremely tiny probabilities that can be hard to visualize. Again, it can be helpful to conceptualize these probabilities with a more familiar reference:

probability	*equivalent*
2^{-10}	*full house in 5-card poker*
2^{-20}	*royal flush in 5-card poker*
2^{-28}	*you win this week's Powerball jackpot*
2^{-40}	*royal flush in 2 consecutive poker games*
2^{-60}	*the next meteorite that hits Earth lands in this square →*

As before, it is not clear exactly where to draw the line between "reasonable" and "unreasonable" success probability for an attack. Just like we did with polynomial running time, we can also use an asymptotic approach to define when a probability is negligibly small. Just as "polynomial time" considers how fast an algorithm's running time approaches infinity as its input grows, we can also consider how fast a success probability approaches zero as the security parameter grows.

In a scheme with λ-bit keys, a blind-guessing attack succeeds with probability $1/2^{\lambda}$. Now what about an attacker who makes 2 blind guesses, or λ guesses, or λ^{42} guesses? Such an attacker would still run in polynomial time, and has success probability $2/2^{\lambda}, \lambda/2^{\lambda}$, or $\lambda^{42}/2^{\lambda}$. However, no matter what polynomial you put in the numerator, the probability still goes to zero. Indeed, $1/2^{\lambda}$ approaches zero so fast that no polynomial can "rescue" it; or, in other words, it approaches zero faster than 1 over any polynomial. This idea leads to our formal definition:

Definition 4.2 (Negligible): *A function f is negligible if, for every polynomial p, we have* $lim_{\lambda\to\infty} p(\lambda)f(\lambda) = 0$.

In other words, a negligible function approaches zero so fast that you can never catch up when multiplying by a polynomial. This is exactly the property we want from a security guarantee that is supposed to hold against all polynomial-time adversaries. If a polynomial-time attacker succeeds with probability f, then repeating the same attack p independent times would still be an overall polynomial-time attack (if p is a polynomial), and its success probability would be $p \cdot f$.

When you want to check whether a function is negligible, you only have to consider polynomials p of the form $p(\lambda) = \lambda^c$ for some constant c :

Claim 4.3 *If for every integer c, $lim_{\lambda\to\infty} \lambda^c f(\lambda) = 0$, then f is negligible.*

Proof Suppose f has this property, and take an arbitrary polynomial p. We want to show that $\lim_{\lambda\to\infty} p(\lambda)f(\lambda) = 0$.

If d is the degree of p, then $\lim_{\lambda\to\infty} \frac{p(\lambda)}{\lambda^{d+1}} = 0$. Therefore,

$$\lim_{\lambda\to\infty} p(\lambda)f(\lambda) = \lim_{\lambda\to\infty} \left[\frac{p(\lambda)}{\lambda^{d+1}}(\lambda^{d+1} \cdot f(\lambda))\right] = \left(\lim_{\lambda\to\infty} \frac{p(\lambda)}{\lambda^{d+1}}\right)\left(\lim_{\lambda\to\infty} \lambda^{d+1} \cdot f(\lambda)\right) = 0 \cdot 0$$

The second equality is a valid law for limits since the two limits on the right exist and are not an indeterminate expression like $0 \cdot \infty$. The final equality follows from the hypothesis on f.

Example *The function $f(\lambda) = 1/2^\lambda$ is negligible, since for any integer c, we have:*

$$\lim_{\lambda\to\infty} \lambda^c/2^\lambda = \lim_{\lambda\to\infty} 2^{c\log(\lambda)}/2^\lambda = \lim_{\lambda\to\infty} 2^{c\log(\lambda)-\lambda} = 0,$$

since $c\log(\lambda) - \lambda$ approaches $-\infty$ in the limit, for any constant c. Using similar reasoning, one can show that the following functions are also negligible:

$$\frac{1}{2^{\lambda/2}}, \frac{1}{2^{\sqrt{\lambda}}}, \frac{1}{2^{\log^2 \lambda}}, \frac{1}{\lambda^{\log \lambda}}.$$

Functions like $1/\lambda^5$ approach zero but not fast enough to be negligible. To see why, we can take polynomial $p(\lambda) = \lambda^6$ and see that the resulting limit does not satisfy the requirement from Definition 4.2:

$$\lim_{\lambda\to\infty} p(\lambda)\frac{1}{\lambda^5} = \lim_{\lambda\to\infty} \lambda = \infty \neq 0$$

In this class, when we see a negligible function, it will typically always be one that is easy to recognize as negligible (just as in an undergraduate algorithms course, you won't really encounter algorithms where it's hard to tell whether the running time is polynomial).

Definition 4.4 ($f \approx g$) *If $f, g: \mathbb{N} \to \mathbb{R}$ are two functions, we write $f \approx g$ to mean that $|f(\lambda) - g(\lambda)|$ is a negligible function.*

We use the terminology of negligible functions exclusively when discussing probabilities, so the following are common:

$$\begin{aligned} \Pr[X] \approx 0 &\Leftrightarrow \text{"event } X \text{ almost never happens"} \\ \Pr[Y] \approx 1 &\Leftrightarrow \text{"event } Y \text{ almost always happens"} \\ \Pr[A] \approx \Pr[B] &\Leftrightarrow \text{"events } A \text{ and } B \text{ happen with} \\ &\quad\ \text{essentially the same probability"}\ ^{6} \end{aligned}$$

Additionally, the $\approx$ symbol is transitive: [7] if $\Pr[X] \approx \Pr[Y]$ and $\Pr[Y] \approx \Pr[Z]$, then $\Pr[X] \approx \Pr[Z]$ (perhaps with a slightly larger, but still negligible, difference).

4.3 Indistinguishability

So far we have been writing formal security definitions in terms of interchangeable libraries, which requires that two libraries have exactly the same effect on every calling program. Going forward, our security definitions will not be quite as demanding. First, we only consider polynomial-time calling programs; second, we don't require the libraries to have exactly the same effect on the calling program, only that the difference in effects is negligible.

Definition 4.5 (Indistinguishable) Let $\mathcal{L}_{\text{left}}$ and $\mathcal{L}_{\text{right}}$ be two libraries with a common interface. We say that $\mathcal{L}_{\text{left}}$ and $\mathcal{L}_{\text{right}}$ are indistinguishable, and write $\mathcal{L}_{\text{left}} \approx \mathcal{L}_{\text{right}}$, iffor all polynomial-time programs $\mathcal{A}$ that output a single bit, $Pr[\mathcal{A} \diamond \mathcal{L}_{\text{left}} \Rightarrow 1] \approx Pr[\mathcal{A} \diamond \mathcal{L}_{\text{right}} \Rightarrow 1]$.

We call the quantity $|Pr[\mathcal{A} \diamond \mathcal{L}_{left} \Rightarrow 1] - Pr[\mathcal{A} \diamond \mathcal{L}_{right} \Rightarrow 1]|$ the advantage or bias of $\mathcal{A}$ in distinguishing $\mathcal{L}_{left}$ from $\mathcal{L}_{right}$. Two libraries are therefore indistinguishable if all polynomial-time calling programs have negligible advantage in distinguishing them.

From the properties of the " ≈ " symbol, we can see that indistinguishability of libraries is also transitive, which allows us to carry out hybrid proofs of security in the same way as before.

Example *Here is a very simple example of two indistinguishable libraries:*

$\mathcal{L}_{\text{left}}$
PREDICT(x):
$s \leftarrow \{0,1\}^\lambda$
return $x \overset{?}{=} s$

$\mathcal{L}_{\text{right}}$
PREDICT(x):
return false

Imagine the calling program trying to predict which string will be chosen when uniformly sampling from $\{0,1\}^\lambda$. The left library tells the calling program whether its prediction was correct. The right library doesn't even bother sampling a string, it just always says "sorry, your prediction was wrong."

Here is one obvious strategy (maybe not the best one, we will see) to distinguish these libraries. The calling program $\mathcal{A}_{obvious}$ calls predict many times and outputs 1 if it ever received true as a response. Since it seems like the argument to PREDICT might not have any effect, let's just use the string of all-0s as argument every time.

$\mathcal{A}_{\text{obvious}}$
do q times:
if PREDICT(0^λ) = true
return 1
return 0

- $\mathcal{L}_{right}$ *can never return true, so* $Pr[\mathcal{A}_{obvious} \diamond \mathcal{L}_{right} \Rightarrow 1] = 0$.
- *In* $\mathcal{L}_{left}$ *each call to predict has an independent probability* $1/2^\lambda$ *of returning true. So* $Pr[\mathcal{A}_{obvious} \diamond \mathcal{L}_{left} \Rightarrow 1]$ *is surely non-zero. Actually, the exact probability is a bit cumbersome to write:*

$$\begin{aligned} Pr[\mathcal{A}_{obvious} \diamond \mathcal{L}_{left} \Rightarrow 1] &= 1 - Pr[\mathcal{A}_{obvious} \diamond \mathcal{L}_{left} \Rightarrow 0] \\ &= 1 - Pr[\text{ all } q \text{ independent calls to PREDICT return false }] \\ &= 1 - \left(1 - \frac{1}{2^\lambda}\right)^q \end{aligned}$$

Rather than understand this probability, we can just compute an upper bound for it. Using the union bound, we get:

$$\begin{aligned} Pr[\mathcal{A}_{obvious} \diamond \mathcal{L}_{left} \Rightarrow 1] \leqslant & Pr[\textit{ first call to PREDICT returns true }] \\ & + Pr[\textit{ second call to PREDICT returns true }] + \cdots \\ = & q\frac{1}{2^\lambda} \end{aligned}$$

This is an overestimate of some probabilities (e.g., if the first call to PREDICT returns true, then the second call isn't made). More fundamentally, $q/2^\lambda$ exceeds 1 when q is large. But nevertheless, $Pr[\mathcal{A}_{obvious} \diamond \mathcal{L}_{left} \Rightarrow 1] \leqslant q/2^\lambda$.

We showed that $\mathcal{A}_{obvious}$ has non-zero advantage. This is enough to show that $\mathcal{L}_{left} \not\equiv \mathcal{L}_{right}$.

We also showed that $\mathcal{A}_{obvious}$ has advantage at most $q/2^\lambda$. Since $\mathcal{A}_{obvious}$ runs in polynomial time, it can only make a polynomial number q of queries to the library, so $q/2^\lambda$ is negligible. However, this is not enough to show that $\mathcal{L}_{left} \approx \mathcal{L}_{right}$ since it considers only a single calling program. To show that the libraries are indistinguishable, we must show that every calling program's advantage is negligible.

In a few pages, we will prove that for any $\mathcal{A}$ that makes q calls to predict,

$$\left|Pr[\mathcal{A} \diamond \mathcal{L}_{left} \Rightarrow 1] - Pr[\mathcal{A} \diamond \mathcal{L}_{right} \Rightarrow 1]\right| \leqslant \frac{q}{2^\lambda}$$

For any polynomial-time $\mathcal{A}$, the number q of calls to predict will be a polynomial in λ, making $q/2^\lambda$ a negligible function. Hence, $\mathcal{L}_{left} \approx \mathcal{L}_{right}$.

Other Properties

Lemma 4.6 ($\approx$ facts) If $\mathcal{L}_1 \equiv \mathcal{L}_2$ then $\mathcal{L}_1 \approx \mathcal{L}_2$. Also, if $\mathcal{L}_1 \approx \mathcal{L}_2 \approx \mathcal{L}_3$ then $\mathcal{L}_1 \approx \mathcal{L}_3$.

Analogous to Lemma 2.11, we also have the following library chaining lemma, which you are asked to prove as an exercise:

Lemma 4.7 (Chaining) *If $\mathcal{L}_{left} \approx \mathcal{L}_{right}$ then $\mathcal{L}^* \diamond \mathcal{L}_{left} \approx \mathcal{L}^* \diamond \mathcal{L}_{right}$ for any polynomial-time library $\mathcal{L}^*$.*

Bad-Event Lemma

A common situation is when two libraries are expected to execute exactly the same statements, until some rare & exceptional condition happens. In that case, we can bound an attacker's distinguishing advantage by the probability of the exceptional condition.

More formally,

Lemma 4.8 (Bad events) *Let $\mathcal{L}_{left}$ and $\mathcal{L}_{right}$ be libraries that each define a variable named 'bad' that is initialized to 0. If $\mathcal{L}_{left}$ and $\mathcal{L}_{right}$ have identical code, except for code blocks reachable only when bad $= 1$ (e.g., guarded by an "if bad $= 1$ " statement), then*

$$\left|\Pr[\mathcal{A} \diamond \mathcal{L}_{\text{left}} \Rightarrow 1] - \Pr\left[\mathcal{A} \diamond \mathcal{L}_{\text{right}} \Rightarrow 1\right]\right| \leqslant \Pr\left[\mathcal{A} \diamond \mathcal{L}_{\text{left}} \text{ sets bad } = 1\right]$$

Proof Fix an arbitrary calling program $\mathcal{A}$. In this proof, we use conditional probabilites [8] to isolate the cases where bad is changed to 1 . We define the following events:

- $\mathcal{B}_{\text{left}}$: the event that $\mathcal{A} \diamond \mathcal{L}_{\text{left}}$ sets bad to 1 at some point.
- $\mathcal{B}_{\text{right}}$: the event that $\mathcal{A} \diamond \mathcal{L}_{\text{right}}$ sets bad to 1 at some point.

We also write $\overline{\mathcal{B}_{\text{left}}}$ and $\overline{\mathcal{B}_{\text{right}}}$ to denote the corresponding complement events. From conditional probability, we can write:

$$\begin{aligned}
&\Pr[\mathcal{A} \diamond \mathcal{L}_{\text{left}} \Rightarrow 1] = \Pr[\mathcal{A} \diamond \mathcal{L}_{\text{left}} \Rightarrow 1 \mid \mathcal{B}_{\text{left}}]\Pr[\mathcal{B}_{\text{left}}] \\
&+\Pr\left[\mathcal{A} \diamond \mathcal{L}_{\text{left}} \Rightarrow 1 \mid \overline{\mathcal{B}_{\text{left}}}\right]\Pr\left[\overline{\mathcal{B}_{\text{left}}}\right] \\
&\Pr\left[\mathcal{A} \diamond \mathcal{L}_{\text{right}} \Rightarrow 1\right] = \Pr\left[\mathcal{A} \diamond \mathcal{L}_{\text{right}} \Rightarrow 1 \mid \mathcal{B}_{\text{right}}\right]\Pr\left[\mathcal{B}_{\text{right}}\right] \\
&+\Pr\left[\mathcal{A} \diamond \mathcal{L}_{\text{right}} \Rightarrow 1 \mid \overline{\mathcal{B}_{\text{right}}}\right]\Pr\left[\overline{\mathcal{B}_{\text{right}}}\right]
\end{aligned}$$

Our first observation is that $\Pr[\mathcal{B}_{\text{left}}] = \Pr\left[\mathcal{B}_{\text{right}}\right]$. This is because at the time bad is changed to 1 for the first time, the library has only been executing instructions that are the same in $\mathcal{L}_{\text{left}}$ and $\mathcal{L}_{\text{right}}$. In other words, the choice to set bad to 1 is determined by the same sequence of instructions in both libraries, so it occurs with the same probability in both libraries.

As a shorthand notation, we define $p^* \stackrel{\text{def}}{=} \Pr[\mathcal{B}_{\text{left}}] = \Pr\left[\mathcal{B}_{\text{right}}\right]$. Then we can write the advantage of $\mathcal{A}$ as:

$$\text{advantage}_{\mathcal{A}} = \left|\Pr[\mathcal{A} \diamond \mathcal{L}_{\text{left}} \Rightarrow 1] - \Pr\left[\mathcal{A} \diamond \mathcal{L}_{\text{right}} \Rightarrow 1\right]\right|$$

$$= \left| \begin{array}{c} \left(\Pr[\mathcal{A} \diamond \mathcal{L}_{\text{left}} \Rightarrow 1 \mid \mathcal{B}_{\text{left}}] \cdot p^* + \Pr[\mathcal{A} \diamond \mathcal{L}_{\text{left}} \Rightarrow 1 \mid \overline{\mathcal{B}_{\text{left}}}](1 - p^*)\right) \\ -\left(\Pr[\mathcal{A} \diamond \mathcal{L}_{\text{right}} \Rightarrow 1 \mid \mathcal{B}_{\text{right}}] \cdot p^* + \Pr[\mathcal{A} \diamond \mathcal{L}_{\text{right}} \Rightarrow 1 \mid \overline{\mathcal{B}_{\text{right}}}](1 - p^*)\right) \end{array} \right|$$

$$= \left| \begin{array}{c} p^*(\Pr[\mathcal{A} \diamond \mathcal{L}_{\text{left}} \Rightarrow 1 \mid \mathcal{B}_{\text{left}}] - \Pr[\mathcal{A} \diamond \mathcal{L}_{\text{right}} \Rightarrow 1 \mid \mathcal{B}_{\text{right}}]) \\ (1 - p^*)(\Pr[\mathcal{A} \diamond \mathcal{L}_{\text{left}} \Rightarrow 1 \mid \overline{\mathcal{B}_{\text{left}}}] - \Pr[\mathcal{A} \diamond \mathcal{L}_{\text{right}} \Rightarrow 1 \mid \overline{\mathcal{B}_{\text{right}}}]) \end{array} \right|$$

In both of the expressions $\Pr[\mathcal{A} \diamond \mathcal{L}_{\text{left}} \Rightarrow 1 \mid \overline{\mathcal{B}_{\text{left}}}]$ and $\Pr[\mathcal{A} \diamond \mathcal{L}_{\text{right}} \Rightarrow 1 \mid \overline{\mathcal{B}_{\text{right}}}]$, we are conditioning on bad never being set to 0 . In this case, both libraries are executing the same sequence of instructions, so the probabilities are equal (and the difference of the probabilities is zero). Substituting in, we get:

$$\text{advantage}_{\mathcal{A}} = p^* \left|\Pr[\mathcal{A} \diamond \mathcal{L}_{\text{left}} \Rightarrow 1 \mid \mathcal{B}_{\text{left}}] - \Pr[\mathcal{A} \diamond \mathcal{L}_{\text{right}} \Rightarrow 1 \mid \mathcal{B}_{\text{right}}]\right|$$

Intuitively, the proof is confirming the idea that differences can only be noticed between $\mathcal{L}_{\text{left}}$ and $\mathcal{L}_{\text{right}}$ when bad is set to 1 (corresponding to our conditioning on $\mathcal{B}_{\text{left}}$ and $\mathcal{B}_{\text{right}}$).

The quantity within the absolute value is the difference of two probabilities, so the largest it can be is 1 . Therefore,

$$\text{advantage}_{\mathcal{A}} \leqslant p^* \stackrel{\text{def}}{=} \Pr[\mathcal{B}_{\text{left}}] = \Pr[\mathcal{A} \diamond \mathcal{L}_{\text{left}} \text{ sets bad } = 1]$$

This completes the proof.

Example: *Consider $\mathcal{L}_{left}$ and $\mathcal{L}_{right}$ from the previous example (where the calling program tries to "predict" the result of uniformly sampling a λ-bit string). We can prove that they are indistinguishable with the following sequence of hybrids:*

Let us justify each of the steps:

- $\mathcal{L}_{\text{left}} \equiv \mathcal{L}_{\text{hyb-L:}}$: The only difference is that $\mathcal{L}_{\text{hyb-L}}$ maintains a variable "bad." Since it never actually reads from this variable, the change can have no effect.
- $\mathcal{L}_{\text{hyb-L}}$ and $\mathcal{L}_{\text{hyb-R}}$ differ only in the highlighted line, which can only be reached when bad $= 1$. Therefore, from the bad-event lemma:

  $$\left|\Pr[\mathcal{A} \diamond \mathcal{L}_{\text{hyb-L}} \Rightarrow 1] - \Pr[\mathcal{A} \diamond \mathcal{L}_{\text{hyb-R}} \Rightarrow 1]\right| \leqslant \Pr[\mathcal{A} \diamond \mathcal{L}_{\text{hyb-L}} \text{ sets bad } = 1]$$

But $\mathcal{A} \diamond \mathcal{L}_{\text{hyb-L}}$ only sets bad = 1 if the calling program successfully predicts s in one of the calls to predict. With q calls to predict, the total probability of this happening is at most $q/2^{\lambda}$, which is negligible when the calling program runs in polynomial time. Hence $\mathcal{L}_{\text{hyb-L}} \approx \mathcal{L}_{\text{hyb-R}}$.

- *$\mathcal{L}_{\text{hyb-R}} \equiv \mathcal{L}_{\text{right}}$: Similar to above, note how the first 3 lines of predict in $\mathcal{L}_{\text{hyb-R}}$ don't actually do anything. The subroutine is going to return false no matter what. Both libraries have identical behavior.*

Since $\mathcal{L}_{\text{left}} \equiv \mathcal{L}_{\text{hyb-L}} \approx \mathcal{L}_{\text{hyb-R}} \equiv \mathcal{L}_{\text{right}}$, this proves that $\mathcal{L}_{\text{left}} \approx \mathcal{L}_{\text{right}}$.

4.4 Birthday Probabilities & Sampling With/out Replacement

In many cryptographic schemes, the users repeatedly choose random strings (e.g., each time they encrypt a message), and security breaks down if the same string is ever chosen twice. Hence, it is important that the probability of a repeated sample is negligible. In this section we compute the probability of such events and express our findings in a modular way, as a statement about the indistinguishability of two libraries.

Birthday Probabilities

If q people are in a room, what is the probability that two of them have the same birthday (if we assume that each person's birthday is uniformly chosen from among the possible days in a year)? This question is known as the birthday problem, and it is famous because the answer is highly unintuitive to most people. [9]

Let's make the question more general. Imagine taking q independent, uniform samples from a set of N items. What is the probability that the same value gets chosen more than once? In other words, what is the probability that the following program outputs 1 ?

```
B(q, N)
for i := 1 to q:
  s_i ← {1, ..., N}
  for j := 1 to i − 1:
     if s_i = s_j then return 1
return 0
```

Let's give a name to this probability:

$$\text{Birthday Prob}(q, N) \stackrel{\text{def}}{=} \Pr[\mathcal{B}(q, N) \text{ outputs } 1].$$

It is possible to write an exact formula for this probability:

Lemma 4.9 BirthdayProb $(q, N) = 1 - \prod_{i=1}^{q-1} \left(1 - \frac{i}{N}\right)$.

Proof : Let us instead compute the probability that $\mathcal{B}$ outputs 0 , which will allow us to then solve for the probability that it outputs 1 . In order for $\mathcal{B}$ to output 0 , it must avoid the early termination conditions in each iteration of the main loop. Therefore:

$$\begin{aligned} \Pr[\mathcal{B}(q,N) \text{ outputs } 0] =& \Pr[\mathcal{B}(q,N) \text{ doesn't terminate early in iteration } i = 1] \\ &\cdot \Pr[\mathcal{B}(q,N) \text{ doesn't terminate early in iteration } i = 2] \\ &\vdots \\ &\cdot \Pr[\mathcal{B}(q,N) \text{ doesn't terminate early in iteration } i = q] \end{aligned}$$

In iteration i of the main loop, there are $i - 1$ previously chosen values $s_1, \ldots, s_{i-1}$. The program terminates early if any of these are chosen again as s_i, otherwise it continues to the next iteration. Put differently, there are $i - 1$ (out of N) ways to choose s_i that lead to early termination - all other choices of s_i avoid early termination. Since the N possibilities for s_i happen with equal probability:

$$\Pr[\mathcal{B}(q,N) \text{ doesn't terminate early in iteration } i] = 1 - \frac{i-1}{N}.$$

Putting everything together:

$$\begin{aligned} \text{BirthdayProb}(q,N) &= \Pr[\mathcal{B}(q,N) \text{ outputs } 1] \\ &= 1 - \Pr[\mathcal{B}(q,N) \text{ outputs } 0] \\ &= 1 - \left(1 - \frac{1}{N}\right)\left(1 - \frac{2}{N}\right)\cdots\left(1 - \frac{q-1}{N}\right) \\ &= 1 - \prod_{i=1}^{q-1} \left(1 - \frac{i}{N}\right) \end{aligned}$$

This completes the proof.

Example: *This formula for BirthdayProb(q, N) is not easy to understand at a glance. We can get a better sense of its behavior as a function of q by plotting it. Below is a plot with $N = 365$, corresponding to the classic birthday problem:*

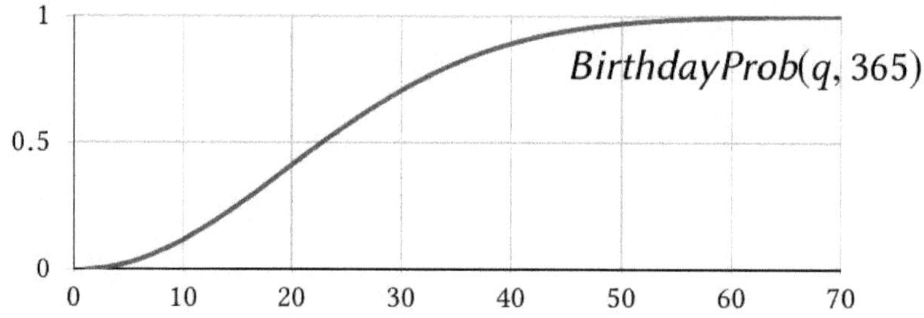

With only $q = 23$ people the probability of a shared birthday already exceeds 50%. The graph could be extended to the right (all the way to $q = 365$), but even at $q = 70$ the probability exceeds 99.9%.

Asymptotic Bounds on the Birthday Probability

It will be helpful to have an asymptotic formula for how BirthdayProb(q, N) grows as a function of q and N. We are most interested in the case where q is relatively small compared to N (e.g., when q is a polynomial function of λ but N is exponential).

Lemma 4.10 (Birthday Bound)

If $q \leqslant \sqrt{2N}$, then

$$0.632\frac{q(q-1)}{2N} \leqslant \mathit{BirthdayProb}(q, N) \leqslant \frac{q(q-1)}{2N}.$$

Since the upper and lower bounds differ by only a constant factor, it makes sense to write BirthdayProb $(q, N) = \Theta(q^2/N)$.

Proof We split the proof into two parts.

- To prove the upper bound, we use the fact that when x and y are positive,

$$\begin{aligned}(1-x)(1-y) &= 1-(x+y)+xy \\ &\geqslant 1-(x+y)\end{aligned}$$

More generally, when all terms x_i are positive, $\prod_i (1-x_i) \geqslant 1-\sum_i x_i$. Hence,

$$1-\prod_i (1-x_i) \leqslant 1-\left(1-\sum_i x_i\right) = \sum_i x_i$$

Applying that fact,

$$\text{BirthdayProb}(q,N) \stackrel{\text{def}}{=} 1-\prod_{i=1}^{q-1}\left(1-\frac{i}{N}\right) \leqslant \sum_{i=1}^{q-1}\frac{i}{N} = \frac{\sum_{i=1}^{q-1} i}{N} = \frac{q(q-1)}{2N}.$$

- To prove the lower bound, we use the fact that when $0 \leqslant x \leqslant 1$,

$$1-x \leqslant e^{-x} \leqslant 1-0.632x$$

This fact is illustrated below. The significance of 0.632 is that $1-\frac{1}{e} = 0.63212\ldots$

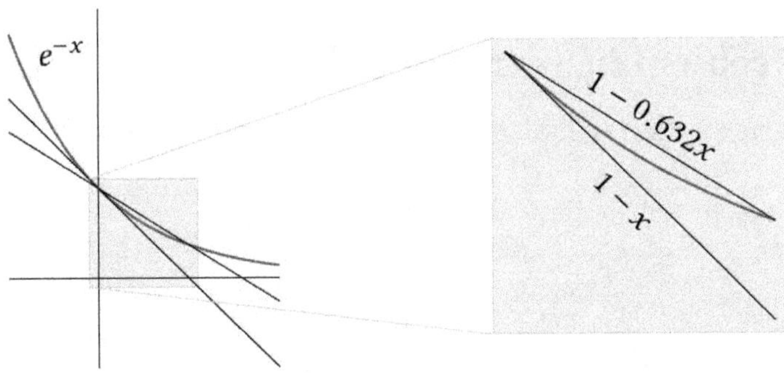

We can use both of these upper and lower bounds on e^{-x} to show the following:

$$\prod_{i=1}^{q-1}\left(1-\frac{i}{N}\right) \leqslant \prod_{i=1}^{q-1} e^{-\frac{i}{N}} = e^{-\sum_{i=1}^{q-1}\frac{i}{N}} = e^{-\frac{q(q-1)}{2N}} \leqslant 1-0.632\frac{q(q-1)}{2N}$$

With the last inequality we used the fact that $q \leqslant \sqrt{2N}$, and therefore $\frac{q(q-1)}{2N} \leqslant 1$ (this is necessary to apply the inequality $e^{-x} \leqslant 1-0.632x$). Hence:

$$\begin{aligned}\text{BirthdayProb}(q,N) &\stackrel{\text{def}}{=} 1-\prod_{i=1}^{q-1}\left(1-\frac{i}{N}\right)\\ &\geqslant 1-\left(1-0.632\frac{q(q-1)}{2N}\right) = 0.632\frac{q(q-1)}{2N}\end{aligned}$$

This completes the proof. □

Example *Below is a plot of these bounds compared to the actual value of BirthdayProb(q, N) (for N = 365):*

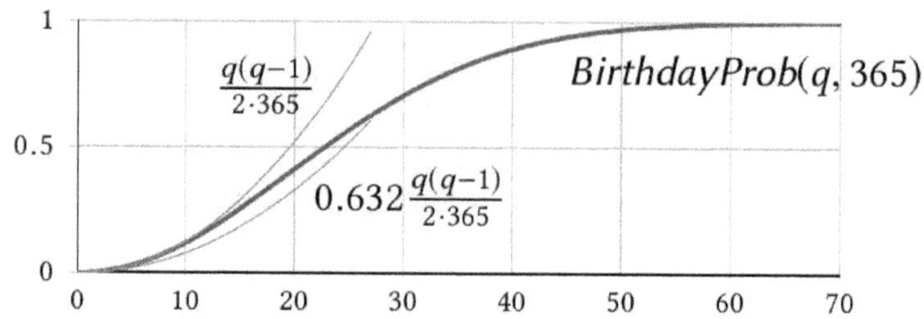

As mentioned previously, BirthdayProb (q, N) grows roughly like q^2/N within the range of values we care about (q small relative to N).

The Birthday Problem in Terms of Indistinguishable Libraries

Below are two libraries which will also be useful for future topics.

$\mathcal{L}_{\text{samp-L}}$
SAMP():
$r \leftarrow \{0,1\}^\lambda$
return r

$\mathcal{L}_{\text{samp-R}}$
$R := \emptyset$
SAMP():
$r \leftarrow \{0,1\}^\lambda \setminus R$
$R := R \cup \{r\}$
return r

Both libraries provide a SAMP subroutine that samples a random element of $\{0,1\}^\lambda$. The implementation in $\mathcal{L}_{\text{samp-L}}$ samples uniformly and independently from $\{0,1\}^\lambda$ each time. It samples with replacement, so it is possible (although maybe unlikely) for multiple calls to samp to return the same value in $\mathcal{L}_{\text{samp-L}}$.

On the other hand, $\mathcal{L}_{\text{samp-R}}$ samples λ-bit strings without replacement. It keeps track of a set R, containing all the values it has previously sampled, and avoids choosing them again (" $\{0,1\}^\lambda \setminus R$ " is the set of λ-bit strings excluding the ones in R). In this library, samp will never output the same value twice.

The "obvious" distinguishing strategy. A natural way (but maybe not the only way) to distinguish these two libraries, therefore, would be to call samp many times. If you ever see a repeated output, then you must certainly be linked to $\mathcal{L}_{\text{samp-L}}$. After some number of calls to samp, if you still don't see any repeated outputs, you might eventually stop and guess that you are linked to $\mathcal{L}_{\text{samp-R}}$.

Let $\mathcal{A}_q$ denote this "obvious" calling program that makes q calls to sAMP and returns 1 if it sees a repeated value. Clearly, the program can never return 1 when it is linked to $\mathcal{L}_{\text{samp-R}}$. On the other hand, when it is linked to $\mathcal{L}_{\text{samp-L}}$, it returns 1 with probability exactly BirthdayProb($q, 2^\lambda$). Therefore, the advantage of $\mathcal{A}_q$ is exactly BirthdayProb($q, 2^\lambda$).

This program behaves differently in the presence of these two libraries, therefore they are not interchangeable. But are the libraries indistinguishable? We have demonstrated a calling program with advantage BirthdayProb $(q, 2^\lambda)$. We have not specified q exactly, but if $\mathcal{A}_q$ is meant to run in polynomial time (as a function of λ), then q must be a polynomial function of λ. Then the advantage of $\mathcal{A}_q$ is BirthdayProb$(q, 2^\lambda) = \Theta(q^2/2^\lambda)$, which is negligible!

To show that the librares are indistinguishable, we have to show that all calling programs have negligible advantage. It is not enough just to show that this particular calling program has negligible advantage. Perhaps surprisingly, the "obvious" calling program that we considered is the best possible distinguisher!

Lemma 4.11 (Repl. Sampling) *Let $\mathcal{L}_{samp\text{-}L}$ and $\mathcal{L}_{samp\text{-}R}$ be defined as above. Then for all calling programs $\mathcal{A}$ that make q queries to the SAMP subroutine, the advantage of $\mathcal{A}$ in distinguishing the libraries is at most BirthdayProb($q, 2^\lambda$).*

In particular, when $\mathcal{A}$ is polynomial-time (in λ), q grows as a polynomial in the security parameter. Hence, $\mathcal{A}$ has negligible advantage. Since this is true for all polynomial-time $\mathcal{A}$, we have $\mathcal{L}_{samp\text{-}L} \approx \mathcal{L}_{samp\text{-}R}$.

Proof Consider the following hybrid libraries:

```
L_hyb-L
R := ∅
bad := 0

SAMP():
  r ← {0,1}^λ
  if r ∈ R then:
    bad := 1

  R := R ∪ {r}
  return r
```

```
L_hyb-R
R := ∅
bad := 0

SAMP():
  r ← {0,1}^λ
  if r ∈ R then:
    bad := 1
    r ← {0,1}^λ \ R
  R := R ∪ {r}
  return r
```

First, let us prove some simple observations about these libraries:

$\mathcal{L}_{\text{hyb-L}} \equiv \mathcal{L}_{\text{samp-L}}$: Note that $\mathcal{L}_{\text{hyb-L}}$ simply samples uniformly from $\{0,1\}^\lambda$. The extra R and bad variables in $\mathcal{L}_{\text{hyb-L}}$ don't actually have an effect on its external behavior (they are used only for convenience later in the proof).

$\mathcal{L}_{\text{hyb-R}} \equiv \mathcal{L}_{\text{samp-R}}$: Whereas $\mathcal{L}_{\text{samp-R}}$ avoids repeats by simply sampling from $\{0,1\}^\lambda \setminus R$, this library $\mathcal{L}_{\text{hyb-R}}$ samples r uniformly from $\{0,1\}^\lambda$ and retries if the result happens to be in R. This method is called rejection sampling, and it has the same effect [10] as sampling r directly from $\{0,1\}^\lambda \setminus R$.

Conveniently, $\mathcal{L}_{\text{hyb-L}}$ and $\mathcal{L}_{\text{hyb-R}}$ differ only in code that is reachable when bad = 1 (highlighted). So, using Lemma 4.8, we can bound the advantage of the calling program:

$$\begin{aligned} &\left| \Pr[\mathcal{A} \diamond \mathcal{L}_{\text{samp-L}} \Rightarrow 1] - \Pr[\mathcal{A} \diamond \mathcal{L}_{\text{samp-R}} \Rightarrow 1] \right| \\ &= \left|\Pr[\mathcal{A} \diamond \mathcal{L}_{\text{hyb-L}} \Rightarrow 1] - \Pr[\mathcal{A} \diamond \mathcal{L}_{\text{hyb-R}} \Rightarrow 1]\right| \\ &\leqslant \Pr[\mathcal{A} \diamond \mathcal{L}_{\text{hyb-L sets bad}} := 1] \end{aligned}$$

Finally, we can observe that $\mathcal{A} \diamond \mathcal{L}_{\text{hyb-L}}$ sets bad := 1 only in the event that it sees a repeated sample from $\{0,1\}^\lambda$. This happens with probability BirthdayProb$(q, 2^\lambda)$.

Discussion

- Stating the birthday problem in terms of indistinguishable libraries makes it a useful tool in future security proofs. For example, when proving the security of a construction we can replace a uniform sampling step with a sampling-without-replacement step. This change has only a negligible effect, but now the rest of the proof can take advantage of the fact that samples are never repeated.
- Another way to say this is that, when you are thinking about a cryptographic construction, it is "safe to assume" that randomly sampled long strings do not repeat, and behave accordingly.
- However, if a security proof does use the indistinguishability of the birthday libraries, it means that the scheme can likely be broken when a user happens to repeat a uniformly sampled value. Since this becomes inevitable as the number of samples approaches $\sqrt{2^{\lambda+1}} \sim 2^{\lambda/2}$, it means the scheme only offers $\lambda/2$ bits of security. When a scheme has this property, we say that it has birthday bound security. It is important to understand when a scheme has this property, since it informs the size of keys that should be chosen in practice.

A Generalization

A calling program can distinguish between the previous libraries if SAMP ever returns the same value twice. In any given call to SAMP, the variable $\mathcal{R}$ denotes the set of "problematic" values that cause the libraries to be distinguished. At any point, $\mathcal{R}$ has only polynomially many values, so the probability of chosing such a problematic one is negligible.

Suppose we considered a different set of values to be problematic. As long as there are only polynomially many problematic values in each call to SAMP, the reasoning behind the proof wouldn't change much. This idea leads to the following generalization, in which the calling program explicitly writes down all of the problematic values:

Lemma 4.12 *The following two libraries are indistinguishable, provided that the argument $\mathcal{R}$ to SAMP is passed as an explicit list of items.*

$\mathcal{L}_{\text{samp-L}}$
SAMP($\mathcal{R} \subseteq \{0,1\}^\lambda$):
$r \leftarrow \{0,1\}^\lambda$
return r

$\mathcal{L}_{\text{samp-R}}$
SAMP($\mathcal{R} \subseteq \{0,1\}^\lambda$):
$r \leftarrow \{0,1\}^\lambda \setminus \mathcal{R}$
return r

Suppose the calling program makes q calls to samp, and in the i th call it uses an argument $\mathcal{R}$ with n_i items. Then the advantage of the calling program is at most:

$$1 - \prod_{i=1}^{q} \left(1 - \frac{n_i}{2^\lambda}\right).$$

We can bound this advantage as before. If $\sum_{i=1}^{q} n_i \leqslant 2^\lambda$, then the advantage is between $0.632(\sum_{i=1}^{q} n_i)/2^\lambda$ and $(\sum_{i=1}^{q} n_i)/2^\lambda$. When the calling program runs in polynomial time and must pass $\mathcal{R}$ as an explicit list (i.e., take the time to "write down" the elements of $\mathcal{R}$), $\sum_{i=1}^{q} n_i$ is a polynomial in the security parameter and the calling program's advantage is negligible.

The birthday scenario corresponds to the special case where $n_i = i$ (in the i th call, $\mathcal{R}$ consists of the $i-1$ results from previous calls to SAMP). In that case, $\sum_{i=1}^{q} n_i = q(q-1)/2$ and the probabilities collapse to the familiar birthday probabilities.

Exercises

4.1. In Section 4.1 we estimated the monetary cost of large computations, using pricing information from Amazon EC2 cloud computing service. This reflects the cost of doing a huge computation using a general-purpose CPU. For long-lived computations, the dominating cost is not the one-time cost of the hardware, but rather the cost of electricity powering the hardware. Because of that, it can be much cheaper to manufacture special-purpose hardware. Depending on the nature of the computation, special-purpose hardware can be significantly more energy-efficient.

This is the situation with the Bitcoin cryptocurrency. Mining Bitcoin requires evaluating the SHA-256 cryptographic hash function as many times as possible, as fast as possible. When mining Bitcoin today, the only economically rational choice is to use specialpurpose hardware that does nothing except evaluate SHA-256, but is millions (maybe billions) of times more energy efficient than a general-purpose CPU evaluating SHA-256.

(a) The relevant specs for Bitcoin mining hardware are wattage and giga-hashes (or terahashes) per second, which can be converted into raw energy required per hash. Search online and find the most energy efficient mining hardware you can (e.g., least joules per hash).

(b) Find the cheapest real-world electricity rates you can, anywhere in the world. Use these to estimate the monetary cost of computing $2^{40}, 2^{50}, \ldots, 2^{120}$ SHA- 256 hashes.

(c) Money is not the only way to measure the energy cost of a huge computation. Search online to find out how much carbon dioxide (CO_2) is placed into the atmosphere per unit of electrical energy produced, under a typical distribution of power production methods. Estimate how many tons of CO_2 are produced as a side-effect of computing $2^{40}, 2^{50}, \ldots, 2^{120}$ SHA-256 hashes.

(d) Estimate the corresponding CO_2 concentration (parts per million) in the atmosphere as a result of computing $2^{40}, 2^{50}, \ldots, 2^{120}$ SHA-256 hashes. If it is possible without a PhD in climate science, try to estimate the increase in average global temperature caused by these computations.

4.2. Which of the following are negligible functions in λ ? Justify your answers.

$$\frac{1}{2^{\lambda/2}} \quad \frac{1}{2^{\log(\lambda^2)}} \quad \frac{1}{\lambda^{\log(\lambda)}} \quad \frac{1}{\lambda^2} \quad \frac{1}{2^{(\log \lambda)^2}} \quad \frac{1}{(\log \lambda)^2} \quad \frac{1}{\lambda^{1/\lambda}} \quad \frac{1}{\sqrt{\lambda}} \quad \frac{1}{2^{\sqrt{\lambda}}}$$

4.3. Suppose f and g are negligible.

(a) Show that $f + g$ is negligible.

(b) Show that $f \cdot g$ is negligible.

(c) Give an example f and g which are both negligible, but where $f(\lambda)/g(\lambda)$ is not negligible.

4.4. Show that when f is negligible, then for every polynomial p, the function $p(\lambda)f(\lambda)$ not only approaches 0 , but it is also negligible itself.

4.5. Prove that the $\approx$ relation is transitive. Let $f, g, h: \mathbb{N} \rightarrow \mathbb{R}$ be functions. Using the definition of the relation, prove that if $f \approx g$ and $g \approx h$ then $f \approx h$. You may find it useful to invoke the triangle inequality: $|a - c| \leqslant |a - b| + |b - c|$.

4.6. Prove Lemma 4.6.

4.7. Prove Lemma 4.7.

4.8. A deterministic program is one that uses no random choices. Suppose $\mathcal{L}_1$ and $\mathcal{L}_2$ are two deterministic libraries with a common interface. Show that either $\mathcal{L}_1 \equiv \mathcal{L}_2$, or else $\mathcal{L}_1$ & $\mathcal{L}_2$ can be distinguished with advantage 1.

4.9. Algorithm $\mathcal{B}$ in Section 4.4 has worst-case running time $O(q^2)$. Can you suggest a way to make it run in $O(q\log\ q)$ time? What about $O(q)$ time?

4.10. Assume that the last 4 digits of student ID numbers are assigned uniformly at this university. In a class of 46 students, what is the exact probability that two students have ID numbers with the same last 4 digits?

Compare this exact answer to the upper and lower bounds given by Lemma 4.10.

4.11. Write a program that experimentally estimates the BirthdayProb(q, N) probabilities.

Given q and N, generate q uniformly chosen samples from $\mathbb{Z}_N$, with replacement, and check whether any element was chosen more than once. Repeat this entire process t times to estimate the true probability of BirthdayProb (q, N).

Generate a plot that compares your experimental findings to the theoretical upper/lower bounds of $0.632 \frac{q(q-1)}{2^{\lambda+1}}$ and $\frac{q(q-1)}{2^{\lambda+1}}$.

4.12. Suppose you want to enforce password rules so that at least 2^{128} passwords satisfy the rules. How many characters long must the passwords be, in each of these cases?

(a) Passwords consist of lowercase a through z only.

(b) Passwords consist of lowercase and uppercase letters a-z and A-Z.

(c) Passwords consist of lower/uppercase letters and digits 0-9.

(d) Passwords consist of lower/uppercase letters, digits, and any symbol characters that appear on a standard US keyboard (including the space character).

Chapter-5

Pseudorandom Generators

One-time pad requires a key that's as long as the plaintext. Let's forget that we know about this limitation. Suppose Alice & Bob share only a short λ-bit secret k, but they want to encrypt a 2λ-bit plaintext m. They don't know that (perfect) one-time secrecy is impossible in this setting (Exercise 2.11), so they try to get it to work anyway using the following reasoning:

- The only encryption scheme they know about is one-time pad, so they decide that the ciphertext will have the form $= m \oplus ??$. This means that the unknown value ?? must be 2λ bits long.
- In order for the security of one-time pad to apply, the unknown value ?? should be uniformly distributed.
- The process of obtaining the unknown value ?? from the shared key k should be deterministic, so that the sender and receiver compute the same value and decryption works correctly.

Let G denote the process that transforms the key k into this mystery value. Then $G : \{0,1\}^\lambda \to \{0,1\}^{2\lambda}$, and the encryption scheme is $\text{Enc}(k,m) = m \oplus G(k)$.

It is not hard to see that if G is a deterministic function, then there are only 2^λ possible outputs of G, so the distribution of $G(k)$ cannot be uniform in $\{0,1\}^{2\lambda}$. We therefore cannot argue that the scheme is secure in the same way as one-time pad.

However, what if the distribution of $G(k)$ values is not perfectly uniform but only "close enough" to uniform? Suppose no polynomial-time algorithm can distinguish the distribution of $G(k)$ values from the uniform distribution. Then surely this ought to be "close enough" to uniform for practical purposes. This is exactly the idea of pseudorandomness. It turns out that if G has a pseudorandomness property, then the encryption scheme described above is actually secure (against polynomial-time adversaries, in the sense discussed in the previous chapter).

5.1 Definitions

A pseudorandom generator (PRG) is a deterministic function G whose outputs are longer than its inputs. When the input to G is chosen uniformly at random, it induces a certain distribution over the possible output. As discussed above, this output distribution cannot be uniform. However, the distribution is pseudorandom if it is indistinguishable from the uniform distribution. More formally:

Definition 5.1 (PRG security) Let $G: \{0,1\}^\lambda \to \{0,1\}^{\lambda+\ell}$ be a deterministic function with $\ell > 0$. We say that G is a **secure pseudorandom generator** (PRG) if $\mathcal{L}^G_{\text{prg-real}} \approx \mathcal{L}^G_{\text{prg-rand}}$, where:

$\mathcal{L}^G_{\text{prg-real}}$	$\mathcal{L}^G_{\text{prg-rand}}$
QUERY():	QUERY():
$s \leftarrow \{0,1\}^\lambda$	$r \leftarrow \{0,1\}^{\lambda+\ell}$
return $G(s)$	return r

The value ℓ is called the stretch of the PRG. The input to the PRG is typically called a seed.

Below is an illustration of the distributions sampled by these libraries, for a lengthdoubling ($\ell = \lambda$) PRG (not drawn to scale):

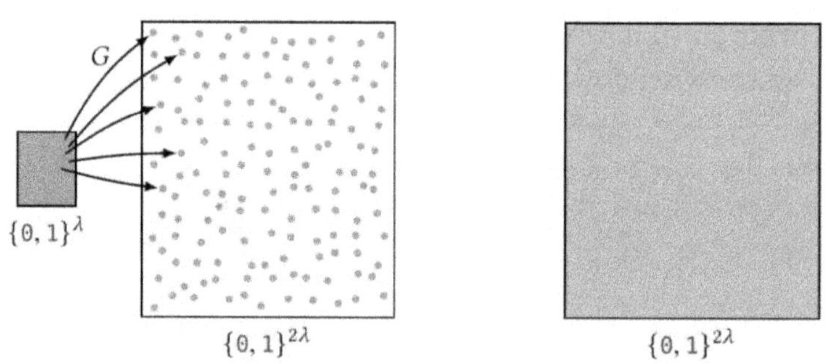

pseudorandom distribution uniform distribution

$\mathcal{L}_{\text{prg-real}}$ samples from distribution of red dots, by first sampling a uniform element of $\{0,1\}^\lambda$ and performing the action of G on that value to get a red result in $\{0,1\}^{2\lambda}$. The other library $\mathcal{L}_{\text{prg-rand}}$ directly samples the uniform distribution on $\{0,1\}^{2\lambda}$ (in green above).

To understand PRGs, you must simultaneously appreciate two ways to compare the PRG's output distribution with the uniform distribution:

- From a relative perspective, the PRG's output distribution is tiny. Out of the $2^{2\lambda}$ strings in $\{0,1\}^{2\lambda}$, only 2^{λ} are possible outputs of G. These strings make up a $2^{\lambda}/2^{2\lambda} = 1/2^{\lambda}$ fraction of $\{0,1\}^{2\lambda}$ - a negligible fraction!

- From an absolute perspective, the PRG's output distribution is huge. There are 2^{λ} possible outputs of G, which is an exponential amount!

The illustration above only captures the relative perspective (comparing the red dots to the entire extent of $\{0,1\}^{2\lambda}$), so it can lead to some misunderstanding. Just looking at this picture, it is hard to imagine how the two distributions could be indistinguishable. How could a calling program not notice whether it's seeing the whole set or just a negligible fraction of the whole set? Well, if you run in polynomial-time in λ, then 2^{λ} and $2^{2\lambda}$ are both so enormous that it doesn't really matter that one is vastly bigger than the other. The relative sizes of the distribution don't really help distinguish, since it is not a viable strategy for the distinguisher to "measure" the size of the distribution it's sampling.

Consider: there are about 2^{75} molecules in a teaspoon of water, and about $2^{2\cdot 75}$ molecules of water in Earth's oceans. Suppose you dump a teaspoon of water into the ocean and let things mix for a few thousand years. Even though the teaspoon accounts for only $1/2^{75}$ of the ocean's contents, that doesn't make it easy to keep track of all 2^{75} water molecules that originated in the teaspoon! If you are small enough to see individual water molecules, then a teaspoon of water looks as big as the ocean.

Discussion & Pitfalls

- Do not confuse the interface of a PRG (it takes in a seed as input) with the interface of the security libraries $\mathcal{L}_{\text{prg-}\star}$ (their query subroutine doesn't take any input)! A PRG is indeed an algorithm into which you can feed any string you like. However, security is only guaranteed when the PRG is being used exactly as described in the security libraries - in particular, when the seed is chosen uniformly/secretly and not used for anything else.

- Nothing prevents a user from putting an adversarially-chosen s into a PRG, or revealing a PRG seed to an adversary, etc. You just get no security guarantee from doing it, since it's not the situation reflected in the PRG security libraries.

- It doesn't really make sense to say that "0010110110 is a random string" or "0000000001 is a pseudorandom string." Randomness and pseudorandomness are properties of the process used to generate a string, not properties of the individual strings themselves. When we have a value $z = G(s)$ where G is a PRG and s is chosen uniformly, you could say that z was "chosen pseudorandomly." You could say that the output of some process is a "pseudorandom distribution." But it is slightly sloppy (although common) to say that a string z "is pseudorandom".

- There are common statistical tests you can run, which check whether some data has various properties that you would expect from a uniform distribution. [1] For example, are there roughly an equal number of 0s and 1s? Does the substring 01010 occur with roughly the frequency I would expect? If I interpret the string as a series of points in the unit square $[0,1)^2$, is it true that roughly $\pi/4$ of them are within Euclidean distance 1 of the origin?
- The definition of pseudorandomness is kind of a "master" definition that encompasses all of these statistical tests and more. After all, what is a statistical test, but a polynomial-time procedure that obtains samples from a distribution and outputs a yes/no decision? Pseudorandomness means that every statistical test that "passes" uniform data will also "pass" pseudorandomly generated data.

5.2 Pseudorandom Generators in Practice

You are probably expecting to now see at least one example of a secure PRG. Unfortunately, things are not so simple. We have no examples of secure PRGs! If it were possible to prove that some function G is a secure PRG, it would resolve the famous Pvs NP problem the most famous unsolved problem in computer science (and arguably, all of mathematics).

The next best thing that cryptographic research can offer are candidate PRGs, which are conjectured to be secure. The best examples of such PRGs are the ones that have been subjected to significant public scrutiny and resisted all attempts at attacks so far.

In fact, the entire rest of this book is based on cryptography that is only conjectured to be secure. How is this possible, given the book's stated focus on provable security? As you progress through the book, pay attention to how all of the provable security claims are conditional - if X is secure then Y is secure. You will be able to trace back through this web of implications and discover that there are only a small number of underlying cryptographic primitives whose security is merely conjectured (PRGs are one example of such a primitive). Everything else builds on these primitives in a provably secure way.

With that disclaimer out of the way, surely now you can be shown an example of a conjectured secure PRG, right? There are indeed some conjectured PRGs that are simple enough to show you at this point, but you won't find them in the book. The problem is that none of these PRG candidates are really used in practice. When you really need a PRG in practice, you would actually use a PRG that is built from something called a block cipher (which we won't see until Chapter 6). A block cipher is conceptually more complicated than a PRG, and can even be built from a PRG (in principle). That explains why this book starts with PRGs. In practice, a block cipher is just a more useful object, so that is what you would find easily available (even implemented with specialized CPU instructions in most CPUs). When we introduce block ciphers (and pseudorandom functions), we will discuss how they can be used to construct PRGs.

How NOT to Build a PRG

We can appreciate the challenges involved in building a PRG "from scratch" by first looking at an obvious idea for a PRG and understanding why it's insecure.

Example *Let's focus on the case of a length-doubling PRG. It should take in λ bits and output 2λ bits. The output should look random when the input is sampled uniformly. A natural idea is for the candidate PRG to simply repeat the input twice. After all, if the input s is random, then $s \| s$ is also random, too, right?*

$G(s)$:
return $s \| s$

To understand why this PRG is insecure, first let me ask you whether the following strings look like they were sampled uniformly from $\{0,1\}^8$:

$$11011101, 01010101, 01110111, 01000100, \cdots$$

Do you see any patterns? Every string has its first half equal to its second half. That is a conspicuous pattern because it is relatively rare for a uniformly chosen string to have this property.

Of course, this is exactly what is wrong with this simplistic PRGG defined above. Every output of G has equal first/second halves. But it is rare for uniformly sampled strings to have this property. We can formalize this observation as an attack against the PRG-security of G:

$\mathcal{A}$
$x \| y := \text{QUERY}()$
return $x \stackrel{?}{=} y$

The first line means to obtain the result of QUERY and set its first half to be the string x and its second half to be y. This calling program simply checks whether the output of QUERY has equal halves.

To complete the attack, we must show that this calling program has non-negligible bias distinguishing the $\mathcal{L}_{\text{prg-}\star}$ libraries.

- *When linked to $\mathcal{L}_{\text{prg-real}}$, the calling program receives outputs of G, which always have matching first/second halves. So $\Pr\left[\mathcal{A} \diamond \mathcal{L}_{\text{prg-real}}^{G} \Rightarrow 1\right] = 1$. Below we have filled in $\mathcal{L}_{\text{prg-real}}$ with the details of our G algorithm:*

$$\mathcal{A}$$
$$x\|y := QUERY()$$
$$return\ x \stackrel{?}{=} y$$
$$\mathcal{L}_{\text{prg-real}}^{G}$$
$$QUERY():$$
$$s \leftarrow \{0,1\}^{\lambda}$$
$$return\ s\|s$$

- *When linked to $\mathcal{L}_{\text{prg-rand}}$, the calling program receives uniform samples from $\{0,1\}^{2\lambda}$.*

$\mathcal{A}$	$\mathcal{L}_{\text{prg-rand}}^{G}$
$x\|y := QUERY()$	$QUERY():$
$return\ x \stackrel{?}{=} y$	$r \leftarrow \{0,1\}^{2\lambda}$
	$return\ r$

$\mathcal{A}$ outputs 1 whenever we sample a string from $\{0,1\}^{2\lambda}$ with equal first/second halves. What exactly is the probability of this happening? There are several ways to see that the probability is $1/2^{\lambda}$ (this is like asking the probability of rolling doubles with two dice, but each die has 2^{λ} sides instead of 6). Therefore, $\Pr\left[\mathcal{A} \diamond \mathcal{L}_{\text{prg-rand}}^{G} \Rightarrow 1\right] = 1/2^{\lambda}$.

The advantage of this adversary is $1 - 1/2^{\lambda}$ which is certainly non-negligible - it does not even approach 0 as λ grows. This shows that G is not a secure PRG.

This example illustrates how randomness/pseudorandomness is a property of the entire process, not of individual strings. If you take a string of 1s and concatenate it with another string of 1 s, you get a long string of 1 s. "Containing only 1 s " is a property of individual strings. If you take a "random string" and concatenate it with another "random string," you might not get a "random long string." Being random is not a property of an individual string, but of the entire process that generates it.

Outputs from this G have equal first/second halves, which is an obvious pattern. The challenge of desiging a secure PRG is that its outputs must have no discernable pattern! Any pattern will lead to an attack similar to the one shown above.

Related Concept: Random Number Generation

The security of a PRG requires the seed to be chosen uniformly. In practice, the seed has to come from somewhere. Generally a source of "randomness" is provided by the hardware or operating system, and the process that generates these random bits is (confusingly) called a random number generator (RNG).

In this course we won't cover low-level random number generation, but merely point out what makes it different than the PRGs that we study:

- The job of a PRG is to take a small amount of "ideal" (in other words, uniform) randomness and extend it.
- By contrast, an RNG usually takes many inputs over time and maintains an internal state. These inputs are often from physical/hardware sources. While these inputs are "noisy" in some sense, it is hard to imagine that they would be statistically uniform. So the job of the RNG is to "refine" (sometimes many) sources of noisy data into uniform outputs.

5.3 Application: Shorter Keys in One-Time-Secret Encryption

We revisit the motivating example from the beginning of this chapter. Alice & Bob share only a λ-bit key but want to encrypt a message of length $\lambda + \ell$. The main idea is to expand the key k into a longer string using a PRG G, and use the result as a one-time pad on the (longer) plaintext. More precisely, let $G: \{0,1\}^\lambda \to \{0,1\}^{\lambda+\ell}$ be a PRG, and define the following encryption scheme:

Construction 5.2 (Pseudo-OTP)

	KeyGen:	Enc(k,m):	Dec(k,c):
$\mathcal{K} = \{0,1\}^\lambda$	$k \leftarrow \mathcal{K}$	return $G(k) \oplus m$	return $G(k) \oplus c$
$\mathcal{M} = \{0,1\}^{\lambda+\ell}$	return k		
$\mathcal{C} = \{0,1\}^{\lambda+\ell}$			

The resulting scheme will not have (perfect) one-time secrecy. That is, encryptions of m_L and m_R will not be identically distributed in general. However, the distributions will be indistinguishable if G is a secure PRG. The precise flavor of security obtained by this construction is the following.

Definition 5.3: *Let Σ be an encryption scheme, and let $\mathcal{L}^{\Sigma}_{\text{ots-L}}$ and $\mathcal{L}^{\Sigma}_{\text{ots-R}}$ be defined as in Definition 2.6 (and repeated below for convenience). Then Σ has (computational) one-time secrecy if $\mathcal{L}^{\Sigma}_{\text{ots-L}} \approx \mathcal{L}^{\Sigma}_{\text{ots-R}}$. That is, if for all polynomial-time distinguishers $\mathcal{A}$, we have $Pr[\mathcal{A} \diamond \mathcal{L}^{\Sigma}_{\text{ots-L}} \Rightarrow 1] \approx Pr[\mathcal{A} \diamond \mathcal{L}^{\Sigma}_{\text{ots-R}} \Rightarrow 1]$.*

$\mathcal{L}^{\Sigma}_{\text{ots-L}}$	$\mathcal{L}^{\Sigma}_{\text{ots-R}}$
EAVESDROP$(m_L, m_R \in \Sigma.\mathcal{M})$:	EAVESDROP$(m_L, m_R \in \Sigma.\mathcal{M})$:
$k \leftarrow \Sigma.\text{KeyGen}$	$k \leftarrow \Sigma.\text{KeyGen}$
$c \leftarrow \Sigma.\text{Enc}(k, m_L)$	$c \leftarrow \Sigma.\text{Enc}(k, m_R)$
return c	return c

This is essentially the same as Definition 2.6, except we are using $\approx$ (indistinguishability) instead of $\equiv$ (interchangeability).

Claim 5.4: *Let pOTP denote Construction 5.2. If pOTP is instantiated using a secure PRG G then pOTP has computational one-time secrecy.*

Proof : We must show that $\mathcal{L}^{\text{pOTP}}_{\text{ots-L}} \approx \mathcal{L}^{\text{pOTP}}_{\text{ots-R}}$. As usual, we will proceed using a sequence of hybrids that begins at $\mathcal{L}^{\text{pOTP}}_{\text{ots-L}}$ and ends at $\mathcal{L}^{\text{pOTP}}_{\text{ots-R}}$. For each hybrid library, we will demonstrate that it is indistinguishable from the previous one. Note that we are allowed to use the fact that G is a secure PRG. In practical terms, this means that if we can express some hybrid library in terms of $\mathcal{L}^{G}_{\text{prg-real}}$ (one of the libraries in the PRG security definition), we can replace it with its counterpart $\mathcal{L}^{G}_{\text{prg-rand}}$ (or vice-versa). The PRG security of G says that such a change will be indistinguishable.

The starting point is $\mathcal{L}^{\text{pOTP}}_{\text{ots-L}}$, shown here with the details of pOTP filled in.

$$\mathcal{L}^{\text{pOTP}}_{\text{ots-L}} : \frac{\mathcal{L}^{\text{pOTP}}_{\text{ots-L}}}{\dfrac{\text{EAVESDROP}(m_L, m_R \in \{0,1\}^{\lambda+\ell}):}{k \leftarrow \{0,1\}^{\lambda}}} \begin{bmatrix} c := G(k) \oplus m_L \\ \text{return } c \end{bmatrix}$$

The first hybrid step is to factor out the computations involving G, in terms of the $\mathcal{L}^{G}_{\text{prg-real}}$ library.

$\mathcal{L}_{\text{hyb-1}}$:

EAVESDROP(m_L, m_R):	$\diamond$	$\mathcal{L}^{G}_{\text{prg-real}}$
$z \leftarrow$ QUERY()		QUERY():
$c := z \oplus m_L$		$s \leftarrow \{0,1\}^{\lambda}$
return c		return $G(s)$

From the PRG security of G, we may replace the instance of $\mathcal{L}^{G}_{\text{prg-real}}$ with $\mathcal{L}^{G}_{\text{prg-rand}}$. The resulting hybrid library $\mathcal{L}_{\text{hyb-2}}$ is indistinguishable from the previous one.

$\mathcal{L}_{\text{hyb-6}}$:

EAVESDROP(m_L, m_R):	$\diamond$	$\mathcal{L}^{G}_{\text{prg-real}}$
$z \leftarrow$ QUERY()		QUERY():
$c := z \oplus m_R$		$s \leftarrow \{0,1\}^{\lambda}$
return c		return $G(s)$

A subroutine has been inlined. Note that the resulting library is precisely $\mathcal{L}^{\text{OTP}}_{\text{ots-L}}$ involving standard one-time pad on plaintexts of size $\lambda + \ell$. We have essentially proven that pOTP is indistinguishable from standard OTP, and therefore we can apply the security of OTP.

$\mathcal{L}^{\text{pOTP}}_{\text{ots-R}}$:

$\mathcal{L}^{\text{pOTP}}_{\text{ots-R}}$
EAVESDROP(m_L, m_R):
$k \leftarrow \{0,1\}^{\lambda}$
$c := G(k) \oplus m_R$
return c

The (perfect) one-time secrecy of r OTP allows us to replace $\mathcal{L}^{\text{OTP}}_{\text{ots-L}}$ with $\mathcal{L}^{\text{OTP}}_{\text{ots-R}}$; they are interchangeable.

$\mathcal{L}_{\text{hyb-4}}$:

$\mathcal{L}^{\text{OTP}}_{\text{ots-R}}$
EAVESDROP(m_L, m_R):
$z \leftarrow \{0,1\}^{\lambda+\ell}$
$c := z \oplus m_R$
return c

The rest of the proof is essentially a "mirror image" of the previous steps, in which we perform the same steps but in reverse (and with m_R being used instead of m_L).

A statement has been factored out into a subroutine, which happens to exactly match $\mathcal{L}^{G}_{\text{prg-rand}}$.

$\mathcal{L}_{\text{hyb-5}}$:

```
EAVESDROP(m_L, m_R):
  z ← QUERY()
  c := z ⊕ m_R
  return c
```

◇

```
L^G_prg-rand
QUERY():
  r ← {0,1}^(λ+ℓ)
  return r
```

From the PRG security of G, we can replace $\mathcal{L}^{G}_{\text{prg-rand}}$ with $\mathcal{L}^{G}_{\text{prg-real}}$. The resulting library is indistinguishable from the previous one.

$\mathcal{L}_{\text{hyb-6}}$:

```
EAVESDROP(m_L, m_R):
  z ← QUERY()
  c := z ⊕ m_R
  return c
```

◇

```
L^G_prg-real
QUERY():
  s ← {0,1}^λ
  return G(s)
```

A subroutine has been inlined. The result is $\mathcal{L}^{\text{pOTP}}_{\text{ots-R}}$.

$\mathcal{L}^{\text{pOTP}}_{\text{ots-R}}$:

```
L^pOTP_ots-R
EAVESDROP(m_L, m_R):
  k ← {0,1}^λ
  c := G(k) ⊕ m_R
  return c
```

Summarizing, we showed a sequence of hybrid libraries satisfying the following:

$$\mathcal{L}^{\text{pOTP}}_{\text{ots-L}} \equiv \mathcal{L}_{\text{hyb-1}} \approx \mathcal{L}_{\text{hyb-2}} \equiv \mathcal{L}_{\text{hyb-3}} \equiv \mathcal{L}_{\text{hyb-4}} \equiv \mathcal{L}_{\text{hyb-5}} \approx \mathcal{L}_{\text{hyb-6}} \equiv \mathcal{L}^{\text{pOTP}}_{\text{ots-R}}.$$

Hence, $\mathcal{L}^{\text{pOTP}}_{\text{ots-L}} \approx \mathcal{L}^{\text{pOTP}}_{\text{ots-R}}$, and pOTP has (computational) one-time secrecy. □

5.4 Extending the Stretch of a PRG

The *stretch* of a PRG measures how much longer its output is than its input. Can we use a PRG with small stretch to construct a PRG with larger stretch? The answer is yes, but only if you do it the right way!

Two Approaches to Increase Stretch

Suppose $G: \{0,1\}^\lambda \to \{0,1\}^{2\lambda}$ is a length-doubling PRG (i.e., a PRG with stretch λ). Below are two ideas for constructing a PRG with longer stretch:

$H_1(s)$:
$x \| y := G(s)$
$u \| v := G(y)$
return $x \| u \| v$

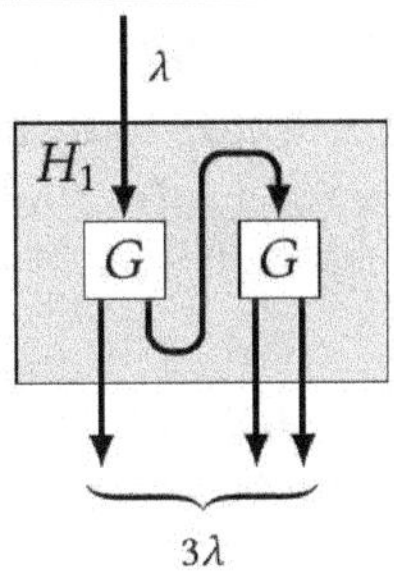

$H_2(s)$:
$x \| y := G(s)$
$u \| v := G(y)$
return $x \| \ y \ \| u \| v$

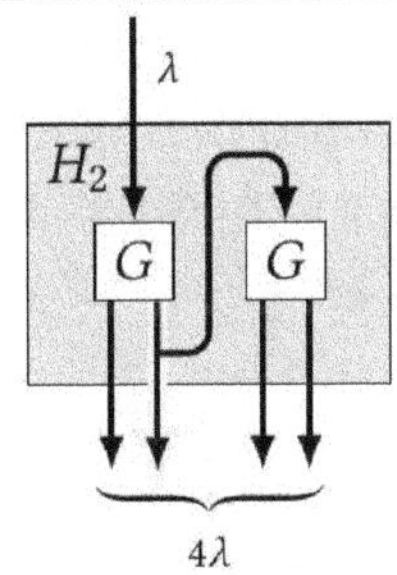

Although the constructions are similar, only one of them is secure. Before reading any further, can you guess which of H_1, H_2 is a secure PRG and which is insecure? By carefully comparing these two approaches, I hope you develop a better understanding of the PRG security definition.

A Security Proof

I think it's helpful to illustrate the "stragey" of security proofs by starting from the desired conclusion and working backwards. What better way to do this than as a Socratic dialogue in the style of Galileo? [2]

Salviati: I'm sure that H_1 is the secure PRG.

Simplicio: If I understand the security definition for PRGs correctly, you mean that the output of H_1 looks indistinguishable from uniform, when the input to H_1 is uniform. Why do you say that?

Salviati: Simple! H_1 's output consists of segments called x, u and v. Each of these are outputs of G, and since G itself is a PRG its outputs look uniform.

Simplicio: I wish I had your boldness, Salviati. I myself am more cautious. If G is a secure PRG, then its outputs are indeed indistinguishable from uniform, but surely only when its input is uniform! Are you so sure that's the case here?

Salviati: You raise a good point, Simplicio. In these endeavors it is always preferable to err on the side of caution. When we want to claim that H_1 is a secure PRG, we consider the nature of its outputs when its seed s is uniform. Since H_1 sends that seed s directly into G, your concern is addressed.

Simplicio: Yes, I can see how in the expression $x\|y := G(s)$ the input to G is uniform, and so its outputs x and y are indistinguishable from random. Since x is part of H_1 's output, we are making progress towards showing that the entire output of H_1 is indistinguishable from random! However, the output of H_1 also contains terms u and v. When I examine how they are generated, as $u\|v := G(y)$, I become concerned again. Surely y is not uniform, so I see no way to apply the security if G !

Salviati: Oh, bless your heart. The answer could not be any more obvious! It is true that y is not uniformly distributed. But did you not just convince yourself that y is indistinguishable from uniform? Should that suffice?

Simplicio: Incredible! I believe I understand now. Let me try to summarize: We suppose the input s to H_1 is chosen uniformly, and examine what happens to H_1 's outputs. In the expression $x\|y := G(s)$, the input to G is uniform, and thus x and y are indistinguishable from uniform. Now, considering the expression $u\|v := G(y)$, the result is indistinguishable from a scenario in which y is truly uniform. But if y were truly uniform, those outputs u and v would be indistinguishable from uniform! Altogether, x, u, and v (the outputs of H_1) are each indistinguishable from uniform!

I hope that was as fun for you as it was for me. [3] The formal security proof and its sequence of hybrids will follow the outline given in Simplicio's summary. We start by applying the PRG security definition to the first call to G, and replace its outputs with truly uniform values. After this change, the input to the second call to G becomes uniform, allowing us to apply the PRG security definition again.

Claim 5.5 *If G is a secure length-doubling PRG, then H_1 (defined above) is a secure (length-tripling) PRG.*

Proof: One of the trickier aspects of this proof is that we are using a secure PRG G to prove the security of another PRG H_1. That means both $\mathcal{L}^{H_1}_{\text{prg-}\star}$ and $\mathcal{L}^{G}_{\text{prg-}\star}$ will appear in this proof. Both libraries/interfaces have a subroutine named "Query", and we will rename these subroutines QUERY $_{H_1}$ and QUERY $_G$ to disambiguate.

We want to show that $\mathcal{L}^{H_1}_{\text{prg-real}} \approx \mathcal{L}^{H_1}_{\text{prg-rand}}$. As usual, we do so with a hybrid sequence. Since we assume that G is a secure PRG, we are allowed to use the fact that $\mathcal{L}^{G}_{\text{prg-real}} \approx \mathcal{L}^{G}_{\text{prg-rand}}$.

The starting point is $\mathcal{L}^{H_1}_{\text{prg-real}}$, shown here with the details of H_1 filled in.

$\mathcal{L}^{H}_{\text{prg-real}}$:

```
L^{H_1}_{prg-real}
QUERY_{H_1}():
  s ← {0,1}^λ
  x‖y := G(s)        }
  u‖v := G(y)        } H_1(s)
  return x‖u‖v       }
```

> The first invocation of G has been factored out into a subroutine. The resulting hybrid library includes an instance of $\mathcal{L}^{G}_{\text{prg-real}}$

```
QUERY_{H_1}():                   L^G_{prg-rand}
  x‖y := QUERY_G()        ◇      QUERY_G():
  u‖v := G(y)                      r ← {0,1}^{2λ}
  return x‖u‖v                     return r
```

```
QUERY_{H_1}():
  x‖y ← {0,1}^{2λ}
  u‖v := G(y)
  return x‖u‖v
```

```
QUERY_{H_1}():
  x ← {0,1}^λ
  y ← {0,1}^λ
  u‖v := G(y)
  return x‖u‖v
```

```
QUERY_{H_1}():                   L^G_{prg-real}
  x ← {0,1}^λ             ◇      QUERY_G():
  u‖v := QUERY_G()                 s ← {0,1}^λ
  return x‖u‖v                     return G(s)
```

```
QUERY_{H_1}():                   L^G_{prg-rand}
  x ← {0,1}^λ             ◇      QUERY_G():
  u‖v := QUERY_G()                 r ← {0,1}^{2λ}
  return x‖u‖v                     return r
```

```
QUERY_{H_1}():                   L^G_{prg-real}
  x‖y := QUERY_G()        ◇      QUERY_G():
  u‖v := G(y)                      s ← {0,1}^λ
  return x‖u‖v                     return G(s)
```

From the PRG security of G, we can replace the instance of $\mathcal{L}^{G}_{\text{prg-real}}$ with $\mathcal{L}^{G}_{\text{prg-rand}}$. The resulting hybrid library is indistinguishable.

```
QUERY_H1():                          L^G_prg-rand
  x||y := QUERY_G()         ⋄        QUERY_G():
  u||v := G(y)                         r ← {0,1}^{2λ}
  return x||u||v                       return r
```

A subroutine has been inlined.

```
QUERY_H1():
  x||y ← {0,1}^{2λ}
  u||v := G(y)
  return x||u||v
```

Choosing 2λ uniformly random bits and then splitting them into two halves has exactly the same effect as choosing λ uniformly random bits and independently choosing λ more.

```
QUERY_H1():
  x ← {0,1}^λ
  y ← {0,1}^λ
  u||v := G(y)
  return x||u||v
```

The remaining appearance of G has been factored out into a subroutine. Now $\mathcal{L}^{G}_{\text{prg-real}}$ makes its second appearance.

```
QUERY_H1():                          L^G_prg-real
  x ← {0,1}^λ               ⋄        QUERY_G():
  u||v := QUERY_G()                    s ← {0,1}^λ
  return x||u||v                       return G(s)
```

Again, the PRG security of G lets us replace $\mathcal{L}^{G}_{\text{prg-real}}$ with $\mathcal{L}^{G}_{\text{prg-rand}}$. The resulting hybrid library is indistinguishable.

```
QUERY_{H_1}():                    ◇   L^G_prg-rand
  x ← {0,1}^λ                         QUERY_G():
  u||v := QUERY_G()                     r ← {0,1}^{2λ}
  return x||u||v                        return r
```

A subroutine has been inlined.

```
QUERY_{H_1}():
  x ← {0,1}^λ
  u||v ← {0,1}^{2λ}
  return x||u||v
```

Similar to above, concatenating λ uniform bits with 2λ independently uniform bits has the same effect as sampling 3λ uniform bits. The result of this change is $\mathcal{L}^{H_1}_{\text{prg-rand}}$.

$\mathcal{L}^{H_1}_{\text{prg-rand}}$:

```
L^{H_1}_prg-rand
QUERY_{H_1}():
  r ← {0,1}^{3λ}
  return r
```

Through this sequence of hybrid libraries, we showed that:

$$\mathcal{L}^{H_1}_{\text{prg-real}} \equiv \mathcal{L}_{\text{hyb-1}} \approx \mathcal{L}_{\text{hyb-2}} \equiv \mathcal{L}_{\text{hyb-3}} \equiv \mathcal{L}_{\text{hyb-4}} \equiv \mathcal{L}_{\text{hyb-5}} \approx \mathcal{L}_{\text{hyb-6}} \equiv \mathcal{L}_{\text{hyb-7}} \equiv \mathcal{L}^{H_1}_{\text{prg-rand}}.$$

Hence, H_1 is a secure PRG.

Where the Proof Breaks Down for H_2

The only difference between H_1 and H_2 is that the variable y is included in the output. How does that minor change affect the reasoning that we applied to H_1 ?

```
H_2(s):
  x||y := G(s)
  u||v := G(y)
  return x||y||u||v
```

We argued that outputs u and v are indistinguishable from uniform since its input y is also indistinguishable from random. But it's not quite so simple: A PRG's output is indistinguishable from random if (1) its seed is uniform, and (2) the seed is not used for anything else! This construction H_2 violates condition (2) because it includes the "seed" y in the output.

We can see this idea reflected in the formal PRG definition. In $\mathcal{L}_{\text{prg-real}}$, the seed s is chosen uniformly, given as input to G, and then goes out of scope! If we try to reproduce the security proof for H_1 with H_2 instead, we'll get stuck when we are trying to factor out the second call to G in terms of $\mathcal{L}_{\text{prg-real}}$:

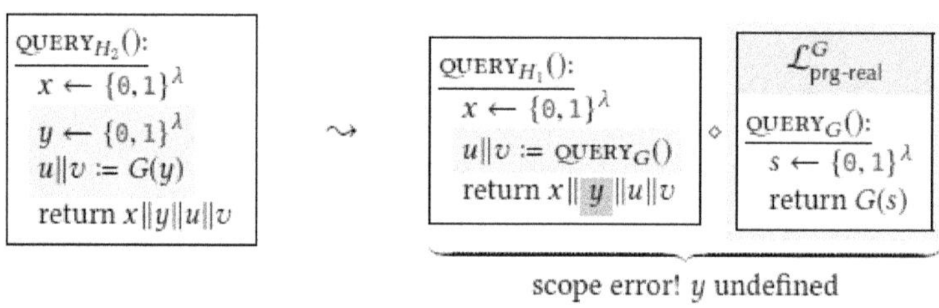

We are trying to factor out the two highlighted lines into a separate library, renaming y into s in the process. But s can only exist inside the private scope of the new library, while there still exists a "dangling reference" y in the original library.

Speaking more generally about PRGs, suppose we have a call to G somewhere and want to argue that its outputs are pseudorandom. We can only express this call to G in terms of $\mathcal{L}^G_{\text{prg-real}}$ if the input to G is uniform and is used nowhere else. That's not true here - we can't express one of the calls to G in terms of $\mathcal{L}^G_{\text{prg-real}}$, so we can't be sure that the outputs of that call to G look random.

These subtle issues are not limited to PRGs. Every hybrid security proof in this course includes steps where we factor out some statements in terms of some pre-existing library. Don't take these steps for granted! They will fail (often because of scoping issues) if the construction isn't using the building block correctly. You should always treat such "factoring out" steps as "sanity checks" for your proof.

A Concrete Attack on H_2

So far, we've only demonstrated that we get stuck when trying to prove the security of H_2. But that doesn't necessarily mean that H_2 is insecure - it could mean that we're just not clever enough to see a different security proof. To show that H_2 is actually insecure, we must demonstrate a successful distinguishing attack.

Attacking a PRG amounts to finding "patterns" in their outputs. Does H_2 have a pattern in its outputs? Yes, in this case the pattern is that if you write the output in the form $x\|y\|u\|v$, then $u\|v$ is always equal to $G(y)$. The calling program can check for this condition, which is unlikely to happen for truly uniform values.

You may wonder, is it legal for the calling program to compute $G(y)$? Well, G is a publicly known algorithm (Kerckhoffs' principle!), and y is right there as part of the input. Nothing prevents the calling program from running G "in its head." [4]

Claim 5.6 *Construction H_2 is not a secure PRG, even if G is.*

Proof Consider the following distinguisher $\mathcal{A}$:

$$x\|y\|u\|v := \text{QUERY}()$$
$$\text{return } G(y) \stackrel{?}{=} u\|v$$

When $\mathcal{A}$ is linked to $\mathcal{L}^{H_2}_{\text{prg-real}}$, the outputs indeed satisfy the condition $G(y) = u\|v$, so $\mathcal{A}$ outputs true with probability 1.

When $\mathcal{A}$ is linked to $\mathcal{L}^{H_2}_{\text{prg-rand}}$, the outputs are truly uniform. It is helpful to imagine x and y being chosen before u and v. As soon as y is chosen, the value $G(y)$ is uniquely determined, since G is a deterministic algorithm. Then $\mathcal{A}$ will output true if $u\|v$ is chosen exactly to equal this $G(y)$. Since u and v are chosen uniformly, and are a total of 2κ bits long, this event happens with probability $1/2^{2\kappa}$.

$\mathcal{A}$'s advantage is the difference in these probabilities: $1 - 1/2^{2\kappa}$, which is nonnegligible.

Discussion

In the attack on H_2, we never tried to distinguish the output of G from uniform. H_2 is insecure even if G is the best PRG in the world! It's insecure because of the incorrect way it uses G.

From now on in this book, we'll be studying higher-level constructions that are assembled from various building blocks - in this chapter, fancy PRGs constructed from simpler PRGs. "Security" means: if the building blocks are secure then the construction is secure. "Insecurity" means: even if the building blocks are secure, the construction can be insecure. So when you're showing insecurity, you shouldn't directly attack the building blocks! You should assume the building blocks are secure and attack the way that the building blocks are being used.

5.5 Applications: Stream Cipher & Symmetric Ratchet

The PRG-feedback construction can be generalized in a natural way, by continuing to feed part of G 's output into G again. The proof works in the same way as for the previous construction - the security of G is applied one at a time to each application of G.

Claim 5.7 If G is a secure length-doubling PRG, then for any n (polynomial function of) the following construction H_n is a secure PRG with stretch $n\lambda$:

```
H_n(s):
  s_0 := s
  for i = 1 to n:
    s_i||t_i := G(s_{i-1})
  return t_1|| ··· ||t_n||s_n
```

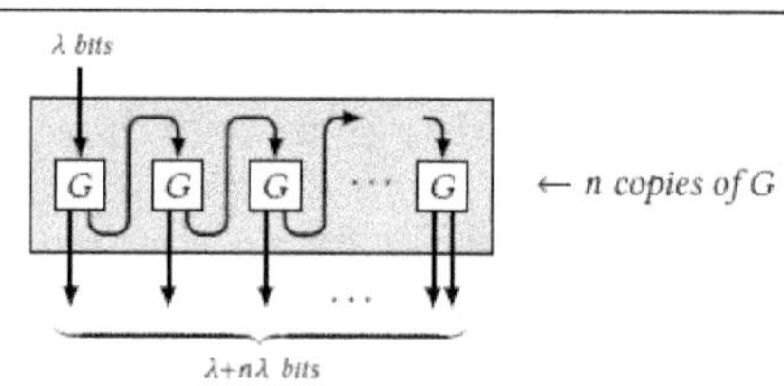

1

The fact that this chain of PRGs can be extended indefinitely gives another useful functionality:

Definition 5.8 (Stream cipher) *A stream cipher is an algorithm G that takes a seed s and length ℓ as input, and outputs a string. It should satisfy the following requirements:*

1. $G(s,\ell)$ is a string of length ℓ.
2. If $i < j$, then $G(s,i)$ is a prefix of $G(s,j)$.
3. For each n, the function $G(\cdot,n)$ is a secure PRG.

Because of the 2nd rule, you might want to think about a single infinitely long string that is the limit of $G(s,n)$ as n goes to infinity. The finite-length strings $G(s,n)$ are all the prefixes of this infinitely long string.

The PRG-feedback construction can be used to construct a secure stream cipher in the natural way: given seed s and length ℓ, keep iterating the PRG-feedback main loop until ℓ bits have been generated.

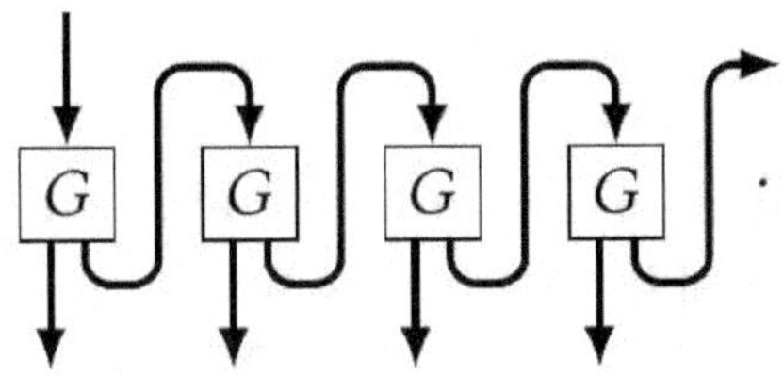

Symmetric Ratchet

Suppose Alice & Bob share a symmetric key k and are using a secure messaging app to exchange messages over a long period of time. Later in the course we will see techniques that Alice & Bob could use to securely encrypt many messages using a single key. However, suppose Bob's device is compromised and an attacker learns k. Then the attacker can decrypt all past, present, and future ciphertexts that it saw!

Alice & Bob can protect against such a key compromise by using the PRG-feedback stream cipher to constantly "update" their shared key. Suppose they do the following, starting with their shared key k :

- They use k to seed a chain of length-doubling PRGs, and both obtain the same stream of pseudorandom keys $t_1, t_2, ...$.
- They use t_i as a key to send/receive the i th message. The details of the encryption are not relevant to this example.
- After making a call to the PRG, they erase the PRG input from memory, and only remember the PRG's output. After using t_i to send/receive a message, they also erase it from memory.

This way of using and forgetting a sequence of keys is called a symmetric ratchet.

Construction 5.9 (Symm Ratchet)

$s_0 = k$
for $i = 1$ to ∞:
  $s_i \| t_i := G(s_{i-1})$
  erase s_{i-1} from memory
  use t_i to encrypt/decrypt the ith message
  erase t_i from memory

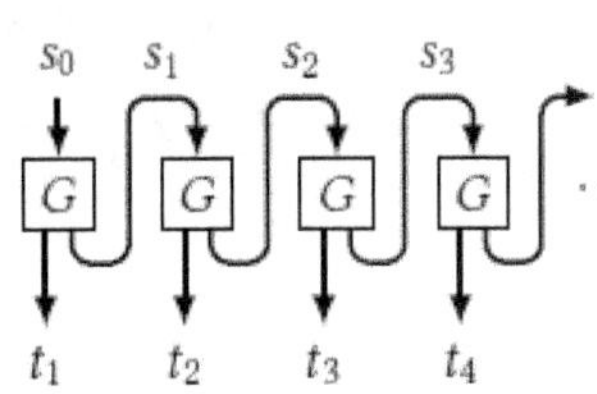

Suppose that an attacker compromises Bob's device after n ciphertexts have been sent. The only value residing in memory is s_n, which the attacker learns. SinceG is deterministic, the attacker can nowcompute t_{n+1}; t_{n+2}; : : : in the usual way and decrypt all future ciphertexts that are sent.

However, we can show that the attacker learns no information about t_1; : : : ; t_n from s_n, which implies that the previous ciphertexts remain safe. By compromising the key s_n, the adversary only compromises the security of future messages, but not past messages.

Sometimes this property is called forward secrecy, meaning that messages in the present are protected against a key-compromise that happens in the future.

This construction is called a ratchet, since it is easy to advance the key sequence in the forward direction (from s_n to s_{n+1}) but hard to reverse it (from s_{n+1} to s_n). The exercises explore the problem of explicitly reversing the ratchet, but the more relevant property for us is whether the attacker learns anything about the ciphertexts that were generated before the compromise.

Claim 5.10 *If the symmetric ratchet (Construction 5.9) is used with a secure PRG G and an encryption scheme Σ that has uniform ciphertexts (and $\Sigma.\mathcal{K} = \{0,1\}^\lambda$), then the first n ciphertexts are pseudorandom, even to an eavesdropper who compromises the key s_n.*

Proof We are considering an attack scenario in which n plaintexts are encrypted, and the adversary sees their ciphertexts as well as the ratchet-key s_n. This situation is captured by the following library:

ATTACK$(m_1, \dots, m_n)$:
$s_0 \leftarrow \{0,1\}^\lambda$ for $i = 1$ to n: $s_i \| t_i := G(s_{i-1})$ $c_i \leftarrow \Sigma.\text{Enc}(t_i, m_i)$ return $(c_1, \dots, c_n, s_n)$

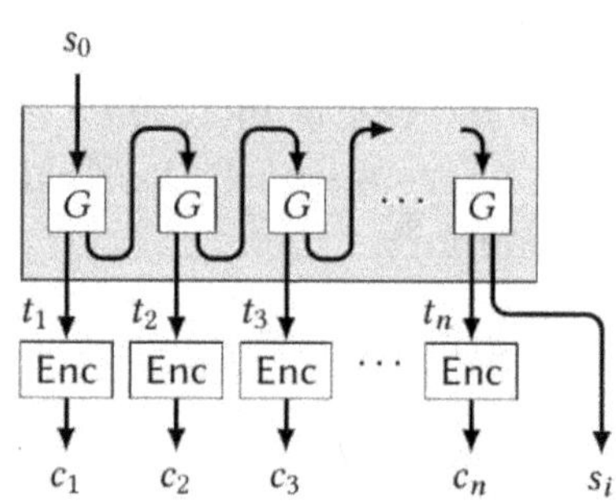

As we have seen, the shaded box (the process that computes $t_1, \dots, t_n$ from s_0) is actually a PRG. Let us rewrite the library in terms of this PRG H_n :

```
ATTACK(m_1, ..., m_n):
  s_0 ← {0,1}^λ
  t_1 ‖ ··· ‖ t_n ‖ s_n := H_n(s_0)
  for i = 1 to n:
    c_i ← Σ.Enc(t_i, m_i)
  return (c_1, ..., c_n, s_n)
```

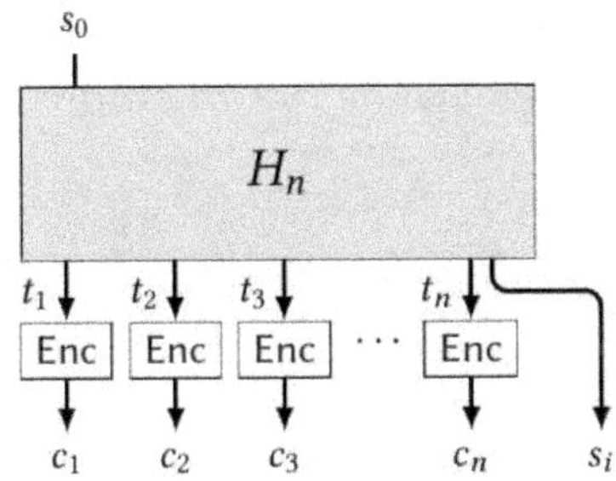

Now, we can apply the PRG security of H_n and instead choose $t_1, \ldots, t_n$ and s_n uniformly. This change is indistinguishable, by the security of the PRG. Note that we have not written out the standard explicit steps (factor out the first two lines of attack in terms of $\mathcal{L}_{\text{prg-real}}$, replace with $\mathcal{L}_{\text{prg-rand}}$, and inline).

```
ATTACK(m_1, ..., m_n):            ATTACK(m_1, ..., m_n):
  for i = 1 to n:                   for i = 1 to n:
    t_i ← {0,1}^λ                     t_i ← {0,1}^λ
  s_n ← {0,1}^λ              ≡        c_i ← Σ.Enc(t_i, m_i)
  for i = 1 to n:                   s_n ← {0,1}^λ
    c_i ← Σ.Enc(t_i, m_i)           return (c_1, ..., c_n, s_n)
  return (c_1, ..., c_n, s_n)
```

At this point, the encryption scheme is being used "as intended," meaning that we generate its keys t_i uniformly/indepenendtly, and use each key only for one encryption and nothing else. Formally speaking, this means we can factor out the body of the for-loop in terms of $\mathcal{L}_{\text{ots\$-real:}}$:

```
ATTACK(m_1, ..., m_n):                 L^Σ_ots$-real
  for i = 1 to n:                 
    c_i ← CTXT(m_i)            ◇       CTXT(m ∈ Σ.M):
  s_n ← {0,1}^λ                          k ← Σ.KeyGen
  return (c_1, ..., c_n, s_n)            c ← Σ.Enc(k, m)
                                         return c
```

We can now replace $\mathcal{L}_{\text{ots \$-real}}$ with $\mathcal{L}_{\text{ots \$-rand}}$ and inline the subroutine (without showing the intermediate library). The result is:

```
ATTACK(m_1, ..., m_n):
  for i = 1 to n:
    c_i ← Σ.C
  s_n ← {0,1}^λ
  return (c_1, ..., c_n, s_n)
```

This final library is indistinguishable from the first one. As promised, we showed that the attacker cannot distinguish the first n ciphertexts from random values, even when seeing s_n.

This proof used the uniform-ciphertexts property, but the same logic applies to basically any encryption property you care about - just imagine factoring out the encryption steps in terms of a different library than $\mathcal{L}_{\text{ots\$-real}}$.

Exercises

5.1. Let $G: \{0,1\}^\lambda \to \{0,1\}^{\lambda+\ell}$ be an injective (i.e., 1-to-1) PRG. Consider the following distinguisher:

```
𝒜
x := QUERY()
for all s' ∈ {0,1}^λ:
  if G(s') = x then return 1
return 0
```

(a) What is the advantage of $\mathcal{A}$ in distinguishing $\mathcal{L}^G_{\text{prg-real}}$ and $\mathcal{L}^G_{\text{prg-rand}}$? Is it negligible?

(b) Does this contradict the fact that G is a PRG? Why or why not?

(c) What happens to the advantage if G is not injective?

5.2. Let $G: \{0,1\}^\lambda \to \{0,1\}^{\lambda+\ell}$ be an injective PRG, and consider the following distinguisher:

```
𝒜
x := QUERY()
s' ← {0,1}^λ
return G(s') =? x
```

What is the advantage of $\mathcal{A}$ in distinguishing $\mathcal{L}^G_{\text{prg-real}}$ from $\mathcal{L}^G_{\text{prg-rand}}$?

5.3. For any PRG $G: \{0,1\}^\lambda \to \{0,1\}^{\lambda+\ell}$ there will be many strings in $\{0,1\}^{\lambda+\ell}$ that are impossible to get as output of G. Let S be any such set of impossible G-outputs, and consider the following adversary that has S hard-coded:

$\mathcal{A}$
$x := \text{QUERY}()$
return $x \overset{?}{\in} S$

What is the advantage of $\mathcal{A}$ in distinguishing $\mathcal{L}^G_{\text{prg-real}}$ from $\mathcal{L}^G_{\text{prg-rand}}$? Why does an adversary like this one not automatically break every PRG?

5.4. Show that the scheme from Section 5.3 does not have perfect one-time secrecy, by showing that there must exist two messages m_1 and m_2 whose ciphertext distributions differ.

5.5. The proof of Claim 5.5 applies the PRG security rule to both of the calls to G, starting with the first one. Describe what happens when you try to apply the PRG security of G to these two calls in the opposite order. Does the proof still work, or does it work only in the order that was presented?

5.6. Let $\ell' > \ell > 0$. Extend the "PRG feedback" construction to transform any PRG of stretch ℓ into a PRG of stretch ℓ'. Formally define the new PRG and prove its security using the security of the underlying PRG.

5.7. Prove that if G is a secure PRG, then so is the function $H(s) = G(\bar{s})$.

5.8. Let $G: \{0,1\}^\lambda \to \{0,1\}^{3\lambda}$ be a secure length-tripling PRG. For each function below, state whether it is also a secure PRG. If the function is a secure PRG, give a proof. If not, then describe a successful distinguisher and explicitly compute its advantage. When we write $a\|b\|c := G(s)$, each of a, b, c have length λ.

(a)
$H(s)$:
$x\|y\|z := G(s)$
return $G(x)\|G(z)$

(b)
$H(s)$:
$x\|y\|z := G(s)$
return $x\|y$

(c)
$H(s)$:
$x := G(s)$
$y := G(s)$
return $x\|y$

(d)
$H(s)$:
$x := G(s)$
$y := G(0^\lambda)$
return $x\|y$

(e)
$H(s)$:
$x := G(s)$
$y := G(0^\lambda)$
return $x \oplus y$

(f)

```
// H : {0,1}^{2λ} → {0,1}^{3λ}

H(s_L||s_R):
  x := G(s_L)
  y := G(s_R)
  return x ⊕ y
```

(g)

```
// H : {0,1}^{2λ} → {0,1}^{6λ}

H(s_L||s_R):
  x := G(s_L)
  y := G(s_R)
  return x||y
```

5.9. Let $G\colon\{0,1\}^{\lambda} \to \{0,1\}^{3\lambda}$ be a secure length-tripling PRG. Prove that each of the following functions is also a secure PRG:

(a)

$$HH\colon\{0,1\}^{2\lambda} \to \{0,1\}^{4\lambda}$$

$$H(s_L\|s_R)\colon$$

$$y := G(s_R)$$

$$\text{return } s_L\|y$$

Note that H includes half of its input directly in the output. How do you reconcile this fact with the conclusion of Exercise 5.14(b)?

(b)

$$//H\colon\{0,1\}^{2\lambda} \to \{0,1\}^{3\lambda}$$

$$H(s_L\|s_R)$$

$$\text{return } G(s_L)$$

⋆ 5.10. Let G be a secure length-doubling PRG. One of the following constructions is a secure PRG and one is not. Which is which? Give a security proof for one and an attack for the other.

```
H_1(s):
  x||y := G(s)
  u||v := G(y)
  return (x ⊕ y)||u||v
```

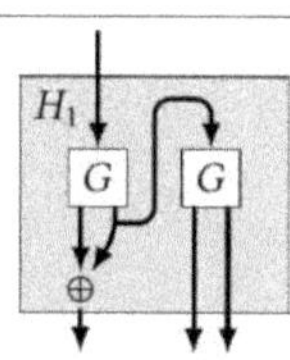


```
H_2(s):
  x||y := G(s)
  u||v := G(y)
  return x||(y ⊕ u)||v
```

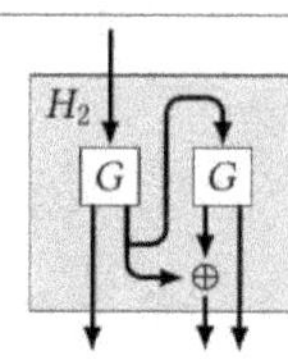

5.11. A frequently asked question in cryptography forums is whether it's possible to determine which PRG implementation was used by looking at output samples.

Let G_1 and G_2 be two PRGs with matching input/output lengths. Define two libraries $\mathcal{L}^{G_1}_{\text{which-prg}}$ and $\mathcal{L}^{G_2}_{\text{which-prg}}$ as follows:

$\mathcal{L}^{G_1}_{\text{which-prg}}$	$\mathcal{L}^{G_2}_{\text{which-prg}}$
QUERY(): $s \leftarrow \{0,1\}^\lambda$ return $G_1(s)$	QUERY(): $s \leftarrow \{0,1\}^\lambda$ return $G_2(s)$

Prove that if G_1 and G_2 are both secure PRGs, then $\mathcal{L}^{G_1}_{\text{which-prg}} \approx \mathcal{L}^{G_2}_{\text{which-prg}}$ - that is, it is infeasible to distinguish which PRG was used simply by receiving output samples.

5.12. Let G_1 and G_2 be deterministic functions, each accepting inputs of length λ and producing outputs of length 3λ.

(a) Define the function $H(s_1 \| s_2) = G_1(s_1) \oplus G_2(s_2)$. Prove that if either of G_1 or G_2 (or both) is a secure PRG, then so is H.

(b) What can you say about the simpler construction $H(s) = G_1(s) \oplus G_2(s)$, when one of G_1, G_2 is a secure PRG?

⋆ 5.13. Prove that if PRGs exist, then $P \neq NP$.

5.14. (a) Let f be any function. Show that the following function G is not a secure PRG, no matter what f is. Describe a successful distinguisher and explicitly compute its advantage:

$$\frac{G(s):}{\text{return } s \| f(s)}$$

(b) Let $G: \{0,1\}^\lambda \to \{0,1\}^{\lambda+\ell}$ be a candidate PRG. Suppose there is a polynomial-time algorithm V with the property that it inverts G with non-negligible probability. That is,

$$\Pr_{s \leftarrow \{0,1\}^\lambda}[V(G(s)) = s] \text{ is non-negligible.}$$

Show that if an algorithm V exists with this property, then G is not a secure PRG. In other words, construct a distinguisher contradicting the PRG-security of G and show that it achieves non-negligible distinguishing advantage.

Note: Don't assume anything about the output of V other than the property shown above. In particular, V might very frequently output the "wrong" thing.

5.15. Let $s_0, s_1, \ldots$ and $t_1, t_2, \ldots$ be defined as in the symmetric ratchet (Construction 5.9).

(a) Prove that if G is a secure PRG then the following two libraries are indistinguishable, for any polynomial-time algorithm :

$\mathcal{L}_{\text{left}}$	$\mathcal{L}_{\text{right}}$
TEST():	TEST():
$s_{n-1} \leftarrow \{0,1\}^\lambda$	$s_n \leftarrow \{0,1\}^\lambda$
$s_n \| t_n := G(s_{n-1})$	$\tilde{t} = \mathcal{A}(s_n)$
$\tilde{t} = \mathcal{A}(s_n)$	$t_n \leftarrow \{0,1\}^\lambda$
return $\tilde{t} \stackrel{?}{=} t_n$	return $\tilde{t} \stackrel{?}{=} t_n$

(b) What is Pr [test outputs true] in $\mathcal{L}_{\text{right}}$?

(c) Prove that for any polynomial-time algorithm $\mathcal{A}$, $\Pr[\mathcal{A}(s_n) = t_n]$ is negligible, where s_n, t_n are generated as in the symmetric ratchet construction.

(d) Prove that for any polynomial-time algorithm $\mathcal{A}$, $\Pr[\mathcal{A}(s_n) = s_{n-1}]$ is negligible. In other words, "turning the ratchet backwards" is a hard problem.

Chapter 6

Pseudorandom Functions & Block Ciphers

Imagine if Alice & Bob had an infinite amount of shared randomness - not just a short key. They could split it up into λ-bit chunks and use each one as a one-time pad whenever they want to send an encrypted message of length λ.

Alice could encrypt by saying, "hey Bob, this message is encrypted with one-time pad using chunk #674696273 as key." Bob could decrypt by looking up location #674696273 in his copy of the shared randomness. As long as Alice doesn't repeat a key/chunk, an eavesdropper (who doesn't have the shared randomness) would learn nothing about the encrypted messages. Although Alice announces (publicly) which location/chunk was used as each one-time pad key, that information doesn't help the attacker know the value at that location.

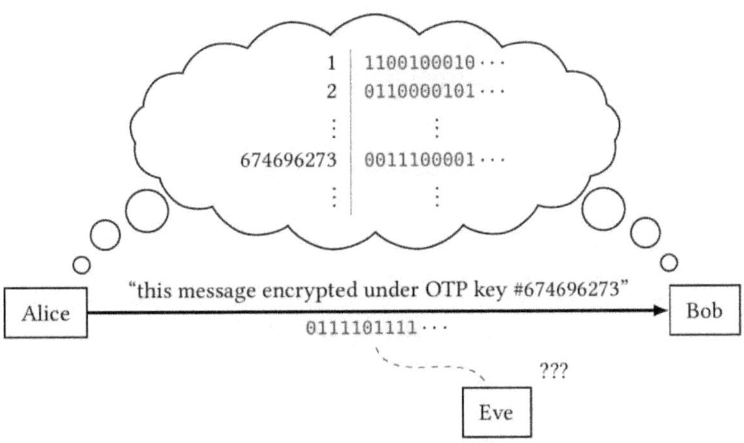

It is silly to imagine an infinite amount of shared randomness. However, an exponential amount of something is often just as good as an infinite amount. A shared table containing "only" 2^λ one-time pad keys would be quite useful for encrypting as many messages as you could ever need.

A pseudorandom function (PRF) is a tool that allows Alice & Bob to achieve the effect of such an exponentially large table of shared randomness in practice. In this chapter we will explore PRFs and their properties. In a later chapter, after introducing new security definitions for encryption, we will see that PRFs can be used to securely encrypt many messages under the same key, following the main idea illustrated above.

6.1 Definition

Continuing our example, imagine a huge table of shared data stored as an array T, so the i th item is referenced as $T[i]$. Instead of thinking of i as an integer, we can also think of i as a binary string. If the array has 2^{in} items, then i will be an in-bit string. If the array contains strings of length "out", then the notation $T[i]$ is like a function that takes an input from $\{0,1\}^{in}$ and gives an output from $\{0,1\}^{\text{out}}$.

A pseudorandom function emulates the functionality of a huge array. It is a function F that takes an input from $\{0,1\}^{\text{in}}$ and gives an output from $\{0,1\}\}^{\text{out}}$. However, F also takes an additional argument called the seed, which acts as a kind of secret key.

The goal of a pseudorandom function is to "look like" a uniformly chosen array / lookup table. Such an array can be accessed through the lookup subroutine of the following library:

$$\begin{array}{c} \text{for } x \in \{0,1\}^{\text{in}}: \\ T[x] \leftarrow \{0,1\}^{\text{out}} \\ \underline{\text{LOOKUP}\left(x \in \{0,1\}^{\text{in}}\right):} \\ \text{return } T[x] \end{array}$$

As you can see, this library initially fills up the array T with uniformly random data, and then allows the calling program to access any position in the array.

A pseudorandom function should produce indistinguishable behavior, when it is used with a uniformly chosen seed. More formally, the following library should be indistinguishable from the one above:

$$\begin{array}{c} k \leftarrow \{0,1\}^{\lambda} \\ \underline{\text{LOOKUP}(x \in \{0,1\}^{in}):} \\ \text{return} F(k,x) \end{array}$$

Note that the first library samples out $\cdot\ 2^{\text{in}}$ bits uniformly at random (out bits for each of 2^{in} entries in the table), while the second library samples only λ bits (the same k is used for all invocations of F). Still, we are asking for the two libraries to be indistinguishable.

This is basically the definition of a PRF, with one technical caveat. We want to allow situations like in $\geqslant \lambda$, but in those cases the first library runs in exponential time. It is generally convenient to build our security definitions with libraries that run in polynomial time.[1] We fix this by taking advantage of the fact that, no matter how big the table T is meant to be, a polynomial-time calling program will only access a polynomial amount of it. In some sense it is "overkill" to actually populate the entire table T upfront. Instead, we can populate T in a lazy / on-demand way. T initially starts uninitialized, and its values are only assigned as the calling program requests them. This changes when each $T[x]$ is sampled (if at all), but does not change how it is sampled (i.e., uniformly & independently). This also changes T from being a typical array to being an associative array ("hash table" or "dictionary" data structure), since it only maps a subset of $\{0,1\}^{\text{in}}$ to values in $\{0,1\}^{\text{out}}$.

Definition 6.1 (PRF security) Let $F: \{0,1\}^{\lambda} \times \{0,1\}^{\text{in}} \rightarrow \{0,1\}^{\text{out}}$ be a deterministic function. We say that F is a secure pseudorandom function (PRF) if $\mathcal{L}^F_{\text{prf-real}} \approx \mathcal{L}^F_{\text{prf-rand}}$, where:

$\mathcal{L}^F_{\text{prf-real}}$
$k \leftarrow \{0,1\}^{\lambda}$
LOOKUP($x \in \{0,1\}^{in}$):
return $F(k,x)$

$\mathcal{L}^F_{\text{prf-rand}}$
T := empty assoc. array
LOOKUP($x \in \{0,1\}^{in}$):
if $T[x]$ undefined:
$T[x] \leftarrow \{0,1\}^{out}$
return $T[x]$

Discussion, Pitfalls

The name "pseudorandom function" comes from the perspective of viewing T not as an (associative) array, but as a function $T: \{0,1\}^{\text{in}} \rightarrow \{0,1\}^{\text{out}}$. There are $2^{\text{out} \cdot 2^{\text{in}}}$ possible functions for T (an incredibly large number), and $\mathcal{L}_{\text{prf-rand}}$ chooses a "random function" by uniformly sampling its truth table as needed.

For each possible seed k, the residual function $F(k,\cdot)$ is also a function from $\{0,1\}^{in} \rightarrow \{0,1\}^{\text{out}}$. There are "only" 2^{λ} possible functions of this kind (one for each choice of k), and $\mathcal{L}_{\text{prf-real}}$ chooses one of these functions randomly. In both cases, the libraries give the calling program input/output access to the function that was chosen. You can think of this in terms of the picture from Section 5.1, but instead of strings, the objects are functions.

Note that even in the case of a "random function" ($\mathcal{L}_{\text{prf-rand}}$), the function T itself is still deterministic! To be precise, this library chooses a deterministic function, uniformly, from the set of all possible deterministic functions. But once it makes this choice, the input/output behavior of T is fixed. If the calling program calls lookup twice with the same x, it receives the same result. The same is true in $\mathcal{L}_{\text{prf-real}}$, since F is a deterministic function and k is fixed throughout the entire execution. To avoid this very natural confusion, it is perhaps better to think in terms of "randomly initialized lookup tables" rather than "random functions."

How NOT to Build a PRF

We can appreciate the challenges involved in building a PRF by looking at a natural approach that doesn't quite work.

Example Suppose we have a length-doubling PRGG : $\{0,1\}^{\lambda} \rightarrow \{0,1\}^{2\lambda}$ and try to use it to construct a PRF F as follows:

$$\frac{F(k,x):}{\text{return } G(k) \oplus x}$$

You might notice that all we have done is rename the encryption algorithm of "pseudo-OTP" (Construction 5.2). We have previously argued that this algorithm is a secure method for onetime encryption, and that the resulting ciphertexts are pseudorandom. Is this enough for a secure PRF? No, we can attack the security of this PRF.

Attacking F means designing distinguisher that behaves as differently as possible in the presence of the two $\mathcal{L}^{F}_{prf-\star}$ libraries. We want to show that F is insecure even if G is an excellent PRG. We should not try to base our attack on distinguishing outputs of G from random. Instead, we must try to break the inappropriate way that G is used to construct a PRF.

The distinguisher must use the interface of the $\mathcal{L}_{prf\text{-}\star}$ libraries - i.e., make some calls to the lOOKUP subroutine and output 0 or 1 based on the answers it gets. The lOOKUP subroutine takes an argument, so the distinguisher has to choose which arguments to use.

One observation we can make is that if a calling program sees only one value of the form $G(k) \oplus x$, it will look pseudorandom. This is essentially what we showed in Section 5.3. So we should be looking for a calling program that makes more than one call to lookup.

If we make two calls to LOOKUP - say, on inputs x_1 and x_2 - the responses from $\mathcal{L}_{prf\text{-}real}$ will be $G(k) \oplus x_1$ and $G(k) \oplus x_2$. To be a secure PRF, these responses must look independent and uniform. Do they? They actually have a pattern that the calling program can notice: their XOR is always $x_1 \oplus x_2$, a value that is already known to the calling program.

We can condense all of our observations into the following distinguisher:

$\mathcal{A}$

```
pick x1, x2 ∈ {0,1}^{2λ} arbitrarily so that x1 ≠ x2
z1 := LOOKUP(x1)
z2 := LOOKUP(x2)
return z1 ⊕ z2 =? x1 ⊕ x2
```

Let's compute its advantage in distinguishing $\mathcal{L}^F_{\text{prf-real}}$ from $\mathcal{L}^F_{\text{prf-rand}}$ by considering 's behavior when linked to these two libraries:

$\mathcal{A}$ ⋄ $\mathcal{L}^F_{\text{prf-real}}$

```
A:
pick x1 ≠ x2 ∈ {0,1}^{2λ}
z1 := LOOKUP(x1)
z2 := LOOKUP(x2)
return z1 ⊕ z2 =? x1 ⊕ x2

L^F_prf-real:
k ← {0,1}^λ

LOOKUP(x):
  return G(k) ⊕ x // F(k,x)
```

When $\mathcal{A}$ is linked to $\mathcal{L}^F_{prf-real}$, the library will choose a key k. Then z_1 is set to $G(k) \oplus x_1$ and z_2 is set to $G(k) \oplus x_2$. So $z_1 \oplus z_2$ is always equal to $x_1 \oplus x_2$, and $\mathcal{A}$ always outputs 1 . That is,

$$\Pr[\mathcal{A} \diamond \mathcal{L}^F_{\text{prf-real}} \Rightarrow 1] = 1.$$

$\mathcal{A}$ ⋄ $\mathcal{L}^F_{\text{prf-rand}}$

```
A:
pick x1 ≠ x2 ∈ {0,1}^{2λ}
z1 := LOOKUP(x1)
z2 := LOOKUP(x2)
return z1 ⊕ z2 =? x1 ⊕ x2

L^F_prf-rand:
T := empty assoc. array

LOOKUP(x):
  if T[x] undefined:
    T[x] ← {0,1}^{2λ}
  return T[x]
```

When $\mathcal{A}$ is linked to $\mathcal{L}^F_{prf\text{-}rand}$, the responses of the two calls to lookup will be chosen uniformly and independently because lookup is being called on distinct inputs. Consider the moment in time when the second call to lookup is about to happen. At that point, x_1, x_2, and z_1 have all been determined, while z_2 is about to be chosen uniformly by the library. Using the properties of XOR, we see that $\mathcal{A}$ will output 1 if and only if z_2 is chosen to be exactly the value $x_1 \oplus x_2 \oplus z_1$. This happens only with probability $1/2^{2\lambda}$. That is,

$$Pr[\mathcal{A} \diamond \mathcal{L}^{F}_{prf-rand} \Rightarrow 1] = 1/2^{2\lambda}.$$

The advantage of $\mathcal{A}$ is therefore $1 - 1/2^{2\lambda}$ which is certainly non-negligible since it doesn't even approach 0. This shows that F is not a secure PRF.

At a more philosophical level, we wanted to identify exactly how G is being used in an inappropriate way. The PRG security libraries guarantee security when G 's seed is chosen freshly for each call to G. This construction of F violates that rule and allows the same seed to be used twice in different calls to G, where the results are supposed to look independent.

This example shows the challenge of building a PRF. Even though we know how to make any individual output pseudorandom, it is difficult to make all outputs collectively appear independent, when in reality they are derived from a single short seed.

6.2 PRFs vs PRGs; Variable-Hybrid Proofs

In this section we show that a PRG can be used to construct a PRF, and vice-versa. The construction of a PRG from PRF is practical, and is one of the more common ways to obtain a PRG in practice. The construction of a PRF from PRG is more of theoretical interest and does not reflect how PRFs are designed in practice.

Constructing a PRG from a PRF

As promised, a PRF can be used to construct a PRG. The construction is quite natural. For simplicity, suppose we have a PRFF: $\{0,1\}^\lambda \times \{0,1\}^\lambda \rightarrow \{0,1\}^\lambda$ (i.e., in $=$ out $= \lambda$). We can build a length-doubling PRG in the following way:

Construction 6.2 (Counter PRG)

```
G(s):
  x := F(s, 0···00)
  y := F(s, 0···01)
  return x||y
```

There is nothing particularly special about the inputs $0\cdots00$ and $0\cdots01$ to F. All that matters is that they are distinct. The construction can be extended to easily give more than 2 blocks of output, by treating the input to F as a simple counter (hence the name of this construction).

The guarantee of a PRF is that when its seed is chosen uniformly and it is invoked on distinct inputs, its outputs look independently uniform. In particular, its output on inputs $0 \cdots 00$ and $0 \cdots 01$ are indistinguishable from uniform. Hence, concatenating them gives a string which is indistinguishable from a uniform 2λ-bit string.

That really is all there is to the security of this construction, but unfortunately there is a slight technical issue which makes the security proof more complicated than you might guess. We will have to introduce a new technique of variable hybrids to cope with it.

Claim 6.3 *If F is a secure PRF, then the counter PRG construction G above is a secure PRG.*

Proof In order to prove that G is a secure PRG, we must prove that the following libraries are indistinguishable:

$\mathcal{L}^G_{\text{prg-real}}$
QUERY():
$s \leftarrow \{0,1\}^\lambda$
$x := F(s, 0\cdots00)$ } // $G(s)$
$y := F(s, 0\cdots01)$ } // $G(s)$
return $x \| y$

$\mathcal{L}^G_{\text{prg-rand}}$
QUERY():
$r \leftarrow \{0,1\}^{2\lambda}$
return r

During the proof, we are allowed to use the fact that F is a secure PRF. That is, we can use the fact that the following two libraries are indistinguishable:

$\mathcal{L}^F_{\text{prf-real}}$
$k \leftarrow \{0,1\}^\lambda$
LOOKUP($x \in \{0,1\}^{in}$):
return $F(k, x)$

$\mathcal{L}^F_{\text{prf-rand}}$
$T :=$ empty assoc. array
LOOKUP($x \in \{0,1\}^{in}$):
if $T[x]$ undefined:
$T[x] \leftarrow \{0,1\}^{out}$
return $T[x]$

The inconvenience in the proof stems from a mismatch of the s variable in $\mathcal{L}_{\text{prg-real}}$ and the k variable in $\mathcal{L}_{\text{prf-real}}$. In $\mathcal{L}_{\text{prg-real}}$, s is local to the query subroutine. Over the course of an execution, s will take on many values. Since s is used as the PRF seed, we must write the calls to F in terms of the lookup subroutine of $\mathcal{L}_{\text{prf-real}}$. But in $\mathcal{L}_{\text{prf-real}}$ the PRF seed is fixed for the entire execution. In other words, we can only use $\mathcal{L}_{\text{prf-real}}$ to deal with a single PRF seed at a time, but $\mathcal{L}_{\text{prg-real}}$ deals with many PRG seeds at a time.

To address this, we will have to apply the security of F (i.e., replace $\mathcal{L}_{\text{prf-real}}$ with $\mathcal{L}_{\text{prf-rand}}$) many times during the proof - in fact, once for every call to QUERY made by the calling program. Previous security proofs had a fixed number of hybrid steps (e.g., the proof of Claim 5.5 used 7 hybrid libraries to show $\mathcal{L}_{\text{prg-real}} \approx \mathcal{L}_{\text{hyb-1}} \approx \cdots \approx \mathcal{L}_{\text{hyb-7}} \approx \mathcal{L}_{\text{prg-rand}}$). This proof will have a variable number of hybrids that depends on the calling program. Specifically, we will prove

$$\mathcal{L}^{G}_{\text{prg-real}} \approx \mathcal{L}_{\text{hyb-1}} \approx \cdots \approx \mathcal{L}_{\text{hyb-}q} \approx \mathcal{L}^{G}_{\text{prg-rand}}$$

where q is the number of times the calling program calls QUERY.

Don't be overwhelmed by all these hybrids. They all follow a simple pattern. In fact, the i th hybrid looks like this:

```
L_hyb-i:
count := 0

QUERY():
  count := count + 1
  if count ≤ i :
    r ← {0,1}^2λ
    return r
  else:
    s ← {0,1}^λ
    x := F(s, 0···00)
    y := F(s, 0···01)
    return x||y
```

In other words, the hybrid libraries all differ in the value i that is inserted into the code above. If you're familiar with C compilers, think of this as adding "#define i 427 " to the top of the code above, to obtain $\mathcal{L}_{\text{hyb-427}}$.

First note what happens for extreme choices of i :

- In $\mathcal{L}_{\text{hyb-}0}$, the if-branch is never taken (count $\leqslant 0$ is never true). This library behaves exactly like $\mathcal{L}^{G}_{\text{prg-real}}$ by giving PRG outputs on every call to QUERY.

- If q is the total number of times that the calling program calls query, then in $\mathcal{L}_{\text{hyb-}q}$, the if-branch is always taken (count $\leqslant q$ is always true). This library behaves exactly like $\mathcal{L}^{G}_{\text{prg-rand}}$ by giving truly uniform output on every call to query.

In general, $\mathcal{L}_{\text{hyb-}i}$ will respond to the first i calls to QUery by giving truly random output. It will respond to all further calls by giving outputs of our PRG construction.

We have argued that $\mathcal{L}^{G}_{\text{prg-real}} \equiv \mathcal{L}_{\text{hyb-}0}$ and $\mathcal{L}^{G}_{\text{prg-rand}} \equiv \mathcal{L}_{\text{hyb-}q}$. To complete the proof, we must show that $\mathcal{L}_{\text{hyb-}(i-1)} \approx \mathcal{L}_{\text{hyb-}i}$ for all i. The main reason for going to all this trouble of defining so many hybrid libraries is that $\mathcal{L}_{\text{hyb-}(i-1)}$ and $\mathcal{L}_{\text{hyb-}i}$ are completely identical except in how they respond to the i th call to query. This difference involves a single call to the PRG (and hence a single PRF seed), which allows us to apply the security of the PRF.

In more detail, let i be arbitrary, and consider the following sequence of steps starting with $\mathcal{L}_{\text{hyb-}(i-1)}$:

We have taken $\mathcal{L}_{\text{hyb-}(i-1)}$ and simply expanded the else-branch (count $\geqslant i$) into two subcases (count $= i$ and count > i). However, both cases lead to the same block of code (apart from a change to a local variable's name), so the change has no effect on the calling program.

```
count := 0

QUERY():
  count := count + 1
  if count < i :
    r ← {0,1}^{2λ}
    return r
  elsif count = i :
    s* ← {0,1}^λ
    x := F(s*, 0···00)
    y := F(s*, 0···01)
    return x||y
  else:
    s ← {0,1}^λ
    x := F(s, 0···00)
    y := F(s, 0···01)
    return x||y
```

We have factored out the calls to F that use seed s^* (corresponding to the count $= i$ case) in terms of $\mathcal{L}_{\text{prf-real}}$. This change no effect on the calling program.

```
count := 0

QUERY():
  count := count + 1
  if count < i :
    r ← {0,1}^2λ
    return r
  elsif count = i :
    x := LOOKUP(0···00)
    y := LOOKUP(0···01)
    return x||y
  else:
    s ← {0,1}^λ
    x := F(s,0···00)
    y := F(s,0···01)
    return x||y
```

◇

```
L^F_prf-real
k ← {0,1}^λ

LOOKUP(x):
  return F(k,x)
```

From the fact that F is a secure PRF, we can replace $\mathcal{L}^F_{\text{prf-real}}$ with $\mathcal{L}^F_{\text{prf-rand}}$, and the overall change is indistinguishable.

```
count := 0

QUERY():
  count := count + 1
  if count < i :
    r ← {0,1}^2λ
    return r
  elsif count = i :
    x := LOOKUP(0···00)
    y := LOOKUP(0···01)
    return x||y
  else:
    s ← {0,1}^λ
    x := F(s,0···00)
    y := F(s,0···01)
    return x||y
```

◇

```
L^F_prf-rand
T := empty assoc. array

LOOKUP(x):
  if T[x] undefined:
    T[x] ← {0,1}^λ
  return T[x]
```

Since count $= i$ happens only once, only two calls to lookup will be made across the entire lifetime of the library, and they are on distinct inputs. Therefore, the if-branch in lookup will always be taken, and T is never needed (it is only needed to "remember" values and give the same answer when the same x is used twice as argument to lookup). Simplifying the library therefore has no effect on the calling program:

```
count := 0

QUERY():
  count := count + 1
  if count < i :
    r ← {0,1}^{2λ}
    return r
  elsif count = i :
    x := LOOKUP(0···00)
    y := LOOKUP(0···01)
    return x‖y
  else:
    s ← {0,1}^λ
    x := F(s, 0···00)
    y := F(s, 0···01)
    return x‖y
```

$\diamond$

```
LOOKUP(x):
  r ← {0,1}^λ
  return r
```

Inlining the subroutine has no effect on the calling program. The resulting library responds with uniformly random output to the first i calls to query, and responds with outputs of our PRG G to the others. Hence, this library has identical behavior to $\mathcal{L}_{\text{hyb-}i}$.

```
count := 0

QUERY():
  count := count + 1
  if count < i :
    r ← {0,1}^{2λ}
    return r
  elsif count = i :
    x ← {0,1}^λ
    y ← {0,1}^λ
    return x‖y
  else:
    s ← {0,1}^λ
    x := F(s, 0···00)
    y := F(s, 0···01)
    return x‖y
```

We showed that $\mathcal{L}_{\text{hyb-}(i-1)} \approx \mathcal{L}_{\text{hyb-}i}$, and therefore:

$$\mathcal{L}^{G}_{\text{prg-real}} \equiv \mathcal{L}_{\text{hyb-}0} \approx \mathcal{L}_{\text{hyb-}1} \approx \cdots \approx \mathcal{L}_{\text{hyb-}q} \equiv \mathcal{L}^{G}_{\text{prg-rand}}$$

This shows that $\mathcal{L}^{G}_{\text{prg-real}} \approx \mathcal{L}^{G}_{\text{prg-rand}}$, so G is a secure PRG. □

A Theoretical Construction of a PRF from a PRG

We have already seen that it is possible to feed the output of a PRG back into the PRG again, to extend its stretch (Claim 5.7). This is done by making a long chain (like a linked list) of PRGs. The trick to constructing a PRF from a PRG is to chain PRGs together in a binary tree (similar to Exercise 5.8(a)). The leaves of the tree correspond to final outputs of the PRF. If we want a PRF with an exponentially large domain (e.g., in $= \lambda$), the binary tree itself is exponentially large! However, it is still possible to compute any individual leaf efficiently by simply traversing the tree from root to leaf. This tree traversal itself is the PRF algorithm. This construction of a PRF is due to Goldreich, Goldwasser, and Micali, in the paper that defined the concept of a PRF .

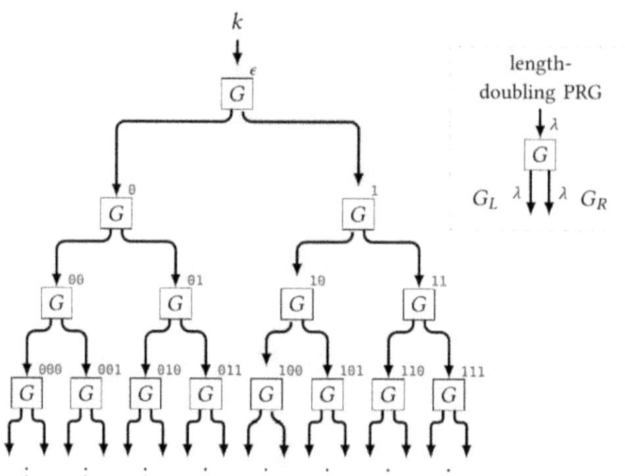

Imagine a complete binary tree of height in (in will be the input length of the PRF). Every node in this tree has a position which can be written as a binary string. Think of a node's position as the directions to get there starting at the root, where a 0 means "go left" and 1 means "go right." For example, the root has position ϵ (the empty string), the right child of the root has position 1 , etc.

The PRF construction works by assigning a label to every node in the tree, using the a length-doubling PRG $G: \{0,1\}^{\lambda} \rightarrow \{0,1\}^{2\lambda}$. For convenience, we will write $G_L(k)$ and $G_R(k)$

to denote the first λ bits and last λ bits of $G(k)$, respectively. Labels in the tree are λ-bit strings, computed according to the following two rules:

1. The root node's label is the PRF seed.
2. If the node at position p has label v, then its left child (at position $p\|0$) gets label $G_L(v)$, and its right child (at position $p\|1$) gets label $G_R(v)$.

In the picture above, a node's label is the string being sent on its incoming edge. The tree has 2^{in} leaves, whose positions are the strings $\{0,1\}^{\text{in}}$. We define $F(k,x)$ to be the label of node/leaf x. To compute this label, we can traverse the tree from root to leaf, taking left and right turns at each node according to the bits of x and computing the labels along that path according to the labeling rule. In the picture above, the highlighted path corresponds to the computation of $F(k, 1001 \cdots)$.

It is important to remember that the binary tree is a useful conceptual tool, but it is exponentially large in general. Running the PRF on some input does not involve computing labels for the entire tree, only along a single path from root to leaf.

Construction 6.4

(GGM PRF)

in = arbitrary out $=\lambda$	$\underline{F(k, x \in \{0,1\}^{in}):}$ $v := k$ for $i = 1$ to in: if $x_i = 0$ then $v := G_L(v)$ if $x_i = 1$ then $v := G_R(v)$ return v

Claim 6.5 *If G is a secure PRG, then Construction 6.4 is a secure PRF.*

Proof We prove the claim using a sequence of hybrids. The number of hybrids in this case depends on the input-length parameter in. The hybrids are defined as follows:

$\mathcal{L}_{\text{hyb-d}}$
T: = empty assoc. array
QUERY (x):

$p := \textbf{first } d \textbf{ bits of } x$
if $T[p]$ **undefined:**
$T[p] \leftarrow \{0,1\}^\lambda$
$v := T[p]$
for $i = d + 1$ **to in:**
if $x_i = 0$ **then** $v := G_L(v)$
if $x_i = 1$ **then** $v := G_R(v)$
return v

The hybrids differ only in their hard-coded value of d. We will show that

$$\mathcal{L}^F_{\text{prf-real}} \equiv \mathcal{L}_{\text{hyb-}0} \approx \mathcal{L}_{\text{hyb-}1} \approx \cdots \approx \mathcal{L}_{\text{hyb-in}} \equiv \mathcal{L}^F_{\text{prf-rand}}$$

We first start by understanding the behavior of $\mathcal{L}_{\text{hyb-}d}$ for extreme choices of d. Simplifications to the code are shown on the right.

In $\mathcal{L}_{\text{hyb-}0}$, we always have $p = \epsilon$, so the only entry of T that is accessed is $T[\epsilon]$. Then renaming $T[\epsilon]$ to k, we see that $\mathcal{L}_{\text{hyb-}0} \equiv \mathcal{L}^F_{\text{prf-real}}$. The only difference is when the PRF seed $k(T[\epsilon])$ is sampled: eagerly at initialization time in $\mathcal{L}^F_{\text{prf-real}}$ vs. at the last possible minute in $\mathcal{L}_{\text{hyb-}0}$.

```
                              L_hyb-0
T := empty assoc. array                   k := undefined
                                          // k is alias for T[ε]
LOOKUP(x):
  p := first 0 bits of x                  p = ε
  if T[p] undefined:                      if k undefined:
    T[p] ← {0,1}^λ                          k ← {0,1}^λ
  v := T[p]                               ⎫
  for i = 1 to in:                        ⎬ v := F(k,x)
    if x_i = 0 then v := G_L(v)           ⎪
    if x_i = 1 then v := G_R(v)           ⎭
  return v                                return F(k,x)
```

In $\mathcal{L}_{\text{hyb-in}}$, we always have $p = x$ and the body of the forloop is always unreachable. In that case, it is easy to see that $\mathcal{L}_{\text{hyb-in}}$ has identical behavior to $\mathcal{L}^F_{\text{prf-rand}}$.

$\mathcal{L}_{\text{hyb-}in}$

```
T := empty assoc. array

LOOKUP(x):
  p := first in bits of x            p = x
  if T[p] undefined:                 if T[x] undefined:
    T[p] ← {0,1}^λ                     T[x] ← {0,1}^λ
  v := T[p]
  for i = in + 1 to in:            }
    if x_i = 0 then v := G_L(v)    } // unreachable
    if x_i = 1 then v := G_R(v)    }
  return v                           return T[x]
```

The general pattern is that $\mathcal{L}_{\text{hyb-}d}$ "chops off" the top d levels of the conceptual binary tree. When computing the output for some string x, we don't start traversing the tree from the root but rather d levels down the tree, at the node whose position is the d-bit prefix of x (called p in the library). We initialize the label of this node as a uniform value (unless it has already been defined), and then continue the traversal to the leaf x.

To finish the proof, we show that $\mathcal{L}_{\text{hyb-}(d-1)}$ and $\mathcal{L}_{\text{hyb-}d}$ are indistinguishable:

The library that is shown here is different from $\mathcal{L}_{\text{hyb-}(d-1)}$ in the highlighted parts. However, these differences have no effect on the calling program. The library here advances $d-1$ levels down the tree (to the node at location p), initializes that node's label as a uniform value, then computes the labels for both its children, and finally continues computing labels toward the leaf. The only significant difference from $\mathcal{L}_{\text{hyb-}(d-1)}$ is that it computes the labels of both of p 's children, even though only one is on the path to x. Since it computes the label correctly, though, it makes no difference when (or if) this extra label is computed.

```
T := empty assoc. array

LOOKUP(x):
  p := first d - 1 bits of x
  if T[p] undefined:
    T[p] ← {0,1}^λ
    T[p‖0] := G_L(T[p])
    T[p‖1] := G_R(T[p])
  p' := first d bits of x
  v := T[p']
  for i = d + 1 to in:
    if x_i = 0 then v := G_L(v)
    if x_i = 1 then v := G_R(v)
  return v
```

We have factored out the body of the if-statement in terms of $\mathcal{L}^{G}_{\text{prg-real}}$ since it involves an call to G on uniform input. Importantly, the seed to G (called $T[p]$ in the previous hybrid) was not used anywhere else - it was a string of length $d-1$ while the library only reads $T[p']$ for p' of length d. The change has no effect on the calling program.

```
T := empty assoc. array                         L^G_prg-real
LOOKUP(x):                                      QUERY():
  p := first d − 1 bits of x               ◇      s ← {0,1}^λ
  if T[p] undefined:                              return G(s)
     T[p‖0]‖T[p‖1] := QUERY()
  p' := first d + 1 bits of x
  v := T[p']
  for i = d + 1 to in:
     if x_i = 0 then v := G_L(v)
     if x_i = 1 then v := G_R(v)
  return v
```

We have applied the security of G and replaced $\mathcal{L}_{\text{prg-real}}$ with $\mathcal{L}_{\text{prg-rand}}$. The change is indistinguishable.

```
T := empty assoc. array                         L^G_prg-rand
LOOKUP(x):                                      QUERY():
  p := first d − 1 bits of x               ◇      r ← {0,1}^2λ
  if T[p] undefined:                              return r
     T[p‖0]‖T[p‖1] := QUERY()
  p' := first d + 1 bits of x
  v := T[p']
  for i = d + 1 to in:
     if x_i = 0 then v := G_L(v)
     if x_i = 1 then v := G_R(v)
  return v
```

We have inlined $\mathcal{L}_{\text{prg-rand}}$ and split the sampling of 2λ bits into two separate statements sampling λ bits each. In this library, we advance d levels down the tree, assign a uniform label to a node (and its sibling), and then proceed to the leaf applying G as usual. The only difference between this library and $\mathcal{L}_{\text{hyb-}d}$ is that we sample the label of a node that is not on our direct path. But since we sample it uniformly, it doesn't matter when (or if) that extra value is sampled. Hence, this library has identical behavior to $\mathcal{L}_{\text{hyb-}d}$.

```
T := empty assoc. array

LOOKUP(x):
  p := first d − 1 bits of x
  if T[p] undefined:
    T[p||0] ← {0,1}^λ
    T[p||1] ← {0,1}^λ
  p' := first d + 1 bits of x
  v := T[p']
  for i = d + 1 to in:
    if x_i = 0 then v := G_L(v)
    if x_i = 1 then v := G_R(v)
  return v
```

We showed that $\mathcal{L}_{\text{hyb-}(d-1)} \approx \mathcal{L}_{\text{hyb-}d}$. Putting everything together, we have:

$$\mathcal{L}^F_{\text{prf-real}} \equiv \mathcal{L}_{\text{hyb-}0} \approx \mathcal{L}_{\text{hyb-}1} \approx \cdots \approx \mathcal{L}_{\text{hyb-in}} \equiv \mathcal{L}^F_{\text{prf-rand}}.$$

Hence, F is a secure PRF. □

6.3 Block Ciphers (Pseudorandom Permutations)

After fixing the seed of a PRF, it computes a function from $\{0,1\}^{\text{in}}$ to $\{0,1\}\}^{\text{out}}$. Let's consider the case where in = out. Some functions from $\{0,1\}^{\text{in}}$ to $\{0,1\}^{\text{out}}$ are invertible, which leads to the question of whether a PRF might realize such a function and be invertible (with knowledge of the seed). In other words, what if it were possible to determine x when given k and $F(k,x)$? While this would be convenient property, it is not guaranteed by the PRF security definition, even in the case of in = out. A function from $\{0,1\}^{\text{in}}$ to $\{0,1\}^{\text{out}}$ chosen at random is unlikely to have an inverse, therefore a PRF instantiated with a random key is unlikely to have an inverse.

A pseudorandom permutation (PRP) - also called a block cipher - is essentially a PRF that is guaranteed to be invertible for every choice of seed. We use both terms (PRP and block cipher) interchangeably. The term "permutation" refers to the fact that, for every k, the function $F(k,\cdot)$ should be a permutation of $\{0,1\}^{in}$. Instead of requiring a PRP to be indistinguishable from a randomly chosen function, we require it to be indistinguishable from a randomly chosen invertible function. [2] This means we must modify one of the libraries from the PRF definition. Instead of populating the associative array T with uniformly random values, it chooses uniformly random but distinct values. As long as T

gives distinct outputs on distinct inputs, it is consistent with some invertible function. The library guarantees distinctness by only sampling values that it has not previously assigned. Thinking of an associative array T as a key-value store, we use the notation T.values to denote the set of values stored in T.

Definition 6.6 (PRP syntax) *Let $F: \{0,1\}^\lambda \times \{0,1\}^{blen} \to \{0,1\}^{blen}$ be a deterministic function. We refer to blen as the blocklength of F and any element of $\{0,1\}^{blen}$ as a block.*

We call F a secure pseudorandom permutation (PRP) (block cipher) if the following two conditions hold:

1. *(Invertible given k) There is a function $F^{-1}: \{0,1\}^\lambda \times \{0,1\}^{blen} \to \{0,1\}^{blen}$ satisfying*

$$F^{-1}(k, F(k,x)) = x,$$

for all $k \in \{0,1\}^\lambda$ and all $x \in \{0,1\}^{blen}$.

2. *(Security)* $\mathcal{L}^F_{\text{prp-real}} \approx \mathcal{L}^F_{\text{prp-rand}}$, *where:*

$\mathcal{L}^F_{\text{prp-real}}$

$k \leftarrow \{0,1\}^\lambda$

LOOKUP($x \in \{0,1\}^{blen}$):
  return $F(k,x)$

$\mathcal{L}^F_{\text{prp-rand}}$

T := empty assoc. array

LOOKUP($x \in \{0,1\}^{blen}$):
  if $T[x]$ undefined:
    $T[x] \leftarrow \{0,1\}^{blen} \setminus T$.values
  return $T[x]$

"T.values" refers to the set $\{v \mid \exists x: T[x] = v\}$.

The changes from the PRF definition are highlighted in yellow. In particular, the $\mathcal{L}_{\text{prp-real}}$ and $\mathcal{L}_{\text{prf-real}}$ libraries are identical.

Discussion, Pitfalls

In the definition, both the functions F and F^{-1} take the seed k as input. Therefore, only someone with k can invert the block cipher. Think back to the definition of a PRF without the seed k, it is hard to compute $F(k,x)$. A block cipher has a forward and reverse direction, and computing either of them is hard without k!

6.4 Relating PRFs and Block Ciphers

In this section we discuss how to obtain PRFs from PRPs/block ciphers, and vice-versa.

Switching Lemma (PRPs are PRFs, Too!)

Imagine you can query a PRP on chosen inputs (as in the $\mathcal{L}_{\text{prp-real}}$ library), and suppose the blocklength of the PRP is blen $= \lambda$. You would only be able to query that PRP on a negligible fraction of its exponentially large input domain. It seems unlikely that you would even be able to tell that it was a PRP (i.e., an invertible function) rather than a PRF (an unrestricted function).

This idea can be formalized as follows.

Lemma 6.7 (PRP switching) *Let $\mathcal{L}_{\text{prf-rand}}$ and $\mathcal{L}_{\text{prp-rand}}$ be defined as in Definitions 6.1 & 6.6, with parameters in = out = blen $= \lambda$ (so that the interfaces match up). Then $\mathcal{L}_{\text{prf-rand}} \approx \mathcal{L}_{\text{prp-rand}}$.*

Proof Recall the replacement-sampling lemma, Lemma 4.11, which showed that the following libraries are indistinguishable:

```
ℒ_samp-L
SAMP():
  r ← {0,1}^λ
  return r
```

```
ℒ_samp-R
R := ∅

SAMP():
  r ← {0,1}^λ \ R
  R := R ∪ {r}
  return r
```

$\mathcal{L}_{\text{samp-L}}$ samples values with replacement, and $\mathcal{L}_{\text{samp-R}}$ samples values without replacement. Now consider the following library $\mathcal{L}^*$:

```
ℒ*
T := empty assoc. array

LOOKUP(x ∈ {0,1}^λ):
  if T[x] undefined:
    T[x] ← SAMP()
  return T[x]
```

When we link $\mathcal{L}^* \diamond \mathcal{L}_{\text{samp-L}}$ we obtain $\mathcal{L}_{\text{prf-rand}}$ since the values in $T[x]$ are sampled uniformly. When we link $\mathcal{L}^* \diamond \mathcal{L}_{\text{samp-R}}$ we obtain $\mathcal{L}_{\text{prp-rand}}$ since the values in $T[x]$ are sampled uniformly subject to having no repeats (consider R playing the role of T.values in $\mathcal{L}_{\text{prp-rand}}$). Then from Lemma 4.11, we have:

$$\mathcal{L}_{\text{prf-rand}} \equiv \mathcal{L}^* \diamond \mathcal{L}_{\text{samp-L}} \approx \mathcal{L}^* \diamond \mathcal{L}_{\text{samp-R}} \equiv \mathcal{L}_{\text{prp-rand}},$$

which completes the proof. □

Using the switching lemma, we can conclude that every PRP (with blen $= \lambda$) is also a PRF:

Corollary 6.8 *Let $F: \{0,1\}^\lambda \times \{0,1\}^\lambda \to \{0,1\}^\lambda$ be a secure PRP (with blen $= \lambda$). Then F is also a secure PRF.*

Proof *As we have observed above, $\mathcal{L}^F_{\textit{prf-real}}$ and $\mathcal{L}^F_{\textit{prp-real}}$ are literally the same library. Since F is a secure PRP, $\mathcal{L}^F_{\textit{prp-real}} \approx \mathcal{L}^F_{\textit{prp-rand}}$. Finally, by the switching lemma, $\mathcal{L}^F_{\textit{prp-rand}} \approx \mathcal{L}^F_{\textit{prf-rand}}$. Putting everything together:*

$$\mathcal{L}^F_{\text{prf-real}} \equiv \mathcal{L}^F_{\text{prp-real}} \approx \mathcal{L}^F_{\text{prp-rand}} \approx \mathcal{L}^F_{\text{prf-rand}},$$

hence F is a secure PRF. □

Keep in mind that the switching lemma applies only when the blocklength is sufficiently large (at least λ bits long). This comes from the fact that $\mathcal{L}_{\text{samp-L}}$ and $\mathcal{L}_{\text{samp-R}}$ in the proof are indistinguishable only when sampling with long (length-) strings (look at the proof of Lemma 4.11 to recall why). Exercise 6.14 asks you to show that a random permutation over a small domain can be distinguished from a random (unconstrained) function; so, a PRP with a small blocklength is not a PRF.

Constructing a PRP from a PRF: The Feistel Construction

How can you build an invertible block cipher out of a PRF that is not necessarily invertible? In this section, we show a simple technique called the Feistel construction (named after IBM cryptographer Horst Feistel).

The main idea in the Feistel construction is to convert a not-necessarily-invertible function $F: \{0,1\}^n \to \{0,1\}^n$ into an invertible function $F^*: \{0,1\}^{2n} \to \{0,1\}^{2n}$. The function F^* is called the Feistel round with round function F and is defined as follows:

Construction 6.9 (Feistel round)

```
F*(x||y):
  // each of x, y are n bits
  return y||(F(y) ⊕ x)
```

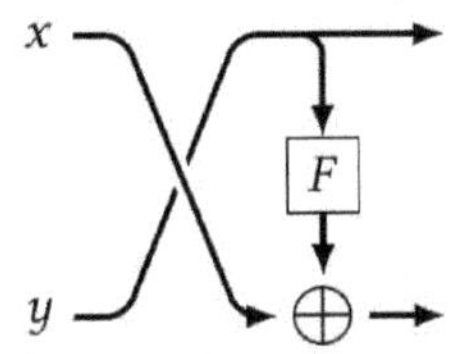

No matter what F is, its Feistel round F^* is invertible. Not only that, but its inverse is a kind of "mirror image" of F^* :

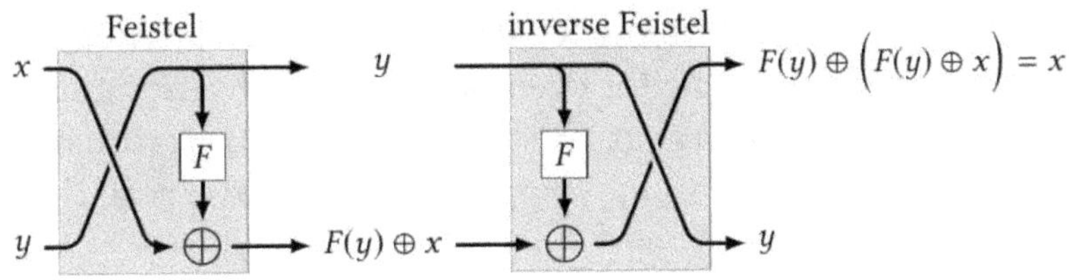

Note how both the forward and inverse Feistel rounds use F in the forward direction!

Example *Let's see what happens in the Feistel construction with a trivial round function. Consider the constant function $F(y) = 0^n$, which is the "least invertible" function imaginable. The Feistel construction gives:*

$$\begin{aligned} F^*(x\|y) &= y\|(F(y) \oplus x) \\ &= y\|(0^n \oplus x) \\ &= y\|x \end{aligned}$$

The result is a function that simply switches the order of its halves - clearly invertible.

Example *Let's try another simple round function, this time the identity function $F(y) = y$. The Feistel construction gives:*

$$\begin{aligned} F^*(x\|y) &= y\|(F(y) \oplus x) \\ &= y\|(y \oplus x) \end{aligned}$$

This function is invertible because given y and $y \oplus x$ we can solve for x as $y \oplus (y \oplus x)$. You can verify that this is what happens when you plug F into the inverse Feistel construction.

We can also consider using a round function F that has a key/seed. The result will be an F^* that also takes a seed. For every seed k, $F^*(k,\cdot)$ will have an inverse (which looks like its mirror image).

Construction 6.10 (Keyed Feistel)

$F^*(k, x \| y)$:
  return $y \| (F(k, y) \oplus x)$

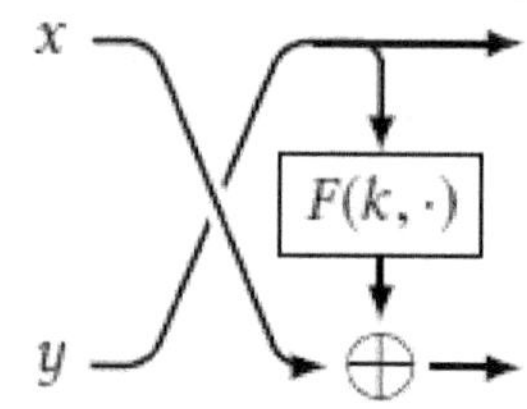

Now suppose F is a secure PRF and we use it as a Feistel round function, to obtain a keyed function F^*. Since $F^*(k,\cdot)$ is invertible for every k, and since F^* uses a secure PRF in some way, you might be tempted to claim that F^* is a secure PRP. Unfortunately, it is not! The output of F^* contains half of its input, making it quite trivial to break the PRP-security of F^*.

We can avoid this trivial attack by performing several Feistel rounds in succession, resulting in a construction called a Feistel cipher. At each round, we can even use a different key to the round function. If we use k_1 in the first round, k_2 in the second round, and so on, then $k_1, k_2, \ldots$ is called the key schedule of the Feistel cipher. The formal definition of an r-round Feistel cipher is given below:

Construction 6.11

(Feistel cipher)

$\mathbb{F}_r((k_1, \ldots, k_r), v_0 \| v_1)$:
  for $i = 1$ to r:
    $v_{i+1} := F(k_i, v_i) \oplus v_{i-1}$
  return $v_r \| v_{r+1}$

$\mathbb{F}_r^{-1}((k_1, \ldots, k_r), v_r \| v_{r+1})$:
  for $i = r$ downto 1:
    $v_{i-1} := F(k_i, v_i) \oplus v_{i+1}$
  return $v_0 \| v_1$

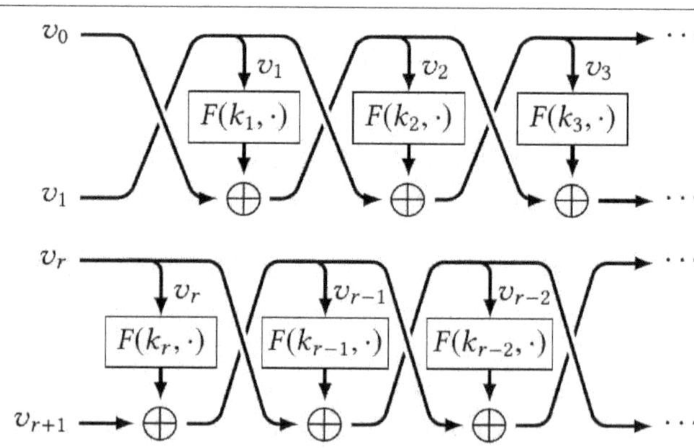

Because each round is invertible (given the appropriate round key), the overall Feistel cipher is also invertible. Note that the inverse of the Feistel cipher uses inverse Feistel rounds and reverses the order of the key schedule.

Surprisingly, a 3-round Feistel cipher can actually be secure, although a 2-round Feistel cipher is never secure (see the exercises). More precisely: when F is a secure PRF with in $=$ out $= \lambda$, then using F as the round function of a 3-round Feistel cipher results in a secure PRP. The Feistel cipher has blocklength 2λ, and it has a key of length 3λ (3 times longer than the key for F). Implicitly, this means that the three round keys are chosen independently.

Theorem 6.12 If $F: \{0,1\}^{\lambda} \times \{0,1\}^{\lambda} \rightarrow \{0,1\}^{\lambda}$ is a secure PRF, then the 3-round Feistel cipher $\mathbb{F}_3$ (Con-(Luby-Rackoff) struction 6.11) is a secure PRP.

Unfortunately, the proof of this theorem is beyond the scope of this book.

6.5 PRFs and Block Ciphers in Practice

Block ciphers are one of the cornerstones of cryptography in practice today. We have shown how (at least in principle) block ciphers can be constructed out of simpler primitives: PRGs and PRFs. However, in practice we use block ciphers that are designed "from scratch," and then use these block ciphers to construct simpler PRGs and PRFs when we need them.

We currently have no proof that any secure PRP exists. As we discussed in Section 5.2, such a proof would resolve the famous P vs NP problem. Without such proofs, what is our basis for confidence in the security of block ciphers being used today? The process that led to the Advanced Encryption Standard (AES) block cipher demonstrates the cryptographic community's best efforts at instilling such confidence.

The National Institute of Standards & Technology (NIST) sponsored a competition to design a block cipher to replace the DES standard from the 1970s. Many teams of cryptographers submitted their block cipher designs, all of which were then subject to years of intense public scrutiny by the cryptographic research community. The designs were evaluated on the basis of their performance and resistance to attacks against the PRP security definition (and other attacks). Some designs did offer proofs that they resist certain

classes of attacks, and proofs that justify certain choices in building the block cipher from simpler components.

The Rijndael cipher, designed by Vincent Rijmen and Joan Daemen, was selected as the winner and became the AES standard in 2001. There may not be another cryptographic algorithm that has been the focus of more scrutiny and attempts at attack. So far no significant weaknesses in AES are known. [3]

The AES block cipher has a blocklength of 128 bits, and offers 3 different variants with 128-bit, 192-bit, and 256-bit keys. As a result of its standardization, AES is available in cryptographic libraries for any programming language. It is even implemented as hardware instructions in most modern processors, allowing millions of AES evaluations per second. As we have seen, once you have access to a good block cipher, it can be used directly also as a secure PRF (Corollary 6.8), and it can be used to construct a simple PRG (Construction 6.2). Even though AES itself is not a provably secure PRP, these constructions of PRFs and PRGs based on AES are secure. Or, more precisely, the PRF-security and PRG-security of these constructions is guaranteed to be as good as the PRP-security of AES.

6.6 Strong Pseudorandom Permutations

Since a block cipher F has a corresponding inverse F^{-1}, it is natural to think of F and F^{-1} as interchangeable in some sense. However, the PRP security definition only guarantees a security property for F and not its inverse. In the exercises, you will see that it is possible to construct F which is a secure PRP, whose inverse F^{-1} is not a secure PRP!

It would be very natural to ask for a PRP whose F and F^{-1} are both secure. We will later see applications where this property would be convenient. An even stronger requirement would allow the distinguisher to query both F and F^{-1} in a single interaction (rather than one security definition where the distinguisher queries only F, and another definition where the distinguisher queries only F^{-1}). If a PRP is indistinguishable from a random permutation under that setting, then we say it is a strong PRP (SPRP).

In the formal security definition, we provide the calling program two subroutines: one for forward queries and one for reverse queries. In $\mathcal{L}_{\text{sprp-real}}$, these subroutines are implemented by calling the PRP or its inverse accordingly. In $\mathcal{L}_{\text{sprp-rand}}$, we emulate the behavior of a randomly chosen permutation that can be queried in both directions. We maintain two associative arrays T and T_{inv} to hold the truth tables of these permutations, and sample their values on-demand. The only restriction is that T and T_{inv} maintain consistency ($T[x] = y$ if and only if $T_{\text{inv}}[y] = x$). This also ensures that they always represent an invertible function. We use the same technique as before to ensure invertibility.

Definition 6.13 (SPRP security) *Let $F: \{0,1\}^{\lambda} \times \{0,1\}^{blen} \to \{0,1\}^{blen}$ be a deterministic function. We say that F is a secure strong pseudorandom permutation (SPRP) if $\mathcal{L}^F_{\text{sprp-real}} \approx \mathcal{L}^F_{\text{sprp-rand}}$, where:*

$\mathcal{L}^F_{\text{sprp-real}}$

```
k ← {0,1}^λ

LOOKUP(x ∈ {0,1}^blen):
  return F(k,x)

INVLOOKUP(y ∈ {0,1}^blen):
  return F^{-1}(k,y)
```

$\mathcal{L}^F_{\text{sprp-rand}}$

```
T, T_inv := empty assoc. arrays

LOOKUP(x ∈ {0,1}^blen):
  if T[x] undefined:
    y ← {0,1}^blen \ T.values
    T[x] := y;  T_inv[y] := x
  return T[x]

INVLOOKUP(y ∈ {0,1}^blen):
  if T_inv[y] undefined:
    x ← {0,1}^blen \ T_inv.values
    T_inv[y] := x;  T[x] := y
  return T_inv[y]
```

Earlier we showed that using a PRF as the round function in a 3-round Feistel cipher results in a secure PRP. However, that PRP is not a strong PRP. Even more surprisingly, adding an extra round to the Feistel cipher does make it a strong PRP! We present the following theorem without proof:

Theorem 6.14 (Luby-Rackoff) *If $F: \{0,1\}^\lambda \times \{0,1\}^\lambda \to \{0,1\}^\lambda$ is a secure PRF, then the 4-round Feistel cipher $\mathbb{F}_4$ (Construction 6.11) is a secure SPRP.*

Exercises

6.1. In this problem, you will show that it is hard to determine the key of a PRF by querying the PRF.

Let F be a candidate PRF, and suppose there exists a program $\mathcal{A}$ such that:

$$\Pr\left[\mathcal{A} \diamond \mathcal{L}^F_{\text{prf-real}} \text{ outputs } k\right] \text{ is non-negligible.}$$

In the above expression, k refers to the private variable within $\mathcal{L}_{\text{prf-real}}$.

Prove that if such an $\mathcal{A}$ exists, then F is not a secure PRF. Use $\mathcal{A}$ to construct a distinguisher that violates the PRF security definition.

6.2. Let F be a secure PRF.

(a) Let $m \in \{0,1\}^{out}$ be a fixed (public, hard-coded, known to the adversary) string. Define:

$$F_m(k,x) = F(k,x) \oplus m.$$

Prove that for every m, F_m is a secure PRF.

(b) Define

$$F'(k,x) = F(k,x) \oplus x$$

Prove that F' is a secure PRF .

6.3. Let F be a secure PRF with λ-bit outputs, and let G be a PRG with stretch ℓ. Define

$$F'(k,r) = G(F(k,r)).$$

So F' has outputs of length $\lambda + \ell$. Prove that F' is a secure PRF.

6.4. Let F be a secure PRF with in $= 2\lambda$, and let G be a length-doubling PRG. Define

$$F'(k,x) = F(k,G(x)).$$

We will see that F' is not necessarily a PRF.

(a) Prove that if G is injective then F' is a secure PRF.

★ (b) Exercise 5.9(b) constructs a secure length-doubling PRG that ignores half of its input. Show that F' is insecure when instantiated with such a PRG. Give a distinguisher and compute its advantage.

Note: You are not attacking the PRF security of F, nor the PRG security of G. You are attacking the invalid way in which they have been combined.

6.5. Let F be a secure PRF, and let $m \in \{0,1\}^{in}$ be a fixed (therefore known to the adversary) string. Define the new function

$$F_m(k,x) = F(k,x) \oplus F(k,m)$$

Show that F_m is not a secure PRF. Describe a distinguisher and compute its advantage.

★6.6. In the previous problem, what happens when m is secret and part of the PRF seed? Let F be a secure PRF, and define the new function: Define the new function

$$F'((k,m),x) = F(k,x) \oplus F(k,m).$$

The seed of F' is (k, m), which you can think of as a $\lambda + in$ bit string. Show that F' is indeed a secure PRF.

6.7. Let F be a secure PRF. Let $\bar{x}$ denote the bitwise complement of the string x. Define the new function:

$$F'(k, x) = F(k, x) \| F(k, \bar{x}).$$

Show that F' is not a secure PRF. Describe a distinguisher and compute its advantage.

6.8. Suppose F is a secure PRF with input length in, but we want to use it to construct a PRF with longer input length. Below are some approaches that don't work. For each one, describe a successful distinguishing attack and compute its advantage:

(a) $F'(k, x\|x') = F(k, x)\|F(k, x')$, where x and x' are each in bits long.

(b) $F'(k, x\|x') = F(k, x) \oplus F(k, x')$, where x and x' are each in bits long.

(c) $F'(k, x\|x') = F(k, x) \oplus F(k, x \oplus x')$, where x and x' are each in bits long.

(d) $F'(k, x\|x') = F(k, 0\|x) \oplus F(k, 1\|x')$, where x and x' are each in -1 bits long.

6.9. Define a PRFF whose key k we write as $(k_1, \ldots, k_{in})$, where each k_i is a string of length out. Then F is defined as:

$$F(k, x) = \bigoplus_{i:x_i=1} k_i.$$

Show that F is not a secure PRF. Describe a distinguisher and compute its advantage.

6.10. Define a PRF F whose key k is an in $\times$ 2 array of out-bit strings, whose entries we refer to as $k[i, b]$. Then F is defined as:

$$F(k, x) = \bigoplus_{i=1}^{in} k[i, x_i]$$

Show that F is not a secure PRF. Describe a distinguisher and compute its advantage.

6.11. A function $\{0,1\}^n \to \{0,1\}^n$ is chosen uniformly at random. What is the probability that the function is invertible?

6.12. Let F be a secure PRP with blocklength blen $= 128$. Then for each k, the function $F(k,\cdot)$ is a permutation on $\{0,1\}^{128}$. Suppose I choose a permutation on $\{0,1\}^{128}$ uniformly at random. What is the probability that the permutation I chose agrees with a permutation of the form $F(k,\cdot)$? Compute the probability as an actual number - is it a reasonable probability or a tiny one?

6.13. Suppose $R: \{0,1\}^n \to \{0,1\}^n$ is chosen uniformly among all such functions. What is the probability that there exists an $x \in \{0,1\}^n$ such that $R(x) = x$?

6.14. In this problem, you will show that the PRP switching lemma holds only for large domains. Let $\mathcal{L}_{\text{prf-rand}}$ and $\mathcal{L}_{\text{prp-rand}}$ be as in Lemma 6.7. Choose any small value of blen $=$ $in =$ out that you like, and show that $\mathcal{L}_{\text{prf-rand}} \Big/ \mathcal{L}\mathcal{L}_{\text{prp-rand}}$ with those parameters. Describe a distinguisher and compute its advantage.

6.15. Let $F: \{0,1\}^{\text{in}} \to \{0,1\}^{\text{out}}$ be a (not necessarily invertible) function. We showed how to use F as a round function in the Feistel construction ony when in = out.

Describe a modification of the Feistel construction that works even when the round function satisfies in $\neq$ out. The result should be an invertible with input/output length in+out. Be sure to show that your proposed transform is invertible! You are not being asked to show any security properties of the Feistel construction.

6.16. Show that a 1 -round keyed Feistel cipher cannot be a secure PRP, no matter what its round functions are. That is, construct a distinguisher that successfully distinguishes $\mathcal{L}^F_{\text{prp-real}}$ and $\mathcal{L}^F_{\text{prp-rand}}$, knowing only that F is a 1-round Feistel cipher. In particular, the purpose is to attack the Feistel transform and not its round function, so your attack should work no matter what the round function is.

6.17. Show that a 2-round keyed Feistel cipher cannot be a secure PRP, no matter what its round functions are. Your attack should work without knowing the round keys, and it should work even with different (independent) round keys.

6.18. Show that any function F that is a 3-round keyed Feistel cipher cannot be a secure strong PRP. As above, your distinguisher should work without knowing what the round functions are, and the attack should work with different (independent) round functions.

6.19. In this problem you will show that PRPs are hard to invert without the key (if the blocklength is large enough). Let F be a candidate PRP with blocklength blen $\geqslant \lambda$. Suppose there is a program $\mathcal{A}$ where:

$$\Pr_{y \leftarrow \{0,1\}^{blen}} \left[\mathcal{A}(y) \diamond \mathcal{L}^F_{\text{prf-real}} \text{ outputs } F^{-1}(k,y) \right] \text{ is non-negligible.}$$

The notation means that $\mathcal{A}$ receives a random block y as an input (and is also linked to $\mathcal{L}_{\text{prf-real}}$). k refers to the private variable within $\mathcal{L}_{\text{prf-real}}$. So, when given the ability to evaluate F in the forward direction only (via $\mathcal{L}_{\text{prf-real}}$), $\mathcal{A}$ can invert a uniformly chosen block y.

Prove that if such an $\mathcal{A}$ exists, then F is not a secure PRP. Use $\mathcal{A}$ to construct a distinguisher that violates the PRP security definition. Where do you use the fact that blen $\geqslant \lambda$? How do you deal with the fact that $\mathcal{A}$ may give the wrong answer with high probability?

6.20. Let F be a secure PRP with blocklength blen $= \lambda$, and consider $\hat{F}(k,x) = F(k,k) \oplus F(k,x)$.

(a) Show that $\hat{F}$ is not a strong PRP (even if F is).

⋆ (b) Show that $\hat{F}$ is a secure (normal) PRP.

Chapter 7

Security Against Chosen Plaintext Attacks

Our previous security definitions for encryption capture the case where a key is used to encrypt only one plaintext. Clearly it would be more useful to have an encryption scheme that allows many plaintexts to be encrypted under the same key.

Fortunately we have arranged things so that we get the "correct" security definition when we modify the earlier definition in a natural way. We simply let the libraries choose a secret key once and for all, which is used to encrypt all plaintexts. More formally:

Definition 7.1 Let Σ be an encryption scheme. We say that Σ has security against chosen-plaintext (CPA security) attacks (CPA security) if $\mathcal{L}^{\Sigma}_{\text{cpa-L}} \approx \mathcal{L}^{\Sigma}_{\text{cpa-R}}$, where:

$\mathcal{L}^{\Sigma}_{\text{cpa-L}}$
$k \leftarrow \Sigma.\text{KeyGen}$
$\text{EAVESDROP}(m_L, m_R \in \Sigma.\mathcal{M})$:
$c := \Sigma.\text{Enc}(k, m_L)$
return c

$\mathcal{L}^{\Sigma}_{\text{cpa-R}}$
$k \leftarrow \Sigma.\text{KeyGen}$
$\text{EAVESDROP}(m_L, m_R \in \Sigma.\mathcal{M})$:
$c := \Sigma.\text{Enc}(k, m_R)$
return c

Notice how the key k is chosen at initialization time and is static for all calls to Enc. CPA security is often called "IND-CPA" security, meaning "indistinguishability of ciphertexts under chosen-plaintext attack."

7.1 Limits of Deterministic Encryption

We have already seen block ciphers / PRPs, which seem to satisfy everything needed for a secure encryption scheme. For a block cipher, F corresponds to encryption, F^{-1} corresponds to decryption, and all outputs of F look pseudorandom. What more could you ask for in a good encryption scheme?

Example We will see that a block cipher, when used "as-is," is not a CPA-secure encryption scheme. Let F denote the block cipher and suppose its block length is blen.

Consider the following adversary $\mathcal{A}$, that tries to distinguish the $\mathcal{L}_{cpa\text{-}\star}$ libraries:

$\mathcal{A}$
$c_1 :=$ EAVESDROP$(0^{blen}, 0^{blen})$
$c_2 :=$ EAVESDROP$(0^{blen}, 1^{blen})$
return $c_1 \stackrel{?}{=} c_2$

When $\mathcal{A}$ is linked to $\mathcal{L}_{\text{cpa-L}}$, the EAVESDROP algorithm will encrypt its first argument. So, c_1 and c_2 will both be computed as $F(k, 0^{\text{blen}})$. Since F is a deterministic function, this results in identical outputs from EAVESDROP. In other words $c_1 = c_2$, and $\mathcal{A} \diamond \mathcal{L}_{\text{cpa-L}}$ always outputs 1.

$\mathcal{A}$		$\mathcal{L}^{\Sigma}_{\text{cpa-L}}$
$c_1 :=$ EAVESDROP$(0^{blen}, 0^{blen})$	$\diamond$	$k \leftarrow \{0,1\}^{\lambda}$
$c_2 :=$ EAVESDROP$(0^{blen}, 1^{blen})$		EAVESDROP(m_L, m_R):
return $c_1 \stackrel{?}{=} c_2$		$c := F(k, m_L)$
		return c

When $\mathcal{A}$ is linked to $\mathcal{L}_{\text{cpa-R}}$, the EAVESDROP algorithm will encrypt its second argument. So, c_1 and c_2 are computed as $c_1 = F(k, 0^{\text{blen}})$ and $c_2 = F(k, 1^{\text{blen}})$. Since F is a permutation, $c_1 \neq c_2$, so $\mathcal{A} \diamond \mathcal{L}_{\text{cpa-R}}$ never outputs 1 .

$\mathcal{A}$		$\mathcal{L}^{\Sigma}_{\text{cpa-R}}$
$c_1 :=$ EAVESDROP$(0^{blen}, 0^{blen})$	$\diamond$	$k \leftarrow \{0,1\}^{\lambda}$
$c_2 :=$ EAVESDROP$(0^{blen}, 1^{blen})$		EAVESDROP(m_L, m_R):
return $c_1 \stackrel{?}{=} c_2$		$c := F(k, m_R)$
		return c

This adversary has advantage 1 in distinguishing the libraries, so the bare block cipher F is not a CPA-secure encryption scheme.

Impossibility of Deterministic Encryption

The reason a bare block cipher does not provide CPA security is that it is deterministic. Calling $\text{Enc}(k, m)$ twice - with the same key and same plaintext - leads to the same ciphertext. Even one-time pad is deterministic. [1] One of the first and most important aspects of CPA security is that it is incompatible with deterministic encryption. Deterministic encryption can never be CPA-secure! In other words, we can attack the CPA-security of any scheme Σ, knowing only that it has deterministic encryption. The attack is a simple generalization of our attack against a bare PRP:

A
arbitrarily choose distinct plaintexts $x, y \in \mathcal{M}$
$c_1 := \text{EAVESDROP}(x, x)$
$c_2 := \text{EAVESDROP}(x, y)$
return $c_1 \stackrel{?}{=} c_2$

A good way to think about what goes wrong with deterministic encryption is that it leaks whether two ciphertexts encode the same plaintext, and this is not allowed by CPA security. Think of sealed envelopes as an analogy for encryption. I shouldn't be able to tell whether two sealed envelopes contain the same text! We are only now seeing this issue because this is the first time our security definition allows an adversary to see multiple ciphertexts encrypted under the same key.

Avoiding Deterministic Encryption

Is CPA security even possible? How exactly can we make a non-deterministic encryption scheme? This sounds challenging! We must design an Enc algorithm such that calling it twice with the same plaintext and key results in different ciphertexts (otherwise the attack $\mathcal{A}$ above violates CPA security). What's more, it must be possible to decrypt all of those different encryptions of the same plaintext to the correct value!

There are 3 general ways to design an encryption scheme that is not deterministic:

- Encryption/decryption can be stateful, meaning that every call to Enc or Dec will actually modify the value of k. The symmetric ratchet construction described in Section 5.5 could be thought of as such a stateful construction. The key is updated via the ratchet mechanism for every encryption. A significant drawback with stateful encryption is that synchronization between sender and receiver is fragile and can be broken if a ciphertext is lost in transit.
- Encryption can be randomized. Each time a plaintext is encrypted, the Enc algorithm chooses fresh, independent randomness specific to that encryption. The

main challenge in designing a randomized encryption method is to incorporate randomness into each ciphertext in such a way that decryption is still possible. Although this sounds quite challenging, we have already seen such a method, and we will prove its CPA security in the next sections. In this book we will focus almost entirely on randomized encryption.

- Encryption can be nonce-based. A "nonce" stands for "number used only once," and it refers to an extra argument that is passed to the Enc and Dec algorithms. A nonce does not need to be chosen randomly; it does not need to be secret; it only needs to be distinct among all calls made to Enc. By guaranteeing that some input to Enc will be different every time (even when the key and plaintext are repeated), the Enc algorithm can be deterministic and still provide CPA security.
- Nonce-based encryption requires a change to the interface of encryption, and therefore a change to the correctness & security definitions as well. The encryption/decryption algorithms syntax is updated to $\text{Enc}(k, v, m)$ and $\text{Dec}(k, v, c)$, where v is a nonce. The correctness property is that $\text{Dec}(k, v, \text{Enc}(k, v, m)) = m$ for all k, v, m, so both encryption & decryption algorithms should use the same nonce. The security definition allows the adversary to choose the nonce, but gives an error if the adversary tries to encrypt multiple ciphertexts with the same nonce. In this way, the definition enforces that the nonces are distinct.

$k \leftarrow \Sigma.\text{KeyGen}$ $V := \emptyset$ EAVESDROP($v, m_L, m_R \in \Sigma.\mathcal{M}$): if $v \in V$: return err $V := V \cup \{v\}$ $c := \Sigma.\text{Enc}(k, v, m_L)$ return c	$\approx$	$k \leftarrow \Sigma.\text{KeyGen}$ $V := \emptyset$ EAVESDROP($v, m_L, m_R \in \Sigma.\mathcal{M}$): if $v \in V$: return err $V := V \cup \{v\}$ $c := \Sigma.\text{Enc}(k, v, m_R)$ return c

Note that the calling program provides a single value v (not a v_L and v_R). Both libraries use the nonce v that is given, and this implies that the encryption scheme does not need to hide v. If something is the same between both libraries, then it is not necessary to hide it in order to make the libraries indistinguishable.

If an encryption scheme does not fall into one of these three categories, it cannot satisfy our definition of CPA-security. You can and should use deterministic encryption as a sanity check against any proposed encryption algorithm.

7.2 Pseudorandom Ciphertexts

When we introduced one-time security of encryption (in Section 2.2), we had two variants of the definition. The more general variant said, roughly, that encryptions of m_L should look like encryptions of m_R. The more specific variant said that encryptions of every m should look uniform.

We can do something similar for CPA security, by defining a security definition that says "encryptions of m look uniform." Note that it is not sufficient to use the same security libraries from the one-time security definition. It is important for the library to allow multiple encryptions under the same key. Just because a single encryption is pseudorandom, it doesn't mean that multiple encryptions appear jointly pseudorandom. In particular, they may not look independent (this was an issue we saw when discussing the difficulty of constructing a PRF from a PRG).

Definition 7.2 (CPA$ security): *Let Σ be an encryption scheme. We say that Σ has pseudorandom ciphertexts in the presence of chosen-plaintext attacks (CPA$security) if* $\mathcal{L}^{\Sigma}_{cpa\$rreal} \approx \mathcal{L}^{\Sigma}_{cpa\$rrand}$, *where:*

$\mathcal{L}^{\Sigma}_{\text{cpa\$-real}}$
$k \leftarrow \Sigma.\text{KeyGen}$
$\text{CTXT}(m \in \Sigma.\mathcal{M})$:
$c := \Sigma.\text{Enc}(k, m)$
return c

$\mathcal{L}^{\Sigma}_{\text{cpa\$-rand}}$
$\text{CTXT}(m \in \Sigma.\mathcal{M})$:
$c \leftarrow \Sigma.\mathcal{C}$
return c

This definition is also called "IND$-CPA", meaning "indistinguishable from random under chosen plaintext attacks." This definition will be useful to use since:

- It is easier to prove CPA$ security than to prove CPA security. Proofs for CPA security tend to be about twice as long and twice as repetitive, since they involve getting to a "half-way hybrid" and then performing the same sequence of hybrids steps in reverse. Taking the proof only to the same half-way point is generally enough to prove CPA$ security
- CPA$ security implies CPA security. We show this below, but the main idea is the same as in the case of one-time security. If encryptions of all plaintexts look uniform, then encryptions of m_L look like encryptions of m_R.
- Most of the schemes we will consider achieve CPA$ anyway.

Still, most of our high-level discussion of security properties will be based on CPA security. It is the "minimal" (i.e., least restrictive) definition that appears to capture our security intuitions.

Claim 7.3 *If an encryption scheme has CPA$ security, then it also has CPA security.*

Proof We want to prove that $\mathcal{L}^{\Sigma}_{\text{cpa-L}} \approx \mathcal{L}^{\Sigma}_{\text{cpa-R}}$, using the assumption that $\mathcal{L}^{\Sigma}_{\text{cpa \$-real}} \approx \mathcal{L}^{\Sigma}_{\text{cpa \$-rand}}$. The sequence of hybrids follows:

The starting point is $\mathcal{L}^{\Sigma}_{\text{cpa-L}}$, as expected.

$\mathcal{L}^{\Sigma}_{\text{cpa-L}}$:

```
L^Σ_cpa-L
---------------------------
k ← Σ.KeyGen

EAVESDROP(m_L, m_R):
  c := Σ.Enc(k, m_L)
  return c
```

It may look strange, but we have further factored out the call to Enc into a subroutine. It looks like everything from $\mathcal{L}_{\text{cpa-L}}$ has been factored out, but actually the original library still "makes the choice" of which of m_L, m_R to encrypt.

```
EAVESDROP(m_L, m_R):          L^Σ_cpa$-real
  c := CTXT(m_L)         ◇    k ← Σ.KeyGen
  return c
                              CTXT(m):
                                c := Σ.Enc(k, m)
                                return c
```

We have replaced $\mathcal{L}^{\Sigma}_{\text{cpa\$-real}}$ with $\mathcal{L}^{\Sigma}_{\text{cpa\$-rand.}}$. By our assumption, the change is indistinguishable.

EAVESDROP(m_L, m_R):	$\diamond$	$\mathcal{L}^{\Sigma}_{\text{cpa\$-rand}}$
$c :=$ CTXT(m_L)		CTXT(m):
return c		$c \leftarrow \Sigma.\mathcal{C}$
		return c

We have changed the argument being passed to CTXT. This has no effect on the library's behavior since CTXT completely ignores its argument in these hybrids.

EAVESDROP(m_L, m_R):	$\diamond$	$\mathcal{L}^{\Sigma}_{\text{cpa\$-rand}}$
$c :=$ CTXT(m_R)		CTXT(m):
return c		$c \leftarrow \Sigma.\mathcal{C}$
		return c

The mirror image of a previous step; we replace $\mathcal{L}_{\text{cpa\$-rand}}$ with $\mathcal{L}_{\text{cpa\$-real}}$.

EAVESDROP(m_L, m_R):	$\diamond$	$\mathcal{L}^{\Sigma}_{\text{cpa\$-real}}$
$c :=$ CTXT(m_R)		$k \leftarrow \Sigma$.KeyGen
return c		CTXT(m):
		$c := \Sigma.\text{Enc}(k, m)$
		return c

The $\mathcal{L}_{\text{cpa\$-real}}$ library has been inlined, and the result is $\mathcal{L}^{\Sigma}_{\text{cpa-R}}$.

$\mathcal{L}^{\Sigma}_{\text{cpa-R}}$:

$\mathcal{L}^{\Sigma}_{\text{cpa-R}}$
$k \leftarrow \Sigma$.KeyGen
EAVESDROP(m_L, m_R):
$c := \Sigma.\text{Enc}(k, m_R)$
return c

The sequence of hybrids shows that $\mathcal{L}^{\Sigma}_{\text{cpa-L}} \approx \mathcal{L}^{\Sigma}_{\text{cpa-R}}$, as desired.

7.3 CPA-Secure Encryption Based On PRFs

CPA security presents a significant challenge; its goals seem difficult to reconcile. On the one hand, we need an encryption method that is randomized, so that each plaintext m is mapped to a large number of potential ciphertexts. On the other hand, the decryption method must be able to recognize all of these various ciphertexts as being encryptions of m.

However, we have already seen a way to do this! In Chapter 6 we motivated the concept of a PRF with the following encryption technique. If Alice and Bob share a huge table T initialized with uniform data, then Alice can encrypt a plaintext m to Bob by saying something like "this is encrypted with one-time pad, using key #674696273" and sending $T[674696273] \oplus m$. Seeing the number 674696273 doesn't help the eavesdropper know what $T[674696273]$ is. A PRF allows Alice & Bob to do the same encryption while sharing only a short key k. Instead of a the huge table T, they can instead use a PRF$F(k,\cdot)$ to derive a common pseudorandom value. Knowing a value r doesn't help the adversary predict $F(k,r)$, when k is secret.

So, translated into more precise PRF notation, an encryption of m will look like $(r, F(k,r) \oplus m)$. Since Bob also has k, he can decrypt any ciphertext of this form by computing $F(k,r)$ and xor'ing the second ciphertext component to recover m.

It remains to decide how exactly Alice will choose r values. We argued, informally, that as long as these r values don't repeat, security is preserved. This is indeed true, and the distinctness of the r values is critical. Recall that there are 3 ways to avoid deterministic encryption, and all 3 of them would work here:

- In a stateful encryption, r could be used as a counter. Use $r = i$ to encrypt/decrypt the i th ciphertext.
- In a randomized encryption, choose r uniformly at random for each encryption. If the r values are long enough strings, then repeating an r value should be negligibly likely.
- In a nonce-based encryption, we can simply let r be the nonce. In the nonce-based setting, it is guaranteed that these values won't repeat.

In this section we will show the security proof for the case of randomized encryption, since it is the most traditional setting and also somewhat more robust than the others.

The exercises explore how the nonce-based approach is more fragile when this scheme is extended in natural ways.

Construction 7.4 *Let F be a secure PRF with in = λ. Define the following encryption scheme based on F :*

$$\mathcal{K} = \{0,1\}^\lambda \quad \mathcal{M} = \{0,1\}^{out} \quad \mathcal{C} = \{0,1\}^\lambda \times \{0,1\}^{out}$$

KeyGen:
$k \leftarrow \{0,1\}^\lambda$
return k

Enc(k, m):
$r \leftarrow \{0,1\}^\lambda$
$x := F(k,r) \oplus m$
return (r, x)

Dec$(k, (r, x))$:
$m := F(k,r) \oplus x$
return m

It is easy to check that the scheme satisfies the correctness property.

Claim 7.5 *Construction 7.4 has CPA$ security (and therefore CPA security) if F is a secure PRF.*

The proof has more steps than other proofs we have seen before, and some steps are subtle. So let us use a Socratic dialogue to illustrate the strategy behind the proof:

Salviati: The ciphertexts of Construction 7.4 are indistinguishable from uniform randomness.

Simplicio: Salviati, you speak with such confidence! Do tell me why you say that these ciphertexts appear pseudorandom.

Salviati: Simple! The ciphertexts have the form $(r, F(k,r) \oplus m)$. By its very definition, r is chosen uniformly, while $F(k,r) \oplus m$ is like a one-time pad ciphertext which is also uniformly distributed.

Simplicio: Your statement about r is self-evident but $F(k,r) \oplus m$ confuses me. This does not look like the one-time pad that we have discussed. For one thing, the same k is used "every time," not "one-time."

Salviati: I did say it was merely "like" one-time pad. The one-time pad "key" is not k but $F(k,r)$. And since F is a pseudorandom function, all its outputs will appear independently uniform (not to mention uncorrelated with their respective r), even when the same seed is used every time. Is this not what we require from a one-time pad key?

Simplicio: I see, but surely the outputs of F appear independent only when its inputs are distinct? I know that F is deterministic, and this may lead to the same "onetime pad key" being used on different occasions.

Salviati: Your skepticism serves you well in this endeavor, Simplicio. Indeed, the heart of your concern is that Alice may choose r such that it repeats. I say that this is negligibly likely, so that we can safely ignore such a bothersome event.

Simplicio: Bothersome indeed, but why do you say that r is unlikely to repeat?

Salviati: Oh Simplicio, now you are becoming bothersome! This value r is λ bits long and chosen uniformly at random each time. Do you not recall our agonizingly long discussion about the birthday paradox?

Simplicio: Oh yes, now I remember it well. Now I believe I understand all of your reasoning: Across all ciphertexts that are generated, r is unlikely to repeat because of the birthday paradox. Now, provided that r never repeats, Alice invokes the PRF on distinct inputs. A PRF invoked on distinct inputs provides outputs that are uniformly random for all intents and purposes. Hence, using these outputs as one-time pads completely hides the plaintext. Is that right, Salviati?

Salviati: Excellent! Now we may return to discussing the motion of the Sun and Earth...

Look for Simplicio's final summary to be reflected in the sequence of hybrids used in the formal proof:

Proof We prove that $\mathcal{L}^{\Sigma}_{\text{cpa\$-real}} \approx \mathcal{L}^{\Sigma}_{\text{cpa\$-rand}}$ using the hybrid technique:

The starting point is $\mathcal{L}^{\Sigma}_{\text{cpa\$-real}}$. The details of Σ have been filled in and highlighted.

$\mathcal{L}^{\Sigma}_{\text{cpa\$-real}}$:

$\mathcal{L}^{\Sigma}_{\text{cpa\$-real}}$
$k \leftarrow \{0,1\}^{\lambda}$
CTXT(m): $r \leftarrow \{0,1\}^{\lambda}$ $x := F(k,r) \oplus m$ return (r,x)

The statements pertaining to the PRF have been factored out in terms of the $\mathcal{L}^F_{\text{prf-real}}$ library.

```
CTXT(m):                     ◇   L^F_prf-real
  r ← {0,1}^λ                    k ← {0,1}^λ
  z := LOOKUP(r)
  x := z ⊕ m                     LOOKUP(r):
  return (r, x)                    return F(k, r)
```

We have replaced $\mathcal{L}^F_{\text{prf-real}}$ with $\mathcal{L}^F_{\text{prf-rand}}$. From the PRF security of F, these two hybrids are indistinguishable.

```
CTXT(m):                     ◇   L^F_prf-rand
  r ← {0,1}^λ                    T := empty
  z := LOOKUP(r)
  x := z ⊕ m                     LOOKUP(r):
  return (r, x)                    if T[r] undefined:
                                     T[r] ← {0,1}^out
                                   return T[r]
```

At this point in the proof, it is easy to imagine that we are done. Ciphertexts have the form (r, x), where r is chosen uniformly and x is the result of encrypting the plaintext with what appears to be a one-time pad. Looking more carefully, however, the "one-time pad key" is $T[r]$ - a value that could potentially be used more than once if r is ever repeated!

As Simplicio rightly pointed out, a PRF gives independently random(-looking) outputs when called on distinct inputs. But in our current hybrid there is no guarantee that PRF inputs are distinct! Our proof must explicitly contain reasoning about why PRF inputs are unlikely to be repeated. We do so by appealing to the sampling-with-replacement lemma of Lemma 4.11.

We first factor out the sampling of r values into a subroutine. The subroutine corresponds to the $\mathcal{L}_{\text{samp-L}}$ library of Lemma 4.11:

```
ctxt(m):                  ◇   L^F_prf-rand               ◇   L_samp-L
  r ← samp()                  T := empty                     samp():
  z := lookup(r)                                               r ← {0,1}^λ
  x := z ⊕ m                  lookup(r):                       return r
  return (r, x)                 if T[r] undefined:
                                  T[r] ← {0,1}^out
                                return T[r]
```

Next, $\mathcal{L}_{\text{samp-L}}$ is replaced by $\mathcal{L}_{\text{samp-R}}$. By Lemma 4.11, the difference is indistinguishable:

```
ctxt(m):                  ◇   L^F_prf-rand               ◇   L_samp-R
  r ← samp()                  T := empty                     R := ∅
  z := lookup(r)
  x := z ⊕ m                  lookup(r):                     samp():
  return (r, x)                 if T[r] undefined:             r ← {0,1}^λ \ R
                                  T[r] ← {0,1}^out             R := R ∪ {r}
                                return T[r]                    return r
```

Inspecting the previous hybrid, we can reason that the arguments to lookup are guaranteed to never repeat. Therefore the $\mathcal{L}_{\text{prf-rand}}$ library can be greatly simplified. In particular, the if-condition in $\mathcal{L}_{\text{prf-rand}}$ is always true. Simplifying has no effect on the library's output behavior:

```
ctxt(m):                  ◇   lookup(r):                 ◇   L_samp-R
  r ← samp()                    t ← {0,1}^out                R := ∅
  z := lookup(r)                return t
  x := z ⊕ m                                                 samp():
  return (r, x)                                                r ← {0,1}^λ \ R
                                                               R := R ∪ {r}
                                                               return r
```

Now we are indeed using unique one-time pads to mask the plaintext. We are in much better shape than before. Recall that our goal is to arrive at a hybrid in which the outputs of ctxt are chosen uniformly. These outputs include the value r, but now r is no longer being chosen uniformly! We must revert r back to being sampled uniformly, and then we are nearly to the finish line.

CTXT(m): $r \leftarrow$ SAMP() $z :=$ LOOKUP(r) $x := z \oplus m$ return (r, x)	$\diamond$ LOOKUP(r): $t \leftarrow \{0,1\}^{out}$ return t	$\diamond$ $\mathcal{L}_{\text{samp-L}}$ SAMP(): $r \leftarrow \{0,1\}^{\lambda}$ return r		As promised, $\mathcal{L}_{\text{samp-R}}$ has been replaced by $\mathcal{L}_{\text{samp-L}}$. The difference is indistinguishable due to Lemma 4.11.
CTXT(m): $r \leftarrow \{0,1\}^{\lambda}$ $z \leftarrow \{0,1\}^{out}$ $x := z \oplus m$ return (r, x)				All of the subroutine calls have been inlined; no effect on the library's output behavior.

$\mathcal{L}^{\Sigma}_{\text{cpa\$-rand}}$:

$\mathcal{L}^{\Sigma}_{\text{cpa\$-rand}}$
CTXT(m): $r \leftarrow \{0,1\}^{\lambda}$ $x \leftarrow \{0,1\}^{out}$ return (r, x)

We have applied the one-time pad rule with respect to variables z and x, but omitted the very familiar steps (factor out, replace library, inline) that we have seen several times before. The resulting library is precisely $\mathcal{L}^{\Sigma}_{\text{cpa\$-rand}}$ since it samples uniformly from $\Sigma.C = \{0,1\}^{\lambda} \times \{0,1\}^{out}$.

The sequence of hybrids shows that $\mathcal{L}^{\Sigma}_{\text{cpa\$-real}} \approx \mathcal{L}^{\Sigma}_{\text{cpa\$-rand}}$, so Σ has pseudorandom ciphertexts. □

Exercises

7.1. Let Σ be an encryption scheme, and suppose there is a program $\mathcal{A}$ that recovers the key from a chosen plaintext attack. More precisely, $\Pr[\mathcal{A} \diamond \mathcal{L} \text{ outputs } k]$ is non-negligible, where $\mathcal{L}$ is defined as:

$\mathcal{L}$
$k \leftarrow \Sigma.\text{KeyGen}$
CHALLENGE($m \in \Sigma.\mathcal{M}$): $c := \Sigma.\text{Enc}(k, m)$ return c

Prove that if such an $\mathcal{A}$ exists, then Σ does not have CPA security. Use $\mathcal{A}$ as a subroutine in a distinguisher that violates the CPA security definition.

In other words, CPA security implies that it should be hard to determine the key from seeing encryptions of chosen plaintexts.

7.2. Let Σ be an encryption scheme with CPA \$ security. Let Σ' be the encryption scheme defined by:

$$\Sigma'.\mathrm{Enc}(k,m) = 00\|\Sigma.\mathrm{Enc}(k,m)$$

The decryption algorithm in Σ' simply throws away the first two bits of the ciphertext and then calls Σ.Dec.

(a) Does Σ' have CPA \$ security? Prove or disprove (if disproving, show a distinguisher and calculate its advantage).

(b) Does Σ' have CPA security? Prove or disprove (if disproving, show a distinguisher and calculate its advantage).

7.3. Suppose a user is using Construction 7.4 and an adversary observes two ciphertexts that have the same r value.

(a) What exactly does the adversary learn about the plaintexts in this case?

(b) How do you reconcile this with the fact that in the proof of Claim 7.5 there is a hybrid where r values are never repeated?

7.4. Construction 7.4 is a randomized encryption scheme, but we could also consider defining it as a nonce-based scheme, interpreting r as the nonce: $\mathrm{Enc}(k,r,m) = (r, F(k,r) \oplus m)$. Formally prove that it is secure as a deterministic, nonce-based scheme. In other words, show that the following two libraries are indistinguishable, where Σ refers to Construction 7.4.

$k \leftarrow \Sigma.\mathrm{KeyGen}$
$V := \emptyset$
 	
EAVESDROP($v, m_L, m_R \in \Sigma.\mathcal{M}$):
  if $v \in V$: return err
  $V := V \cup \{v\}$
  $c := \Sigma.\mathrm{Enc}(k, v, m_L)$
  return c
	$k \leftarrow \Sigma.\mathrm{KeyGen}$
	$V := \emptyset$
	
	EAVESDROP($v, m_L, m_R \in \Sigma.\mathcal{M}$):
	  if $v \in V$: return err
	  $V := V \cup \{v\}$
	  $c := \Sigma.\mathrm{Enc}(k, v, m_R)$
	  return c

7.5. Let F be a secure PRP with blocklength blen $= \lambda$. Consider the following randomized encryption scheme:

$$\begin{array}{lll} \mathcal{K} = \{0,1\}^\lambda & \underline{\text{KeyGen}:} & \underline{\text{Enc}(k,m):} \\ \mathcal{M} = \{0,1\}^\lambda & \quad k \leftarrow \{0,1\}^\lambda & \quad v \leftarrow \{0,1\}^\lambda \\ \mathcal{C} = (\{0,1\}^\lambda)^2 & \quad \text{return } k & \quad x := F(k, v \oplus m) \\ & & \quad \text{return } (v, x) \end{array}$$

(a) Give the decryption algorithm for this scheme.

(b) Prove that the scheme has CPA$ security.

(c) Suppose that we interpret this scheme as a nonce-based scheme, where v is the nonce. Show that the scheme does not have nonce-based CPA security. The libraries for this definition are given in the previous problem.

Note: Even in the standard CPA libraries, v is given to the adversary and it is unlikely to repeat. However, in the nonce-based libraries the adversary can choose v, and this is what leads to problems.

7.6. Let F be a secure PRP with blocklength blen $= \lambda$. Show the the following scheme has pseudorandom ciphertexts:

$$\begin{array}{ll} \mathcal{K} = \{0,1\}^\lambda & \underline{\text{Enc}(k,m):} \\ \mathcal{M} = \{0,1\}^\lambda & \quad s \leftarrow \{0,1\}^\lambda \\ \mathcal{C} = (\{0,1\}^\lambda)^2 & \quad z := F(k, s \oplus m) \oplus m \\ & \quad \text{return } (s \oplus m, z) \\ \underline{\text{KeyGen}:} & \underline{\text{Dec}(k,(r,z)):} \\ \quad k \leftarrow \{0,1\}^\lambda & \quad \text{return } F(k,r) \oplus z \\ \quad \text{return } k & \end{array}$$

7.7. Let F be a secure PRP with blocklength blen $= \lambda$. Below are several encryption schemes, each with $\mathcal{K} = \mathcal{M} = \{0,1\}^\lambda$ and $\mathcal{C} = (\{0,1\}^\lambda)^2$. For each one:

- Give the corresponding Dec algorithm.
- State whether the scheme has CPA security. (Assume KeyGen samples the key uniformly from $\{0,1\}^\lambda$.) If so, then give a security proof. If not, then describe a successful adversary and compute its distinguishing bias.

(a)
```
Enc(k, m):
  r ← {0,1}^λ
  z := F(k, m) ⊕ r
  return (r, z)
```

(b)
```
Enc(k, m):
  r ← {0,1}^λ
  s := r ⊕ m
  x := F(k, r)
  return (s, x)
```

(c)
```
Enc(k, m):
  r ← {0,1}^λ
  x := F(k, r)
  y := r ⊕ m
  return (x, y)
```

(d)
```
Enc(k, m):
  r ← {0,1}^λ
  x := F(k, r)
  y := F(k, r) ⊕ m
  return (x, y)
```

(e)
```
Enc(k, m):
  r ← {0,1}^λ
  x := F(k, r)
  y := r ⊕ F(k, m)
  return (x, y)
```

(f)
```
Enc(k, m):
  s1 ← {0,1}^λ
  s2 := s1 ⊕ m
  x := F(k, s1)
  y := F(k, s2)
  return (x, y)
```

★ (g)
```
Enc(k, m):
  r ← {0,1}^λ
  x := F(k, m ⊕ r) ⊕ r
  return (r, x)
```

7.8. Suppose F is a secure PRP with blocklength $n + \lambda$. Below is the encryption algorithm for a scheme that supports plaintext space $\mathcal{M} = \{0,1\}^n$:

```
Enc(k, m):
  r ← {0,1}^λ
  return F(k, m||r)
```

(a) Describe the corresponding decryption algorithm.

(b) Prove that the scheme satisfies CPA$ security.

★ 7.9. Suppose F is a secure PRP with blocklength λ. Give the decryption algorithm for the following scheme and prove that it does not have CPA security:

$$\begin{array}{lll} \mathcal{K} = \{0,1\}^\lambda & \underline{\text{KeyGen}:} & \underline{\text{Enc}(k, m_1 \| m_2):} \\ \mathcal{M} = \{0,1\}^{2\lambda} & k \leftarrow \{0,1\}^\lambda & r \leftarrow \{0,1\}^\lambda \\ C = (\{0,1\}^\lambda)^3 & \text{return } k & s := F(k, r \oplus m_1) \\ & & t := F(k, r \oplus m_1 \oplus F(k, m_1) \oplus m_2) \\ & & \text{return } (r, s, t) \end{array}$$

⋆ 7.10. Suppose F is a secure PRP with blocklength λ. Give the decryption algorithm for the following scheme and prove that it satisfies CPA$ security:

$$\begin{array}{lll} \mathcal{K} = (\{0,1\}^\lambda)^2 & \underline{\text{KeyGen}:} & \underline{\text{Enc}((k,r), m):} \\ \mathcal{M} = \{0,1\}^\lambda & k \leftarrow \{0,1\}^\lambda & s \leftarrow \{0,1\}^\lambda \\ C = (\{0,1\}^\lambda)^2 & r \leftarrow \{0,1\}^\lambda & x := F(k, s) \\ & \text{return } (k, r) & y := F(k, s \oplus m \oplus r) \\ & & \text{return } (x, y) \end{array}$$

Note: If $r = 0^\lambda$ then the scheme reduces to Exercise 7.7 (f). So it is important that r is secret and random.

7.11. Let Σ be an encryption scheme with plaintext space $\mathcal{M} = \{0,1\}^n$ and ciphertext space $C = \{0,1\}^n$. Prove that Σ cannot have CPA security.

Conclude that direct application of a PRP to the plaintext is not a good choice for an encryption scheme.

⋆ 7.12. In all of the CPA-secure encryption schemes that we'll ever see, ciphertexts are at least λ bits longer than plaintexts. This problem shows that such ciphertext expansion is essentially unavoidable for CPA security.

Let Σ be an encryption scheme with plaintext space $\mathcal{M} = \{0,1\}^n$ and ciphertext space $C = \{0,1\}^{n+\ell}$. Show that there exists a distinguisher that distinguishes the two CPA libraries with advantage $\Omega(1/2^\ell)$.

7.13. Show that an encryption scheme Σ has CPA security if and only if the following two libraries are indistinguishable:

$\mathcal{L}^{\Sigma}_{\text{left}}$
$k \leftarrow \Sigma.\text{KeyGen}$
CHALLENGE($m \in \Sigma.\mathcal{M}$):
return $\Sigma.\text{Enc}(k, m)$

$\mathcal{L}^{\Sigma}_{\text{right}}$
$k \leftarrow \Sigma.\text{KeyGen}$
CHALLENGE($m \in \Sigma.\mathcal{M}$):
$m' \leftarrow \Sigma.\mathcal{M}$
return $\Sigma.\text{Enc}(k, m')$

In plain language: if these libraries are indistinguishable, then encryptions of chosen plaintexts are indistinguishable from encryptions of random plaintexts. You must prove both directions!

7.14. Let Σ_1 and Σ_2 be encryption schemes with $\Sigma_1 \cdot \mathcal{M} = \Sigma_2 \cdot \mathcal{M} = \{0,1\}^n$.

Consider the following approach for encrypting plaintext $m \in \{0,1\}^n$: First, secret-share m using any 2-out-of-2 secret-sharing scheme. Then encrypt one share under Σ_1 and the other share under Σ_2. Release both ciphertexts.

(a) Formally describe the algorithms of this encryption method.

(b) Prove that the scheme has CPA security if at least one of $\{\Sigma_1, \Sigma_2\}$ has CPA security. In other words, it is not necessary that both Σ_1 and Σ_2 are secure. This involves proving two cases (assuming Σ_1 is secure, and assuming Σ_2 is secure).

Chapter-8

Block Cipher Modes of Operation

One of the drawbacks of the previous CPA-secure encryption scheme is that its ciphertexts are λ bits longer than its plaintexts. In the common case that we are using a block cipher with blocklength blen $= \lambda$, this means that ciphertexts are twice as long as plaintexts. Is there any way to encrypt data (especially lots of it) without requiring such a significant overhead?

A block cipher mode refers to a way to use a block cipher to efficiently encrypt a large amount of data (more than a single block). In this chapter, we will see the most common modes for CPA-secure encryption of long plaintexts.

8.1 A Tour of Common Modes

As usual, blen will denote the blocklength of a block cipher F. In our diagrams, we'll write F_k as shorthand for $F(k,\cdot)$. When m is the plaintext, we will write $m = m_1 \| m_2 \| \cdots \| m_\ell$, where each m_i is a single block (so ℓ is the length of the plaintext measured in blocks). For now, we will assume that m is an exact multiple of the block length.

ECB: Electronic Codebook (never never use this! never!!)

The most obvious way to use a block cipher to encrypt a long message is to just apply the block cipher independently to each block. The only reason to know about this mode is to know never to use it (and to publicly shame anyone who does). It can't be said enough times: never use ECB mode! It does not provide security of encryption; can you see why?

Construction 8.1 (ECB Mode)

$\underline{\text{Enc}(k, m_1 \| \cdots \| m_\ell):}$
for $i = 1$ to ℓ:
  $c_i := F(k, m_i)$
return $c_1 \| \cdots \| c_\ell$

$\underline{\text{Dec}(k, c_1 \| \cdots \| c_\ell):}$
for $i = 1$ to ℓ:
  $m_i := F^{-1}(k, c_i)$
return $m_1 \| \cdots \| m_\ell$

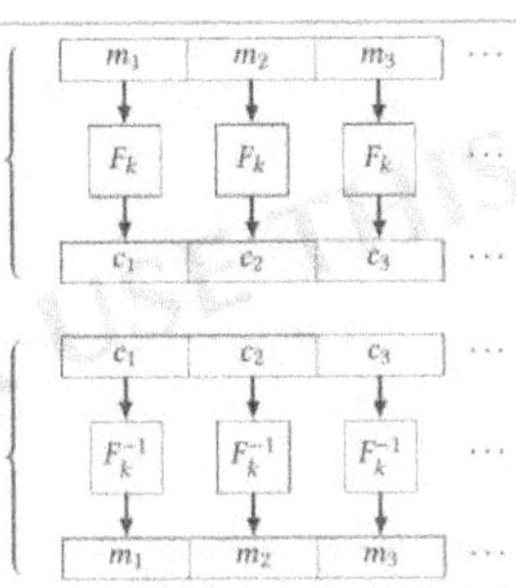

CBC: Cipher Block Chaining

CBC (which stands for cipher block chaining) is the most common mode in practice. The CBC encryption of an ℓ-block plaintext is $\ell + 1$ blocks long. The first ciphertext block is called an initialization vector (IV). Here we have described CBC mode as a randomized encryption, with the IV of each ciphertext being chosen uniformly. As you know, randomization is necessary (but not sufficient) for achieving CPA security, and indeed CBC mode provides CPA security.

Construction 8.2 (CBC Mode)

$\underline{\text{Enc}(k, m_1 \| \cdots \| m_\ell)}$:
$\quad c_0 \leftarrow \{0,1\}^{blen}$;
$\quad$for $i = 1$ to ℓ:
$\quad\quad c_i := F(k, m_i \oplus c_{i-1})$
$\quad$return $c_0 \| c_1 \| \cdots \| c_\ell$

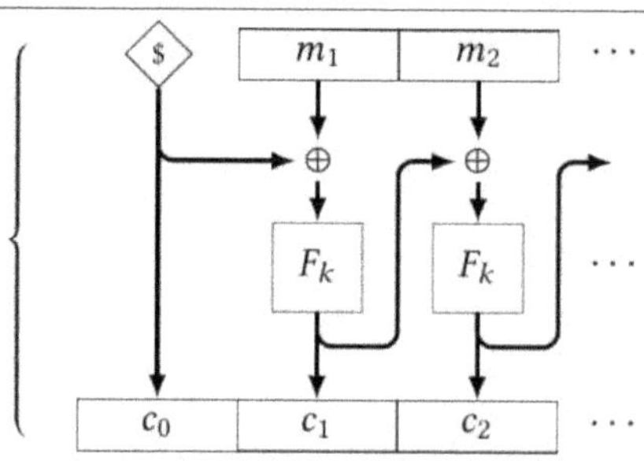

$\underline{\text{Dec}(k, c_0 \| \cdots \| c_\ell)}$:
$\quad$for $i = 1$ to ℓ:
$\quad\quad m_i := F^{-1}(k, c_i) \oplus c_{i-1}$
$\quad$return $m_1 \| \cdots \| m_\ell$

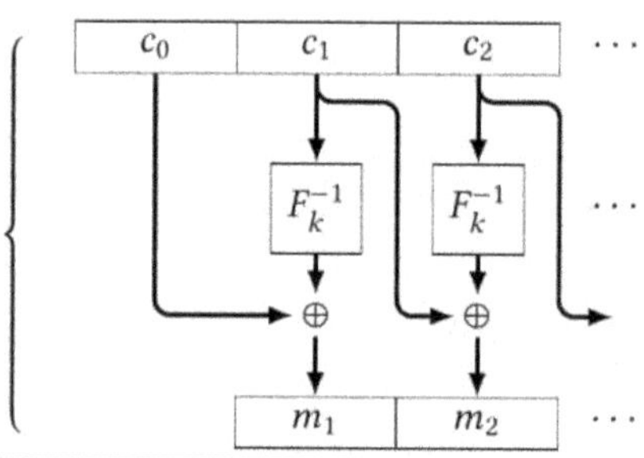

CTR: Counter

The next most common mode in practice is counter mode (usually abbreviated as CTR mode). Just like CBC mode, it involves an additional IV block r that is chosen uniformly. The idea is to then use the sequence

$$F(k,r);\ F(k,r+1);\ F(k,r+2);\ \cdots$$

as a long one-time pad to mask the plaintext. Since r is a block of bits, the addition expressions like $r + 1$ refer to addition modulo 2^{blen} (this is the typical behavior of unsigned addition in a processor).

Construction 8.3 (CTR Mode)

$\underline{\text{Enc}(k, m_1 \| \cdots \| m_\ell)\text{:}}$

$r \leftarrow \{0,1\}^{blen}$

$c_0 := r$

for $i = 1$ to ℓ:

$\quad c_i := F(k,r) \oplus m_i$

$\quad r := r + 1 \% 2^{blen}$

return $c_0 \| \cdots \| c_\ell$

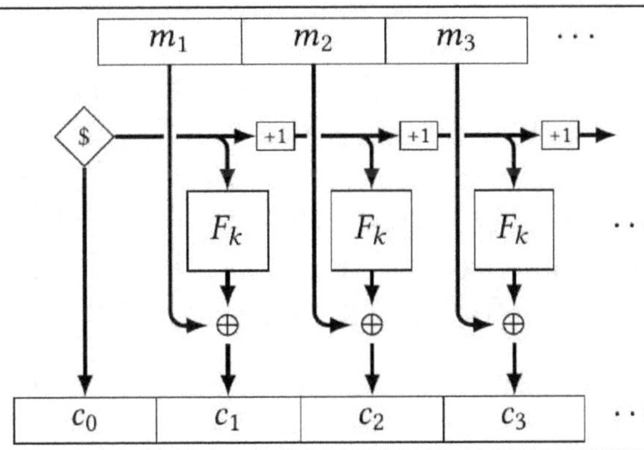

OFB: Output Feedback

OFB (output feedback) mode is rarely used in practice. We'll include it in our discussion because it has the easiest security proof. As with CBC and CTR modes, OFB starts with a random IV r, and then uses the sequence:

$$F(k,r);\ F(k,F(k,r));\ F(k,F(k,F(k,r)));\ \cdots$$

as a one-time pad to mask the plaintext.

Construction 8.4 (OFB Mode)

$\underline{\text{Enc}(k, m_1 \| \cdots \| m_\ell)\text{:}}$

$r \leftarrow \{0,1\}^{blen}$

$c_0 := r$

for $i = 1$ to ℓ:

$\quad r := F(k,r)$

$\quad c_i := r \oplus m_i$

return $c_0 \| \cdots \| c_\ell$

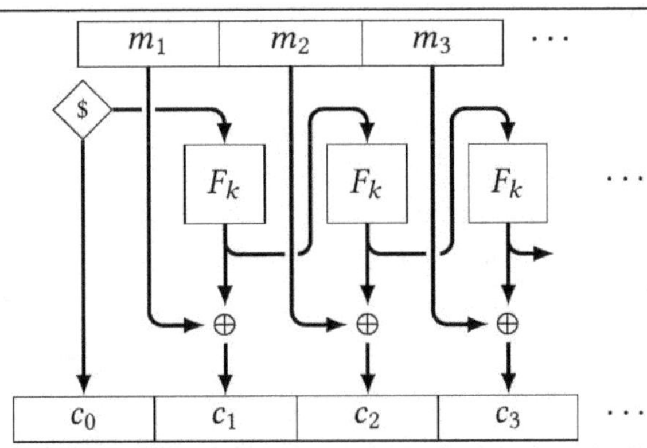

Compare & Contrast

CBC and CTR modes are essentially the only two modes that are ever considered in practice for CPA security. Both provide the same security guarantees, and so any comparison between the two must be based on factors outside of the CPA security definition. Here are a few properties that are often considered when choosing between these modes:

- Although we have not shown the decryption algorithm for CTR mode, it does not even use the block cipher's inverse F^{-1}. This is similar to our PRF-based encryption scheme from the previous chapter (in fact, CTR mode collapses to that construction when restricted to 1-block plaintexts). Strictly speaking, this means CTR mode can be instantiated from a PRF; it doesn't need a PRP. However, in practice it is rare to encounter an efficient PRF that is not a PRP.
- CTR mode encryption can be parallelized. Once the IV has been chosen, the i th block of ciphertext can be computed without first computing the previous $i - 1$
- blocks. CBC mode does not have this property, as it is inherently sequential. Both modes have a parallelizable decryption algorithm, though.
- If calls to the block cipher are expensive, it might be desirable to pre-compute and store them before the plaintext is known. CTR mode allows this, since only the IV affects the input given to the block cipher. In CBC mode, the plaintext influences the inputs to the block cipher, so these calls cannot be pre-computed before the plaintext is known.
- It is relatively easy to modify CTR to support plaintexts that are not an exact multiple of the blocklength. (This is left as an exercise.) We will see a way to make CBC mode support such plaintexts as well, but it is far from trivial.
- So far all of the comparisons have favored CTR mode, so here is one important property that favors CBC mode. It is common for implementers to misunderstand the security implications of the IV in these modes. Many careless implementations allow an IV to be reused. Technically speaking, reusing an IV (other than by accident, as the birthday bound allows) means that the scheme was not implemented correctly. But rather than dumping the blame on the developer, it is good design practice to anticipate likely misuses of a system and, when possible, try to make them non-catastrophic.

The effects of IV-reuse in CTR mode are quite devastating to message privacy (see the exercises). In CBC mode, reusing an IV can actually be safe, if the two plaintexts have different first blocks!

8.2 CPA Security and Variable-Length Plaintexts

Here's a big surprise: none of these block cipher modes achieve CPA security, or at least CPA security as we have been defining it.

Example *Consider a block cipher with blen = λ, used in CBC mode. As you will see, there is nothing particularly specific to CBC mode, and the same observations apply to the other modes.*

In CBC mode, a plaintext consisting of ℓ blocks is encrypted into a ciphertext of $\ell + 1$ blocks. In other words, the ciphertext leaks the number of blocks in the plaintext. We can leverage this observation into the following attack:

$$\begin{gathered}\mathcal{A}: \\ c := \text{EAVESDROP}(0^{\lambda}, 0^{2\lambda}) \\ \text{return } |c| \overset{?}{=} 2\lambda\end{gathered}$$

The distinguisher chooses a 1-block plaintext and a 2-block plaintext. If this distinguisher is linked to $\mathcal{L}_{cpa-L}$, the 1 -block plaintext is encrypted and the resulting ciphertext is 2 blocks (2λ bits) long. If the distinguisher is linked to $\mathcal{L}_{cpa-R}$, the 2-block plaintext is encrypted and the resulting ciphertext is 3 blocks (3λ bits) long. By simply checking the length of the ciphertext, this distinguisher can tell the difference and achieve advantage 1.

So, technically speaking, these block cipher modes do not provide CPA security, since ciphertexts leak the length (measured in blocks) of the plaintext. But suppose we don't really care about hiding the length of plaintexts. [1] Is there a way to make a security definition that says: ciphertexts hide everything about the plaintext, except their length?

It is clear from the previous example that a distinguisher can successfully distinguish the CPA libraries if it makes a query eavesdrop(m_L, m_R) with $|m_L| \neq |m_R|$. A simple way to change the CPA security definition is to just disallow this kind of query. The libraries will give an error message if $|m_L| \neq |m_R|$. This would allow the adversary to make the challenge plaintexts differ in any way of his/her choice, except in their length. It doesn't really matter whether $|m|$ refers to the length of the plaintext in bits or in blocks - whichever makes the most sense for a particular scheme.

From now on, when discussing encryption schemes that support variable-length plaintexts, CPA security will refer to the following updated libraries:

$\mathcal{L}^{\Sigma}_{\text{cpa-L}}$
$k \leftarrow \Sigma.\text{KeyGen}$
$\text{CTXT}(m_L, m_R \in \Sigma.\mathcal{M})$:
if $\lvert m_L \rvert \neq \lvert m_R \rvert$ return err
$c := \Sigma.\text{Enc}(k, m_L)$
return c

$\mathcal{L}^{\Sigma}_{\text{cpa-R}}$
$k \leftarrow \Sigma.\text{KeyGen}$
$\text{CTXT}(m_L, m_R \in \Sigma.\mathcal{M})$:
if $\lvert m_L \rvert \neq \lvert m_R \rvert$ return err
$c := \Sigma.\text{Enc}(k, m_R)$
return c

In the definition of CPA$ security (pseudorandom ciphertexts), the $\mathcal{L}_{\text{cpa\$-rand}}$ library responds to queries with uniform responses. Since these responses must look like ciphertexts, they must have the appropriate length. For example, for the modes discussed in this chapter, an ℓ-block plaintext is expected to be encrypted to an $(\ell + 1)$-block ciphertext. So, based on the length of the plaintext that is provided, the library must choose the appropriate ciphertext length. We are already using $\Sigma.C$ to denote the set of possible ciphertexts of an encryption scheme Σ. So let's extend the notation slightly and write $\Sigma.C(\ell)$ to denote the set of possible ciphertexts for plaintexts of length ℓ. Then when discussing encryption schemes supporting variable-length plaintexts, CPA$ security will refer to the following libraries:

$\mathcal{L}^{\Sigma}_{\text{cpa\$-real}}$
$k \leftarrow \Sigma.\text{KeyGen}$
$\text{CHALLENGE}(m \in \Sigma.\mathcal{M})$:
$c := \Sigma.\text{Enc}(k, m)$
return c

$\mathcal{L}^{\Sigma}_{\text{cpa\$-rand}}$
$\text{CHALLENGE}(m \in \Sigma.\mathcal{M})$:
$c \leftarrow \Sigma.C(\lvert m \rvert)$
return c

Note that the $\mathcal{L}_{\text{cpa\$-rand}}$ library does not use any information about m other than its length. This again reflects the idea that ciphertexts leak nothing about plaintexts other than their length.

In the exercises, you are asked to prove that, with respect to these updated security definitions, CPA$ security implies CPA security as before.

Don't Take Length-Leaking for Granted!

We have just gone from requiring encryption to leak no partial information to casually allowing some specific information to leak. Let us not be too hasty about this!

If we want to truly support plaintexts of arbitrary length, then leaking the length is in fact unavoidable. But "unavoidable" doesn't mean "free of consequences." By observing only the length of encrypted network traffic, many serious attacks are possible. Here are several examples:

- When accessing Google maps, your browser receives many image tiles that comprise the map that you see. Each image tile has the same pixel dimensions. However, they are compressed to save resources, and not all images compress as significantly as others. Every region of the world has its own rather unique "fingerprint" of imagetile lengths. So even though traffic to and from Google maps is encrypted, the sizes of the image tiles are leaked. This can indeed be used to determine the region for which a user is requesting a map. [2] The same idea applies to auto-complete suggestions in a search form.
- Variable-bit-rate (VBR) encoding is a common technique in audio/video encoding. When the data stream is carrying less information (e.g., a scene with a fixed camera position, or a quiet section of audio), it is encoded at a lower bit rate, meaning that each unit of time is encoded in fewer bits. In an encrypted video stream, the changes in bit rate are reflected as changes in packet length. When a user is watching a movie on Netflix or a Youtube video (as opposed to a live event stream), the bit-rate changes are consistent and predictable. It is therefore rather straightforward to determine which video is being watched, even on an encrypted connection, just by observing the packet lengths.
- VBR is also used in many encrypted voice chat programs. Attacks on these tools have been increasing in sophistication. The first attacks on encrypted voice programs showed how to identify who was speaking (from a set of candidates), just by observing the stream of ciphertext sizes. Later attacks could determine the language being spoken. Eventually, when combined with sophisticated linguistic models, it was shown possible to even identify individual words to some extent!

It's worth emphasizing again that none of these attacks involve any attempt to break the encryption. The attacks rely solely on the fact that encryption leaks the length of the plaintexts.

8.3 Security of OFB Mode

In this section we will prove that OFB mode has pseudorandom ciphertexts (when the blocklength is blen $= \lambda$ bits). OFB encryption and decryption both use the forward direction of F, so OFB provides security even when F is not invertible. Therefore we will prove security assuming F is simply a PRF .

Claim 8.5 *OFB mode (Construction 8.4) has CPA\$ security, if its underlying block cipher F is a secure PRF with parameters $in = out = \lambda$.*

Proof The general structure of the proof is very similar to the proof used for the PRF-based encryption scheme in the previous chapter (Construction 7.4). This is no coincidence: if OFB mode is restricted to plaintexts of a single block, we obtain exactly Construction 7.4!

The idea is that each ciphertext block (apart from the IV) is computed as $c_i := r \oplus m_i$. By the one-time pad rule, it suffices to show that the r values are independently pseudorandom. Each r value is the result of a call to the PRF. These PRF outputs will be independently pseudorandom only if all of the inputs to the PRF are distinct. In OFB mode, we use the output r of a previous PRF call as input to the next, so it is highly unlikely that this PRF output r matches a past PRF-input value. To argue this more precisely, the proof includes hybrids in which r is chosen without replacement (before changing r back to uniform sampling).

The formal sequence of hybrid libraries is given below:

$\mathcal{L}^{\text{OFB}}_{\text{cpa\$-real}}$:

$\mathcal{L}^{\text{OFB}}_{\text{cpa\$-real}}$
$k \leftarrow \{0,1\}^\lambda$
$\text{CTXT}(m_1 \| \cdots \| m_\ell)$:
$\quad r \leftarrow \{0,1\}^\lambda$
$\quad c_0 := r$
$\quad$ for $i = 1$ to ℓ:
$\qquad r := F(k, r)$
$\qquad c_i := r \oplus m_i$
$\quad$ return $c_0 \| c_1 \| \cdots \| c_\ell$

The starting point is $\mathcal{L}^{\text{OFB}}_{\text{cpa\$-real}}$, shown here with the details of OFB filled in.

```
◇  L^F_prf-real
   k ← {0,1}^λ

   LOOKUP(r):
     return F(k, r)
```

The statements pertaining to the PRF F have been factored out in terms of $\mathcal{L}^F_{\text{prf-real}}$.

```
CTXT(m_1 || ··· || m_ℓ):                    L^F_prf-real
  r ← {0,1}^λ                           k ← {0,1}^λ
  c_0 := r                          ◇
  for i = 1 to ℓ:                       LOOKUP(r):
    r := LOOKUP(r)                        return F(k, r)
    c_i := r ⊕ m_i
  return c_0 || c_1 || ··· || c_ℓ
```

$\mathcal{L}^F_{\text{prf-real}}$ has been replaced by $\mathcal{L}^F_{\text{prf-rand}}$. By the PRF security of F, the change is indistinguishable.

```
CTXT(m_1 || ··· || m_ℓ):                    L^F_prf-rand
  r ← {0,1}^λ                           T := empty
  c_0 := r
  for i = 1 to ℓ:                   ◇   LOOKUP(x):
    r := LOOKUP(r)                        if T[x] undefined:
    c_i := r ⊕ m_i                          T[x] ← {0,1}^λ
  return c_0 || c_1 || ··· || c_ℓ         return T[x]
```

Next, all of the statements that involve sampling values for the variable r are factored out in terms of the $\mathcal{L}_{\text{samp-L}}$ library from Lemma 4.11:

```
CHALLENGE(m_1 || ··· || m_ℓ):         T := empty                    L_samp-L
  r := SAMP()
  c_0 := r                            LOOKUP(x):                SAMP():
  for i = 1 to ℓ:               ◇       if T[x] undefined:  ◇     r ← {0,1}^λ
    r := LOOKUP(r)                        T[x] := SAMP()          return r
    c_i := r ⊕ m_i                      return T[x]
  return c_0 || c_1 || ··· || c_ℓ
```

$\mathcal{L}_{\text{samp-L}}$ is then replaced by $\mathcal{L}_{\text{samp-R}}$. By Lemma 4.11, this change is indistinguishable:

CTXT($m_1 \| \cdots \| m_\ell$):				$\mathcal{L}_{\text{samp-R}}$

$r :=$ SAMP()
$c_0 := r$
for $i = 1$ to ℓ:
  $r :=$ LOOKUP(r)
  $c_i := r \oplus m_i$
return $c_0 \| c_1 \| \cdots \| c_\ell$
	$\diamond$	$T :=$ empty
		
		LOOKUP(x):
		  if $T[x]$ undefined:
		    $T[x] :=$ SAMP()
		  return $T[x]$
			$\diamond$	$R := \emptyset$
				
				SAMP():
				  $r \leftarrow \{0,1\}^\lambda \setminus R$
				  $R := R \cup \{r\}$
				  return r

Arguments to lookup are never repeated in this hybrid, so the middle library can be significantly simplified:

CTXT($m_1 \| \cdots \| m_\ell$):				$\mathcal{L}_{\text{samp-R}}$

$r :=$ SAMP()
$c_0 := r$
for $i = 1$ to ℓ:
  $r :=$ LOOKUP(r)
  $c_i := r \oplus m_i$
return $c_0 \| c_1 \| \cdots \| c_\ell$
	$\diamond$	LOOKUP(x):
		  $t :=$ SAMP()
		  return t
			$\diamond$	$R := \emptyset$
				
				SAMP():
				  $r \leftarrow \{0,1\}^\lambda \setminus R$
				  $R := R \cup \{r\}$
				  return r

Next, $\mathcal{L}_{\text{samp-R}}$ is replaced by $\mathcal{L}_{\text{samp-L}}$. By Lemma 4.11, this change is indistinguishable:

CTXT($m_1 \| \cdots \| m_\ell$):				$\mathcal{L}_{\text{samp-L}}$

$r :=$ SAMP()
$c_0 := r$
for $i = 1$ to ℓ:
  $r :=$ LOOKUP(r)
  $c_i := r \oplus m_i$
return $c_0 \| c_1 \| \cdots \| c_\ell$
	$\diamond$	LOOKUP(x):
		  $t :=$ SAMP()
		  return t
			$\diamond$	SAMP():
				  $r \leftarrow \{0,1\}^\lambda$
				  return r

Subroutine calls to lookup and samp are inlined:

```
CTXT(m_1||···||m_ℓ):
  r ← {0,1}^λ
  c_0 := r
  for i = 1 to ℓ:
    r ← {0,1}^λ
    c_i := r ⊕ m_i
  return c_0||c_1||···||c_ℓ
```

Finally, the one-time pad rule is applied within the for-loop (omitting some common steps). Note that in the previous hybrid, each value of r is used only once as a one-time pad. The $i = 0$ case has also been absorbed into the for-loop. The result is $\mathcal{L}^{\text{OFB}}_{\text{cpa\$-rand}}$, since OFB encrypts plaintexts of ℓ blocks into $\ell + 1$ blocks.

$\mathcal{L}^{\text{OFB}}_{\text{cpa\$-rand}}$

```
CTXT(m_1||···||m_ℓ):
  for i = 0 to ℓ:
    c_i ← {0,1}^λ
  return c_0||c_1||···||c_ℓ
```

The sequence of hybrids shows that $\mathcal{L}^{\text{OFB}}_{\text{cpa \$-real}} \approx \mathcal{L}^{\text{OFB}}_{\text{cpa \$-rand}}$, and so OFB mode has pseudorandom ciphertexts. □

We proved the claim assuming F is a PRF only, since OFB mode does not require F to be invertible. Since we assume a PRF with parameters in $=$ out $= \lambda$, the PRP switching lemma (Lemma 6.7) shows that OFB is secure also when F is a PRP with blocklength $n = \lambda$.

8.4 Padding & Ciphertext Stealing

So far we have assumed that all plaintexts are exact multiples of the blocklength. But data in the real world is not always so accommodating. How are block ciphers used in practice with data that has arbitrary length?

Padding

Padding just refers to any approach to encode arbitrary-length data into data that is a multiple of the blocklength. The only requirement is that this encoding is reversible. More formally, a padding scheme should consist of two algorithms:

- pad: takes as input a string of any length, and outputs a string whose length is a multiple of the blocklength
- unpad: the inverse of pad. We require that unpad (pad(x)) $= x$ for all strings x.

The idea is that the sender can encrypt pad (x), which is guaranteed to be a multiple of the blocklength; the receiver can decrypt and run unpad on the result to obtain x.

In the real world, data almost always comes in bytes and not bits, so that will be our assumption here. In this section we will write bytes in hex, for example 8f. Typical blocklengths are 128 bits (16 bytes) or 256 bits (32 bytes).

Here are a few common approaches for padding:

Null padding: The simplest padding approach is to just fill the final block with null bytes (00). The problem with this approach is that it is not always reversible. For example, pad(314159) and pad(31415900) will give the same result. It is not possible to distinguish between a null byte that was added for padding and one that was intentionally the last byte of the data.

ANSI X. 923 standard: Data is padded with null bytes, except for the last byte of padding which indicates how many padding bytes there are. In essence, the last byte of the padded message tells the receiver how many bytes to remove to recover the original message.

Note that in this padding scheme (and indeed in all of them), if the original unpadded data is already a multiple of the block length, then an entire extra block of padding must be added. This is necessary because it is possible for the original data to end with some bytes that look like valid padding (e.g., 000003), and we do not want these bytes to be removed erroneously.

Example Below are some examples of valid and invalid X. 923 padding (using 16-byte blocks):

01	34	11	d9	81	88	05	57	1d	73	c3	00	00	00	00	05	$\Rightarrow$ *valid*
95	51	05	4a	d6	5a	a3	44	af	b3	85	00	00	00	00	03	$\Rightarrow$ *valid*
71	da	77	5a	5e	77	eb	a8	73	c5	50	b5	81	d5	96	01	$\Rightarrow$ *valid*
5b	1c	01	41	5d	53	86	4e	e4	94	13	e8	7a	89	c4	71	$\Rightarrow$ *invalid*
d4	0d	d8	7b	53	24	c6	d1	af	5f	d6	f6	00	c0	00	04	$\Rightarrow$ *invalid*

PKCS#7 standard: If *b* bytes of padding are needed, then the data is padded not with null bytes but with *b* bytes. Again, the last byte of the padded message tells the receiver how many bytes to remove.

Example Below are some examples of valid and invalid PKCS#7 padding (using 16-byte blocks):

```
01 34 11 d9 81 88 05 57 1d 73 c3 05 05 05 05 05 ⇒ valid
95 51 05 4a d6 5a a3 44 af b3 85 03 03 03 03 03 ⇒ valid
71 da 77 5a 5e 77 eb a8 73 c5 50 b5 81 d5 96 01 ⇒ valid
5b 1c 01 41 5d 53 86 4e e4 94 13 e8 7a 89 c4 71 ⇒ invalid
d4 0d d8 7b 53 24 c6 d1 af 5f d6 f6 04 c0 04 04 ⇒ invalid
```

ISO/IEC 7816-4 standard: The data is padded with a 80 byte followed by null bytes. To remove the padding, remove all trailing null bytes and ensure that the last byte is 80 (and then remove it too).

The significance of 80 is clearer when you write it in binary as 10000000. So another way to describe this padding scheme is: append a 1 bit, and then pad with 0 bits until reaching the blocklength. To remove the padding, remove all trailing 0 bits as well as the rightmost 1 bit. Hence, this approach generalizes easily to padding data that is not a multiple of a byte.

Example Below are some examples of valid and invalid ISO/IEC 7816-4 padding (using 16-byte blocks):

```
01 34 11 d9 81 88 05 57 1d 73 c3 80 00 00 00 00 ⇒ valid
95 51 05 4a d6 5a a3 44 af b3 85 03 03 80 00 00 ⇒ valid
71 da 77 5a 5e 77 eb a8 73 c5 50 b5 81 d5 96 80 ⇒ valid
5b 1c 01 41 5d 53 86 4e e4 94 13 e8 7a 89 c4 71 ⇒ invalid
d4 0d d8 7b 53 24 c6 d1 af 5f d6 f6 c4 00 00 00 ⇒ invalid
```

The choice of padding scheme is not terribly important, and any of these is generally fine. Just remember that padding schemes are not a security feature! Padding is a public method for encoding data, and it does not involve any secret keys. The only purpose of padding is to enable functionality - using block cipher modes like CBC with data that is not a multiple of the block length.

Furthermore, as we will see in the next chapter, padding is associated with certain attacks against improper use of encryption. Even though this is not really the fault of the padding (rather, it is the fault of using the wrong flavor of encryption), it is such a common pitfall that it is always worth considering in a discussion about padding.

Ciphertext Stealing

Another approach with a provocative name is ciphertext stealing (CTS, if you are not yet tired of three-leter acronyms), which results in ciphertexts that are not a multiple of the blocklength. The main idea behind ciphertext stealing is to use a standard block-cipher mode that only supports full blocks (e.g., CBC mode), and then simply throw away some bits of the ciphertext, in such a way that decryption is still possible. If the last plaintext blocks is j bits short of being a full block, it is generally possible to throw away j bits of the ciphertext. In this way, a plaintext of n bits will be encrypted to a ciphertext of blen $+n$ bits, where blen is the length of the extra IV block.

As an example, let's see ciphertext stealing as applied to CBC mode. Suppose the blocklength is blen and the last plaintext block m_ℓ is j bits short of being a full block. We start by extending m_ℓ with j zeroes (i.e., null-padding the plaintext) and performing CBC encryption as usual.

Now our goal is to identify j bits of the CBC ciphertext that can be thrown away while still making decryption possible. In this case, the appropriate bits to throw away are the last j bits of $c_{\ell-1}$ (the next-to-last block of the CBC ciphertext). The reason is illustrated in the figure below:

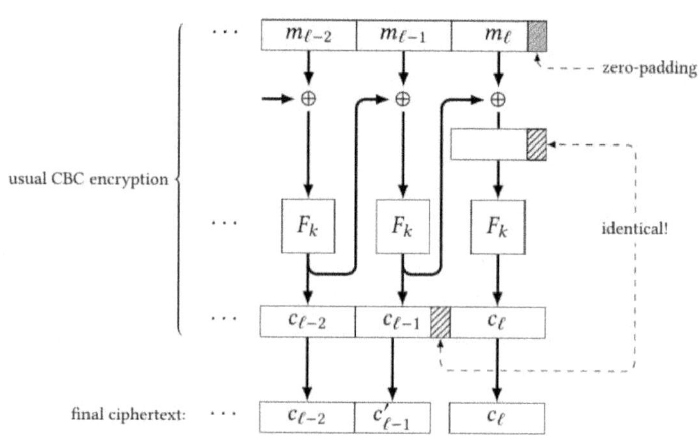

Suppose the receiver obtains this CBC ciphertext but the last j bits of $c_{\ell-1}$ have been deleted. How can he/she decrypt? The important idea is that those missing j bits were redundant, because there is another way to compute them.

In CBC encryption, the last value given as input into the block cipher is $c_{\ell-1} \oplus m_\ell$. Let us give this value a name $x^* := c_{\ell-1} \oplus m_\ell$. Since the last j bits of m_ℓ are $0's$, [3] the last j bits of x^* are the last j bits of $c_{\ell-1}$ - the missing bits. Even though these bits are missing from $c_{\ell-1}$, the receiver has a different way of computing them as $x^* := F^{-1}(k, c_\ell)$.

Putting it all together, the receiver does the following: First, it observes that the ciphertext is j bits short of a full block. It computes $F^{-1}(k, c_\ell)$ and takes the last j bits of this value to be the missing bits from $c_{\ell-1}$. With the missing bits recovered, the receiver does CBC decryption as usual. The result is a plaintext consisting of ℓ full blocks, but we know that the last j bits of that plaintext are 0 padding that the receiver can remove.

It is convenient in an implementation for the boundaries between blocks to be in predictable places. For that reason, it is slightly awkward to remove j bits from the middle of the ciphertext during encryption (or add them during decryption), as we have done here. So in practice, the last two blocks of the ciphertext are often interchanged. In the example above, the resulting ciphertext (after ciphertext stealing) would be:

$$c_0 \parallel c_1 \parallel c_2 \cdots c_{\ell-3} \parallel c_{\ell-2} \parallel c_\ell \parallel c'_{\ell-1}, \text{ where } c'_{\ell-1} \text{ is the first } blen - j \text{ bits of } c_{\ell-1}.$$

That way, all ciphertext blocks except the last one are the full blen bits long, and the boundaries between blocks appear consistently every blen bits. This "optimization" does add some significant edge cases to any implementation. One must also decide what to do when the plaintext is already an exact multiple of the blocklength - should the final two ciphertext blocks be swapped even in this case? Below we present an implementation of ciphertext stealing (CTS) that does not swap the final two blocks in this case. This means that it collapses to plain CBC mode when the plaintext is an exact multiple of the block length.

Construction 8.6

(CBC-CTS)

```
Enc(k, m_1 || ··· || m_ℓ):
  // each m_i is blen bits,
  // except possibly m_ℓ

  j := blen − |m_ℓ|
  m_ℓ := m_ℓ || 0^j
| c_0 ← {0,1}^blen;
| for i = 1 to ℓ:
|    c_i := F(k, m_i ⊕ c_{i−1})
  if j ≠ 0:
     remove final j bits of c_{ℓ−1}
     swap c_{ℓ−1} and c_ℓ
  return c_0 || c_1 || ··· || c_ℓ
```

```
Dec(k, c_0 || ··· || c_ℓ):
  // each c_i is blen bits,
  // except possibly c_ℓ

  j := blen − |c_ℓ|
  if j ≠ 0:
     swap c_{ℓ−1} and c_ℓ
     x := last j bits of F^{−1}(k, c_ℓ)
     c_{ℓ−1} := c_{ℓ−1} || x
| for i = 1 to ℓ:
|    m_i := F^{−1}(k, c_i) ⊕ c_{i−1}
  remove final j bits of m_ℓ
  return m_1 || ··· || m_ℓ
```

The marked lines correspond to plain CBC mode.

Exercises

8.1. Prove that a block cipher in ECB mode does not provide CPA security. Describe a distinguisher and compute its advantage.

8.2. Describe OFB decryption mode.

8.3. Describe CTR decryption mode.

8.4 CBC mode:

(a) In CBC-mode encryption, if a single bit of the plaintext is changed, which ciphertext blocks are affected (assume the same IV is used)?

(b) In CBC-mode decryption, if a single bit of the ciphertext is changed, which plaintext blocks are affected?

8.5. Prove that CPA$ security for variable-length plaintexts implies CPA security for variablelength plaintexts. Where in the proof do you use the fact that $|m_L| = |m_R|$?

8.6. Suppose that instead of applying CBC mode to a block cipher, we apply it to one-time pad. In other words, we replace every occurrence of $F(k,\star)$ with $k \oplus \star$ in the code for CBC encryption. Show that the result does not have CPA security. Describe a distinguisher and compute its advantage.

8.7. Prove that there is an attacker that runs in time $O(2^{\lambda/2})$ and that can break CPA security of CBC mode encryption with constant probability.

8.8. Below are several block cipher modes for encryption, applied to a PRP F with blocklength blen $= \lambda$. For each of the modes:

- Describe the corresponding decryption procedure.
- Show that the mode does not have CPA-security. That means describe a distinguisher and compute its advantage.

(a)

$$\begin{array}{l} \underline{\text{Enc}(k, m_1 \| \cdots \| m_\ell):} \\ \quad r_0 \leftarrow \{0,1\}^\lambda \\ \quad c_0 := r_0 \\ \quad \text{for } i = 1 \text{ to } \ell: \\ \quad\quad r_i := F(k, m_i) \\ \quad\quad c_i := r_i \oplus r_{i-1} \\ \quad \text{return } c_0 \| \cdots \| c_\ell \end{array}$$

(b)

$$\begin{array}{l} \underline{\text{Enc}(k, m_1 \| \cdots \| m_\ell):} \\ \quad c_0 \leftarrow \{0,1\}^\lambda \\ \quad \text{for } i = 1 \text{ to } \ell: \\ \quad\quad c_i := F(k, m_i) \oplus c_{i-1} \\ \quad \text{return } c_0 \| \cdots \| c_\ell \end{array}$$

(c)

$$\begin{array}{l} \underline{\text{Enc}(k, m_1 \| \cdots \| m_\ell):} \\ \quad c_0 \leftarrow \{0,1\}^\lambda \\ \quad m_0 := c_0 \\ \quad \text{for } i = 1 \text{ to } \ell: \\ \quad\quad c_i := F(k, m_i) \oplus m_{i-1} \\ \quad \text{return } c_0 \| \cdots \| c_\ell \end{array}$$

(d)

$$\begin{array}{l} \underline{\text{Enc}(k, m_1 \| \cdots \| m_\ell):} \\ \quad c_0 \leftarrow \{0,1\}^\lambda \\ \quad r_0 := c_0 \\ \quad \text{for } i = 1 \text{ to } \ell: \\ \quad\quad r_i := r_{i-1} \oplus m_i \\ \quad\quad c_i := F(k, r_i) \\ \quad \text{return } c_0 \| \cdots \| c_\ell \end{array}$$

Mode (a) is similar to CBC, except the xor happens after, rather than before, the block cipher application. Mode (c) is essentially the same as CBC decryption.

8.9. Suppose you observe a CBC ciphertext and two of its blocks happen to be identical. What can you deduce about the plaintext? State some non-trivial property of the plaintext that doesn't depend on the encryption key.

8.10. The CPA\$-security proof for CBC encryption has a slight complication compared to the proof of OFB encryption. Recall that an important part of the proof is arguing that all inputs to the PRF are distinct.

In OFB, outputs of the PRF were fed directly into the PRF as inputs. The adversary had no influence over this process, so it wasn't so bad to argue that all PRF inputs were distinct (with probability negligibly close to 1).

By contrast, CBC mode takes an output block from the PRF, xor's it with a plaintext block (which is after all chosen by the adversary), and uses the result as input to the next PRF call. This means we have to be a little more careful when arguing that CBC mode gives distinct inputs to all PRF calls (with probability negligibly close to 1).

(a) Prove that the following two libraries are indistinguishable:

$\mathcal{L}_{\text{left}}$
SAMP$(m \in \{0,1\}^\lambda)$:
$r \leftarrow \{0,1\}^\lambda$
return r

$\mathcal{L}_{\text{right}}$
$R := \emptyset$
SAMP$(m \in \{0,1\}^\lambda)$:
$r \leftarrow \{r' \in \{0,1\}^\lambda \mid r' \oplus m \notin R\}$
$R := R \cup \{r \oplus m\}$
return r

(b) Using part (a), and the security of the underlying PRF, prove the CPA\$-security of CBC mode.

Note: Appreciate how important it is that the adversary chooses plaintext block m before "seeing" the output r from the PRF (which is included in the ciphertext).

⋆ 8.11. Prove that CTR mode achieves CPA\$ security.

8.12. Let F be a secure PRF with out $=$ in $= \lambda$ and let $F^{(2)}$ denote the function $F^{(2)}(k,r) = F(k,F(k,r))$.

(a) Prove that $F^{(2)}$ is also a secure PRF.

(b) What if F is a secure PRP with blocklength blen? Is $F^{(2)}$ also a secure PRP?

8.13. This question refers to the nonce-based notion of CPA security.

(a) Show a definition for CPA\$ security that incorporates both the nonce-based syntax of Section 7.1 and the variable-length plaintexts of Section 8.2.

(b) Show that CBC mode not secure as a nonce-based scheme (where the IV is used as a nonce).

(c) Show that CTR mode is not secure as a nonce-based scheme (where the IV is used as a nonce). Note that if we restrict (randomized) CTR mode to a single plaintext block, we get the CPA-secure scheme of Construction 7.4, which is is secure as a nonce-based scheme. The attack must therefore use the fact that plaintexts can be longer than one block. (Does the attack in part (b) work with single-block plaintexts?)

8.14. One way to convert a randomized-IV-based construction into a nonce-based construction is called the synthetic IV approach.

(a) The synthetic-IV (SIV) approach applied to CBC mode is shown below. Prove that it is CPA/CPA$ secure as a nonce-based scheme (refer to the security definitions from the previous problem):

$$\begin{array}{l}
\underline{\text{SIV-CBC.Enc}\Big((k_1,k_2),v,m_1\|\cdots\|m_\ell\Big):}\\
c_0 := F(k_1,v)\\
\text{for } i=1 \text{ to } \ell:\\
\quad c_i := F(k_2, m_i \oplus c_{i-1})\\
\text{return } c_0\|c_1\|\cdots\|c_\ell
\end{array}$$

Instead of chosing a random IV c_0, it is generated deterministically from the nonce v using the block cipher F. In your proof, you can use the fact that randomized CBC mode has CPA$ security, and that F is also a secure PRF.

(b) It is important that the SIV construction uses two keys for different purposes. Suppose that we instead used the same key throughout:

$$\begin{array}{l}
\underline{\text{BadSIV-CBC.Enc}(k,v,m_1\|\cdots\|m_\ell):}\\
c_0 := F(k,v)\\
\text{for } i=1 \text{ to } \ell:\\
\quad c_i := F(k, m_i \oplus c_{i-1})\\
\text{return } c_0\|c_1\|\cdots\|c_\ell
\end{array}$$

Show that the resulting scheme does not have CPA$ security (in the nonce-based sense). Ignore the complication of padding, and only consider plaintexts that are a multiple of the blocklength. Describe a successful distinguisher and compute its advantage.

(c) For randomized encryption, it is necessary to include the IV in the ciphertext; otherwise the receiver cannot decrypt. In the nonce-based setting we assume that the receiver knows the correct nonce (e.g., from some out-of-band communication). With that in mind, we could modify the scheme from part (b) to remove c_0, since the receiver could reconstruct it anyway from v.

Show that even with this modification, the scheme still fails to be CPA-secure under the nonce-based definition.

8.15. Implementers are sometimes cautious about IVs in block cipher modes and may attempt to "protect" them. One idea for protecting an IV is to prevent it from directly appearing in the ciphertext. The modified CBC encryption below sends the IV through the block cipher before including it in the ciphertext:

$$\begin{array}{l}\underline{\text{Enc}(k, m_1 \| \cdots \| m_\ell):}\\ \quad c_0 \leftarrow \{0,1\}^{\text{blen}}\\ c_0' := F(k, c_0)\\ \text{for } i = 1 \text{ to } \ell:\\ c_i := F(k, m_i \oplus c_{i-1})\\ \text{return } c_0' \| c_1 \| \cdots \| c_\ell\end{array}$$

This ciphertext can be decrypted by first computing $c_0 := F^{-1}(k, c_0')$ and then doing usual CBC decryption on $c_0 \| \cdots \| c_\ell$.

Show that this new scheme is not CPA-secure (under the traditional definitions for randomized encryption).

8.16. Suppose a bad implementation leads to two ciphertexts being encrypted with the same IV, rather than a random IV each time.

(a) Characterize as thoroughly as you can what information is leaked about the plaintexts when CBC mode was used and an IV is repeated.

(b) Characterize as thoroughly as you can what information is leaked about the plaintexts when CTR mode was used and an IV is repeated.

8.17. Describe how to extend CTR and OFB modes to deal with plaintexts of arbitrary length (without using padding). Why is it so much simpler than CBC ciphertext stealing?

8.18. The following technique for ciphertext stealing in CBC was proposed in the 1980s and was even adopted into commercial products. Unfortunately, it's insecure.

Suppose the final plaintext block m_ℓ is blen $-j$ bits long. Rather than padding the final block with zeroes, it is padded with the last j bits of ciphertext block $c_{\ell-1}$. Then the padded block m_ℓ is sent through the PRP to produce the final ciphertext block c_ℓ. Since the final j bits of $c_{\ell-1}$ are recoverable from c_ℓ, they can be discarded.

If the final block of plaintext is already blen bits long, then standard CBC mode is used.

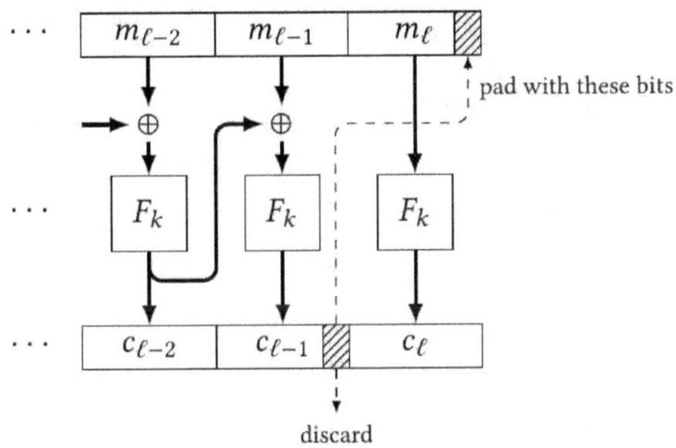

Show that the scheme does not satisfy CPA$ security. Describe a distinguisher and compute its advantage.

8.19. Prove that any CPA-secure encryption remains CPA-secure when augmented by padding the input.

8.20. Prove that CBC with ciphertext stealing has CPA$ security. You may use the fact that CBC mode has CPA$ security when restricted to plaintexts whose length is an exact multiple of the blocklength (i.e., CBC mode without padding or ciphertext stealing).

8.21. Propagating CBC (PCBC) mode refers to the following variant of CBC mode:

$\text{Enc}(k, m_1 \| \cdots \| m_\ell)$:
- $c_0 \leftarrow \{0,1\}^{blen}$;
- $m_0 := 0^{blen}$
- for $i = 1$ to ℓ:
  - $c_i := F(k, m_i \oplus c_{i-1} \oplus m_{i-1})$
- return $c_0 \| c_1 \| \cdots \| c_\ell$

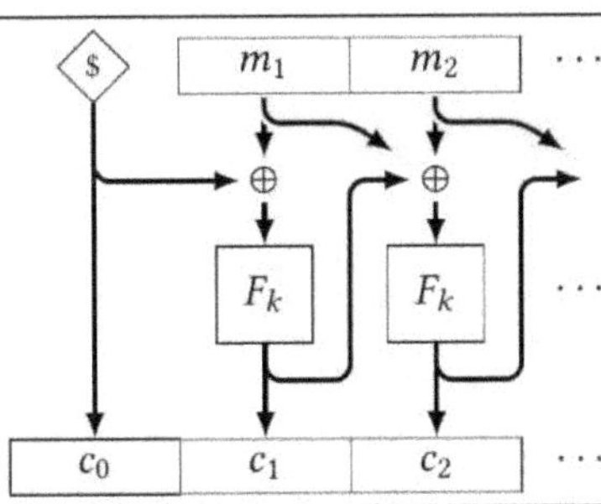

(a) Describe PCBC decryption.

(b) Assuming that standard CBC mode has CPA \$-security (for plaintexts that are exact multiple of the block length), prove that PCBC mode also has CPA\$-security (for the same plaintext space).

(c) Consider the problem of adapting CBC ciphertext stealing to PCBC mode. Suppose the final plaintext block m_ℓ has blen $-j$ bits, and we pad it with the final j bits of the previous plaintext block $m_{\ell-1}$. Show that discarding the last j bits of $c_{\ell-1}$ still allows for correct decryption and results in CPA\$ security.

(d) Suppose the final plaintext block is padded using the final j bits of the previous ciphertext block $c_{\ell-1}$. Although correct decryption is still possible, the construction is no longer secure. Show an attack violating the CPA\$-security of this construction. Why doesn't the proof approach from part (c) work?

Chapter 9

Chosen Ciphertext Attacks

In this chapter we discuss the limitations of the CPA security definition. In short, the CPA security definition considers only the information leaked to the adversary by honestlygenerated ciphertexts. It does not, however, consider what happens when an adversary is allowed to inject its own maliciously crafted ciphertexts into an honest system. If that happens, then even a CPA-secure encryption scheme can fail in spectacular ways. We begin by seeing such an example of spectacular and surprising failure, called a padding oracle attack:

9.1 Padding Oracle Attacks

Imagine a webserver that receives CBC-encrypted ciphertexts for processing. When receiving a ciphertext, the webserver decrypts it under the appropriate key and then checks whether the plaintext has valid X. 923 padding (Section 8.4).

Importantly, suppose that the observable behavior of the webserver changes depending on whether the padding is valid. You can imagine that the webserver gives a special error message in the case of invalid padding. Or, even more cleverly (but still realistic), the difference in response time when processing a ciphertext with invalid padding is enough to allow the attack to work. [1] The mechanism for learning padding validity is not important what is important is simply the fact that an attacker has some way to determine whether a ciphertext encodes a plaintext with valid padding. No matter how the attacker comes by this information, we say that the attacker has access to a padding oracle, which gives the same information as the following subroutine:

```
PADDINGORACLE( $c$ ):
$m:=\operatorname{Dec}(k, c)$
return validpad( $m$ )
```

We call this a padding oracle because it answers only one specific kind of question about the input. In this case, the answer that it gives is always a single boolean value.

It does not seem like a padding oracle is leaking useful information, and that there is no cause for concern. Surprisingly, we can show that an attacker who doesn't know the encryption key k can use a padding oracle alone to decrypt any ciphertext of its choice! This is true no matter what else the webserver does. As long as it leaks this one bit of information on ciphertexts that the attacker can choose, it might as well be leaking everything.

Malleability of CBC Encryption

Recall the definition of CBC decryption. If the ciphertext is $c = c_0 \cdots c_\ell$ then the i th plaintext block is computed as:

$$m_i := F^{-1}(k, c_i) \oplus c_{i-1}.$$

From this we can deduce two important facts:

- Two consecutive blocks (c_{i-1}, c_i) taken in isolation are a valid encryption of m_i. Looking ahead, this fact allows the attacker to focus on decrypting a single block at a time.
- xoring a ciphertext block with a known value (say, x) has the effect of xoring the corresponding plaintext block by the same value. In other words, for all x, the ciphertext ($c_{i-1} \oplus x, c_i$) decrypts to $m_i \oplus x$:

$$\mathrm{Dec}\big(k, (c_{i-1} \oplus x, c_i)\big) = F^{-1}(k, c_i) \oplus (c_{i-1} \oplus x) = (F^{-1}(k, c_i) \oplus c_{i-1}) \oplus x = m_i \oplus x.$$

If we send such a ciphertext ($c_{i-1} \oplus x, c_i$) to the padding oracle, we would therefore learn whether $m_i \oplus x$ is a (single block) with valid padding. Instead of thinking in terms of padding, it might be best to think of the oracle as telling you whether $m_i \oplus x$ ends in one of the suffixes 01,0002,000003, etc.

By carefully choosing different values x and asking questions of this form to the padding oracle, we will show how it is possible to learn all of m_i. We summarize the capability so far with the following subroutine:

```
// suppose c encrypts an (unknown) plaintext m_1 || ··· ||m_ℓ
// does m_i ⊕ x end in one of the valid pading strings?

CHECKXOR(c, i, x):
  return PADDINGORACLE(c_{i-1} ⊕ x, c_i)
```

Given a ciphertext c that encrypts an unknown message m, we can see that an adversary can generate another ciphertext whose contents are related to m in a predictable way. This property of an encryption scheme is called malleability.

Learning the Last Byte of a Block

We now show how to use the checkxor subroutine to determine the last byte of a plaintext block m. There are two cases to consider, depending on the contents of m. The attacker does not initially know which case holds:

For the first (and easier) of the two cases, suppose the second-to-last byte of m is nonzero. We will try every possible byte b and ask whether $m \oplus b$ has valid padding. Since m is a block and b is a single byte, when we write $m \oplus b$ we mean that b is extended on the left with zeroes. Since the second-to-last byte of m (and hence $m \oplus b$) is nonzero, only one of these possibilities will have valid padding - the one in which $m \oplus b$ ends in byte 01. Therefore, if b is the candidate byte that succeeds (i.e., $m \oplus b$ has valid padding) then the last byte of m must be $b \oplus 01$.

Example *Using LEARNLASTBYTE to learn the last byte of a plaintext block:*

For the other case, suppose the second-to-last byte of m is zero. Then $m \oplus b$ will have valid padding for several candidate values of b :

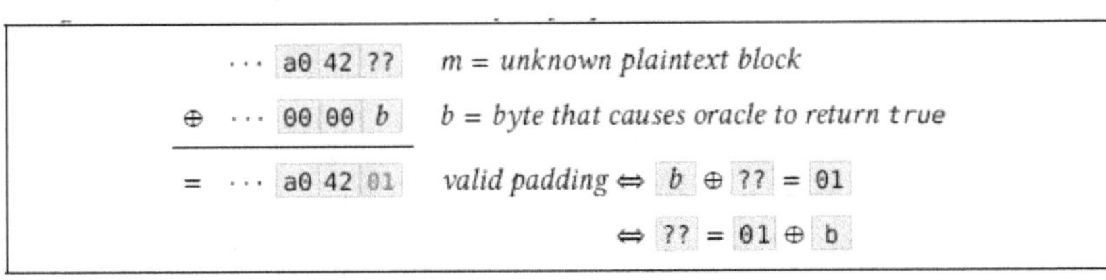

Example Using learnlastbyte to learn the last byte of a plaintext block:

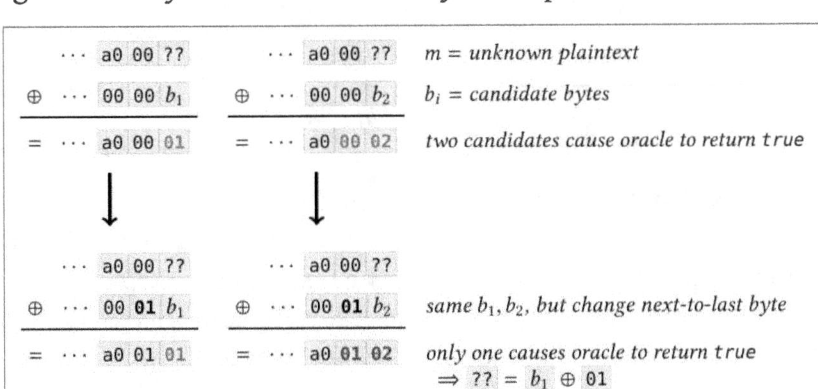

Whenever more than one candidate b value yields valid padding, we know that the second-to-last byte of m is zero (in fact, by counting the number of successful candidates, we can know exactly how many zeroes precede the last byte of m).

If the second-to-last byte of m is zero, then the second-to-last byte of $m \oplus 01b$ is nonzero. The only way for both strings $m \oplus 01b$ and $m \oplus b$ to have valid padding is when $m \oplus b$ ends in byte `01` . We can re-try all of the successful candidate b values again, this time with an extra nonzero byte in front. There will be a unique candidate b that is successful in both rounds, and this will tell us that the last byte of m is $b \oplus 01$.

The overall approach for learning the last byte of a plaintext block is summarized in the learnlastbyte subroutine in Figure 9.1. The set B contains the successful candidate bytes from the first round. There are at most 16 elements in B after the first round, since there are only 16 valid possibilities for the last byte of a properly padded block. In the worst case, learnlastbyte makes $256 + 16 = 272$ calls to the padding oracle (via checkxor).

Learning Other Bytes of a Block

Once we have learned one of the trailing bytes of a plaintext block, it is slightly easier to learn additional ones. Suppose we know the last 3 bytes of a plaintext block, as in the example below. We would like to use the padding oracle to discover the 4th-to-last byte.

Example Using learnprevbyte to learn the 4th-to-last byte when the last 3 bytes of the block are already known.

	$\cdots$ `?? a0 42 3c`	*m = partially unknown plaintext block*
$\oplus$	$\cdots$ `00 00 00 04`	*p = string ending in* `04`
$\oplus$	$\cdots$ `00 a0 42 3c`	*s = known bytes of m*
$\oplus$	$\cdots$ b `00 00 00`	*y = candidate byte b shifted into place*
$=$	$\cdots$ `00 00 00 04`	*valid padding* $\Leftrightarrow$ `??` $=$ b

Since we know the last 3 bytes of m, we can calculate a string x such that $m \oplus x$ ends in `000004` . Now we can try xor'ing the 4th-to-last byte of $m \oplus x$ with different candidate bytes b, and asking the padding oracle whether the result has valid padding. Valid padding only occurs when the result has `00` in its 4th-to-last byte, and this happens exactly when the 4th-to-last byte of m exactly matches our candidate byte b.

The process is summarized in the learnprevbyte subroutine in Figure 9.1. In the worst case, this subroutine makes 256 queries to the padding oracle.

Putting it all together. We now have all the tools required to decrypt any ciphertext using only the padding oracle. The process is summarized below in the learnall subroutine.

In the worst case, 256 queries to the padding oracle are required to learn each byte of the plaintext. [2] However, in practice the number can be much lower. The example in this section was inspired by a real-life padding oracle attack [3] which includes optimizations that allow an attacker to recover each plaintext byte with only 14 oracle queries on average.

9.2 What Went Wrong?

CBC encryption provides CPA security, so why didn't it save us from padding oracle attacks? How was an attacker able to completely obliterate the privacy of encryption?

1. First, CBC encryption (in fact, every encryption scheme we've seen so far) has a property called malleability. Given an encryption c of an unknown plaintext m, it is possible to generate another ciphertext c' whose contents are related to m in a predictable way. In the case of CBC encryption, if ciphertext $c_0 \| \cdots \| c_\ell$ encrypts a plaintext $m_1 \| \cdots \| m_\ell$, then ciphertext $(c_{i-1} \oplus x, c_i)$ encrypts the related plaintext $m_i \oplus x$.

In short, if an encryption scheme is malleable, then it allows information contained in one ciphertext to be "transferred" to another ciphertext.

2. Second, you may have noticed that the CPA security definition makes no mention of the Dec algorithm. The Dec algorithm shows up in our definition for correctness, but it is nowhere to be found in the $\mathcal{L}_{\text{cpa-}\star}$ libraries. Decryption has no impact on CPA security!

But the padding oracle setting involved the Dec algorithm - in particular, the adversary was allowed to see some information about the result of Dec applied to adversarially-chosen ciphertexts. Because of that, the CPA security definition does not capture the padding oracle attack scenario.

The bottom line is: give an attacker a malleable encryption scheme and access to any partial information related to decryption, and he/she can get information to leak out in surprising ways. As the padding-oracle attack demonstrates, even if only a single bit of information (i.e., the answer to a yes/no question about a plaintext) is leaked about the result of decryption, this is frequently enough to extract the entire plaintext.

```
CHECKXOR(c, i, x):
  // if c encrypts (unknown)
  // plaintext m_1 ··· m_ℓ; then
  // does m_i ⊕ x (by itself)
  // have valid padding?
  return PADDINGORACLE(c_{i-1} ⊕ x, c_i)

LEARNLASTBYTE(c, i):
  // deduce the last byte of
  // plaintext block m_i
  B := ∅
  for b = 00 to ff:
    if CHECKXOR(c, i, b):
      B := B ∪ {b}
  if |B| = 1:
    b := only element of B
    return b ⊕ 01
  else:
    for each b ∈ B:
      if CHECKXOR(c, i, 01 b ):
        return b ⊕ 01

LEARNPREVBYTE(c, i, s):
  // knowing that m_i ends in s,
  // find rightmost unknown
  // byte of m_i
  p := |s| + 1
  for b = 00 to ff:
    y := b 00 ··· 00   (|s| bytes of 00)
    if CHECKXOR(c, i, p ⊕ s ⊕ y):
      return b

LEARNBLOCK(c, i):
  // learn entire plaintext block m_i
  s := LEARNLASTBYTE(c, i)
  do 15 times:
    b := LEARNPREVBYTE(c, i, s)
    s := b||s
  return s

LEARNALL(c):
  // learn entire plaintext m_1 ··· m_ℓ
  m := ϵ
  ℓ := number of non-IV blocks in c
  for i = 1 to ℓ:
    m := m||LEARNBLOCK(c, i)
  return m
```

Figure 9.1: Summary of padding oracle attack.

If we want security even under the padding-oracle scenario, we need a better security definition and encryption schemes that achieve it. That's what the rest of this chapter is about.

Discussion

- Is this a realistic concern? You may wonder whether this whole situation is somewhat contrived just to give cryptographers harder problems to solve. That was probably a common attitude towards the security definitions introduced in this chapter. However, in 1998, Daniel Bleichenbacher demonstrated a devastating attack against early versions of the SSL protocol. By presenting millions of carefully crafted ciphertexts to a webserver, an attacker could eventually recover arbitrary SSL session keys.

- In practice, it is hard to make the external behavior of a server not depend on the result of decryption. This makes CPA security rather fragile in the real world. In the case of padding oracle attacks, mistakes in implementation can lead to different error messages for invalid padding. In other cases, even an otherwise careful implementation can provide a padding oracle through a timing side-channel (if the server's response time is different for valid/invalid padded plaintexts).

- As we will see, it is in fact possible to provide security in these kinds of settings, and with low additional overhead. These days there is rarely a good excuse for using encryption which is only CPA-secure.
- Padding is in the name of the attack. But padding is not the culprit. The culprit is using a (merely) CPA-secure encryption scheme while allowing some information to leak about the result of decryption. The exercises expand on this idea further.
- If padding is added to only the last block of the plaintext, how can this attack recover the entire plaintext? This common confusion is another reason to not place so much blame on the padding scheme. A padding oracle has the following behavior: "give me an encryption of $m_1 \| \cdots \| m_\ell$ and I'll tell you some information about m_ℓ (whether it ends with a certain suffix)." Indeed, the padding oracle checks only the last block. However, CBC mode has the property that if you have an encryption of $m_1 \| \cdots \| m_\ell$, then you can easily construct a different ciphertext that encrypts $m_1 \| \cdots \| m_{\ell-1}$. If you send this ciphertext to the padding oracle, you will get information about $m_{\ell-1}$. By modifying the ciphertext (via the malleability of CBC), you give different plaintext blocks the chance to be the "last block" that the padding oracle looks at.
- The attack seems superficially like brute force, but it is not: The attack makes 256 queries per byte of plaintext, so it costs about 256ℓ queries for a plaintext of ℓ bytes. Brute-forcing the entire plaintext would cost 256^ℓ since that's how many ℓ-byte plaintexts there are. So the attack is exponentially better than brute force. The lesson is: brute-forcing small pieces at a time is much better then brute-forcing the entire thing.

9.3 Defining CCA Security

Our goal now is to develop a new security definition - one that considers an adversary that can construct malicious ciphertexts and observe the effects caused by their decryption. We will start with the basic approach of CPA security, with left and right libraries that differ only in which of two plaintexts they encrypt.

In a typical system, an adversary might be able to learn only some specific partial information about the Dec process. In the padding oracle attack, the adversary was able to learn only whether the result of decryption had valid padding.

However, we are trying to come up with a security definition that is useful no matter how the encryption scheme is deployed. How can we possibly anticipate every kind of partial information that might make its way to the adversary in every possible usage of the encryption scheme? The safest choice is to be as pessimistic as possible, as long as we end up with a security notion that we can actually achieve in the end. So let's just allow the adversary to totally decrypt arbitrary ciphertexts of its choice. In other words, if we can guarantee security when the adversary has full information about decrypted ciphertexts, then we certainly have security when the adversary learns only partial information about decrypted ciphertexts (as in a typical real-world system).

But this presents a significant problem. An adversary can do $c^* := \text{eavesdrop}(m_L, m_R)$ to obtain a challenge ciphertext, and then immediately ask for that ciphertext c^* to be decrypted. This will obviously reveal to the adversary whether it is linked to the left or right library.

So, simply providing unrestricted Dec access to the adversary cannot lead to a reasonable security definition (it is a security definition that can never be satisfied). The simplest way to patch this obvious problem with the definition is to allow the adversary to ask for the decryption of any ciphertext, except those produced in response to eavesdrop queries. In doing so, we arrive at the final security definition: security against chosenciphertext attacks, or CCA-security:

Definition 9.1 (CCA security) *Let Σ be an encryption scheme. We say that Σ has security against chosen-ciphertext attacks (CCA security) if $\mathcal{L}^{\Sigma}_{cca\text{-}L} \approx \mathcal{L}^{\Sigma}_{cca\text{-}R}$, where:*

$\mathcal{L}^{\Sigma}_{\text{cca-L}}$

```
k ← Σ.KeyGen
S := ∅

EAVESDROP(m_L, m_R ∈ Σ.M):
  if |m_L| ≠ |m_R| return err
  c := Σ.Enc(k, m_L)
  S := S ∪ {c}
  return c

DECRYPT(c ∈ Σ.C):
  if c ∈ S return err
  return Σ.Dec(k, c)
```

$\mathcal{L}^{\Sigma}_{\text{cca-R}}$

```
k ← Σ.KeyGen
S := ∅

EAVESDROP(m_L, m_R ∈ Σ.M):
  if |m_L| ≠ |m_R| return err
  c := Σ.Enc(k, m_R)
  S := S ∪ {c}
  return c

DECRYPT(c ∈ Σ.C):
  if c ∈ S return err
  return Σ.Dec(k, c)
```

In this definition, the set $\mathcal{S}$ keeps track of the ciphertexts that have been generated by the eavesdrop subroutine. The decrypt subroutine refuses to decrypt these ciphertexts, but will gladly decrypt any other ciphertext of the adversary's choice.

An Example

The padding oracle attack already demonstrates that CBC mode does not provide security in the presence of chosen ciphertext attacks. But that attack was quite complicated since the adversary was restricted to learn just 1 bit of information at a time about a decrypted ciphertext. An attack against full CCA security can be much more direct, since the adversary has full access to decrypted ciphertexts.

Example: Consider the adversary below attacking the CCA security of CBC mode (with block length blen)

$\mathcal{A}$
$c = c_0 \| c_1 \| c_2 :=$ EAVESDROP$(0^{2blen}, 1^{2blen})$ $m :=$ DECRYPT$(c_0 \| c_1)$ return $m \stackrel{?}{=} 0^{blen}$

It can easily be verified that this adversary achieves advantage 1 distinguishing $\mathcal{L}_{cca\text{-}L}$ from $\mathcal{L}_{cca-R}$. The attack uses the fact (also used in the padding oracle attack) that if $c_0 \| c_1 \| c_2$ encrypts $m_1 \| m_2$, then $c_0 \| c_1$ encrypts m_1. To us, it is obvious that ciphertext $c_0 \| c_1$ is related to $c_0 \| c_1 \| c_2$. Unfortunately for CBC mode, the security definition is not very clever - since $c_0 \| c_1$ is simply different than $c_0 \| c_1 \| c_2$, the DECRYPT subroutine happily decrypts it.

Example *Perhaps unsurprisingly, there are many very simple ways to catastrophically attack the CCA security of CBC-mode encryption. Here are some more (where $\bar{x}$ denotes the result of flipping every bit in x):*

$\mathcal{A}'$
$c_0 \| c_1 \| c_2 :=$ EAVESDROP$(0^{2blen}, 1^{2blen})$ $m :=$ DECRYPT$(c_0 \| c_1 \| \overline{c_2})$ if m begins with 0^{blen} return 1 else return 0

$\mathcal{A}''$
$c_0 \| c_1 \| c_2 :=$ EAVESDROP$(0^{2blen}, 1^{2blen})$ $m :=$ DECRYPT$(\overline{c_0} \| c_1 \| c_2)$ return $m \stackrel{?}{=} 1^{blen} \| 0^{blen}$

The first attack uses the fact that modifying c_2 has no effect on the first plaintext block. The second attack uses the fact that flipping every bit in the IV flips every bit in m_1.

Again, in all of these cases, the decrypt subroutine is being called on a different (but related) ciphertext than the one returned by eavesdrop.

Discussion

So if I use a CCA-secure encryption scheme, I should never decrypt a ciphertext that I encrypted myself?

Remember: when we define the Enc and Dec algorithms of an encryption scheme, we are describing things from the normal user's perspective. As a user of an encryption scheme, you can encrypt and decrypt whatever you like. It would indeed be strange if you encrypted something knowing that it should never be decrypted. What's the point?

The security definition describes things from the attacker's perspective. The $\mathcal{L}_{\text{cca-}\star}$ libraries tell us what are the circumstances under which the encryption scheme provides security? They say (roughly):

> an attacker can't tell what's inside a ciphertext c^*, even if she has some partial information about that plaintext, even if she had some partial influence over the choice of that plaintext, and even if she is allowed to decrypt any other ciphertext she wants.

Of course, if a real-world system allows an attacker to learn the result of decrypting c^*, then by definition the attacker learns what's inside that ciphertext.

CCA security is deeply connected with the concept of malleability. Malleability means that, given a ciphertext that encrypts an unknown plaintext m, it is possible to generate a different ciphertext that encrypts a plaintext that is related to m in a predictable way. For example:

- If $c_0\|c_1\|c_2$ is a CBC encryption of $m_1\|m_2$, then $c_0\|c_1$ is a CBC encryption of m_1.
- If $c_0\|c_1\|c_2$ is a CBC encryption of $m_1\|m_2$, then $c_0\|c_1\|c_2\|0^{\text{blen}}$ is a CBC encryption of some plaintext that begins with $m_1\|m_2$.
- If $c_0\|c_1$ is a CBC encryption of m_1, then $(c_0 \oplus x)\|c_1$ is a CBC encryption of $m_1 \oplus x$.

Note from the second example that we don't need to know exactly the relationship between the old and new ciphertexts.

If an encryption scheme is malleable, then a typical attack against its CCA security would work as follows:

1. Request an encryption c of some plaintext.
2. Applying the malleability of the scheme, modify c to some other ciphertext c'.
3. Ask for c' to be decrypted.

Since $c' \neq c$, the security library allows c' to be decrypted. The malleability of the scheme says that the contents of c' should be related to the contents of c. In other words, seeing the contents of c' should allow the attacker to determine what was initially encrypted in c.

Pseudorandom Ciphertexts

We can also modify the pseudorandom-ciphertexts security definition (CPA$ security) in a similar way:

Definition 9.2 *Let Σ be an encryption scheme. We say that Σ has pseudorandom ciphertexts in the (CCA$ security) presence of chosen-ciphertext attacks (CCA$ security) if* $\mathcal{L}^{\Sigma}_{cca\$real} \approx \mathcal{L}^{\Sigma}_{cca\$\ s=rand}$, *where:*

$\mathcal{L}^{\Sigma}_{\text{cca\$-real}}$	$\mathcal{L}^{\Sigma}_{\text{cca\$-rand}}$
$k \leftarrow \Sigma.\text{KeyGen}$ $\mathcal{S} := \emptyset$	$k \leftarrow \Sigma.\text{KeyGen}$ $\mathcal{S} := \emptyset$

CTXT($m \in \Sigma.\mathcal{M}$):
  $c := \Sigma.\text{Enc}(k, m)$
  $\mathcal{S} := \mathcal{S} \cup \{c\}$
  return c
	CTXT($m \in \Sigma.\mathcal{M}$):
	  $c \leftarrow \Sigma.\mathcal{C}(\lvert m\rvert)$
	  $\mathcal{S} := \mathcal{S} \cup \{c\}$
	  return c

DECRYPT($c \in \Sigma.\mathcal{C}$):
  if $c \in \mathcal{S}$ return err
  return $\Sigma.\text{Dec}(k, c)$
	DECRYPT($c \in \Sigma.\mathcal{C}$):
	  if $c \in \mathcal{S}$ return err
	  return $\Sigma.\text{Dec}(k, c)$

Just like for CPA security, if a scheme has CCA$ security, then it also has CCA security, but not vice-versa. See the exercises.

9.4 A Simple CCA-Secure Scheme

Recall the definition of a strong pseudorandom permutation (PRP) (Definition 6.13). A strong PRP is one that is indistinguishable from a randomly chosen permutation, even to an adversary that can make both forward (i.e., to F) and reverse (i.e., to F^{-1}) queries.

This concept has some similarity to the definition of CCA security, in which the adversary can make queries to both Enc and its inverse Dec. Indeed, a strong PRP can be used to construct a CCA-secure encryption scheme in a natural way:

Construction 9.3 *Let F be a pseudorandom permutation with block length blen $= n + \lambda$. Define the following encryption scheme with message space $\mathcal{M} = \{0,1\}^n$:*

KeyGen:	Enc(k, m):	Dec(k, c):
$k \leftarrow \{0,1\}^\lambda$	$r \leftarrow \{0,1\}^\lambda$	$v := F^{-1}(k, c)$
return k	return $F(k, m \| r)$	return first n bits of v

In this scheme, m is encrypted by appending a random value r to it, then applying a PRP. While this scheme is conceptually quite simple, it is generally not used in practice since it requires a block cipher with a fairly large block size, and these are rarely encountered.

We can informally reason about the security of this scheme as follows:

- Imagine an adversary linked to one of the CCA libraries. As long as the random value r does not repeat, all inputs to the PRP are distinct. The guarantee of a pseudorandom function/permutation is that its outputs (which are the ciphertexts in this scheme) will therefore all look independently uniform.

- The CCA library prevents the adversary from asking for c to be decrypted, if c was itself generated by the library. For any other value c' that the adversary asks to be decrypted, the guarantee of a strong PRP is that the result will look independently random. In particular, the result will not depend on the choice of plaintexts used to generate challenge ciphertexts. Since this choice of plaintexts is the only difference between the two CCA libraries, these decryption queries (intuitively) do not help the adversary.

We now prove the CCA security of Construction 9.3 formally:

Claim 9.4 *If F is a strong PRP (Definition 6.13) then Construction 9.3 has CCA$ security (and therefore CCA security).*

Proof As usual, we prove the claim in a sequence of hybrids.

$\mathcal{L}^{\Sigma}_{\text{cca\$-real}}$:

The starting point is $\mathcal{L}^{\Sigma}_{\text{cca\$-real}}$, as expected, where Σ refers to Construction 9.3.

$\mathcal{L}^{\Sigma}_{\text{cca\$-real}}$:

$\mathcal{L}^{\Sigma}_{\text{cca\$-real}}$
$k \leftarrow \{0,1\}^{\lambda}$ $\mathcal{S} := \emptyset$

CTXT(m):
  $r \leftarrow \{0,1\}^{\lambda}$
  $c := F(k, m \Vert r)$
  $\mathcal{S} := \mathcal{S} \cup \{c\}$
  return c

DECRYPT($c \in \Sigma.\mathcal{C}$):
  if $c \in \mathcal{S}$ return err
  return first n bits of $F^{-1}(k, c)$

We have applied the strong PRP security (Definition 6.13) of F, skipping some standard intermediate steps. We factored out all invocations of F and F^{-1} in terms of the $\mathcal{L}_{\text{sprp-real}}$ library, replaced that library with $\mathcal{L}_{\text{sprp-rand}}$, and finally inlined it.

$\mathcal{S} := \emptyset$ T, T_{inv} := empty assoc. arrays

CTXT(m):
  $r \leftarrow \{0,1\}^{\lambda}$
  if $T[m \Vert r]$ undefined:
    $c \leftarrow \{0,1\}^{blen} \setminus T.\text{values}$
    $T[m \Vert r] := c$; $T_{inv}[c] := m \Vert r$
  $c := T[m \Vert r]$
  $\mathcal{S} := \mathcal{S} \cup \{c\}$
  return c

DECRYPT($c \in \Sigma.\mathcal{C}$):
  if $c \in \mathcal{S}$ return err
  if $T_{inv}[c]$ undefined:
    $m \Vert r \leftarrow \{0,1\}^{blen} \setminus T_{inv}.\text{values}$
    $T_{inv}[c] := m \Vert r$; $T[m \Vert r] := c$
  return first n bits of $T_{inv}[c]$

This proof has some subtleties, so it's a good time to stop and think about what needs to be done. To prove CCA$-security, we must reach a hybrid in which the responses of CTXT are uniform. In the current hybrid there are two properties in the way of this goal:

- The ciphertext values c are sampled from $\{0,1\}^{\text{blen}} \setminus T.$ values, rather than $\{0,1\}^{\text{blen}}$.
- When the if-condition in ctxt is false, the return value of ctxt is not a fresh random value but an old, repeated one. This happens when $T[m\|r]$ is already defined. Note that both ctxt and decrypt assign to T, so either one of these subroutines may be the cause of a pre-existing $T[m\|r]$ value.

Perhaps the most subtle fact about our current hybrid is that arguments of ctxt can affect responses from decrypt! In ctxt, the library assigns $m\|r$ to a value $T_{\text{inv}}[c]$. Later calls to decrypt will not read this value directly; these values of c are off-limits due to the guard condition in the first line of decrypt. However, decrypt samples a value from $\{0,1\}^{\text{blen}} \setminus T_{\text{inv}}$ .values, which indeed uses the values $T_{\text{inv}}[c]$. To show CCA $ security, we must remove this dependence of decrypt on previous values given to CTXT

We have added some book-keeping that is not used anywhere. Every time an assignment of the form $T[m\|r]$ happens, we add r to the set $\mathcal{R}$. Looking ahead, we eventually want to ensure that r is chosen so that the if-statement in CTXT is always taken, and the return value of CTXT is always a fresh random value.

```
S := ∅;    R := ∅
T, T_inv := empty assoc. arrays

CTXT(m):
  r ← {0,1}^λ
  if T[m||r] undefined:
    c ← {0,1}^blen \ T.values
    T[m||r] := c; T_inv[c] := m||r
    R := R ∪ {r}
  c := T[m||r]
  S := S ∪ {c}
  return c

DECRYPT(c ∈ Σ.C):
  if c ∈ S return err
  if T_inv[c] undefined:
    m||r ← {0,1}^blen \ T_inv.values
    T_inv[c] := m||r; T[m||r] := c
    R := R ∪ {r}
  return first n bits of T_inv[c]
```

We have applied Lemma 4.12 three separate times. The standard intermediate steps (factor out, swap library, inline) have been skipped, and this shows only the final result.

In ctxt, we've added a restriction to how r is sampled. Looking ahead, sampling r in this way means that the if-statement in CTXT is always taken.

In cTXT, we've removed the restriction in how c is sampled. Since c is the final return value of CTXT, this gets us closer to our goal of this return value being uniformly random.

In DECRYPT, we have removed the restriction in how $m\|r$ is sampled. As described above, this is because T_{inv}.values contains previous arguments of CTXT, and we don't want these arguments to affect the result of DECRYPT in any way.

```
S := ∅;   R := ∅
T, T_inv := empty assoc. arrays

CTXT(m):
  r ← {0,1}^λ \ R
  if T[m||r] undefined:
    c ← {0,1}^blen
    T[m||r] := c; T_inv[c] := m||r
    R := R ∪ {r}
  c := T[m||r]
  S := S ∪ {c}
  return c

DECRYPT(c ∈ Σ.C):
  if c ∈ S return err
  if T_inv[c] undefined:
    m||r ← {0,1}^blen
    T_inv[c] := m||r; T[m||r] := c
    R := R ∪ {r}
  return first n bits of T_inv[c]
```

In the previous hybrid, the if-statement in ctxt is always taken. This is because if $T[m\|r]$ is already defined, then r would already be in $\mathcal{R}$, but we are sampling r to avoid everything in $\mathcal{R}$. We can therefore simply execute the body of the if-statement without actually checking the condition.

```
S := ∅;   R := ∅
T, T_inv := empty assoc. arrays

CTXT(m):
  r ← {0,1}^λ \ R
  c ← {0,1}^blen
  T[m||r] := c; T_inv[c] := m||r
  R := R ∪ {r}
  S := S ∪ {c}
  return c

DECRYPT(c ∈ Σ.C):
  if c ∈ S return err
  if T_inv[c] undefined:
    m||r ← {0,1}^blen
    T_inv[c] := m||r; T[m||r] := c
    R := R ∪ {r}
  return first n bits of T_inv[c]
```

In the previous hybrid, no line of code ever reads from T; they only write to T. It has no effect to remove a line that assigns to T, so we do so in cTXT.

cTXT also writes to $T_{\text{inv}}[c]$, but for a value $c \in \mathcal{S}$. The only line that reads from T_{inv} is in decrypt, but the first line of decrypt prevents it from being reached for such a $c \in \mathcal{S}$. It therefore has no effect to remove this assignment to T_{inv}.

```
S := ∅;   R := ∅
T, T_inv := empty assoc. arrays

CTXT(m):
  r ← {0,1}^λ \ R
  c ← {0,1}^blen
  // T[m||r] := c; T_inv[c] := m||r
  R := R ∪ {r}
  S := S ∪ {c}
  return c

DECRYPT(c ∈ Σ.C):
  if c ∈ S return err
  if T_inv[c] undefined:
    m||r ← {0,1}^blen
    T_inv[c] := m||r; T[m||r] := c
    R := R ∪ {r}
  return first n bits of T_inv[c]
```

Consider all the ways that $\mathcal{R}$ is used in the previous hybrid. The first line of ctxt uses $\mathcal{R}$ to sample r, but then r is subsequently used only to further update $\mathcal{R}$ and nowhere else. Both subroutines use $\mathcal{R}$ only to update the value of $\mathcal{R}$. It has no effect to simply remove all lines that refer to variable $\mathcal{R}$.

```
S := ∅;    // R := ∅
T, T_inv := empty assoc. arrays

CTXT(m):
  // r ← {0,1}^λ \ R
  c ← {0,1}^blen
  // R := R ∪ {r}
  S := S ∪ {c}
  return c

DECRYPT(c ∈ Σ.C):
  if c ∈ S return err
  if T_inv[c] undefined:
    m||r ← {0,1}^blen
    T_inv[c] := m||r; T[m||r] := c
    // R := R ∪ {r}
  return first n bits of T_inv[c]
```

We have applied Lemma 4.12 to the sampling step in decrypt. The standard intermediate steps have been skipped. Now the second if-statement in decrypt exactly matches $\mathcal{L}_{\text{sprp-rand}}$.

```
S := ∅
T, T_inv := empty assoc. arrays

CTXT(m):
  c ← {0,1}^blen
  S := S ∪ {c}
  return c

DECRYPT(c ∈ Σ.C):
  if c ∈ S return err
  if T_inv[c] undefined:
    m||r ← {0,1}^blen \ T_inv.values
    T_inv[c] := m||r; T[m||r] := c
  return first n bits of T_inv[c]
```

We have applied the strong PRP security of F to replace $\mathcal{L}_{\text{sprp-rand}}$ with $\mathcal{L}_{\text{sprp-real}}$. The standard intermediate steps have been skipped. The result is $\mathcal{L}_{\text{cca\$-rand}}$.

$\mathcal{L}^{\Sigma}_{\text{cca\$-rand}}$:

```
L^Σ_cca$-rand
------------------------------
k ← {0,1}^λ
S := ∅

CTXT(m):
  c ← {0,1}^blen
  S := S ∪ {c}
  return c

DECRYPT(c ∈ Σ.C):
  if c ∈ S return err
  return first n bits of F^{-1}(k, c)
```

We showed that $\mathcal{L}^{\Sigma}_{\text{cca\$-real}} \approx \mathcal{L}^{\Sigma}_{\text{cca\$-rand}}$, so the scheme has CCA$ security. □

Exercises

9.1. There is nothing particularly bad about padding schemes. They are only a target because padding is a commonly used structure in plaintexts that is verified at the time of decryption.

A null character is simply the byte 00. We say that a string is properly null terminated if its last character is null, but no other characters are null. Suppose you have access to the following oracle:

```
NULLTERMORACLE(c):
  m := Dec(k, c)
  if m is properly null terminated:
    return true
  else return false
```

Suppose you are given a CTR-mode encryption of an unknown (but properly null terminated) plaintext m^* under unknown key k. Suppose that plaintexts of arbitrary length are supported by truncating the CTR-stream to the appropriate length before xoring with the plaintext.

Show how to completely recover m^* in the presence of this null-termination oracle.

9.2. Show how to completely recover the plaintext of an arbitrary CBC-mode ciphertext in the presence of the following oracle:

```
NULLORACLE(c):
  m := Dec(k, c)
  if m contains a null character:
    return true
  else return false
```

Assume that the victim ciphertext encodes a plaintext that does not use any padding (its plaintext is an exact multiple of the blocklength).

9.3. Show how to perform a padding oracle attack, to decrypt arbitrary messages that use PKCS#7 padding (where all padded strings end with 01,0202,030303, etc.).

9.4. Sometimes encryption is as good as decryption, to an adversary.

(a) Suppose you have access to the following encryption oracle, where s is a secret that is consistent across all calls:

```
ECBORACLE(m):
  // k, s are secret
  return ECB.Enc(k, m||s)
```

Yes, this question is referring to the awful ECB encryption mode (Construction 8.1). Describe an attack that efficiently recovers all of s using access to ecboracle. Assume that if the length of $m\|s$ is not a multiple of the blocklength, then ECB mode will pad it with null bytes.

(b) Now suppose you have access to a CBC encryption oracle, where you can control the IV that is used:

```
CBCORACLE(iv, m):
  // k, s are secret
  return CBC.Enc(k, iv, m||s)
```

Describe an attack that efficiently recovers all of s using access to cbcoracle. As above, assume that $m\|s$ is padded to a multiple of the blocklength in some way. It is possible to carry out the attack no matter what the padding method is, as long as the padding method is known to the adversary.

★ 9.5. Show how a padding oracle (for CBC-mode encryption with X. 923 padding) can be used to generate a valid encryption of any chosen plaintext, under the same (secret) key that the padding oracle uses. In this problem, you are not given access to an encryption subroutine, or any valid ciphertexts - only the padding oracle subroutine.

9.6. Prove formally that CCA$ security implies CCA security.

9.7. Let Σ be an encryption scheme with message space $\{0,1\}^n$ and define Σ^2 to be the following encryption scheme with message space $\{0,1\}^{2n}$:

KeyGen:	Enc(k,m): $c_1 := \Sigma.\mathrm{Enc}(k, m_{\text{left}})$ $c_2 := \Sigma.\mathrm{Enc}(k, m_{\text{right}})$ return (c_1, c_2)	Dec$(k,(c_1,c_2))$: $m_1 := \Sigma.\mathrm{Dec}(k, c_1)$ $m_2 := \Sigma.\mathrm{Dec}(k, c_2)$ if err $\in \{m_1, m_2\}$: return err else return $m_1 \| m_2$

(a) Prove that if Σ has CPA security, then so does Σ^2.

(b) Show that even if Σ has CCA security, Σ^2 does not. Describe a successful distinguisher and compute its distinguishing advantage.

9.8. Show that the following block cipher modes do not have CCA security. For each one, describe a successful distinguisher and compute its distinguishing advantage.

(a) OFB mode

(b) CBC mode

(c) CTR mode

9.9. Show that none of the schemes in Exercise 7.7 have CCA security. For each one, describe a successful distinguisher and compute its distinguishing advantage.

9.10. Let F be a secure block cipher with blocklength λ. Below is an encryption scheme for plaintexts $\mathcal{M} = \{0,1\}^\lambda$. Formally describe its decryption algorithm and show that it does not have CCA security.

$$\begin{array}{ll}
\underline{\text{KeyGen:}} & \underline{\text{Enc}(k,m):} \\
\quad k \leftarrow \{0,1\}^\lambda & \quad r \leftarrow \{0,1\}^\lambda \\
\quad \text{return } k & \quad c_1 := F(k,r) \\
 & \quad c_2 := r \oplus F(k,m) \\
 & \quad \text{return } (c_1, c_2)
\end{array}$$

9.11. Let F be a secure block cipher with blocklength λ. Below is an encryption scheme for plaintexts $\mathcal{M} = \{0,1\}^\lambda$. Formally describe its decryption algorithm and show that it does not have CCA security.

$$\begin{array}{ll}
\underline{\text{KeyGen:}} & \underline{\text{Enc}\big((k_1,k_2),m\big):} \\
\quad k_1 \leftarrow \{0,1\}^\lambda & \quad r \leftarrow \{0,1\}^\lambda \\
\quad k_2 \leftarrow \{0,1\}^\lambda & \quad c_1 := F(k_1,r) \\
\quad \text{return } (k_1,k_2) & \quad c_2 := F(k_1, r \oplus m \oplus k_2) \\
 & \quad \text{return } (c_1, c_2)
\end{array}$$

9.12. Alice has the following idea for a CCA-secure encryption. To encrypt a single plaintext block m, do normal CBC encryption of $0^{\text{blen}} \| m$. To decrypt, do normal CBC decryption but give an error if the first plaintext block is not all zeroes. Her reasoning is:

- The ciphertext has 3 blocks (including the IV). If an adversary tampers with the IV or the middle block of a ciphertext, then the first plaintext block will no longer be all zeroes and the ciphertext is rejected.
- If an adversary tampers with the last block of a ciphertext, then the CBC decryption results in $0^{\text{blen}} \| m'$ where m' is unpredictable from the adversary's point of view. Hence the result of decryption (m') will leak no information about the original m.

More formally, let CBC denote the encryption scheme obtained by using a secure PRF in CBC mode. Below we define an encryption scheme Σ' with message space $\{0,1\}^{\text{blen}}$ and ciphertext space $\{0,1\}^{3\,\text{blen}}$:

Σ'.KeyGen:
$k \leftarrow$ CBC.KeyGen
return k

Σ'.Enc(k, m):
return CBC.Enc$(k, 0^{blen} \| m)$

Σ'.Dec(k, c):
$m_1 \| m_2 :=$ CBC.Dec(k, c)
if $m_1 = 0^{blen}$:
  return m_2
else return err

Show that Σ' does not have CCA security. Describe a distinguisher and compute its distinguishing advantage. What part of Alice's reasoning was not quite right?

9.13. CBC and OFB modes are malleable in very different ways. For that reason, Mallory claims that encrypting a plaintext (independently) with both modes results in CCA security, when the Dec algorithm rejects ciphertexts whose OFB and CBC plaintexts don't match. The reasoning is that it will be hard to tamper with both ciphertexts in a way that achieves the same effect on the plaintext.

Let CBC denote the encryption scheme obtained by using a secure PRF in CBC mode. Let OFB denote the encryption scheme obtained by using a secure PRF in OFB mode. Below we define an encryption scheme Σ' :

Σ'.KeyGen:
$k_{cbc} \leftarrow$ CBC.KeyGen
$k_{ofb} \leftarrow$ OFB.KeyGen
return (k_{cbc}, k_{ofb})

Σ'.Enc$((k_{cbc}, k_{ofb}), m)$:
$c :=$ CBC.Enc(k_{cbc}, m)
$c' :=$ OFB.Enc(k_{ofb}, m)
return (c, c')

Σ'.Dec$((k_{cbc}, k_{ofb}), (c, c'))$:
$m :=$ CBC.Dec(k_{cbc}, c)
$m' :=$ OFB.Dec(k_{ofb}, c')
if $m = m'$:
  return m
else return err

Show that Σ' does not have CCA security. Describe a distinguisher and compute its distinguishing advantage.

9.14. This problem is a generalization of the previous one. Let Σ_1 and Σ_2 be two (possibly different) encryption schemes with the same message space $\mathcal{M}$. Below we define an encryption scheme Σ' :

$\Sigma'.\text{KeyGen}$:	$\Sigma'.\text{Enc}((k_1,k_2),m)$:	$\Sigma'.\text{Dec}((k_1,k_2),(c_1,c_2))$:
$k_1 \leftarrow \Sigma_1.\text{KeyGen}$ $k_2 \leftarrow \Sigma_2.\text{KeyGen}$ return (k_1,k_2)	$c_1 := \Sigma_1.\text{Enc}(k_1,m)$ $c_2 := \Sigma_2.\text{Enc}(k_2,m)$ return (c_1,c_2)	$m_1 := \Sigma_1.\text{Dec}(k_1,c_1)$ $m_2 := \Sigma_2.\text{Dec}(k_2,c_2)$ if $m_1 = m_2$: return m_1 else return err

Show that Σ' does not have CCA security, even if both Σ_1 and Σ_2 have CCA (yes, CCA) security. Describe a distinguisher and compute its distinguishing advantage.

9.15. Consider any padding scheme consisting of subroutines PAD (which adds valid padding to its argument) and validpad (which checks its argument for valid padding and returns true/false). Assume that validpad(pad(x)) = true for all strings x.

Show that if an encryption scheme Σ has CCA security, then the following two libraries are indistinguishable:

$\mathcal{L}^{\Sigma}_{\text{pad-L}}$	$\mathcal{L}^{\Sigma}_{\text{pad-R}}$
$k \leftarrow \Sigma.\text{KeyGen}$	$k \leftarrow \Sigma.\text{KeyGen}$

EAVESDROP($m_L, m_R \in \Sigma.\mathcal{M}$):
  if $\lvert m_L\rvert \neq \lvert m_R\rvert$ return err
  return $\Sigma.\text{Enc}(k, \text{PAD}(m_L))$
	EAVESDROP($m_L, m_R \in \Sigma.\mathcal{M}$):
	  if $\lvert m_L\rvert \neq \lvert m_R\rvert$ return err
	  return $\Sigma.\text{Enc}(k, \text{PAD}(m_R))$

PADDINGORACLE($c \in \Sigma.\mathcal{C}$):
  return VALIDPAD($\Sigma.\text{Dec}(k,c)$)
	PADDINGORACLE($c \in \Sigma.\mathcal{C}$):
	  return VALIDPAD($\Sigma.\text{Dec}(k,c)$)

That is, a CCA-secure encryption scheme hides underlying plaintexts in the presence of padding-oracle attacks.

Note: The distinguisher can even send a ciphertext c obtained from eavesdrop as an argument to paddingoracle. Your proof should somehow account for this when reducing to the CCA security of Σ.

9.16. Show that an encryption scheme Σ has CCA \$ security if and only if the following two libraries are indistinguishable:

$\mathcal{L}^{\Sigma}_{\text{left}}$

$k \leftarrow \Sigma.\text{KeyGen}$

EAVESDROP($m \in \Sigma.\mathcal{M}$):
  return $\Sigma.\text{Enc}(k, m)$

DECRYPT($c \in \Sigma.\mathcal{C}$):
  return $\Sigma.\text{Dec}(k, c)$

$\mathcal{L}^{\Sigma}_{\text{right}}$

$k \leftarrow \Sigma.\text{KeyGen}$
$D :=$ empty assoc. array

EAVESDROP($m \in \Sigma.\mathcal{M}$):
  $c \leftarrow \Sigma.\mathcal{C}(|m|)$
  $D[c] := m$
  return c

DECRYPT($c \in \Sigma.\mathcal{C}$):
  if $D[c]$ exists: return $D[c]$
  else: return $\Sigma.\text{Dec}(k, c)$

Note: In $\mathcal{L}_{\text{left}}$, the adversary can obtain the decryption of any ciphertext via decrypt. In $\mathcal{L}_{\text{right}}$, the decrypt subroutine is "patched" (via D) to give reasonable answers to ciphertexts generated in eavesdrop.

Chapter-10

Message Authentication Codes

The challenge of CCA-secure encryption is dealing with ciphertexts that were generated by an adversary. Imagine there was a way to "certify" that a ciphertext was not adversarially generated - i.e., it was generated by someone who knows the secret key. We could include such a certification in the ciphertext, and the Dec algorithm could raise an error if it asked to decrypt something with invalid certification.

What we are asking for is not to hide the ciphertext but to authenticate it: to ensure that it was generated by someone who knows the secret key. The tool for the job is called a message authentication code. One of the most important applications of a message authentication code is to transform a CPA-secure encryption scheme into a CCA-secure one.

As you read this chapter, keep in mind that privacy and authentication are indeed different properties. It is possible to have one or the other or indeed both simultaneously. But one does not imply the other, and it is crucial to think about them separately.

10.1 Definition

A MAC is like a signature that can be added to a piece of data, which certifies that someone who knows the secret key attests to this particular data. In cryptography, the term "signature" means something specific, and slightly different than a MAC. Instead of calling the output of a MAC algorithm a signature, we call it a "tag" (or, confusingly, just "a MAC").

Our security requirement for a MAC scheme is that only someone with the secret key can generate a valid tag. To check whether a tag is valid, you just recompute the tag for a given message and see whether it matches the claimed tag. This implies that both generating and verifying a MAC tag requires the secret key.

Definition 10.1 *A message authentication code (MAC) scheme for message space $\mathcal{M}$ consists of the fol(MAC scheme) lowing algorithms:*

- *KeyGen: samples a key.*

- *MAC: takes a key k and message $m \in \mathcal{M}$ as input, and outputs a tagt. The MAC algorithm is deterministic.*

Think About Authenticity Properties

Every security definition we've seen so far is about hiding information, so how do we make a formal definition about authenticity?

Before we see the security definition for MACs, let's start with a much simpler (potentially obvious?) statement: "an adversary should not be able to guess a uniformly chosen λ-bit value." We can formalize this idea with the following two libraries:

$\mathcal{L}_{\text{left}}$

$r \leftarrow \{0,1\}^{\lambda}$

GUESS(g):
  return $g \stackrel{?}{=} r$

$\mathcal{L}_{\text{right}}$

GUESS(g):
  return false

The left library allows the calling program to attempt to guess a uniformly chosen "target" string. The right library doesn't even bother to verify the calling program's guess - in fact it doesn't even bother to sample a random target string!

The guess subroutines of these libraries give the same output on nearly all inputs. There is only one input r on which they disagree. If a calling program can manage to find the value r, then it can easily distinguish the libraries. Therefore, by saying that these libraries are indistinguishable, we are really saying that it's hard for an adversary to find/generate this special value! That's the kind of property we want to express.

Indeed, in this case, an adversary who makes q queries to the guess subroutine achieves an advantage of at most $q/2^{\lambda}$. For polynomial-time adversaries, this is a negligible advantage (since q is a polynomial function of λ).

More generally, suppose we have two libraries, and a subroutine in one library checks some condition (and could return either true or false), while in the other library this subroutine always returns false. If the two libraries are indistinguishable, the calling program can't tell whether the library is actually checking the condition or always saying false. This means it must be very hard to find an input for which the "correct" answer is true.

The MAC Security Definition

We want to say that only someone who knows the secret key can come up with valid MAC tags. In other words, the adversary cannot come up with valid MAC tags.

Actually, that property is not quite enough to be useful. A more useful property is: even if the adversary knows valid MAC tags corresponding to various messages, she cannot produce a valid MAC tag for a different message. We call it a forgery if the adversary can produce a "new" valid MAC tag.

To translate this security property to a formal definition, we define two libraries that allow the adversary to request MAC tags on chosen messages. The libraries also provide a mechanism to let the adversary check whether it has successfully found a forgery (since there is no way of checking this property without the secret key). One library will actually perform the check, and the other library will simply assume that forgeries are impossible. The two libraries are different only in how they behave when the adversary calls this verification subroutine on a forgery. By demanding that the two libraries be indistinguishable, we are actually demanding that it is difficult for the calling program to generate a forgery.

Definition 10.2 Let Σ be a MAC scheme. We say that Σ is a secure MAC if $\mathcal{L}^{\Sigma}_{\text{mac-real}} \approx \mathcal{L}^{\Sigma}_{\text{mac-fake}}$, where: (MAC security)

$\mathcal{L}^{\Sigma}_{\text{mac-real}}$

$k \leftarrow \Sigma.\text{KeyGen}$

GETTAG($m \in \Sigma.\mathcal{M}$):
  return $\Sigma.\text{MAC}(k, m)$

CHECKTAG($m \in \Sigma.\mathcal{M}, t$):
  return $t \stackrel{?}{=} \Sigma.\text{MAC}(k, m)$

$\mathcal{L}^{\Sigma}_{\text{mac-fake}}$

$k \leftarrow \Sigma.\text{KeyGen}$
$\mathcal{T} := \emptyset$

GETTAG($m \in \Sigma.\mathcal{M}$):
  $t := \Sigma.\text{MAC}(k, m)$
  $\mathcal{T} := \mathcal{T} \cup \{(m, t)\}$
  return t

CHECKTAG($m \in \Sigma.\mathcal{M}, t$):
  return $(m, t) \stackrel{?}{\in} \mathcal{T}$

Discussion:

- The adversary can see valid tags of chosen messages, from the gettag subroutine. However, these tags shouldn't count as a successful forgery. The way this is enforced is in the checktag subroutine of $\mathcal{L}_{\text{mac-fake}}$ – instead of always responding false, it gives the correct answer (true) for any tags generated by gettag.

In order for the two libraries to behave differently, the adversary must call checktag on input (m, t) such that m was never used as an argument to gettag (so that $\mathcal{L}_{\text{mac-fake}}$ responds false) but where the tag is actually correct (so that $\mathcal{L}_{\text{mac-real}}$ responds true).

- The adversary can successfully distinguish if it finds any forgery - a valid MAC tag of any "fresh" message. The definition doesn't care whether it's the tag of any particular meaningful message.

MAC Applications

Although MACs are less embedded in public awareness than encryption, they are extremely useful. A frequent application of MACs is to store some information in an untrusted place, where we don't intend to hide the data, only ensure that the data is not changed.

- A browser cookie is a small piece of data that a webserver stores in a user's web browser. The browser presents the cookie data to the server upon each request.

Imagine a webserver that stores a cookie when a user logs in, containing that user's account name. What stops an attacker from modifying their cookie to contain a different user's account name? Adding a MAC tag of the cookie data (using a key known only to the server) ensures that such an attack will not succeed. The server can trust any cookie data whose MAC tag is correct.

- When Alice initiates a network connection to Bob, they must perform a TCP handshake:

1. Alice sends a special SYN packet containing her initial sequence number A. In TCP, all packets from Alice to Bob include a sequence number, which helps the parties detect when packets are missing or out of order. It is important that the initial sequence number be random, to prevent other parties from injecting false packets.
2. Bob sends a special SYN+ACK packet containing $A + 1$ (to acknowledge Alice's A value) and the initial sequence number B for his packets.
3. Alice sends a special ACK packet containing $B + 1$, and then the connection is established.

When Bob is waiting for step 3, the connection is considered "half-open." While waiting, Bob must remember B so that he can compare to the $B + 1$ that Alice is supposed to send in her final ACK. Typically the operating system allocates only a very limited amount of resources for these half-open connections.

In the past, it was possible to perform a denial of service attack by starting a huge number of TCP connections with a server, but never sending the final ACK packet. The server's queue for half-open connections fills up, which prevents other legitimate connections from starting.

A clever backwards-compatible solution to this problem is called SYN cookies. The idea is to let Bob choose his initial sequence number B to be a MAC of the client's IP address, port number, and some other values. Now there is nothing to store for half-open connections. When Alice sends the final ACK of the handshake, Bob can recompute the initial sequence number from his MAC key.

These are all cases where the person who generates the MAC is the same person who later verifies the MAC. You can think of this person as choosing not to store some information, but rather leaving the information with someone else as a "note to self."

There are other useful settings where one party generates a MAC while the other verifies.

- In two-factor authentication, a user logs into a service using something they know (e.g., a password) and something they have (e.g., a mobile phone). The most common two-factor authentication mechanism is called timed one-time passwords (TOTP). When you (as a user) enable two-factor authentication, you generate a secret key k and store it both on your phone and with the service provider. When you wish to log in, you open a simple app on your phone which computes $p = \text{MAC}(k, T)$, where T is the current date + time (usually rounded to the nearest 30 seconds). The value p is the "timed one-time password." You then log into the service using your usual (long-term) password and the one-time password p. The service provider has k and also knows the current time, so can verify the MAC p.

- From the service provider's point of view, the only other place k exists in in the phone of this particular user. Intuitively, the only way to generate a valid one-time password at time T is to be in posession of this phone at time T. Even if an attacker sees both your long-term and one-time password over your shoulder, this does not help him gain access to your account in the future (well, not after 30 seconds in the future).

10.2 A PRF is a MAC

The definition of a PRF says (more or less) that even if you've seen the output of the PRF on several chosen inputs, all other outputs look independently & uniformly random. Furthermore, uniformly chosen values are hard to guess, as long as they are sufficiently long (e.g., λ bits).

In other words, after seeing some outputs of a PRF, any other PRF output will be hard to guess. This is exactly the intuitive property we require from a MAC. And indeed, we will prove in this section that a PRF is a secure MAC. While the claim makes intuitive sense, proving it formally is a little tedious. This is due to the fact that that in the MAC security game, the adversary can make many verification queries checktag (m, t) before asking to see the correct MAC of m. Dealing with this event is the source of all the technical difficulty in the proof.

We start with a technical claim that captures the idea that "if you can blindly guess at uniformly chosen values and can also ask to see the values, then it is hard to guess a random value before you have seen it."

Claim 10.3 The following two libraries are indistinguishable:

$\mathcal{L}_{\text{guess-L}}$	$\mathcal{L}_{\text{guess-R}}$
T := empty assoc. array	T := empty assoc. array
GUESS($m \in \{0,1\}^{in}, g \in \{0,1\}^{\lambda}$):	GUESS($m \in \{0,1\}^{in}, g \in \{0,1\}^{\lambda}$):
if $T[m]$ undefined: $T[m] \leftarrow \{0,1\}^{\lambda}$ return $g \stackrel{?}{=} T[m]$	// *returns* false *if* $T[m]$ *undefined* return $g \stackrel{?}{=} T[m]$
REVEAL($m \in \{0,1\}^{in}$):	REVEAL($m \in \{0,1\}^{in}$):

if $T[m]$ undefined:
  $T[m] \leftarrow \{0,1\}^{\lambda}$
return $T[m]$
	if $T[m]$ undefined:
	  $T[m] \leftarrow \{0,1\}^{\lambda}$
	return $T[m]$

Both libraries maintain an associative array T whose values are sampled uniformly the first time they are needed. Calling programs can try to guess these values via the guess subroutine, or simply learn them via reveal. Note that the calling program can call guess $(m,\cdot)$ both before and after calling reveal(m).

Intuitively, since the values in T are λ bits long, it should be hard to guess $T[m]$ before calling reveal(m). That is exactly what we formalize in $\mathcal{L}_{\text{guess-r.}}$ In fact, this library doesn't bother to even choose $T[m]$ until reveal (m) is called. All calls to guess$(m,\cdot)$ made before the first call to reveal (m) will return false.

Proof Let q be the number of queries that the calling program makes to guess. We will show that the libraries are indistinguishable with a hybrid sequence of the form:

$$\mathcal{L}_{\text{guess-L}} \equiv \mathcal{L}_{\text{hyb-}0} \approx \mathcal{L}_{\text{hyb-}1} \approx \cdots \approx \mathcal{L}_{\text{hyb-}q} \equiv \mathcal{L}_{\text{guess-R}}$$

The h th hybrid library in the sequence is defined as:

```
ℒhyb-h
count := 0
T := empty assoc. array

GUESS(m, g):
  count := count + 1
  if T[m] undefined and count > h :
    T[m] ← {0,1}^λ
  return g =? T[m]
  // returns false if T[m] undefined

REVEAL(m):
  if T[m] undefined:
    T[m] ← {0,1}^λ
  return T[m]
```

This hybrid library behaves like $\mathcal{L}_{\text{guess-R}}$ for the first h queries to guess, in the sense that it will always just return falsewhen $T[m]$ is undefined. After h queries, it will behave like $\mathcal{L}_{\text{guess-L}}$ by actually sampling $T[m]$ in these cases.

In $\mathcal{L}_{\text{hyb- }0}$, the clause "count > 0 " is always true so this clause can be removed from the if-condition. This modification results in $\mathcal{L}_{\text{guess-L}}$, so we have $\mathcal{L}_{\text{guess-L}} \equiv \mathcal{L}_{\text{hyb- }0}$.

In $\mathcal{L}_{\text{hyb- }q}$, the clause "count $> q$ " in the if-statement is always false since the calling program makes only q queries. Removing the unreachable if-statement it results in $\mathcal{L}_{\text{guess-R}}$, so we have $\mathcal{L}_{\text{guess-R}} \equiv \mathcal{L}_{\text{hyb- }q}$.

It remains to show that $\mathcal{L}_{\text{hyb- }h} \approx \mathcal{L}_{\text{hyb- }(h+1)}$ for all h. We can do so by rewriting these two libraries as follows:

```
ℒhyb-h
count := 0
T := empty assoc. array

GUESS(m, g):
  count := count + 1
  if T[m] undefined and count > h :
    T[m] ← {0,1}^λ
    if g = T[m] and count = h + 1:
      bad := 1
  return g =? T[m]
  // returns false if T[m] undefined

REVEAL(m):
  if T[m] undefined:
    T[m] ← {0,1}^λ
  return T[m]
```

```
ℒhyb-(h+1)
count := 0
T := empty assoc. array

GUESS(m, g):
  count := count + 1
  if T[m] undefined and count > h :
    T[m] ← {0,1}^λ
    if g = T[m] and count = h + 1:
      bad := 1; return false
  return g =? T[m]
  // returns false if T[m] undefined

REVEAL(m):
  if T[m] undefined:
    T[m] ← {0,1}^λ
  return T[m]
```

The library on the left is equivalent to $\mathcal{L}_{\text{hyb-}h}$ since the only change is the highlighted lines, which don't actually affect anything. In the library on the right, if $T[m]$ is undefined during the first $h+1$ calls to guess, the subroutine will return false (either by avoiding the if-statement altogether or by triggering the highlighted lines). This matches the behavior of $\mathcal{L}_{\text{hyb-}(h+1)}$, except that the library shown above samples the value $T[m]$ which in $\mathcal{L}_{\text{hyb-}(h+1)}$ would not be sampled until the next call of the form guess $(m,\cdot)$ or reveal (m). But the method of sampling is the same, only the timing is different. This difference has no effect on the calling program.

So the two libraries above are indeed equivalent to $\mathcal{L}_{\text{hyb-}h}$ and $\mathcal{L}_{\text{hyb-}(h+1)}$. They differ only in code that is reachable when bad $= 1$. From Lemma 4.8, we know that these two libraries are indistinguishable if Pr[bad $= 1$] is negligible. In these libraries there is only one chance to set bad = 1, and that is by guessing/predicting uniform $T[m]$ on the ($h+1$)th call to guess. This happens with probability $1/2^{\lambda}$, which is indeed negligible.

This shows that $\mathcal{L}_{\text{hyb-}h} \approx \mathcal{L}_{\text{hyb-}(h+1)}$, and completes the proof. □

We now return to the problem of proving that a PRF is a MAC.

Claim 10.4 *Let F be a secure PRF with input length in and output length out $= \lambda$. Then the scheme $MAC(k,m) = F(k,m)$ is a secure MAC for message space $\{0,1\}^{in}$.*

Proof We show that $\mathcal{L}^{F}_{\text{mac-real}} \approx \mathcal{L}^{F}_{\text{mac-fake}}$, using a standard sequence of hybrids.

The starting point is the $\mathcal{L}_{\text{mac-real}}$ library, with the details of this MAC scheme filled in.

$\mathcal{L}^{F}_{\text{mac-real}}$

$k \leftarrow \{0,1\}^{\lambda}$

GETTAG(m):
  return $F(k,m)$

CHECKTAG(m,t):
  return $t \overset{?}{=} F(k,m)$

We have factored out the PRF operations in terms of the library $\mathcal{L}_{\text{prf-real}}$ from the PRF security definition.

```
GETTAG(m):
  return LOOKUP(m)

CHECKTAG(m, t):
  return t =? LOOKUP(m)
```

$\diamond$

```
L^F_prf-real
k ← {0,1}^λ

LOOKUP(x):
  return F(k, x)
```

We have applied the PRFsecurity of F and replaced $\mathcal{L}_{\text{prf-real}}$ with $\mathcal{L}_{\text{prf-rand}}$.

```
GETTAG(m):
  return LOOKUP(m)

CHECKTAG(m, t):
  return t =? LOOKUP(m)
```

$\diamond$

```
L^F_prf-rand
T := empty assoc. array

LOOKUP(x):
  if T[x] undefined:
    T[x] ← {0,1}^out
  return T[x]
```

We can express the previous hybrid in terms of the $\mathcal{L}_{\text{guess-L}}$ library from Claim 10.3. The change has no effect on the calling program.

```
GETTAG(m):
  return REVEAL(m)

CHECKTAG(m, t):
  return GUESS(m, t)
```

$\diamond$

```
L_guess-L
T := empty assoc. array

GUESS(m, g):
  if T[m] undefined:
    T[m] ← {0,1}^λ
  return g =? T[m]

REVEAL(m):
  if T[m] undefined:
    T[m] ← {0,1}^λ
  return T[m]
```

We have applied Claim 10.3 to replace $\mathcal{L}_{\text{guess-L}}$ with $\mathcal{L}_{\text{guess-R}}$. This involves simply removing the if-statement from guess. As a result, Guess(m, g) will return false if $T[m]$ is undefined.

```
GETTAG(m):
  return REVEAL(m)

CHECKTAG(m, t):
  return GUESS(m, t)
```

◇

```
L_guess-R
T := empty assoc. array

GUESS(m, g):
  return g =? T[m]

REVEAL(m):
  if T[m] undefined:
    T[m] ← {0,1}^λ
  return T[m]
```

Extra bookkeeping information is added, but not used anywhere. There is no e_ect on the calling program.

```
𝒯 := ∅

GETTAG(m):
  t := REVEAL(m)
  𝒯 := 𝒯 ∪ {(m, t)}
  return t

CHECKTAG(m, t):
  return GUESS(m, t)
```

◇

```
L_guess-R
T := empty assoc. array

GUESS(m, g):
  return g =? T[m]

REVEAL(m):
  if T[m] undefined:
    T[m] ← {0,1}^λ
  return T[m]
```

Consider the hybrid experiment above, and suppose the calling program makes a call to checktag (m, t). There are two cases:

- Case 1: there was a previous call to gettag(m). In this case, the value $T[m]$ is defined in $\mathcal{L}_{\text{guess-R}}$ and ($m, T[m]$) already exists in $\mathcal{T}$. In this case, the result of Guess(m, t) (and hence, of checktag(m, t)) will be $t \stackrel{?}{=} T[m]$.
- Case 2: there was no previous call to gettag(m). Then there is no value of the form $(m,\star)$ in $\mathcal{T}$. Furthermore, $T[m]$ is undefined in $\mathcal{L}_{\text{guess-R}}$. The call to guess (m, t) will
- return false, and so will the call to checktag (m, t) that we consider.
- In both cases, the result of checktag(m, t) is true if and only if $(m, t) \in \mathcal{T}$.

We have modified checktag according to the discussion above.

```
𝒯 := ∅

GETTAG(m):
  t := REVEAL(m)
  𝒯 := 𝒯 ∪ {(m, t)}
  return t

CHECKTAG(m, t):
  return (m, t) ∈? 𝒯
```

◇

```
ℒ_guess-R

T := empty assoc. array

GUESS(m, g):
  return g =? T[m]

REVEAL(m):
  if T[m] undefined:
    T[m] ← {0,1}^λ
  return T[m]
```

In the previous hybrid, the guess subroutine is never called. Removing that unused subroutine and renaming reveal to lookup results in the $\mathcal{L}_{\text{prf-ideal}}$ library from the PRF security definition.

```
𝒯 := ∅

GETTAG(m):
  t := LOOKUP (m)
  𝒯 := 𝒯 ∪ {(m, t)}
  return t

CHECKTAG(m, t):
  return (m, t) ∈? 𝒯
```

◇

```
ℒ^F_prf-rand

T := empty assoc. array

LOOKUP(x):
  if T[x] undefined:
    T[x] ← {0,1}^out
  return T[x]
```

We have applied the PRF security of F again, replacing Lprf-ideal with Lprf-real.

```
𝒯 := ∅

GETTAG(m):
  t := LOOKUP(m)
  𝒯 := 𝒯 ∪ {(m, t)}
  return t

CHECKTAG(m, t):
  return (m, t) ∈? 𝒯
```

◇

```
ℒ^F_prf-real

k ← {0,1}^λ

LOOKUP(x):
  return F(k, x)
```

Inlining $\mathcal{L}_{\text{prf-real}}$ in the final hybrid, we see that the result is exactly $\mathcal{L}^F_{\text{mac-fake}}$. Hence, we have shown that $\mathcal{L}^F_{\text{mac-real}} \approx \mathcal{L}^F_{\text{mac-fake}}$, which completes the proof. □

Discussion

If PRFs are MACs, why do we even need a definition for MACs? The simplest answer to this question is that the concepts of PRF and MAC are indeed different:

- Not every PRF is a MAC. Only sufficiently long random values are hard to guess, so only PRFs with long outputs (out $\geqslant \lambda$) are MACs. It is perfectly reasonable to consider a PRF with short outputs.

- Not every MAC is a PRF. Just like not every encryption scheme has pseudorandom ciphertexts, not every MAC scheme has pseudorandom tags. Imagine taking a secure MAC scheme and modifying it as $\text{MAC}'(k, m) = \text{MAC}(k, m) \| 0^\lambda$. Adding 0s to every tag prevents the tags from looking pseudorandom, but does not make the tags any easier to guess. Something doesn't have to be uniformly random in order to be hard to guess.

It is true that in the vast majority of cases we will encounter MAC schemes with random tags, and PRFs with long outputs (out $\geqslant \lambda$). But it is good practice to know whether you really need something that is pseudorandom or hard to guess.

10.3 MACs for Long Messages

Using a PRF as a MAC is useful only for short, fixed-length messages, since most PRFs that exist in practice are limited to such inputs. Can we somehow extend a PRF to construct a MAC scheme for long messages, similar to how we used block cipher modes to construct encryption for long messages?

How NOT to do it

To understand the challenges of constructing a MAC for long messages, we first explore some approaches that don't work. The things that can go wrong in an insecure MAC are quite different in character to the things that can go wrong in a block cipher mode, so pay attention closely!

Example *Let F be a PRF with in = out $= \lambda$. Below is a MAC approach for messages of length 2λ. It is inspired by ECB mode, so you know it's going to be a disaster:*

$$
\begin{array}{l}
\underline{\text{ECBMAC}(k, m_1 \| m_2):} \\
t_1 := F(k, m_1) \\
t_2 := F(k, m_2) \\
\text{return } t_1 \| t_2
\end{array}
$$

One problem with this approach is that, although the PRF authenticates each block m_1, m_2 individually, it does nothing to authenticate that m_1 is the first block but m_2 is the second one. Translating this observation into an attack, an adversary can ask for the MAC tag of $m_1 \| m_2$ and then predict/forge the tag for $m_2 \| m_1$:

```
𝒜:
t1||t2 := GETTAG(0^λ||1^λ)
return CHECKTAG(1^λ||0^λ, t2||t1)
```

When $\mathcal{A}$ is linked to $\mathcal{L}_{\text{mac-real}}$, it always return true, since we can tell that $t_2 \| t_1$ is indeed the valid tag for $1^\lambda \| 0^\lambda$. When $\mathcal{A}$ is linked to $\mathcal{L}_{\text{mac-fake}}$, it always return false, since the calling program never called gettag with input $1^\lambda \| 0^\lambda$. Hence, $\mathcal{A}$ distinguishes the libraries with advantage 1.

This silly MAC construction treats both m_1 and m_2 identically, and an obvious way to try to fix the problem is to treat the different blocks differently somehow:

Example *Let F be a PRF with in* $= \lambda + 1$ *and out* $= \lambda$. *Below is another MAC approach for messages of length* 2λ *:*

```
ECB++MAC(k, m1||m2):
  t1 := F(k, 0||m1)
  t2 := F(k, 1||m2)
  return t1||t2
```

This MAC construction does better, as it treats the two message blocks m_1 and m_2 differently. Certainly the previous attack of swapping the order of m_1 and m_2 doesn't work anymore. (Can you see why?)

The construction authenticates (in some sense) the fact that m_1 is the first message block, and m_2 is the second block. However, this construction doesn't authenticate the fact that this particular m_1 and m_2 belong together. More concretely, we can "mix and match" blocks of the tag corresponding to different messages:

```
𝒜:
t1||t2 := GETTAG(0^2λ)
t1'||t2' := GETTAG(1^2λ)
return CHECKTAG(0^λ||1^λ, t1||t2')
```

In this attack, we combine the t_1 block from the first tag and the t_2 block from the second tag.

We are starting to see the challenges involved in constructing a MAC scheme for long messages. A secure MAC should authenticate each message block, the order of the message blocks, and the fact that these particular message blocks are appearing in a single message. In short, it must authenticate the entirety of the message.

Think about how authentication is significantly different than privacy/hiding in this respect. At least for CPA security, we can hide an entire plaintext by hiding each individual piece of the plaintext separately (encrypting it with a CPA-secure encryption). Authentication is fundamentally different.

How to do it: CBC-MAC

We have seen some insecure ways to construct a MAC for longer messages. Now let's see a secure way. A common approach to constructing a MAC for long messages involves the CBC block cipher mode.

```
CBCMAC^F(k, m_1 ··· m_ℓ):
  t := 0^λ
  for i = 1 to ℓ:
    t := F(k, m_i ⊕ t)
  return t
```

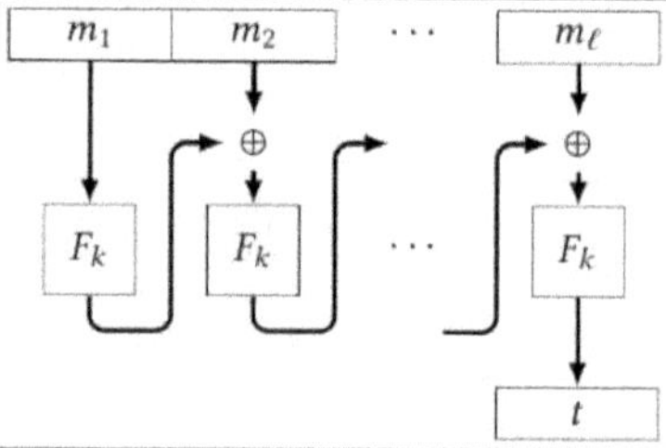

Unlike CBC encryption, CBC-MAC uses no initialization vector (or, you can think of it as using the all-zeroes IV), and it outputs only the last block.

Theorem 10.6 *If F is a secure PRF with $in = out = \lambda$, then for any fixed ℓ, $CBC - MAC$ is a secure MAC when used with message space $\mathcal{M} = \{0,1\}^{\lambda\ell}$.*

Pay close attention to the security statement. It says that if you only ever authenticate 4-block messages, CBC-MAC is secure. If you only ever authenticate 24-block messages, CBC-MAC is secure. However, if you want to authenticate both 4-block and 24-block messages (i.e., under the same key), then CBC-MAC is not secure. In particular, seeing the CBC-MAC of several 4-block messages allows an attacker to generate a forgery of a 24-block message. The exercises explore this property.

More Robust CBC-MAC

If CBC-MAC is so fragile, is there a way to extend it to work for messages of mixed lengths? One approach is called ECBC-MAC, and is shown below. It works by treating the last block differently - specifically, it uses an independent PRF key for the last block in the CBC chain.

Construction 10.7 (ECBC-MAC)

Let F be a PRF with in = out = λ. $ECBC - $ MAC refers to the following scheme:

```
ECBCMAC^F((k1, k2), m1 ··· mℓ):
  t := 0^λ
  for i = 1 to ℓ − 1 :
     t := F( k1 , mi ⊕ t)
  return F( k2 , mℓ ⊕ t)
```

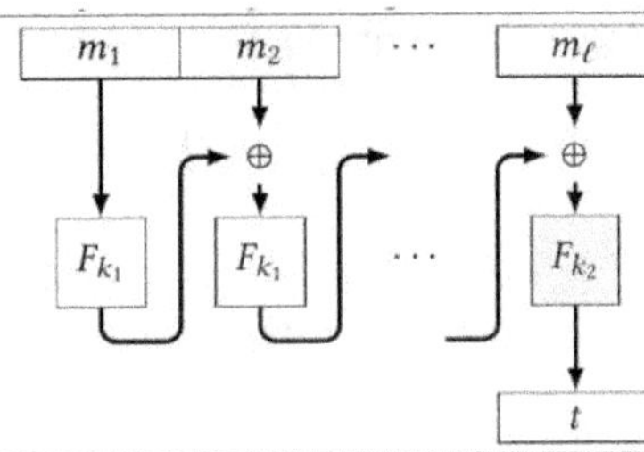

Theorem 10.8 *If F is a secure PRF with in = out = λ, then $ECBC - MAC$ is a secure MAC for message space $\mathcal{M} = \left(\{0,1\}^\lambda\right)^*$.*

In other words, ECBC-MAC is safe to use with messages of any length (that is a multiple of the block length).

To extend ECBC-MAC to messages of any length (not necessarily a multiple of the block length), one can use a padding scheme as in the case of encryption. [1]

10.4 Encrypt-Then-MAC

Our motivation for studying MACs is that they seem useful in constructing a CCA-secure encryption scheme. The idea is to add a MAC to a CPA-secure encryption scheme. The decryption algorithm can raise an error if the MAC is invalid, thereby ensuring that adversarially-generated (or adversarially-modified) ciphertexts are not accepted. There are several natural ways to combine a MAC and encryption scheme, but not all are secure! (See the exercises.) The safest way is known as encrypt-then-MAC:

Construction 10.9 (Enc-then-MAC)

Let E denote an encryption scheme, and M denote a MAC scheme where $E.\mathcal{C} \subseteq M.\mathcal{M}$ (i.e., the MAC scheme is capable of generating MACs of ciphertexts in the E scheme). Then let EtM denote the encrypt-then-MAC construction given below:

```
K = E.K × M.K                 Enc((k_e, k_m), m):
M = E.M                         c := E.Enc(k_e, m)
C = E.C × M.T                   t := M.MAC(k_m, c)
                                return (c, t)
KeyGen:
  k_e ← E.KeyGen              Dec((k_e, k_m), (c, t)):
  k_m ← M.KeyGen                if t ≠ M.MAC(k_m, c):
  return (k_e, k_m)                 return err
                                return E.Dec(k_e, c)
```

Importantly, the scheme computes a MAC of the CPA ciphertext, and not of the plaintext! The result is a CCA-secure encryption scheme:

Claim 10.10 If E has CPA security and M is a secure MAC, then EtM (Construction 10.9) has CCA security.

Proof As usual, we prove the claim with a sequence of hybrid libraries:

The starting point is $\mathcal{L}^{EtM}_{\text{cca-L}}$, shown here with the details of the encrypt-then-MAC construction highlighted. Our goal is to eventually swap m_L with m_R. But the CPA security of E should allow us to do just that, so what's the catch?

To apply the CPA-security of E, we must factor out the relevant call to E. Enc in terms of the CPA library $\mathcal{L}^{E}_{\text{cpa-L}}$. This means that k_e becomes private to the $\mathcal{L}_{\text{cpa-L}}$ library. But k_e is also used in the last line of the library as $E.\text{Dec}(k_e, c)$. The *CPA* security library for E provides no way to carry out such E.Dec statements!

```
L^EtM_cca-L
k_e ← E.KeyGen
k_m ← M.KeyGen
S := ∅

EAVESDROP(m_L, m_R):
  if |m_L| ≠ |m_R|
      return null
  c := E.Enc(k_e, m_L)
  t ← M.MAC(k_m, c)
  S := S ∪ { (c, t) }
  return (c, t)

DEC(c, t):
  if (c, t) ∈ S return null
  if t ≠ M.MAC(k_m, c):
      return err
  return E.Dec(k_e, c)
```

◇The operations of the MAC scheme have been factored out in terms of $\mathcal{L}^{M}_{\text{mac-real}}$. Notably, in the dec subroutine the condition " $t \neq M.MAC(k_M, c)$ " has been replaced with "not checktag(c, t)."

```
k_e ← E.KeyGen                            |  L^M_mac-real
S := ∅                                    |
                                          |  k_m ← M.KeyGen
EAVESDROP(m_L, m_R):                      |
  if |m_L| ≠ |m_R|                        |  GETTAG(c):
    return null                           |    return M.MAC(k_m, c)
  c := E.Enc(k_e, m_L)                    |
  t := GETTAG(c)                      ◇   |  CHECKTAG(c, t):
  S := S ∪ {(c, t)}                       |    return t =? M.MAC(k_m, c)
  return (c, t)

DEC(c, t):
  if (c, t) ∈ S
    return null
  if not CHECKTAG(c, t) :
    return err
  return E.Dec(k_e, c)
```

We have applied the security of the MAC scheme, and replaced $\mathcal{L}_{\text{mac-real}}$ with $\mathcal{L}_{\text{mac-fake}}$.

```
k_e ← E.KeyGen                            |  L^M_mac-fake
S := ∅                                    |
                                          |  k_m ← M.KeyGen
EAVESDROP(m_L, m_R):                      |  T := ∅
  if |m_L| ≠ |m_R|                        |
    return null                           |  GETTAG(c):
  c := E.Enc(k_e, m_L)                    |    t := M.MAC(k_m, c)
  t := GETTAG(c)                      ◇   |    T := T ∪ {(c, t)}
  S := S ∪ {(c, t)}                       |    return t
  return (c, t)                           |
                                          |  CHECKTAG(c, t):
DEC(c, t):                                |    return (c, t) ∈? T
  if (c, t) ∈ S
    return null
  if not CHECKTAG(c, t):
    return err
  return E.Dec(k_e, c)
```

We have inlined the $\mathcal{L}_{\text{mac-fake}}$ library. This library keeps track of a set $\mathcal{S}$ of values for the purpose of the CCA interface, but also a set $\mathcal{T}$ of values for the purposes of the MAC. However, it is clear from the code of this library that $\mathcal{S}$ and $\mathcal{T}$ always have the same contents.

Therefore, the two conditions " $(c,t) \in \mathcal{S}$ " and " $(c,t) \notin \mathcal{T}$ " in the dec subroutine are exhaustive! The final line of dec is unreachable. This hybrid highlights the intuitive idea that an adversary can either query DEC with a ciphertext generated by EAVESDROP (the $(c,t) \in \mathcal{S}$ case) - in which case the response is null - or with a different ciphertext - in which case the response will be err since the MAC will not verify.

```
k_e ← E.KeyGen
k_m ← M.KeyGen
T := ∅
S := ∅

EAVESDROP(m_L, m_R):
  if |m_L| ≠ |m_R|
    return null
  c := E.Enc(k_e, m_L)
  t := M.MAC(k_m, c)
  T := T ∪ {(c,t)}
  S := S ∪ {(c,t)}
  return (c,t)

DEC(c,t):
  if (c,t) ∈ S
    return null
  if (c,t) ∉ T :
    return err
  return E.Dec(k_e, c)
```

The unreachable statement has been removed and the redundant variables $\mathcal{S}$ and $\mathcal{T}$ have been unified. Note that this hybrid library never uses E.Dec, making it possible to express its use of the E encryption scheme in terms of $\mathcal{L}_{\text{cpa-L}}$.

```
k_e ← E.KeyGen
k_m ← M.KeyGen
S := ∅

EAVESDROP(m_L, m_R):
  if |m_L| ≠ |m_R|
    return null
  c := E.Enc(k_e, m_L)
  t := M.MAC(k_m, c)
  S := S ∪ {(c,t)}
  return (c,t)

DEC(c,t):
  if (c,t) ∈ S
    return null
  if (c,t) ∉ S :
    return err
  // unreachable
```

The statements involving the encryption scheme E have been factored out in terms of $\mathcal{L}_{\text{cpa-L}}$.

```
k_m ← M.KeyGen
S := ∅

EAVESDROP(m_L, m_R):
  if |m_L| ≠ |m_R|
    return null
  c := CPA.EAVESDROP(m_L, m_R)
  t := M.MAC(k_m, c)
  S := S ∪ {(c, t)}
  return (c, t)

DEC(c, t):
  if (c, t) ∈ S
    return null
  if (c, t) ∉ S:
    return err
```

$\diamond$

```
L^E_cpa-L

k_e ← E.KeyGen

CPA.EAVESDROP(m_L, m_R):
  c := E.Enc(k_e, m_L)
  return c
```

We have now reached the half-way point of the proof. The proof proceeds by replacing $\mathcal{L}_{\text{cpa-L}}$ with $\mathcal{L}_{\text{cpa-R}}$ (so that m_R rather than m_L is encrypted), applying the same modifications as before (but in reverse order), to finally arrive at $\mathcal{L}_{\text{cca-R}}$. The repetitive details have been omitted, but we mention that when listing the same steps in reverse, the changes appear very bizarre indeed. For instance, we add an unreachable statement to the dec subroutine; we create a redundant variable $\mathcal{T}$ whose contents are the same as $\mathcal{S}$; we mysteriously change one instance of $\mathcal{S}$ (the condition of the second if-statement in dec) to refer to the other variable $\mathcal{T}$. Of course, all of this is so that we can factor out the statements referring to the MAC scheme (along with) in terms of $\mathcal{L}_{\text{mac-fake}}$ and finally replace $\mathcal{L}_{\text{mac-fake}}$ with $\mathcal{L}_{\text{mac-real}}$. □

Exercises

10.1. Consider the following MAC scheme, where F is a secure PRF with in = out = λ:

```
KeyGen:                MAC(k, m_1 || ··· || m_ℓ): // each m_i is λ bits
  k ← {0,1}^λ            m* := 0^λ
  return k               for i = 1 to ℓ:
                           m* := m* ⊕ m_i
                         return F(k, m*)
```

Show that the scheme is not a secure MAC. Describe a distinguisher and compute its advantage.

10.2. Consider the following MAC scheme, where F is a secure PRF with in = out = λ :

```
KeyGen:                 MAC(k, m_1 || ··· || m_ℓ): // each m_i is λ bits
  k ← {0,1}^λ             t := 0^λ
  return k                for i = 1 to ℓ:
                              t := t ⊕ F(k, m_i)
                          return t
```

Show that the scheme is not a secure MAC. Describe a distinguisher and compute its advantage.

10.3. Suppose MAC is a secure MAC algorithm. Define a new algorithm $\text{MAC}'(k,m) = \text{MAC}(k,m)\|\text{MAC}(k,m)$. Prove that MAC′ is also a secure MAC algorithm.

Note: MAC′ cannot be a secure PRF. This shows that MAC security is different than PRF security.

10.4. Suppose MAC is a secure MAC scheme, whose outputs are ℓ bits long. Show that there is an efficient adversary that breaks MAC security (i.e., distinguishes the relevant libraries) with advantage $\Theta(1/2^{\ell})$. This implies that MAC tags must be reasonably long in order to be secure.

10.5. Suppose we use CBC-MAC with message space $\mathcal{M} = (\{0,1\}^{\lambda})^*$. In other words, a single MAC key will be used on messages of any length that is an exact multiple of the block length. Show that the result is not a secure MAC. Construct a distinguisher and compute its advantage.

⋆ 10.6. Here is a different way to extend CBC-MAC for mixed-length messages, when the length of each message is known in advance. Assume that F is a secure PRF with in = out = λ.

```
NEWMAC^F(k, m_1 || ··· || m_ℓ):
  k* := F(k, ℓ)
  return CBCMAC^F( k* , m_1 || ··· || m_ℓ)
```

Prove that this scheme is a secure MAC for message space $\mathcal{M} = (\{0,1\}^{\lambda})^*$. You can use the fact that CBC-MAC is secure for messages of fixed-length.

10.7. Let E be a CPA-secure encryption scheme and M be a secure MAC. Show that the following encryption scheme (called encrypt & MAC) is not CCA-secure:

E&M.KeyGen: $k_e \leftarrow$ E.KeyGen $k_m \leftarrow$ M.KeyGen return (k_e, k_m)	$\underline{E\&M.Enc((k_e, k_m), m)}$: $c :=$ $E.\mathrm{Enc}(k_e, m)t :=$ $M.MAC(k_m, m)$ return (c, t)	$E\&M.\mathrm{Dec}((k_e, k_m), (c, t))$: $m := E.\mathrm{Dec}(k_e, c)$ if $t \neq$ $M.MAC(k_m, m)$: return err return m

Describe a distinguisher and compute its advantage.

10.8. Let E be a CPA-secure encryption scheme and M be secure MAC. Show that the following encryption scheme Σ (which I call encrypt-and-encrypted-MAC) is not CCA-secure:

$\underline{\Sigma.\mathrm{KeyGen}}$: $k_e \leftarrow E.\mathrm{KeyGen}$ $k_m \leftarrow M.\mathrm{KeyGen}$ return (k_e, k_m)	$\underline{\Sigma.\mathrm{Enc}((k_e, k_m), m)}$: $c := E.\mathrm{Enc}(k_e, m)$ $t := M.\mathrm{MAC}(k_m, m)$ $c' \leftarrow E.\mathrm{Enc}(k_e, t)$ return (c, c')	$\underline{\Sigma.\mathrm{Dec}((k_e, k_m), (c, c'))}$: $m := E.\mathrm{Dec}(k_e, c)$ $t := E.\mathrm{Dec}(k_e, c')$ if $t \neq M.\mathrm{MAC}(k_m, m)$: return err return m

Describe a distinguisher and compute its advantage.

⋆ 10.9. In Construction 7.4, we encrypt one plaintext block into two ciphertext blocks. Imagine applying the Encrypt-then-MAC paradigm to this encryption scheme, but (erroneously) computing a MAC of only the second ciphertext block.

In other words, let F be a PRF with in = out = λ, and let M be a MAC scheme for message space $\{0,1\}^\lambda$. Define the following encryption scheme:

$\underline{\mathrm{KeyGen}}$: $k_e \leftarrow \{0,1\}^\lambda$ $k_m \leftarrow M.\mathrm{KeyGen}$ return (k_e, k_m)	$\underline{\mathrm{Enc}((k_e, k_m), m)}$: $r \leftarrow \{0,1\}^\lambda$ $x := F(k_e, r) \oplus m$ $t := M.\mathrm{MAC}(k_m, x)$ return (r, x, t)	$\underline{\mathrm{Dec}((k_e, k_m), (r, x, t))}$: if $t \neq M.\mathrm{MAC}(k_m, x)$: return err else return $F(k_e, r) \oplus x$

Show that the scheme does not have CCA security. Describe a successful attack and compute its advantage.

10.10. When we combine different cryptographic ingredients (e.g., combining a CPA-secure encryption scheme with a MAC to obtain a CCA-secure scheme) we generally require the two ingredients to use separate, independent keys. It would be more convenient if the entire scheme just used a single λ-bit key.

(a) Suppose we are using Encrypt-then-MAC, where both the encryption scheme and MAC have keys that are λ bits long. Refer to the proof of security of Claim 12.5 and describe where it breaks down when we modify Encrypt-then-MAC to use the same key for both the encryption & MAC components:

KeyGen:	Enc(k , m):	Dec(k , (c,t)):
$k \leftarrow \{0,1\}^\lambda$	$c := E.\text{Enc}(k, m)$	if $t \neq M.\text{MAC}(k, c)$:
return k	$t := M.\text{MAC}(k, c)$	return err
	return (c, t)	return $E.\text{Dec}(k, c)$

(b) While Encrypt-then-MAC requires independent keys k_e and k_m for the two components, show that they can both be derived from a single key using a PRF.

In more detail, let F be a PRF with in $= 1$ and out $= \lambda$. Prove that the following modified Encrypt-then-MAC construction is CCA-secure:

KeyGen:	Enc(k^* , m):	Dec(k^* , (c,t)):
$k^* \leftarrow \{0,1\}^\lambda$	$k_e := F(k^*, 0)$	$k_e := F(k^*, 0)$
return k^*	$k_m := F(k^*, 1)$	$k_m := F(k^*, 1)$
	$c := E.\text{Enc}(k_e, m)$	if $t \neq M.\text{MAC}(k_m, c)$:
	$t := M.\text{MAC}(k_m, c)$	return err
	return (c, t)	return $E.\text{Dec}(k_e, c)$

You should not have to re-prove all the tedious steps of the Encrypt-then-MAC security proof. Rather, you should apply the security of the PRF in order to reach the original Encrypt-then-MAC construction, whose security we already proved (so you don't have to repeat).

Chapter-11

Hash Functions

Suppose you share a huge file with a friend, but you are not sure whether you both have the same version of the file. You could send your version of the file to your friend and they could compare to their version. Is there any way to check that involves less communication than this?

Let's call your version of the file x (a string) and your friend's version y. The goal is to determine whether $x = y$. A natural approach is to agree on some deterministic function H, compute $H(x)$, and send it to your friend. Your friend can compute $H(y)$ and, since H is deterministic, compare the result to your $H(x)$. In order for this method to be fool-proof, we need H to have the property that different inputs always map to different outputs - in other words, H must be injective (1-to-1). Unfortunately, if H is injective and $H: \{0,1\}^{\text{in}} \to \{0,1\}^{\text{out}}$ is injective, then out $\geqslant$ in. This means that sending $H(x)$ is no better/shorter than sending x itself!

Let us call a pair (x, y) a collision in H if $x \neq y$ and $H(x) = H(y)$. An injective function has no collisions. One common theme in cryptography is that you don't always need something to be impossible; it's often enough for that thing to be just highly unlikely. Instead of saying that H should have no collisions, what if we just say that collisions should be hard (for polynomial-time algorithms) to find? An H with this property will probably be good enough for anything we care about. It might also be possible to construct such an H with outputs that are shorter than its inputs!

What we have been describing is exactly a cryptographic hash function. A hash function has long inputs and short outputs - typically $H: \{0,1\}^* \to \{0,1\}^n$. Such an H must necessarily have many collisions. The security property of a hash function is that it is hard to find any such collision. Another good name for a hash function (which I just made up, and no one else uses) would be a "pseudo-injective" function. Although it is not injective, it behaves like one for our purposes.

11.1 Security Properties for Hash Functions

There are two common security properties of hash functions:

Collision resistance. It should be hard to compute any collision $x \neq x'$ such that $H(x) = H(x')$.

Second-preimage resistance. Given x, it should be hard to compute any collision involving x. In other words, it should be hard to compute $x' \neq x$ such that $H(x) = H(x')$.

Brute Force Attacks on Hash Functions

There is an important difference between collision resistance and second-preimage resistance, which is reflected in the difficulty of their respective brute force attacks. Suppose H is a hash function whose outputs are n bits long. Let's make a simplifying assumption that for any $m > n$, the following distribution is roughly uniform over $\{0,1\}^n$:

$$\begin{array}{c} x \leftarrow \{0,1\}^m \\ \text{return } H(x) \end{array}$$

This is quite a realistic assumption for practical hash functions. If this were not true, then H would introduce some bias towards some outputs and away from other outputs, which would be perceived as suspicious. Also, as the output of H deviates farther from a uniform distribution, it only makes finding collisions easier.

Below are straight-forward brute-force attacks for collision resistance (left) and second-preimage resistance (right):

Collision brute force:

$\mathcal{A}_{cr}()$:
- for $i = 1, \ldots$:
  - $x_i \leftarrow \{0,1\}^m$
  - $y_i := H(x_i)$
  - if there is some $j < i$ with $x_i \neq x_j$ but $y_i = y_j$:
    - return (x_i, x_j)

Second preimage brute force:

$\mathcal{A}_{2pi}(x)$:
- while true:
  - $x' \leftarrow \{0,1\}^m$
  - $y' := H(x')$
  - if $y' = H(x)$: return x'

Under the simplifying assumption on H, the collision-resistance brute force attack $\mathcal{A}_{cr}$ is essentially choosing each y_i uniformly at random. Since each $y_i \in \{0,1\}^n$, the probability of finding a repeated value after q times through the main loop is roughly $\Theta(q^2/2^n)$ by the birthday bound. While in the worst case it could take 2^n steps to find collision in H, the birthday bound implies that it takes only $2^{n/2}$ attempts to find a collision with 99% probability (or any constant probability).

On the other hand, the second-preimage brute force attack $\mathcal{A}_{2pi}$ is given y as input and (under our simplifying assumption on H) essentially samples y' uniformly at random until y is the result. It will therefore take $\Theta(2^n)$ attempts in expectation to terminate successfully. [1]

There is a fundamental difference in how hard it is to break collision resistance and second-preimage resistance. Breaking collision-resistance is like inviting more people into the room until the room contains 2 people with the same birthday. Breaking secondpreimage resistance is like inviting more people into the room until the room contains another person with your birthday. One of these fundamentally takes longer than the other.

This difference explains why you will typically see cryptographic hash functions in practice that have 256 - to 512 -bit output length (but not 128 -bit output length), while you only typically see block ciphers with 128-bit or 256-bit keys. In order to make brute force attacks cost 2^n, a block cipher needs only an n-bit key while a collision-resistant hash function needs a $2n$-bit output.

Discussion of these attacks in terms of graphs, where # of edges is the "number of chances" to get a collision. Collision-resistance brute force is a complete graph (need $\sqrt{N}$ vertices to have N edges / chances for a collision). Second-preimage brute force is a star graph (need N vertices to N edges). Can generalize to consider complete bipartite graph between $\sqrt{N} + \sqrt{N}$ vertices.

Hash Function Security in Practice

We will focus on developing a formal definition for collision resistance. We can take some inspiration from the security definition for MACs. Security for a MAC means that it should be hard to produce a forgery. The MAC security definition formalized that idea with one library that checks for a forgery and another library that assumes a forgery is impossible. If the two libraries are indistinguishable, then it must be hard to find a forgery.

We can take a similar approach to say that it should be hard to produce a collision. Here is an attempt:

$$\frac{\text{TEST}(x, x'):}{\text{if } x \neq x'} \text{ and } H(x) = H(x')\text{: return true} \approx \frac{\text{TEST}(x, x'):}{\text{return false}}$$

else: return false

This corresponds to what I would call the "folk definition" of collision resistance. It makes intuitive sense (as long as you're comfortable with our style of security definition), but unfortunately the definition suffers from a very subtle technical problem.

Because of Kerckhoffs' principle, we allow calling programs to depend arbitrarily on the source code of the two libraries. This is a way of formalizing the idea that "the attacker knows everything about the algorithms." Our security definitions restrict calling programs to be polynomial-time algorithms, but they never consider the effort that goes into finding the source code of the calling program!

This strange loophole leads to the following valid attack. When we consider the security of some function H, we know that there exists many collisions (x, x') in H. These collisions may be hard to find, but they certainly exist. With exponential time, we could find such an (x, x') pair and write down the code of an attacker:

$\mathcal{A}$:
return test(x, x')

Here, the values x and x' are hard-coded into $\mathcal{A}$. The algorithm $\mathcal{A}$ is clearly polynomialtime (in fact, constant time). The "loophoole" is that the definition considers only the cost of running the algorithm $\mathcal{A}$, and not the cost of finding the source code of $\mathcal{A}$.

The way this kind of situation is avoided in other security definitions is that the libraries have some secret randomness. While the attacker is allowed to depend arbitrarily on the source code of the libraries, it is not allowed to depend on the choice of outcomes for random events in the libraries, like sampling a secret key. Since the calling program can't "prepare" for the random choice that it will be faced with, we don't have such trivial attacks. On the other hand, these two libraries for collision resistance are totally deterministic. There are no "surprises" about which function H the calling program will be asked to compute a collision for, so there is nothing to prevent a calling program from being "prepared" with a pre-computed collision in H.

Hash Function Security in Theory

The way around this technical issue is to introduce some randomness into the libraries and into the inputs of H. We define hash functions to take two arguments: a randomly chosen, public value s called a salt, and an adversarially chosen input x.

Definition 11.1 *A hash function H is collision-resistant if* $\mathcal{L}^{\mathcal{H}}_{\text{cr-real}} \approx \mathcal{L}^{\mathcal{H}}_{\text{cr-fake}}$, *where:*

$\mathcal{L}^{\mathcal{H}}_{\text{cr-real}}$
$s \leftarrow \{0,1\}^\lambda$
GETSALT():
return s
TEST($x, x' \in \{0,1\}^*$):
if $x \neq x'$ and $H(s,x) = H(s,x')$: return `true`
return `false`

$\mathcal{L}^{\mathcal{H}}_{\text{cr-fake}}$
$s \leftarrow \{0,1\}^\lambda$
GETSALT():
return s
TEST($x, x' \in \{0,1\}^*$):
return `false`

The library initially samples the salt s. Unlike in other libraries, this value s is meant to be provided to the calling program, and so the library provides a way (getsalt) for the calling program to learn it. The calling program then attempts to find a collision $x \neq x'$ where $H(s,x) = H(s,x')$.

I don't know why the term "salt" is used with hash functions. The reason appears to be a mystery to the Internet. [2] Think of salt as an extra value that "personalizes" the hash function for a given application. Here is a good analogy: an encryption scheme can be thought of as a different encryption algorithm Enc(k,·) for each choice of key k. When I choose a random k, I get a personalized encryption algorithm Enc(k,·) that is unrelated to the algorithm Enc(k',·) that someone else would get when they choose their own k. When I choose a salt s, I get a personalized hash function $H(s,\cdot)$ that is unrelated to other $H(s',\cdot)$ functions. Because the salt is chosen uniformly from $\{0,1\}^\lambda$, a calling program cannot predict what salt (which personalized hash function) it will be challenged with.

Definition 11.1 is a valid definition for collision resistance, free of strange loopholes like the "folklore" definition. However, it is not a particularly useful definition to use in security proofs, when a hash function is used as a building block in a bigger system.

It becomes cumbersome to use in those cases, because when you use a hash function, you typically don't explicitly check whether you've seen a collision. Instead, you simply proceed as if collisions are not going to happen.

In this chapter, we won't see provable statements of security referring to this definition.

Salts in Practice

When we define hash functions in theory, we require that the hash function accept two inputs, the first of which is interpreted as a salt. The hash functions that you see in practice have only one input, a string of arbitrary length. You can simulate the effect of a salt for such a hash function by simply concatenating the two inputs - e.g., $H(s\|x)$ instead of $H(s,x)$.

The concept of a salted hash is not just useful to make a coherent security definition, it is also just good practice. Hash functions are commonly used to store passwords. A server may store user records of the form (username, $h = H$ (password)). When a user attempts to login with password p', the server computes $H(p')$ and compares it to h. Storing hashed passwords means that, in the event that the password file is stolen, an attacker would need to find a preimage of h in order to impersonate the user.

Best practice is to use a separate salt for each user. Instead of storing (username, H(password)), choose a random salt s for each user and store (username, $s, H(s$, password)). The security properties of a hash function do not require s to be secret, although there is also no good reason to broadcast a user's salt publicly. The salt is only needed by the server, when it verifies a password during a login attempt.

A user-specific salt means that each user gets their own "personalized" hash function to store their password. Salts offer the following benefits:

- Without salts, it would be evident when two users have the same password - they would have the same password hashes. The same password hashed with different salts will result in unrelated hash outputs.
- An attacker can compute a dictionary of $(p, H(p))$ for common passwords. Without salts, this dictionary makes it easy to attack all users at once, since all users are using the same hash function. With salts, each user has a personalized hash function, each of which would require its own dictionary. Salt makes an attacker's effort scale with the number of victims.

11.2 Merkle-Damgård Construction

Building a hash function, especially one that accepts inputs of arbitrary length, seems like a challenging task. In this section, we'll see one approach for constructing hash functions, called the Merkle-Damgård construction.

Instead of a full-fledged hash function, imagine that we had a collision-resistant function whose inputs were of a single fixed length, but longer than its outputs. In other words, $h: \{0,1\}^{n+t} \rightarrow \{0,1\}^n$, where $t > 0$. We call such an h a compression function. This is not compression in the usual sense of the word - we are not concerned about recovering the input from the output. We call it a compression function because it "compresses" its input by t bits (analogous to how a pseudorandom generator "stretches" its input by some amount).

The following construction is one way to build a full-fledged hash function (supporting inputs of arbitrary length) out of such a compression function:

Construction 11.2 (Merkle-Damgård)

Let $h: \{0,1\}^{n+t} \to \{0,1\}^n$ *be a compression function. Then the Merkle-Damgård transformation of* h *is* $MD_h: \{0,1\}^* \to \{0,1\}^n$*, where:*

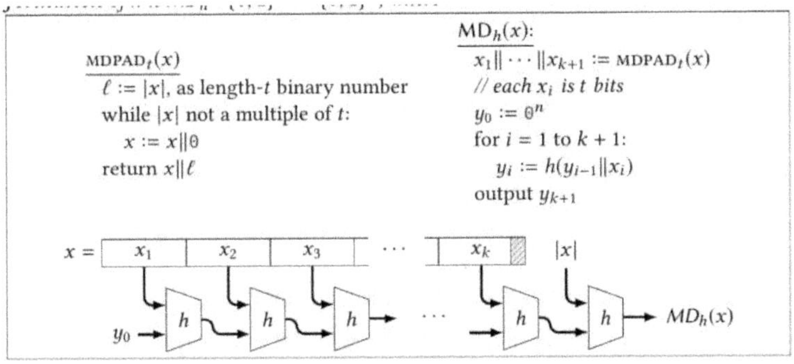

The idea of the Merkle-Damgård construction is to split the input x into blocks of size t. The end of the string is filled out with 0s if necessary. A final block called the "padding block" is added, which encodes the (original) length of x in binary.

Example: *Suppose we have a compression function* $h: \{0,1\}^{48} \to \{0,1\}^{32}$*, so that* $t = 16$*. We build a Merkle-Damgård hash function out of this compression function and wish to compute the hash of the following 5-byte (40-bit) string:*

$$x = 0110001111001101010000111001011101010000$$

We must first pad x appropriately (mDPAD(x)) :

- Since x is not a multiple of $t = 16$ bits, we need to add 8 bits to make it so.
- Since $|x| = 40$, we need to add an extra 16-bit block that encodes the number 40 in binary (101000).

After this padding, and splitting the result into blocks of length 16, we have the following:

$$\underbrace{0110001111001101}_{x_1}\,\underbrace{0100001110010111}_{x_2}\,\underbrace{0101000000000000}_{x_3}\,\underbrace{0000000000101000}_{x_4}$$

The final hash of x is computed as follows:

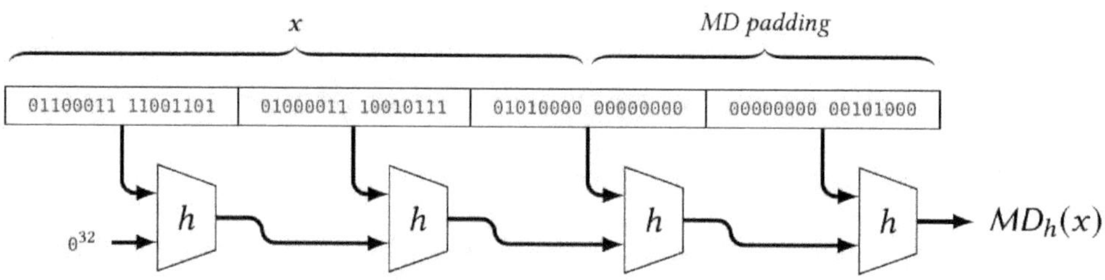

We are presenting a simplified version, in which MD_h accepts inputs whose maximum length is $2^t - 1$ bits (the length of the input must fit into t bits). By using multiple padding blocks (when necessary) and a suitable encoding of the original string length, the construction can be made to accommodate inputs of arbitrary length (see the exercises).

The value y_0 is called the initialization vector (IV), and it is a hard-coded part of the algorithm.

As discussed above, we will not be making provable security claims using the librarystyle definitions. However, we can justify the Merkle-Damgård construction with the following claim:

Claim 11.3 *Suppose h is a compression function and MD_h is the Merkle-Damgård construction applied to h. Given a collision x, x' in MD_h, it is easy to find a collision in h. In other words, if it is hard to find a collision in h, then it must also be hard to find a collision in MD_h.*

Proof Suppose that x, x' are a collision under MD_h. Define the values $x_1, \ldots, x_{k+1}$ and $y_1, \ldots, y_{k+1}$ as in the computation of $\mathrm{MD}_h(x)$. Similarly, define $x'_1, \ldots, x'_{k'+1}$ and $y'_1, \ldots, y'_{k'+1}$ as in the computation of $\mathrm{MD}_h(x')$. Note that, in general, k may not equal k'.

Recall that:

$$\mathrm{MD}_h(x) = y_{k+1} = h(y_k \| x_{k+1})$$
$$\mathrm{MD}_h(x') = y'_{k'+1} = h(y'_{k'} \| x'_{k'+1})$$

Since we are assuming $\mathrm{MD}_h(x) = \mathrm{MD}_h(x')$, we have $y_{k+1} = y'_{k'+1}$. We consider two cases:

Case 1: If $|x| \neq |x'|$, then the padding blocks x_{k+1} and $x'_{k'+1}$ which encode $|x|$ and $|x'|$ are not equal. Hence we have $y_k \| x_{k+1} \neq y'_{k'} \| x'_{k'+1}$, so $y_k \| x_{k+1}$ and $y'_{k'} \| x'_{k'+1}$ are a collision under h and we are done.

Case 2: If $|x| = |x'|$, then x and x' are broken into the same number of blocks, so $k = k'$. Let us work backwards from the final step in the computations of $\mathrm{MD}_h(x)$ and $\mathrm{MD}_h(x')$. We know that:

$$\begin{array}{c} y_{k+1} = h(y_k \| x_{k+1}) \\ = \\ y'_{k+1} = h(y'_k \| x'_{k+1}) \end{array}$$

If $y_k \| x_{k+1}$ and $y'_k \| x'_{k+1}$ are not equal, then they are a collision under h and we are done. Otherwise, we can apply the same logic again to y_k and y'_k, which are equal by our assumption.

More generally, if $y_i = y'_i$, then either $y_{i-1} \| x_i$ and $y'_{i-1} \| x'_i$ are a collision under h (and we say we are "lucky"), or else $y_{i-1} = y'_{i-1}$(and we say we are "unlucky"). We start with the

premise that $y_k = y'_k$. Can we ever get "unlucky" every time, and not encounter a collision when propagating this logic back through the computations of $\mathrm{MD}_h(x)$ and $\mathrm{MD}_h(x')$? The answer is no, because encountering the unlucky case every time would imply that $x_i = x'_i$ for all i. That is, $x = x'$. But this contradicts our original assumption that $x \neq x'$. Hence we must encounter some "lucky" case and therefore a collision in h.

11.3 Hash Functions vs. MACs: Length-Extension Attacks

When we discuss hash functions, we generally consider the salt s to be public. A natural question is, what happens when we make the salt private? Of all the cryptographic primitives we have discussed so far, a hash function with secret salt most closely resembles a MAC. So, do we get a secure MAC by using a hash function with private salt?

Unfortunately, the answer is no in general (although it can be yes in some cases, depending on the hash function). In particular, the method is insecure when H is constructed using the Merkle-Damgård approach. The key observation is that:

knowing $H(x)$ allows you to predict the hash of any string that begins with MDPAD(x).

This concept is best illustrated by example.

Example *Let's return to our previous example, with a compression function $h: \{0,1\}^{48} \to \{0,1\}^{32}$. Suppose we construct a Merkle-Damgård hash out of this compression function, and use the construction $MAC(k, m) = H(k \| m)$ as a MAC.*

Suppose the MAC key is chosen as $k = 01100011$ *11001101, and an attacker sees the MAC tag* t *of the message* $m = 0100001110010111010100000$. *Then* $t = H(k\|m)$ *corresponds exactly to the example from before:*

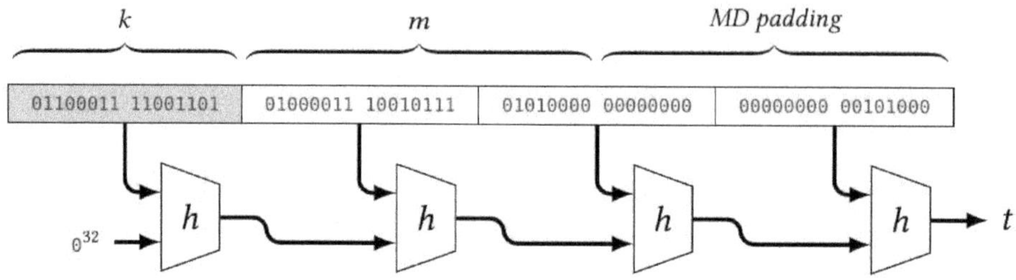

The only difference from before is that the first block contains the MAC key, so its value is not known to the attacker. We have shaded it in gray here. The attacker knows all other inputs as well as the output tag t.

I claim that the attacker can now exactly predict the tag of:

$$m' = 0100001110010111010100000000000000000000000101000$$

The correct MAC tag t' *of this value would be computed by someone with the key as:*

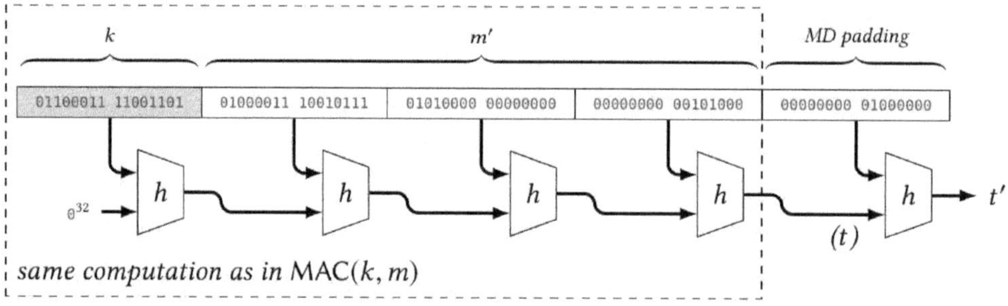

The attacker can compute the output t' *in a different way, without knowing the key. In particular, the attacker knows all inputs to the last instance of* h. *Since the* h *function itself is public, the attacker can compute this value herself as* $t' = h(t\|0000000001000000)$. *Since she can predict the tag of* m', *having seen only the tag of* m, *she has broken the MAC scheme.*

Discussion

- In our example, the attacker sees the MAC tag for m (computed as $(k\|m)$) and then forges the tag for $m' = m\|p$, where p is the padding you must add when hashing $k\|m$. Note that the padding depends only on the length of k, which we assume is public.

- The same attack works to forge the tag of any m' that begins with $m\|p$. The attacker would simply have to compute the last several rounds (not just one round) of MerkleDamgård herself.
- This is not an attack on collision resistance! Length-extension does not result in collisions! We are not saying that $k\|m$ and $k\|m\|p$ have the same hash under H, only that knowing the hash of $k\|m$ allows you to also compute the hash of $k\|m\|p$.

Knowing how $H(k\|m)$ fails to be a MAC helps us understand better ways to build a secure MAC from a hash function:

- The Merkle-Damgård approach suffers from length-extension attacks because it outputs its entire internal state. In the example picture above, the value t is both the output of $H(k\|m)$ as well as the only information about $k\|m$ needed to compute the last call to h in the computation $H(k\|m\|p)$.
- One way to avoid this problem is to only output part of the internal state. In MerkleDamgård, we compute $y_i := h(y_{i-1}\|x_i)$ until reaching the final output y_{k+1}. Suppose instead that we only output half of y_{k+1} (the y_i values may need to be made longer in order for this to make sense). Then just knowing half of y_{k+1} is not enough to predict what the hash output will be in a length-extension scenario.
- The hash function SHA-3 was designed in this way (often called a "wide pipe" construction). One of the explicit design criteria of SHA-3 was that $H(k\|m)$ would be a secure MAC.
- Length extension with Merkle-Damgård is possible because the computation of $H(k\|m)$ exactly appears during the computation of $H(k\|m\|p)$. Similar problems
- appear in plain CBC-MAC when used with messages of mixed lengths. To avoid this, we can "do something different" to mark the end of the input. In a "wide pipe" construction, we throw away half of the internal state at the end. In ECBC-MAC, we use a different key for the last block of CBC chaining.
- We can do something similar to the $H(k\|m)$ construction, by doing $H\big(k_2\|H(k_1\|m)\big)$, with independent keys. This change is enough to mark the end of the input. This construction is known as NMAC, and it can be proven secure for MerkleDamgård hash functions, under certain assumptions about their underlying compression function. A closely related (and popular) construction called HMAC allows k_1 and k_2 to even be related in some way.

Exercises

11.1. Sometimes when I verify an MD5 hash visually, I just check the first few and the last few hex digits, and don't really look at the middle of the hash.

Generate two files with opposite meanings, whose MD5 hashes agree in their first 16 bits (4 hex digits) and in their last 16 bits (4 hex digits). It could be two text files that say opposite things. It could be an image of Mario and an image of Bowser. I don't know, be creative.

As an example, the strings "subtitle illusive planes" and "wantings premises forego" actually agree in the first 20 and last 20 bits (first and last 5 hex digits) of their MD5 hashes, but it's not clear that they're very meaningful.

```
$ echo -n "subtitle illusive planes" | md5sum

4188d4cdcf2be92a112bdb8ce4500243 -

$ echo -n "wantings premises forego" | md5sum

4188d209a75e1a9b90c6fe3efe300243 -
```

Describe how you generated the files, and how many MD5 evaluations you had to make.

11.2. Let $h: \{0,1\}^{n+t} \to \{0,1\}^n$ be a fixed-length compression function. Suppose we forgot a few of the important features of the Merkle-Damgård transformation, and construct a hash function H from h as follows:

- Let x be the input.
- Split x into pieces $y_0, x_1, x_2, \dots, x_k$, where y_0 is n bits, and each x_i is t bits. The last piece x_k should be padded with zeroes if necessary.
- For $i = 1$ to k, set $y_i = h(y_{i-1} \| x_i)$.
- Output y_k.

Basically, it is similar to the Merkle-Damgård except we lost the IV and we lost the final padding block.

1. Describe an easy way to find two messages that are broken up into the same number of pieces, which have the same hash value under H.

2. Describe an easy way to find two messages that are broken up into different number of pieces, which have the same hash value under H.

Neither of your collisions above should involve finding a collision in h.

11.3. I've designed a hash function $H: \{0,1\}^* \to \{0,1\}^n$. One of my ideas is to make $H(x) = x$ if x is an n-bit string (assume the behavior of H is much more complicated on inputs of other lengths). That way, we know with certainty that there are no collisions among n-bit strings. Have I made a good design decision?

11.4. Same as above, but now if x is n bits long, then $H(x) = x \oplus m$, where m is a fixed, public string. Can this be a good hash function?

11.5. Let H be a hash function and let t be a fixed constant. Define $H^{(t)}$ as:

$$H^{(t)}(x) = \underbrace{H(\cdots H(H}_{t \text{ times}}(x))\cdots).$$

Show that if you are given a collision under $H^{(t)}$ then you can efficiently find a collision under H.

11.6. In this problem, if x and y are strings of the same length, then we write $x \sqsubseteq y$ if $x = y$ or x comes before y in standard dictionary ordering.

Suppose a function $H: \{0,1\}^* \to \{0,1\}^n$ has the following property. For all strings x and y of the same length, if $x \sqsubseteq y$ then $H(x) \sqsubseteq H(y)$. Show that H is not collision resistant (describe how to efficiently find a collision in such a function).

⋆ 11.7. Suppose a function $H: \{0,1\}^* \to \{0,1\}^n$ has the following property. For all strings x and y of the same length, $H(x \oplus y) = H(x) \oplus H(y)$. Show that H is not collision resistant (describe how to efficiently find a collision in such a function).

⋆ 11.8. Let H be a salted hash function with n bits of output, and define the following function:

$$\frac{H^*(x_1 \| x_2 \| x_3 \| \cdots \| x_k):}{\text{return} H(1, x_1) \oplus H(2, x_2) \oplus \cdots \oplus H(k, x_k)}$$

Note that H^* can take inputs of any length (k). Show how to find collisions in H^* when $k > n$.

11.9. Generalize the Merkle-Damgård construction so that it works for arbitrary input lengths (and arbitrary values of t in the compression function). Extend the proof of Claim 11.3 to your new construction.

⋆ 11.10. Let F be a secure PRF with n-bit inputs, and let H be a collision-resistant (salted) hash function with n-bit outputs. Define the new function $F'((k,s),x) = F(k,H(s,x))$, where we interpret (k,s) to be its key. Prove that F' is a secure PRF with arbitrary-length inputs.

⋆ 11.11. Let MAC be a secure MAC algorithm with n-bit inputs, and let H be a collision-resistant (salted) hash function with n-bit outputs. Define the new function $\text{MAC}'((k,s),x) = \text{MAC}(k,H(s,x))$, where we interpret (k,s) to be its key. Prove that MAC' is a secure MAC with arbitrary-length inputs.

11.12. More exotic issues with the Merkle-Damgård construction:

(a) Let H be a hash function with n-bit output, based on the Merkle-Damgård construction. Show how to compute (with high probability) 4 messages that all hash to the same value under H, using only $\sim 2 \cdot 2^{n/2}$ calls to H.

(b) Show how to construct 2^d messages that all hash to the same value under H, using only $O(d \cdot 2^{n/2})$ evaluations of H.

(c) Suppose H_1 and H_2 are (different) hash functions, both with n-bit output. Consider the function $H^*(x) = H_1(x) \| H_2(x)$. Since H^* has $2n$-bit output, it is tempting to think that finding a collision in H^* will take $2^{(2n)/2} = 2^n$ effort.

However, this intuition is not true when H_1 is a Merkle-Damgård hash. Show that when H_1 is Merkle-Damgård, then it is possible to find collisions in H^* with only $O(n2^{n/2})$ effort. The attack should assume nothing about H_2 (i.e., H_2 need not be Merkle-Damgård).

11.13. Let H be a collision-resistant hash function with output length n. Let H^* denote iterating H in a manner similar to CBC-MAC:

$H^*(x_1 \cdots x_\ell)$:
// each x_i is n bits
$y_0 := 0^n$
for $i = 1$ to ℓ:
  $y_i := H(x_i \oplus y_{i-1})$
return y_i

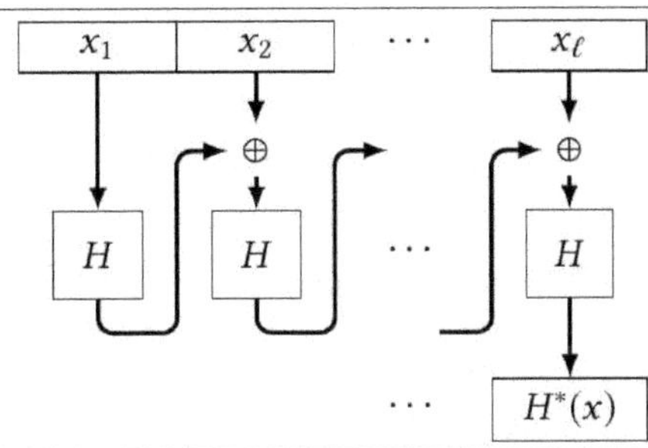

Show that H^* is not collision-resistant. Describe a successful attack.

11.14. Show that a bare PRP is not collision resistant. In other words, if F is a secure PRP, then show how to efficiently find collisions in $H(x\|y) = F(x, y)$.

11.15. Show that the CBC-MAC construction applied to a PRP is not collision-resistant. More precisely, let F be a secure PRP. Show how to efficiently find collisions in the following

salted hash function H :

$$\begin{array}{l} \underline{H(k, m_1\|m_2\|m_3):} \\ c_1 := F(k, m_1) \\ c_2 := F(k, m_2 \oplus c_1) \\ c_3 := F(k, m_3 \oplus c_2) \\ \text{return } c_3 \end{array}$$

Here we are interpreting k as the salt. This is yet another example of how collisionresistance is different than authenticity (MAC).

11.16. Let $H: \{0,1\}^\lambda \to \{0,1\}^\lambda$ be any function, and define the following function $H^*: \{0,1\}^{2\lambda} \to \{0,1\}^\lambda$:

$$\begin{array}{l} \underline{H^*(x\|y):} \\ z := H(x) \oplus y \\ \text{return } H(z) \oplus x \end{array}$$

Show how to succeed in an efficient second-preimage attack on H^*.

11.17. Adding a plain hash to a plaintext does not result in CCA security. Consider the following approach for encryption, that uses a plain (unsalted) hash function H. To encrypt plaintext m, simply encrypt $m||H(m)$ under CTR mode. To decrypt, use normal CTR mode decryption but return err if the plaintext does not have the form $m||H(m)$ (i.e., if the last n bits are not a hash of the rest of the CTR-plaintext).

Show that the scheme does not have CCA security.

11.18. In the discussion of length-extension attacks, we noted that a natural way to stop them is to "do something different" for the last block of Merkle-Damgård. Suppose after performing the final call to h in Merkle-Damgård, we complement the value (y_{k+1}). Does this modified scheme still have length-extension properties?

Chapter 12

Authenticated Encryption & AEAD

It can be helpful to think of encryption as providing a secure logical channel between two users who only have access to an insecure physical channel. Below are a few things that an attacker might do to the insecure physical channel:

- An attacker may passively eavesdrop; i.e., simply observe the channel. A CPAsecure encryption scheme provides confidentiality and prevents the attacker from learning anything by eavesdropping.
- An attacker may drop messages sent along the channel, resulting in a denial of service. If the attacker can do this on the underlying physical channel, then it cannot be overcome through cryptography.
- An attacker may try to modify messages that are sent along the channel, by tampering with their ciphertexts. This sounds like what CCA-secure encryption protects against, right?
- An attacker may try to inject new messages into the channel. If successful, Bob might receive a message and mistake it for something that Alice meant to send. Does CCA security protect against this? If it is indeed possible to inject new messages into the channel, then an attacker can delete Alice's ciphertexts and replace them with their own. This would seem to fall under the category of "modifying" messages on the channel, so message-injection and message-modification are somewhat connected.
- An attacker may try to replay messages that were sent. For example, if Bob was convinced that a ciphertext c came from Alice, then an attacker can re-send the same c many times, and Bob may interpret this as Alice wanting to re-send the same plaintext many times. Does CCA security protect against this?

Although it might seem that CCA-secure encryption guarantees protection against many of these kinds of attacks, it does not!

To see why, consider the SPRP-based encryption scheme of Construction 9.3. We proved that this scheme has CCA security. However, it never raises any errors during decryption.

Every ciphertext is interpreted as a valid encryption of some plaintext. An attacker can choose an arbitrary ciphertext, and when Bob decrypts it he might think Alice was trying to send some (presumably garbled) message. The only thing that CCA security guarantees is that if an attacker is able to make a ciphertext that decrypts without error, then it must decrypt to something that is unrelated to the contents of other ciphertexts.

In order to achieve protection against message-modification and message-injection on the secure channel, we need a stronger/better security definition. Authenticated encryption (AE) formalizes the extra property that only someone with the secret key can find ciphertexts that decrypt without error. For example, encrypt-then-MAC (Construction 10.9) already has this property.

In this chapter we will discuss authenticated encryption and a closely-related concept of encryption with associated data (AD), which is designed to help prevent messagereplay attacks. These two concepts are the "gold standard" for encryption.

12.1 Definitions

Authenticated Encryption

As with CPA and CCA flavors of security, we can define AE security in both a "left-vsright" style or a "pseudorandom ciphertexts" style. Both are reasonable choices. To make life simpler we will only define the pseudorandom-ciphertexts-style of AE security in this chapter.

In CCA$ security, the attacker has access to the decryption algorithm (except for ciphertexts generated by the library itself). This captures the idea that the result of decrypting adversarially-generated ciphertexts cannot help distinguish the contents of other ciphertexts. For AE security, we want a stronger condition that $\text{Dec}(k, c) = \text{err}$ for every adversarially-generated ciphertext c. Using the same ideas used to define security for MACs, we express this requirement by saying that the attacker shouldn't be able to distinguish access to the "real" Dec algorithm, or one that always outputs err:

Definition 12.1 Let Σ be an encryption scheme. We say that Σ has authenticated encryption (AE) security

(AE) if $\mathcal{L}^{\Sigma}_{\text{ae\$-real}} \approx \mathcal{L}^{\Sigma}_{\text{ae\$-rand}}$, where:

$\mathcal{L}^{\Sigma}_{\text{ae\$-real}}$
$k \leftarrow \Sigma.\text{KeyGen}$ $\mathcal{S} := \emptyset$
$\text{CTXT}(m \in \Sigma.\mathcal{M})$: $c := \Sigma.\text{Enc}(k, m)$ $\mathcal{S} := \mathcal{S} \cup \{c\}$ return c
$\text{DECRYPT}(c \in \Sigma.\mathcal{C})$:   if $c \in \mathcal{S}$: return err   return $\Sigma.\text{Dec}(k, c)$

$\mathcal{L}^{\Sigma}_{\text{ae\$-fake}}$
$\text{CTXT}(m \in \Sigma.\mathcal{M})$: $c \leftarrow \Sigma.\mathcal{C}(\lvert m \rvert)$ return c
$\text{DECRYPT}(c \in \Sigma.\mathcal{C})$:   return err

Discussion

The two libraries are different from each other in two major ways: whether the calling program sees real ciphertexts or random strings (that have nothing to do with the given plaintext), and whether the calling program sees the true result of decryption or an error message. With these two differences, we are demanding that two conditions be true: the calling program can't tell whether it is seeing real or fake ciphertexts, it also cannot generate a ciphertext (other than the ones it has seen) that would cause Dec to output anything except err.

Whenever the calling program calls decrypt(c) for a ciphertext c that was produced by the library (in cTXT), both libraries will return err by construction. Importantly, the difference in the libraries is the behavior of decrypt on ciphertexts that were not generated by the library (i.e., generated by the attacker).

Associated Data

AE provides a secure channel between Alice and Bob that is safe from messagemodification and message-injection by the attacker (in addition to providing confidentiality). However, AE still does not protect from replay of messages. If Alice sends a ciphertext c to Bob, we know that Bob will decrypt c without error. The guarantee of AE security is that Bob can be sure that the message originated from Alice in this case. If an attacker re-sends the same c at a later time, Bob will likely interpret that as a sign that Alice wanted to say the same thing again, even though this was not Alice's intent. It is still true that Alice was the originator of the message, but just not at this time.

You may wonder how it is possible to prevent this sort of attack. If a ciphertext c is a valid ciphertext when Alice sends it, then it will always be a valid ciphertext, right? A clever way around this problem is for Alice to not only authenticate the ciphertext as coming from her, but to authenticate it also to a specific context. For example, suppose that Alice & Bob are exchanging encrypted messages, and the 5th ciphertext is c, sent by Alice. The main idea is to let Alice authenticate the fact that "I meant to send c as the 5th ciphertext in the conversation." If an attacker re-sends c later (e.g., as the 11th ciphertext, a different context), Bob will attempt to authenticate the fact that "Alice meant to send c as the 11th ciphertext," and this authentication will fail.

What I have called "context" is called associated data in an encryption scheme. In order to support associated data, we modify the syntax of the encryption and decryption algorithms to take an additional argument d. The ciphertext $c = \text{Enc}(k, d, m)$ is an encryption of m with associated data d. In an application, d could be a sequence number of a conversation, a hash of the entire conversation up to this point, an IP address + port number, etc. - basically, as much information as you can think of regarding this ciphertext's intended context. Decrypting c with the "correct" associated data d via $\text{Dec}(k, d, c)$ should result in the correct plaintext m. Decrypting c with any other associated data should result in an error, since that reflects a mismatch between the sender's and receiver's contexts.

The intuitive security requirement for authenticated encryption with associated data (AEAD) is that an attacker who sees many encryptions c_i of chosen plaintexts, each authenticated to a particular associated data d_i, cannot generate a different (c^*, d^*) that decrypts successfully. The security definition rules out attempts to modify some c_i under the same d_i, or modify some d_i for the same c_i, or produce a completely new (c^*, d^*).

Definition 12.2 (AEAD): Let Σ be an encryption scheme. We write $\Sigma.\mathcal{D}$ to denote the space of supported associated data signifiers ("contexts"). We say that Σ has authenticated encryption with associated data (AEAD) security if $\mathcal{L}^{\Sigma}_{\text{aead\$-real}} \approx \mathcal{L}^{\Sigma}_{\text{aead\$-rand}}$, where:

$\mathcal{L}^{\Sigma}_{\text{aead\$-real}}$

$k \leftarrow \Sigma.\text{KeyGen}$
$\mathcal{S} := \emptyset$

$\text{CTXT}(d \in \Sigma.\mathcal{D}, m \in \Sigma.\mathcal{M})$:
  $c := \Sigma.\text{Enc}(k, d, m)$
  $\mathcal{S} := \mathcal{S} \cup \{(d, c)\}$
  return c

$\text{DECRYPT}(d \in \Sigma.\mathcal{D}, c \in \Sigma.\mathcal{M})$:
  if $(d, c) \in \mathcal{S}$: return err
  return $\Sigma.\text{Dec}(k, d, c)$

$\mathcal{L}^{\Sigma}_{\text{aead\$-fake}}$

$\text{CTXT}(c \in \Sigma.\mathcal{D}, m \in \Sigma.\mathcal{M})$:
  $c \leftarrow \Sigma.\mathcal{C}(|m|)$
  return c

$\text{DECRYPT}(d \in \Sigma.\mathcal{D}, c \in \Sigma.\mathcal{M})$:
  return err

Discussion

One way to "authenticate a message to some context " is to encrypt $m \| d$ instead of just m (in an AE scheme). This would indeed work! Including d as part of the plaintext would indeed authenticate it, but it would also hide it. The point of differentiating between plaintext and associated data is that we assume the associated data is shared context between both participants. In other words, we assume that the sender and receiver both already know the context d. Therefore, hiding d is overkill - only authentication is needed. By making a distinction between plaintext and associated data separately in AEAD, the ciphertext length can depend only on the length of the plaintext, and not depend on the length of the associated data.

The fact that associated data d is public is reflected in the fact that the calling program chooses it in the security definition.

"Standard" AE corresponds to the case where d is always empty: all ciphertexts are authenticated to the same context.

12.2 Achieving AE/AEAD

The Encrypt-then-MAC construction (Construction 10.9) has the property that the attacker cannot generate ciphertexts that decrypt correctly. Even though we introduced encrypt-then-MAC to achieve CCA security, it also achieves the stronger requirement of AE.

Claim 12.3: *If E has CPA security and M is a secure MAC, then EtM (Construction 10.9) has AE security.*

The security proof is essentially the same as the proof of CCA security (Claim 12.5). In that proof, there is a hybrid in which the decrypt subroutine always returns an error. Stopping the proof at that point would result in a proof of AE security.

Encrypt-then-MAC with Associated Data

Recall that the encrypt-then-MAC construction computes a MAC of the ciphertext. To incorporate associated data, we simply need to compute a MAC of the ciphertext along with the associated data.

Recall that most MACs in practice support variable-length inputs, but the length of the MAC tag does not depend on the length of the message. Hence, this new variant of encrypt-then-MAC has ciphertexts whose length does not depend on the length of the associated data.

Construction 12.4 (Enc+MAC+AD):

$\underline{\text{Enc}((k_e, k_m), d, m)}$: $c \leftarrow E.\text{Enc}(k_e, m)$ $t := M.MAC(k_m, d\|c)$ return (c, t)	$\text{Dec}((k_e, k_m), d, (c, t))$: if $t \neq M.MAC(k_m, d\|c)$: return err return $E.\text{Dec}(k_e, c)$

Claim 12.5 : *If E has CPA security and M is a secure MAC, then Construction 12.4 has AEAD security, when the associated data has fixed length (i.e.,* $\mathcal{D} = \{0,1\}^n$ *for some fixed* n *).*

12.3 Carter-Wegman MACs

Suppose we construct an AE[AD] scheme using the encrypt-then-MAC paradigm. A good choice for the CPA-secure encryption scheme would be CBC mode; a good choice for the MAC scheme would be ECBC-MAC. Combining these two building blocks would result in an AE[AD] scheme that invokes the block cipher t wice for each plaintext block - once for the CBC encryption (applied to the plaintext) and once more for the ECBC-MAC (applied to that ciphertext block).

Is it possible to achieve AE[AD] with less cost? In this section we will explore a more efficient technique for variable-length MACs, which requires only one multiplication operation per message block along with a single invocation of a block cipher.

Universal Hash Functions

The main building block in Carter-Wegman-style MACs is a kind of hash function called a universal hash function (UHF). While the name "universal hash function" sounds like it must be an incredibly strong primitive, a UHF actually gives a much weaker security guarantee than a collision-resistant or second-preimage-resistant hash function.

Recall that (x, x') is a collision under salt s if $x \neq x'$ and $H(s, x) = H(s, x')$. A universal hash function has the property that it is hard to find such a collision ...

... when x and x' are chosen without knowledge of the salt,

... and when the attacker has only one attempt at finding a collision for a particular salt value.

These constraints are equivalent to choosing the salt after x and x' are chosen, and a collision should be negligibly likely under such circumstances.

The definition can be stated more formally:

Definition 12.6 : A hash function H with set of salts $\mathcal{S}$ is called a universal hash function (UHF) if (UHF) $\mathcal{L}^{H}_{\text{uhf-real}} \approx \mathcal{L}^{H}_{\text{uhf-fake}}$, where:

$\mathcal{L}^{H}_{\text{uhf-real}}$

```
TEST(x, x' ∈ {0,1}*):
  s ← S
  b := [H(s,x) =? H(s,x')]
  return (s, b)
```

$\mathcal{L}^{H}_{\text{uhf-fake}}$

```
TEST(x, x' ∈ {0,1}*):
  s ← S
  return (s, false)
```

This definition is similar in spirit to the formal definition of collision resistance (Definition 11.1). Just like that definition, this one is cumbersome to use in a security proof. When using a hash function, one typically does not explicitly check for collisions, but instead just proceeds as if there was no collision.

In the case of UHFs, there is a different and helpful way of thinking about security. Consider a "blind collision-resistance" game, where you try to find a collision under H without access to the salt, and even without seeing the outputs of H ! It turns out that if H is a UHF, then it is hard to find collisions in such a game:

Claim 12.7 : If H is a UHF, then the following libraries are indistinguishable:

$\mathcal{L}^{H}_{\text{bcr-real}}$

```
s ← S
H_inv := empty assoc. array

TEST(x ∈ {0,1}*):
  y := H(s, x)
  if H_inv[y] defined and H_inv[y] ≠ x:
    return H_inv[y]
  H_inv[y] := x
  return false
```

$\approx$

$\mathcal{L}^{H}_{\text{bcr-fake}}$

```
TEST(x ∈ {0,1}*):
  return false
```

In these libraries, the calling program chooses inputs x to the UHF. The $\mathcal{L}_{\text{bcr-real}}$ library maintains a private record of all of the x values and their hashes, in the form of a reverse lookup table. H_{inv} $[y]$ will hold the value x that was hashed to result in y.

If the calling program calls test(x) on a value that collides with a previous x', then $\mathcal{L}_{\text{bcr-real}}$ will respond with this x' value (the purpose of this is just to be helpful to security proofs that use these libraries); otherwise it will respond with false, giving no information about

s or $H(s, x)$. The other library always responds with false. Hence, the two are indistinguishable only if finding collisions is hard.

to-do Proof to come. It's not hard but tedious.

Constructing UHFs using Polynomials

UHFs have much weaker security than other kinds of hashing, and they can in fact be constructed unconditionally. One of the mathematically simplest constructions has to do with polynomials.

Claim 12.8: *Let p be a prime and g be a nonzero polynomial with coefficients in $\mathbb{Z}_p$ and degree at most d. Then g has at most d zeroes from $\mathbb{Z}_p$.*

This observation leads to a simple UHF construction, whose idea is to interpret the string x as the coefficients of a polynomial, and evaluate that polynomial at point s (the salt of the UHF). In more detail, let p be a prime with $p > 2^\lambda$, and let the salt s be a uniformly chosen element of $\mathbb{Z}_p$. To compute the hash of x, first split x into λ-bit blocks, which will be convenient to index as $x_{d-1} \| x_{d-2} \| \ldots \| x_0$. Interpret each x_i as a number mod$p$. Then, the value of the hash $H(s, x)$ is:

$$s^d + x_{d-1}s^{d-1} + x_{d-2}s^{d-2} + \cdots + x_0 \pmod{p}$$

This is the result of evaluating a polynomial with coefficients $(1, x_{d-1}, x_{d-2}, \ldots, x_0)$ at the point s. A convenient way to evaluate this polynomial is by using Horner's rule:

$$\cdots s \cdot (s \cdot (s + x_{d-1}) + x_{d-2}) + x_{d-3} \cdots$$

Horner's rule can be expressed visually as follows:

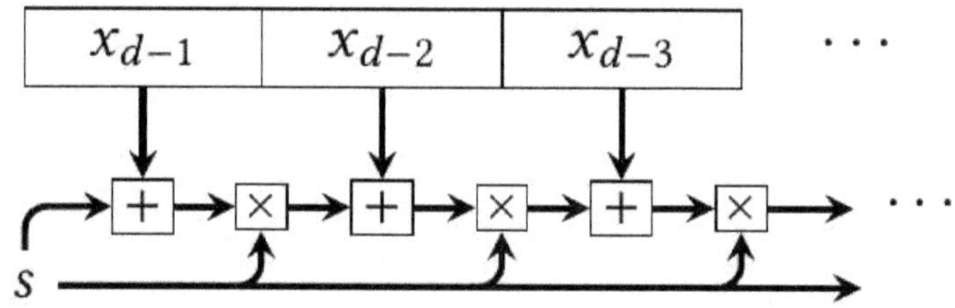

The UHF construction is described formally below.

Construction 12.9 (Poly-UHF)

$p =$ a prime $> 2^\lambda$ $\mathcal{S} = \mathbb{Z}_p$	$\underline{H(s,x)}$: write $x = x_{d-1} \| x_{d-2} \| \cdots \| x_0$, where each $\|x_i\| = \lambda$ $y := 1$ for $i = d-1$ downto 0: $y := s \cdot y + x_i \% p$ return y

Claim 12.10: *The Poly-UHF construction is a secure UHF.*

Proof: It suffices to show that, for any $x \neq x'$, the probability that $H(s,x) = H(s,x')$ (taken over random choice of s) is negligible. Note that $H(s,x) = g(s)$, where g is a polynomial whose coefficients are $(1, x_{d-1}, \dots, x_0)$, and $H(s,x') = g'(s)$, where g' is a similar polynomial derived from x'. Note that x and x' may be split into a different number of blocks, leading to different degrees (d and d') for the two polynomials.

In order to have a collision $H(s,x) = H(s,x')$, we must have

$$g(s) \equiv_p g'(s)$$
$$\Leftrightarrow g(s) - g'(s) \equiv_p 0$$

Note that the left-hand side in this equation is a polynomial of degree at most $d^* = \max\{d, d'\}$. Furthermore, that polynomial $g - g'$ is not the zero polynomial because g and g' are different polynomials. Even if the original strings x and x' differ only in blocks of 0 s , the resulting g and g' will be different polynomials because they include an extra leading coefficient of 1 .

A collision happens if and only if s is chosen to be one of the roots of $g - g'$. From Claim 12.8 , the polynomial has at most d^* roots, so the probability of choosing one of them is at most:

$$d^*/p \leqslant d^*/2^\lambda.$$

This probability is negligible since d^* is polynomial in λ (it is the number of blocks in a string that was written down by the attacker, who runs in polynomial time in λ). □

to-do Fine print: this works but modular multiplication is not fast. If you want this to be fast, you would use a binary finite field. It is not so bad to describe what finite fields are, but doing so involves more polynomials. Then when you make polynomials whose coefficients are finite field elements, it runs the risk of feeling like polynomials over polynomials (because at some level it is). Not sure how I will eventually deal with this.

Carter-Wegman UHF-based MAC

A UHF by itself is not a good MAC, even when its salt s is kept secret. This is because the security of a MAC must hold even when the attacker sees the function's outputs, but a UHF provides security (blind collision-resistance) only when the attacker does not see the UHF outputs.

The Carter-Wegman MAC technique augments a UHF by sending its output through a PRF, so the MAC of m is $F(k, H(s, m))$ where H is a UHF and F is a PRF.

Construction 12.11 (Carter-Wegman)

Let H be a UHF with n bits of output, and let F be a secure PRF with $in = n$. The CarterWegman construction combines them as follows:

KeyGen:	$\text{MAC}\big((k,s),x\big)$:
$k \leftarrow \{0,1\}^\lambda$	$y := H(s,x)$
$s \leftarrow \mathcal{S}$	return $F(k,y)$
return (k,s)	

We will show that the Carter-Wegman construction is a secure PRF. Recall that this implies that the construction is also a secure MAC (Claim 10.4). Note that the CarterWegman construction also uses a PRF as a building block. However, it uses a PRF for short messages, to construct a PRF for arbitrary-length messages. Furthermore, it only calls the underlying PRF once, and all other computations involving the UHF are comparitively "cheap."

To understand the security of Carter-Wegman, we work backwards. The output $F(k, H(s, x))$ comes directly from a PRF. These outputs will look random as long as the inputs to the PRF are distinct. In this construction, the only way for PRF inputs to repeat is for there to be a collision in the UHF H. However, we have to be careful. We can only reason about the collision-resistance of H when its salt is secret and its outputs are hidden from the attacker. The salt is indeed hidden in this case (kept as part of the Carter-Wegman key), but its outputs are being used as PRF inputs. Fortunately, the guarantee of a PRF is that its outputs appear unrelated to its inputs. In other words, the PRF outputs leak no information about the PRF inputs (H-outputs). Indeed, this appears to be a situation where the UHF outputs are hidden from the attacker, so we can argue that collisions in H are negligibly likely.

Claim 12.12: If H is a secure UHF and F is a secure PRF, then the Carter-Wegman construction (Construction 12.11) is a secure PRF, and hence a secure MAC as well.

Proof: We will show that $\mathcal{L}^{\text{CW}}_{\text{prf-real}} \approx \mathcal{L}^{\text{CW}}_{\text{prf-rand}}$ using a standard hybrid technique.

The starting point is $\mathcal{L}^{\text{CW}}_{\text{prf-real}}$.

$\mathcal{L}^{\text{CW}}_{\text{prf-real}}$

$k \leftarrow \{0,1\}^{\lambda}$
$s \leftarrow \mathcal{S}$

LOOKUP(x):
  $y := H(s,x)$
  return $F(k,y)$

We have applied the security of F, by factoring out in terms of $\mathcal{L}^{F}_{\text{prf-real}}$, replacing it with $\mathcal{L}^{F}_{\text{prf-rand}}$, and inlining the result.

$T :=$ empty assoc. array
$s \leftarrow \mathcal{S}$

LOOKUP(x):
  $y := H(s,x)$
  if $T[y]$ undefined:
    $T[y] \leftarrow \{0,1\}^{out}$
  return $T[y]$

The lookup subroutine has the property that if it is called on the same x twice, it will return the same result. It therefore does no harm to cache the answer every time. The second time lookup is called on the same value x, the previous value is loaded from cache rather than recomputed. This change has no effect on the calling program.

```
cache := empty assoc. array
T := empty assoc. array
s ← S

LOOKUP(x):
  if cache[x] undefined:
    y := H(s, x)
    if T[y] undefined:
      T[y] ← {0,1}^out
    cache[x] := T[y]
  return cache[x]
```

Note that if lookup is first called on x' and then later on x, where $H(s, x) = H(s, x')$, lookup will return the same result. We therefore modify the library to keep track of H-outputs and inputs. Whenever the library computes $y = H(s, x)$, it stores $H_{\text{inv}}[y] = x$. However, if $H_{\text{inv}}[y]$ already exists, it means that this x and $x' = H_{\text{inv}}[y]$ are a collision under H. In that case, the library directly returns whatever it previously returned on input x'. This change has no effect on the calling program.

```
cache := empty assoc. array
H_inv := empty assoc. array
T := empty assoc. array
s ← S

LOOKUP(x):
  if cache[x] undefined:
    y := H(s, x)
    if H_inv[y] defined:
      x' := H_inv[y]
      return cache[x']
    if T[y] undefined:
      T[y] ← {0,1}^out
    H_inv[y] := x
    cache[x] := T[y]
  return cache[x]
```

In the previous hybrid, $T[y]$ is set at the same time $H_{\text{inv}}[y]$ is set - on the first call lookup (x) such that $H(s, x) = y$. Therefore, it has no effect on the calling program to check whether $T[y]$ is defined or check whether $H_{\text{inv}}[y]$ is defined.

```
cache := empty assoc. array
H_inv := empty assoc. array
T := empty assoc. array
s ← S

LOOKUP(x):
  if cache[x] undefined:
    y := H(s,x)
    if H_inv[y] defined:
      x' := H_inv[y]
      return cache[x']
    if H_inv[y] undefined:
      T[y] ← {0,1}^out
    H_inv[y] := x
    cache[x] := T[y]
  return cache[x]
```

Note that if $H_{\text{inv}}[y]$ is defined, then lookup returns within that if-statement. The line cache $[x] := T[y]$ is therefore only executed in the case that $H_{\text{inv}}[y]$ was not initially defined. Instead of choosing $T[y]$ only to immediately assign it to cache $[x]$, we just assign directly to cache $[x]$. This change has no effect on the calling program, and it does away with the T associative array entirely.

```
cache := empty assoc. array
H_inv := empty assoc. array
s ← S

LOOKUP(x):
  if cache[x] undefined:
    y := H(s,x)
    if H_inv[y] defined:
      x' := H_inv[y]
      return cache[x']
    if H_inv[y] undefined:
      cache[x] ← {0,1}^out
    H_inv[y] := x
  return cache[x]
```

The if-statements involving H_{inv} in this hybrid are checking whether x has collided with any previous x' under H. All of this logic, including the evaluation of H, can be factored out in terms of $\mathcal{L}^{H}_{\text{bcr-real}}$. At this point in the sequence of hybrids, the output of H is not needed, except to check whether a collision has been encountered (and if so, what the offending inputs are). Again, this change has no effect on the calling program. The result is:

```
cache := empty assoc. array

LOOKUP(x):
  if cache[x] undefined:
    if TEST(x) = x' ≠ false :
      return cache[x']
    else:
      cache[x] ← {0,1}^out
  return cache[x]
```

$\diamond$

$\mathcal{L}^H_{\text{bcr-real}}$

```
s ← S
H_inv := empty assoc. array

TEST(x):
  y := H(s,x)
  if H_inv[y] defined:
    return H_inv[y]
  H_inv[y] := x
  return false
```

The security of H is that we can swap $\mathcal{L}^H_{\text{bcr-real}}$ for $\mathcal{L}^H_{\text{bcr-fake}}$, with negligible effect on the calling program. Note that test algorithm in $\mathcal{L}_{\text{bcr-fake}}$ always returns false. This leads us to simply remove the "if test(x) $\neq f$ false" clause, resulting in the following:

$\mathcal{L}^{\text{CW}}_{\text{prf-rand}}$

```
cache := empty assoc. array
LOOKUP(x):
  if cache[x] undefined:
    cache[x] ← {0,1}^out
  return cache[x]
```

Since this is exactly $\mathcal{L}^{\text{CW}}_{\text{prf-rand}}$, we are done. We have shown that $\mathcal{L}^{\text{CW}}_{\text{prf-rand}} \approx \mathcal{L}^{\text{CW}}_{\text{prf-rand}}$. □

12.4 Galois Counter Mode for AEAD

The most common block cipher mode for AEAD is called Galois Counter Mode (GCM). GCM is essentially an instance of encrypt-then-MAC, combining CTR mode for encryption and the polynomial-based Carter-Wegman MAC for authentication. GCM is relatively inexpensive since it requires only one call to the block cipher per plaintext block, plus one multiplication for each block of ciphertext + associated data.

Rather than using polynomials over $\mathbb{Z}_p$, GCM mode uses polynomials defined over a finite field with 2^λ elements. Such fields are often called "Galois fields," which leads to the name Galois counter mode.

To do: *More information about GCM will go here. Again, would be nice to have a crash course in finite fields.*

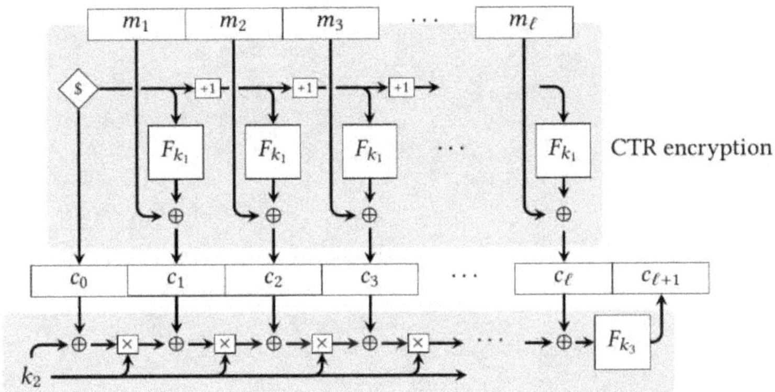

Carter-Wegman MAC of CTR ciphertext

Exercises

12.1. Suppose Enc-then-MAC+AD is instantiated with CBC mode and any secure MAC, as described in Construction 12.4. The scheme is secure for fixed-length associated data. Show that if variable-length associated data is allowed, then the scheme does not provide AEAD security.

Note: you are not attacking the MAC! Take advantage of the fact that $d\|c$ is ambiguous when the length of d is not fixed and publicly known.

12.2. Suggest a way to make Construction 12.4 secure for variable-length associated data. Prove that your construction is secure.

12.3. Show that if you know the salt s of the Poly-UHF construction (Construction 12.9), you can efficiently find a collision.

12.4. Show that if you are allowed to see only the output of Poly-UHF (i.e., the salt remains hidden), on chosen inputs then you can compute the salt.

Chapter 13

RSA & Digital Signatures

RSA was among the first public-key cryptography developed. It was first described in 1978, and is named after its creators, Ron Rivest, Adi Shamir, and Len Adleman. [1] RSA can be used as a building block for public-key encryption and digital signatures. In this chapter we discuss only the application of RSA for digital signatures.

13.1 "Dividing" Mod n

to-do: I'm considering moving some of this material to Chapter 3 (secret sharing) - enough to understand that every nonzero element has a multiplicative inverses modulo a prime (totients, etc can stay here). That way, I don't have to say "trust me, this can be made to work" when describing Lagrange interpolation over a prime field, and students can play around with secret sharing using Sage. Also, students will see that there is "serious math" in the course already in chapter 3 so they don't get blindsided as we transition into public-key crypto. (Not to mention, this chapter is too long.)

Please review the material from Section 0.2, to make sure your understanding of basic modular arithmetic is fresh. You should be comfortable with the definitions of $\mathbb{Z}_n$, congruence ($\equiv_n$), the modulus operator (%), and how to do addition, multiplication, and subtraction mod$n$.

Note that we haven't mentioned division mod$n$. Does it even make sense to talk about division mod$n$?

Example

Consider the following facts which hold mod 15:

$$\begin{array}{ll} 2 \cdot 8 \equiv_{15} 1 & 10 \cdot 8 \equiv_{15} 5 \\ 4 \cdot 8 \equiv_{15} 2 & 12 \cdot 8 \equiv_{15} 6 \\ 6 \cdot 8 \equiv_{15} 3 & 14 \cdot 8 \equiv_{15} 7 \\ 8 \cdot 8 \equiv_{15} 4 & \end{array}$$

Now imagine replacing " $\cdot\ 8$ *" with "* $\div\ 2$ *" in each of these examples:*

$$\begin{array}{ll} 2 \div 2 \equiv_{15} 1 & 10 \div 2 \equiv_{15} 5 \\ 4 \div 2 \equiv_{15} 2 & 12 \div 2 \equiv_{15} 6 \\ 6 \div 2 \equiv_{15} 3 & 14 \div 2 \equiv_{15} 7 \\ 8 \div 2 \equiv_{15} 4 & \end{array}$$

Everything still makes sense! Somehow, multiplying by $8 mod 15$ seems to be the same thing as "dividing by 2 " mod 15.

The previous examples all used $x \cdot 8(x \div 2)$ where x was an even number. What happens when x is an odd number?

$$3 \cdot 8 \equiv_{15} 9 \Leftrightarrow \text{ " } 3 \div 2 \equiv_{15} 9 \text{ "??}$$

This might seem non-sensical, but if we make the substitutions $3 \equiv_{15} - 12$ and $9 \equiv_{15} - 6$, then we do indeed get something that makes sense:

$$-12 \cdot 8 \equiv_{15} - 6 \Leftrightarrow -12 \div 2 \equiv_{15} - 6$$

This example shows that there is surely some interesting relationship among the numbers 2,8 , and 15 . It seems reasonable to interpret "multiplication by 8 " as "division by 2 " when working mod15.

Is there a way we can do something similar for "division by 3 " mod 15 ? Can we find some y where "multiplication by $y$mod15 " has the same behavior as "division by 3mod 15 ?" In particular, we would seek a value y that satisfies $3 \cdot y \equiv_{15} 1$, but you can check for yourself that no such value of y exists.

Why can we "divide by 2 " mod15 but we apparently cannot "divide by 3 " mod15 ? We will explore this question in the remainder of this section.

Multiplicative Inverses

We usually don't directly use the terminology of "division" with modular arithmetic. Instead of saying "division by 2 ", we say "multiplication by 2^{-1} ", where 2^{-1} is just another name for 8.

Definition 13.1 (x^{-1}mod$n$):

The multiplicative inverse of $x$mod$n$ is the integer y that satisfies $x \cdot y \equiv_n 1$ (if such a number exists). We usually refer to the multiplicative inverse of x as " $x - 1$."

Example: *Contuining to work mod 15, we have:*

- $4^{-1} \equiv_{15} 4$ since $4 \cdot 4 = 16 \equiv_{15} 1$. Hence 4 is its own multiplicative inverse! You can also understand this as:

$$4^{-1} = (2^2)^{-1} = (2^{-1})^2 \equiv_{15} 8^2 = 64 \equiv_{15} 4$$

- $7^{-1} \equiv_{15} 13$ since $7 \cdot 13 = 91 \equiv_{15} 1$.

We are interested in which numbers have a multiplicative inverse mod$n$.

Definition 13.2 ($\mathbb{Z}_n^*$): The multiplicative group [2] modulo n is defined as:

$$\mathbb{Z}_n^* = \{x \in \mathbb{Z}_n \mid x \text{ has a multiplicative inverse mod} n\}$$

For example, we have seen that $\mathbb{Z}_n^*$ contains the numbers 2, 4, and 7 (and perhaps others), but it doesn't contain the number 3 since 3 does not have a multiplicative inverse.

So which numbers have a multiplicative inverse mod$n$, in general? (Which numbers belong to $\mathbb{Z} *_n$?) The answer is quite simple:

Theorem 13.3: x has a multiplicative inverse mod$n$ if and only if $\gcd(x, n) = 1$. In other words, $\mathbb{Z}_n^* = \{x \in \mathbb{Z}_n \mid \gcd(x, n) = 1\}$.

We prove the theorem using another fact from abstract algebra which is often useful:

Theorem 13.4 (Bezout's Theorem) For all integers x and y, there exist integers a and b such that $ax + by = \gcd(x, y)$. In fact, $\gcd(x, y)$ is the smallest positive integer that can be written as an integral linear combination of x and y.

We won't prove Bezout's theorem, but we will show how it is used to prove Theorem 13.3:

Proof (of Theorem 13.3): ($\Leftarrow$) Suppose $\gcd(x, n) = 1$. We will show that x has a multiplicative inverse mod$n$. From Bezout's theorem, there exist integers a, b satisfying $ax + bn = 1$. By reducing both sides of this equation modulo n, we have

$$1 = ax + bn \equiv_n ax + b \cdot 0 = ax$$

Thus the integer a that falls out of Bezout's theorem is the multiplicative inverse of x modulo n.

($\Rightarrow$) Suppose x has a multiplicative inverse mod$n$, so $xx^{-1} \equiv_n 1$. We need to show that $\gcd(x, n) = 1$. From the definition of $\equiv_n$, we know that n divides $xx^{-1} - 1$, so we can write $xx^{-1} - 1 = kn$ (as an expression over the integers) for some integer k. Rearranging, we have $xx^{-1} - kn = 1$. Since we can write 1 as an integral linear combination of x and n, Bezout's theorem says that we must have $\gcd(x, n) = 1$.

Example:

$\mathbb{Z}_{15} = \{0,1, \dots ,14\}$, and to obtain $\mathbb{Z}_{15}^*$ we exclude any of the numbers that share a common factor with 15. In other words, we exclude the multiples of 3 and multiples of 5 . The remaining numbers are $\mathbb{Z}_{15}^* = \{1,2,4,7,8,11,13,14\}$.

Since 11 is a prime, 0 is the only number in $\mathbb{Z}_{11}$ that shares a common factor with 11. All the rest satisfy $\gcd(x, 11) = 1$. Hence, $\mathbb{Z}_{11}^* = \{1,2, \cdots ,10\}$.

Example

We can use Sage [3] to play around with these concepts. Sage supports the % operator for modulus:

```
sage: 2 * 8 % 15
```

It also supports a convenient way to generate " $\mathbb{Z}_n$-objects," or Mod-objects as they are called. An object like Mod (2,15) represents the value $2 \in \mathbb{Z}_{15}$, and all of its operations are overloaded to be the mod-15 operations:

```
sage: Mod(2,15)*8

1

sage: Mod(2,15)+31415926

3

sage: Mod(-1,15)

14
```

In Sage, you can compute multiplicative inverses in a few different ways:

```
sage: Mod(2,15)^-1

8

sage: 1/Mod(2,15)

8
```

```
sage: 2.inverse_mod(15)

8

sage: (1/2) % 15

8
```

Sage is smart enough to know when a multiplicative inverse doesn't exist:

```
sage: Mod(3,15)^-1

ZeroDivisionError: inverse of Mod(3, 15) does not exist
```

Sage supports huge integers, with no problem:

```
sage: n = 3141592653589793238462643383279502884197169399375105820974944

sage: x = 123456789012345678901234567890123456789012345678901

sage: 1/Mod(x,n)

2234412539909122491686747985730075304931040310346724620855837
```

The relationship between multiplicative inverses and GCD goes even farther than Theorem 13.3. Recall that we can compute $\gcd(x, n)$ efficiently using Euclid's algorithm. There is a relatively simple modification to Euclid's algorithm that also computes the corresopnding Bezout coefficients with little extra work. In other words, given x and n, it is possible to efficiently compute integers a, b, and d such that

$$ax + bn = d = \gcd(x, n)$$

In the case where $\gcd(x, n) = d = 1$, the integer a is a multiplicative inverse of $x \mathrm{mod} n$. The "extended Euclidean algorithm" for GCD is given below:

```
EXTGCD(x, y):
  // returns (d, a, b) such that gcd(x, y) = d = ax + by
  if y = 0:
    return (x, 1, 0)
  else:
    (d, a, b) := EXTGCD(y, x % y)
    return (d, b, a − b⌊x/y⌋)
```

Example

Sage implements the extended Euclidean algorithm as "xgcd":

```
sage: xgcd(427,529)

(1, 223, -180)

sage: 223*427 + (-180)*529

1
```

You can then see that 223 and 427 are multiplicative inverses mod 529:

```
sage: 427*223 % 529

1
```

The Totient Function

Euler's totient function is defined as $\phi(n) \stackrel{\text{def}}{=} |\mathbb{Z}_n^*|$; that is, the number of elements of Z_n that have multiplicative inverses.

As an example, if n is a prime, then $\mathbb{Z}_n^* = \mathbb{Z}_n \setminus \{0\}$ because every integer in $\mathbb{Z}_n$ apart from zero is relatively prime to n. Therefore, $\phi(n) = n - 1$ in this case.

RSA involves a modulus n that is the product of two distinct primes $n = pq$. In that case, $\phi(n) = (p-1)(q-1)$. To see why, let's count how many elements in $\mathbb{Z}_{pq}$ share a common divisor with pq (i.e., are not in $\mathbb{Z}_{pq}^*$).

- The multiples of p share a common divisor with pq. These include $0, p, 2p, 3p, \ldots, (q-1)p$. There are q elements in this list.

- The multiples of q share a common divisor with pq. These include $0, q, 2q, 3q, \dots, (p-1)q$. There are p elements in this list.

We have clearly double-counted element 0 in these lists. But no other element is double counted. Any item that occurs in both lists would be a common multiple of both p and q, but since p and q are relatively prime, their least common multiple is pq, which is larger than any item in these lists.

We count $p + q - 1$ elements of $\mathbb{Z}_{pq}$ which share a common divisor with pq. The rest belong to $\mathbb{Z}^*_{pq}$, and there are $pq - (p + q - 1) = (p - 1)(q - 1)$ of them. Hence $\phi(pq) = (p - 1)(q - 1)$.

General formulas for $\phi(n)$ exist, but they typically rely on knowing the prime factorization of n. We will see more connections between the difficulty of computing $\phi(n)$ and the difficulty of factoring n later in this part of the course.

The reason we consider $\phi(n)$ at all is this fundamental theorem from abstract algebra:

Theorem 13.5 (Euler's Theorem)
If $x \in \mathbb{Z}^*_n$ then $x^{\phi(n)} \equiv_n 1$.

Example
Using the formula for $\phi(n)$, we can see that $\phi(15) = \phi(3 \cdot 5) = (3 - 1)(5 - 1) = 8$. Euler's theorem says that raising any element of $\mathbb{Z}^*_{15}$ to the 8 power results in 1: We can use Sage to verify this:

```
sage: for i in range(15):

....: if gcd(i,15) == 1:

...: print("%d^8 mod 15 = %d" % (i, i^8 % 15))

....:

1^8 mod 15 = 1

2^8 mod 15 = 1

4^8 mod 15 = 1

7^8 mod 15 = 1

8^8 mod 15 = 1

11^8 mod 15 = 1
```

```
13^8 mod 15 = 1

14^8 mod 15 = 1
```

13.2 The RSA Function

The RSA function is defined as follows:

- Let p and q be distinct primes (later we will say more about how they are chosen), and let $N = pq. N$ is called the RSA modulus.
- Let e and d be integers such that $ed \equiv_{\phi(N)} 1$. That is, e and d are multiplicative inverses $\bmod \phi(N)$ – $\operatorname{not} \bmod N$!
- The RSA function is: $x \mapsto x^e \% N$, where $x \in \mathbb{Z}_N$.
- The inverse RSA function is: $y \mapsto y^d \% N$, where $x \in \mathbb{Z}_N$.

Essentially, the RSA function (and its inverse) is a simple modular exponentiation. The most confusing thing to remember about RSA is that e and d "live" in $\mathbb{Z}^*_{\phi(N)}$, while x and y "live" in $\mathbb{Z}_N$.

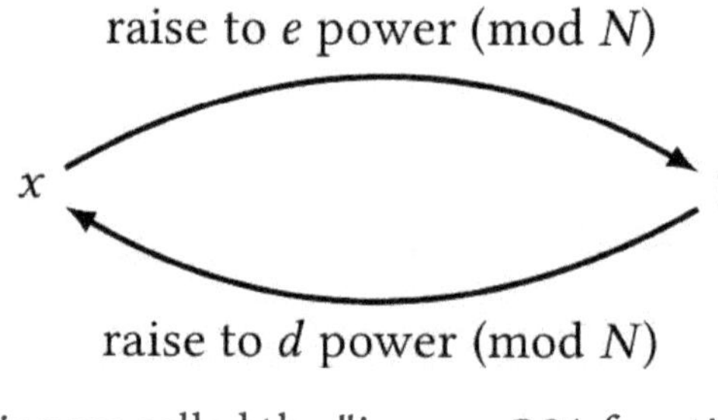

Let's make sure the function we called the "inverse RSA function" is actually an inverse of the RSA function. Let's start with an example:

Example In Sage, we can sample a random prime between 1 and k by using random_prime(k). We use it to sample the prime factors p and q :

```
sage: p = random_prime(10^5)

sage: q = random_prime(10^5)
```

```
sage: N = p*q
sage: N
36486589
```

Then we can compute the exponents e and d. Recall that they must be multiplicative inverses $mod\phi(N)$*, so they cannot share any common factors with* $\phi(N)$*. An easy way to ensure this is to choose e to be a prime:*

```
sage: phi = (p-1)*(q-1)
sage: e = random_prime(phi)
sage: e
2 8 9 3 1 4 3 1
sage: d = 1/Mod(e,phi)
sage: d
31549271
```

We can now raise something to the e power and again to the d power:

```
sage: x = 31415926
sage: y = x^e % N
sage: y
1 7 9 8 9 9 6
sage: y^d % N
3 1 4 1 5 9 2 6
```

As you can see, raising to the e power and then d power $(modN)$ *seems to bring us back to where we started (* x *).*

We can argue that raising-to-the- e-power and raising-to-the- d-power are inverses in general: Since $ed \equiv_{\phi(N)} 1$, we can write $ed = t\phi(N) + 1$ for some integer t. Then:

$$(x^e)^d = x^{ed} = x^{t\phi(N)+1} = \left(x^{\phi(N)}\right)^t x \equiv_N 1^t x = x$$

Note that we have used the fact that $x^{\phi(N)} \equiv_N 1$ from Euler's theorem. [4]

How [Not] to Exponentiate Huge Numbers

When you see an expression like " $x^e \% N$ ", you might be tempted to implement it with the following algorithm:

```
NaiveExponentiate(x, e, N):
  result = 1
  for i = 1 to e: // compute x^e
    result = result × x
  return result % N
```

While this algorithm would indeed give the correct answer, it is a really bad way of doing it. In practice, we use RSA with numbers that are thousands of bits long. Suppose we run the NaiveExponentiate algorithm with arguments x, e, and N which are around a thousand bits each (so the magnitude of these numbers is close to 2^{1000}):

1. The algorithm will spend approximately 2^{1000} iterations in the for-loop!
2. The algorithm computes x^e as an integer first, and then reduces that integer mod$N$. Observe that x^2 is roughly 2000 bits long, x^3 is roughly 3000 bits long, etc. So it would take about $2^{1000} \cdot 1000$ bits just to write down the integer x^e.

As you can see, there is neither enough time nor storage capacity in the universe to use this algorithm. So how can we actually compute values like $x^e \% N$ on huge numbers?

1. Suppose you were given an integer x and were asked to compute x^{17}. You can compute it as:

$$x^{17} = \underbrace{x \cdot x \cdot x \cdots x}_{16 \text{ multiplications}}$$

But a more clever way is to observe that:

$$x^{17} = x^{16} \cdot x = (((x^2)^2)^2)^2 \cdot x$$

This expression can be evaluated with only 5 multiplications (squaring is just muliplying a number by itself).

More generally, you can compute an expression like x^e by following the recurrence below. The method is called exponentiation by repeated squaring, for reasons that are hopefully clear:

$$x^e = \begin{cases} 1 & \text{if } e = 0 \\ (x^{\frac{e}{2}})^2 & \text{if } e \text{ even} \\ (x^{\frac{e-1}{2}})^2 \cdot x & \text{if } e \text{ odd} \end{cases}$$

```
BETTEREXP(x, e):
  if e = 0: return 1
  if e even:
    return BETTEREXP(x, e/2)^2
  if e odd:
    return BETTEREXP(x, (e-1)/2)^2 · x
```

BetterExp divides the e argument by two (more or less) each time it recurses, until reaching the base case. Hence, the number of recursive calls is $O(\log\ e)$. In each recursive call there are only a constant number of multiplications (including squarings). So overall this algorithm requires only $O(\log\ e)$ multiplications (compared to $e - 1$ multiplications by just multiplying m by itself e times). In the case where $e \sim 2^{1000}$, this means only a few thousand multiplications.

2. We care about only $x^e\%N$, not the intermediate integer value x^e. One of the most fundamental features of modular arithmetic is that you can reduce any intermediate values mod$N$ if you care about the final result only mod$N$.

Revisiting our previous example:

$$x^{17}\%N = x^{16} \cdot x\%N = (((x^2\%N)^2\%N)^2\%N)^2 \cdot x\%N$$

More generally, we can reduce all intermediate value mod$N$:

```
MODEXP(x, e, N): // compute x^e % N
  if e = 0: return 1
  if e even:
    return MODEXP(x, e/2, N)^2 % N
  if e odd:
    return MODEXP(x, (e-1)/2, N)^2 · x % N
```

This algorithm avoids the problem of computing the astronomically huge integer x^e. It never needs to store any value (much) larger than N.

Warning: *Even this ModExp algorithm isn't an ideal way to implement exponentiation for cryptographic purposes. Exercise 13.10 explores some unfortunate properties of this exponentiation algorithm.*

Example: *Most math libraries implement exponentiation using repeated squaring. For example, you can use Sage to easily calculate numbers with huge exponents:*

```
sage: 427^31415926 % 100

89
```

However, this expression still tells Sage to compute $427^{31415926}$ *as an integer, before reducing it mod 100. As such, it takes some time to perform this computation.*

If you try an expression like x^e% N with a larger exponent, Sage will give a memory error. How can we tell Sage to perform modular reduction at every intermediate step during repeated squaring? The answer is to use Sage's Mod objects, for example:

```
sage: Mod(427,100)^314159265358979

63
```

This expression performs repeated squaring on the object Mod(427,100). Since a Mod-object's operations are all overloaded (to give the answer only mod n), this has the result of doing a modular reduction after every squaring and multiplication. This expression runs instantaneously, even with very large numbers.

Security Properties & Discussion

RSA is what is called a trapdoor function.

- One user generates the RSA parameters (primarily N, e, and d) and makes N and e public, while keeping d private.
- Functionality properties: Given only the public information N and e, it is easy to compute the RSA function ($x \mapsto x^e \% N$). Given the private information (d) it clearly easy to compute the RSA inverse ($y \mapsto y^d \% N$).

- Security property: Given only the public information, it should be hard to compute the RSA inverse ($y \mapsto y^d \% N$) on randomly chosen values. In other words, the only person who is able to compute the RSA inverse function is the person who generated the RSA parameters.
- to-do The security property is not natural to express in our language of security definitions (libraries).

Currently the best known attacks against RSA (i.e., ways to compute the inverse RSA function given only the public information) involve factoring the modulus. If we want to ensure that RSA is secure as a trapdoor function, we must understand the state of the art for factoring large numbers.

Before discussing the performance of factoring algorithms, remember that we measure performance as a function of the length of the input - how many bits it takes to write the input. In a factoring algorithm, the input is a large number N, and it takes roughly $n = \log_2 N$ bits to write down that number. We will discuss the running time of algorithms as a function of n, not N. Just keep in mind the difference in cost between writing down a 1000 -bit number ($n = 1000$) vs counting up to a 1000 -bit number ($N = 2^{1000}$)

Everyone knows the "trial division" method of factoring: given a number N, check whether i divides N, for every $i \in \{2, \ldots \sqrt{N}\}$. This algorithm requires $\sqrt{N} = 2^{n/2}$ divisions in the worst case. It is an exponential-time algorithm since we measure performance in terms of the bit-length n.

If this were the best-known factoring algorithm, then we would need to make N only as large as 2^{256} to make factoring require 2^{128} effort. But there are much better factoring algorithms than trial division. The fastest factoring algorithm today is called the Generalized Number Field Sieve (GNFS), and its complexity is something like $O\left(n^{\left(\frac{n}{\log n}\right)^{\frac{1}{3}}}\right)$. This is not a polynomial-time algorithm, but it's much faster than trial division.

Example: *Sage can easily factor reasonably large numbers. Factoring the following 200-bit RSA modulus on my modest computer takes about 10 seconds:*

```
sage: p = random_prime(2^100)

sage: q = random_prime(2^100)

sage: N = p * q
```

sage: factor(N)

206533721079613722225064934611 * 517582080563726621130111418123

As of January 2020, the largest RSA modulus that has been (publically) factored is a 795-bit modulus. [5] Factoring this number required the equivalent of 900 CPU-core-years, or roughly 2^{66} total clock cycles.

All of this is to say, the numbers involved in RSA need to be quite large to resist factoring attacks (i.e., require 2^{128} effort for state-of-the-art factoring algorithms). Current best practices suggest to use 2048- or 4096-bit RSA moduli, meaning that p and q are each 1024 or 2048 bits.

to-do "What about quantum computers?" is a common FAQ that I should address here.

13.3 Digital Signatures

MACs are a cryptographic primitive that provide authenticity. A valid MAC tag on m is "proof" that someone who knows the key has vouched for m. MACs are a symmetric-key primitive, in the sense that generating a MAC tag and verifying a MAC tag both require the same key (in fact, a tag is verified by re-computing it).

Digital signatures are similar to MACs, but with separate keys for signing and verification. A digital signature scheme consists of the following algorithms:

- KeyGen: outputs a pair of keys (sk, vk), where sk is the signing key and vk is the verification key.
- Sign: takes the signing key sk and a message m as input, and outputs a signature σ.
- Ver: takes the verification key vk, message m, and a potential signature σ as input; outputs a boolean.

If indeed σ is an output of $\text{Sign}(sk, m)$, then $\text{Ver}(vk, m, \sigma)$ should output true. Intuitively, it should be hard for an attacker to find any other (m, σ) pairs that cause Ver to output true.

The idea behind digital signatures is to make vk public. In other words, anyone (even the attacker) should be able to verify signatures. But only the holder of sk (the person who generated vk and sk) should be able to generate valid signatures. Furthermore, this guarantee should hold even against an attacker who sees many examples of valid signatures. The attacker should not be able to generate new valid signatures.

We formalize this security property in a similar way that we formalized the security of MACs: "only the secret-key holder can generate valid tags, even after seeing chosen examples of valid tags."

Definition 13.6: *Let Σ be a signature scheme. We say that Σ is a secure signature if $\mathcal{L}^{\Sigma}_{\text{sig-real}} \approx \mathcal{L}^{\Sigma}_{\text{sig-fake}}$, where:*

$\mathcal{L}^{\Sigma}_{\text{sig-real}}$

```
(vk, sk) ← Σ.KeyGen

GETVK():
  return vk

GETSIG(m):
  return Σ.Sign(sk, m)

VERSIG(m, σ):
  return Σ.Ver(vk, m, σ)
```

$\mathcal{L}^{\Sigma}_{\text{sig-fake}}$

```
(vk, sk) ← Σ.KeyGen
S := ∅

GETVK():
  return vk

GETSIG(m):
  σ := Σ.Sign(sk, m)
  S := S ∪ {(m, σ)}
  return σ

VERSIG(m, σ):
  return (m, σ) ∈? S
```

Similar to the security definition for MACs, the libraries differ only in how they verify signatures provided by the attacker (versig). If the attacker can generate a messagesignature pair (m, σ) that (1) verifies correctly, but (2) was not generated previously by the library itself, then versig from the $\mathcal{L}_{\text{sig-real}}$ library will return true, while the $\mathcal{L}_{\text{sig-fake}}$ library would return false. By asking for the libraries to be indistinguishable, we are really asking that the attacker cannot find any such message-signature pair (forgery).

The main difference to the MAC definition is that, unlike for the MAC setting, we intend to make a verification key public. The library can run $(vk, sk) \leftarrow$ KeyGen, but these values remain private by default. To make vk public, we explicitly provide an accessor getvk to the attacker.

"Textbook" RSA Signatures

Signatures have an asymmetry: everyone should be able to verify a signature, but only the holder of the signing key should be able to generate a valid signature. The RSA function has a similar asymmetry: if N and e are public, then anyone can raise things to the e power, but only someone with d can raise things to the d power.

This similarity suggests that we can use RSA for signatures in the following way:

- The verification key is (N, e) and the signing key is (N, d), where these values have the appropriate RSA relationship.
- A signature of message m (here m is an element of $\mathbb{Z}_N$) is the value $\sigma = m^d \% N$. Intuitively, only someone with the signing key can generate this value for a given m.
- To verify a signature σ on a message m, our goal is to check whether $\sigma \equiv_N m^d$. However, we are given only N and e, not d. Consider raising both sides of this equation to the e power:

$$\sigma^e \equiv_N (m^d)^e \equiv_N m$$

The second equality is from the standard RSA property. Now this check can be done given only the public information N and e.

A formal description of this scheme is given below:

Construction 13.7: *The key generation algorithm is not listed here, but N, e, d are generated in the usual way for (Textbook RSA) RSA. The signing key is $sk = (N, d)$ and the verification key is $vk = (N, e)$.*

$\text{Sign}(sk = (N, d), m)$:	$\text{Ver}(vk = (N, e), m, \sigma)$:
return $m^d \% N$	$m' := \sigma^e \% N$
	return $m \stackrel{?}{=} m'$

Unfortunately, textbook RSA signatures are useful only as a first intuition. They are not secure! A simple attack is the following:

Suppose an attacker knows the verification key (N, e) and sees a valid signature $\sigma \equiv_N m^d$ for some message m. Then σ^2 is also a valid signature for the message m^2, since:

$$\sigma^2 \equiv_n (m^d)^2 = (m^2)^d$$

The attacker can easily generate a forged signature on a new message m^2, making the scheme insecure.

Hashed RSA Signatures

The problem with textbook RSA signatures is that the signatures and plaintexts had a very strong algebraic relationship. Squaring the signature had the effect of squaring the underlying message. One way to fix the problem is to "break" this algebraic relationship. Hashed RSA signatures break the algebraic structure by applying the RSA function not to m directly, but to $H(m)$, where H is a suitable hash function (with outputs interpreted as elements of $\mathbb{Z}_N$).

Construction 13.8 (Textbook RSA):

$\text{Sign}(sk = (N,d), m)$:	$\text{Ver}(vk = (N,e), m, \sigma)$:
return $H(m)^d \% N$	$y := \sigma^e \% N$
	return $H(m) \stackrel{?}{=} y$

Let's see how this change thwarts the attack on textbook signatures. If σ is a valid signature of m, we have $\sigma \equiv_N H(m)^d$. Squaring both sides leads to $\sigma^2 \equiv_N (H(m)^2)^d$. Is this the valid signature of any m' ? An attacker would have to identify some m' that has $H(m') = H(m)^2$. If the hash function is a good one, then this should be hard.

Of course, this is not a formal proof. It is possible to formally prove the security of hashed RSA signatures. The precise statement of security is: "if RSA is a secure trapdoor function and H is modeled as a random oracle, then hashed RSA signatures are a secure signature scheme." Since we have not given formal definitions for either trapdoor functions or random oracles, we won't see the proof in this book.

13.4 Chinese Remainder Theorem

When doing arithmetic mod$N$, we can sometimes use knowledge of the fact to speed things up. This section discusses the math behind these speedups.

History: *In the Sunzi Suanjing, written some time around the 4th century ce, Chinese mathematician Sunzi posed an interesting puzzle involving remainders:*

> *"We have a number of things, but we do not know exactly how many. If we count them by threes we have two left over. If we count them by fives we have three left over. If we count them by sevens we have two left over. How many things are there?"* [6]

Sunzi's puzzle is the first known instance of a system of simultaneous equations involving modular arithmetic: In our notation, he is asking us to solve for x in the following system of congruences:

$$x \equiv_3 2$$
$$x \equiv_5 3$$
$$x \equiv_7 2$$

We can solve such systems of equations using what is called (in the West) the Chinese Remainder Theorem (CRT). Below is one of the simpler formations of the Chinese Remainder Theorem, involving only two equations/moduli (unlike the example above, which has three moduli 3,5, and 7):

Theorem 13.9 (CRT):

Suppose $\gcd(r, s) = 1$. Then for all integers u, v, there is a solution for x in the following system of equations:

$$x \equiv_r u$$
$$x \equiv_s v$$

Furthermore, this solution is unique modulo rs.

Since $\gcd(r, s) = 1$, we have by Bezout's theorem that $1 = ar + bs$ for some integers a and b. Furthermore, b and s are multiplicative inverses modulo r. Now choose $x = var + ubs$. Then,

$$x = var + ubs \equiv_r (va)0 + u(s^{-1}s) = u$$

So $x \equiv_r u$, as desired. Using similar reasoning mods, we can see that $x \equiv_s v$, so x is a solution to both equations.

Now we argue that this solution is unique modulo rs. Suppose x and x' are two solutions to the system of equations, so we have:

$$x \equiv_r x' \equiv_r u$$

$$x \equiv_s x' \equiv_s v$$

Since $x \equiv_r x'$ and $x \equiv_s x'$, it must be that $x - x'$ is a multiple of r and a multiple of s. Since r and s are relatively prime, their least common multiple is rs, so $x - x'$ must be a multiple of r s. Hence, $x \equiv_{rs} x'$. So any two solutions to this system of equations are congruent modrs. □

Example: *Sage implements the crt function to solve for x in these kinds of systems of equations. Suppose we want to solve for x :*

$$x \equiv_{427} 42$$
$$x \equiv_{529} 123$$

In Sage, the solution can be found as follows:

```
sage: crt( 42,123, 427,529 )

3 2 9 2 1
```

We can check the solution:

```
sage: 32921 % 427

42

sage: 32921 % 529

123
```

CRT Encodings Preserve Structure

Let's call $(u, v) \in \mathbb{Z}_r \times \mathbb{Z}_s$ the CRT encoding of $x \in \mathbb{Z}_{rs}$ if they satisfy the usual relationship:

$$x \equiv_r u$$
$$x \equiv_s v$$

We can convert any $x \in \mathbb{Z}_{rs}$ into its CRT encoding quite easily, via $x \mapsto (x\%r, x\%s)$. The Chinese Remainder Theorem says that any $(u, v) \in \mathbb{Z}_r \times \mathbb{Z}_s$ is a valid CRT encoding of a unique $x \in \mathbb{Z}_{rs}$; and the proof of the theorem shows how to convert from the CRT encoding into the "usual $\mathbb{Z}_{rs}$ encoding."

The amazing thing about these CRT encodings is that they preserve all sorts of arithmetic structure.

Claim 13.10

If (u, v) *is the CRT encoding of* x*, and* (u', v') *is the CRT encoding of* x'*, then* $(u + u'\%r, v + v'\%s)$ *is the CRT encoding of* $x + x'\%rs$*.*

Example: *Taking* $r = 3$ *and* $s = 5$*, let's write down the CRT encodings of every element in* $\mathbb{Z}_{15}$*. In this table, every column contains* x *and its CRT encoding* (u, v) *:*

x	0	1	2	3	4	5	6	7	8	9	10	11	12	13	14
u	0	1	2	0	1	2	0	1	2	0	1	2	0	1	2
v	0	1	2	3	4	0	1	2	3	4	0	1	2	3	4

Highlight the columns for $x = 3$ *and* $x' = 7$ *and their sum* $x + x' = 10$*.*

x	0	1	2	3	4	5	6	7	8	9	10	11	12	13	14
u	0	1	2	0	1	2	0	1	2	0	1	2	0	1	2
v	0	1	2	3	4	0	1	2	3	4	0	1	2	3	4

Focusing on only the highlighted cells, the top row shows a true addition expression $3 + 7 \equiv_{15} 10$*; the second row shows a true addition expression* $0 + 1 \equiv_3 1$*; the third row shows a true addition expression* $3 + 2 \equiv_5 0$*.*

This pattern holds for any x *and* x'*, and I encourage you to try it!*

As if that weren't amazing enough, the same thing holds for multiplication:

Claim 13.11; *If* (u, v) *is the CRT encoding of* x*, and* (u', v') *is the CRT encoding of* x'*, then* $(u \cdot u'\%r, v \cdot v'\%s)$ *is the CRT encoding of* $x \cdot x'\%rs$*.*

Example: *Let's return to the $r = 3, s = 5$ setting for CRT and highlight $x = 6, x' = 7$, and their product $x \cdot x' \equiv_{15} 12$.*

x	0	1	2	3	4	5	6	7	8	9	10	11	12	13	14
u	0	1	2	0	1	2	0	1	2	0	1	2	0	1	2
v	0	1	2	3	4	0	1	2	3	4	0	1	2	3	4

The top row shows a true multiplication expression $6 \cdot 7 \equiv_{15} 12$; the second row shows a true multiplication expression $0 \cdot 1 \equiv_3 0$; the third row shows a true multiplication expression $1 \cdot 2 \equiv_5 2$.

This pattern holds for any x and x', and I encourage you to try it!

The CRT suggests a different, perhaps more indirect, way to do things mod rs. Suppose x has CRT encoding (u, v) and x' has CRT encoding (u', v'), and we want to compute $x + y \mathrm{mod} rs$. One wild idea is to first directly compute the CRT encoding of this answer, and then convert that encoding to the normal integer representation in $\mathbb{Z}_{rs}$.

In this case, we know that the answer $x + x'$ has the CRT encoding $(u + u'\%r, v + v'\%s)$. But this is the same as $(x + x'\%r, x + x'\%s)$ - do you see why? So, to add $x + x' \mathrm{mod} rs$, we just need to add $x + x' \mathrm{mod} r$, and then add$x + x' \mathrm{mods}$. This gives us the CRT encoding of the answer we want, and we can convert that CRT encoding back into a normal $\mathbb{Z}_{rs}$ integer.

The same idea works for multiplication as well, giving us the following:

CRT method for doing some operation [s] mod rs

1. Do the operation[s] you want, but mod r instead of mod rs.
2. Do the operation[s] you want, but mods instead of modrs.
3. Those two results are the CRT encoding of the final answer, so convert them back to the normal representation.

Example

Let's take the example $r = 3359$ *and* $s = 2953$*, which are relatively prime (so the CRT applies). Suppose we want to compute 3141592 + 6535897 % rs. Doing it the usual way in Sage looks like this:*

```
sage: r = 3359

sage: s = 2953

sage: (3141592 + 6535897) % (r*s)

9 6 7 7 4 8 9
```

Doing it in the CRT way looks like this.

```
sage: u = (3141592 + 6535897) % r

sage: v = (3141592 + 6535897) % s

sage: crt( u,v, r,s )

9 6 7 7 4 8 9
```

Both methods give the same answer!

Application to RSA

You might be wondering what the point of all of this is. [7] The CRT method seems like a very indirect and wasteful way to compute anything. This impression might be true for simple operations like addition and single multiplications. However, the CRT method is faster for exponentiation mod$N$, which is the main operation in RSA!

Example

In Sage, we can do basic exponentiation mod n as follows:

```
sage: def modexp(x,e,n): # x^e mod n

...:: return Mod(x,n)^e
```

If we are working over an RSA modulus and know its factorization $p \times q$, then we use the CRT method for exponentiation $mod pq$ as follows. We simply do the exponentiation $mod p$ and (separately) mod q, then use the crt function to convert back to $\mathbb{Z}_{pq}$.

```
sage: def crtmodexp(x,e,p,q): # x^e mod pq, using CRT speedup
...:: u = Mod(x,p)^e
...:: v = Mod(x,q)^e
....: return crt(u.lift(),v.lift(),p,q)
```

We need to use u.lift() and v. lift() to convert u and v from Mod-objects into integers, because that is what crt expects.

We can use both methods to perform an exponentiation, and measure how long it takes with the timeit function. In this example, N is about 2000 bits long, and the difference in speed is noticeable:

```
sage: p = random_prime(2^1000)
sage: q = random_prime(2^1000)
sage: N = p*q
sage: x = 12345678901234567
sage: e = randint(0,N) # random integer between 0 & N-1
sage: timeit('modexp(x,e,N)')
125 loops, best of 3: 5.34 ms per loop
sage: timeit('crtmodexp(x,e,p,q)')
125 loops, best of 3: 2.86 ms per loop
```

And just for good measure, we can check that both approaches give the same answer:

```
sage: modexp(x,e,N) == crtmodexp(x,e,p,q)
True
```

To understand why the CRT method is faster, it's important to know that the cost of standard modular exponentiation over a k-bit modulus is $O(k^3)$. For simplicity, let's pretend that exponentiation takes exactly k^3 steps. Suppose p and q are each k bits long, so that the RSA modulus N is $2k$ bits long. Hence, a standard exponentiation mod$N$ takes $(2k)^3 = 8k^3$ steps.

With the CRT method, we do an exponentiation mod$p$ and an exponentiation mod$q$. Each of these exponentiations takes k^3 steps, since p and q are only k bits long. Overall, we are only doing $2k^3$ steps in this approach, which is $4\times$ faster than the standard exponentiation mod$N$. In this simple analysis, we are not counting the cost of converting the CRT encoding back to the typical mod $-$ N representation. But this cost is much smaller than the cost of an exponentiation (both in practice and asymptotically).

It's worth pointing out that this speedup can only be done for RSA signing, and not verification. In order to take advantage of the CRT method to speed up exponentiation mod$N$, it's necessary to know the prime factors p and q. Only the person who knows the signing key knows these factors.

13.5 The Hardness of Factoring *N*

As previously mentioned, the best known way to break the security of RSA as a trapdoor function (i.e., to compute the inverse RSA function given only the public information N and) involves factoring the RSA modulus.

Factoring integers (or, more specifically, factoring RSA moduli) is believed to be a hard problem for classical computers. In this section we show that some other problems related to RSA are "as hard as factoring." What does it mean for a computational problem to be "as hard as factoring?" More formally, in this section we will show the following:

Theorem 13.12:
Either all of the following problems can be solved in polynomial-time, or none of them can:

1. Given an RSA modulus $N = pq$, compute its factors p and q.
2. Given an RSA modulus $N = pq$ compute $\phi(N) = (p-1)(q-1)$.

Given an RSA modulus $N = pq$ and value e, compute the corresponding d (satisfying $ed \equiv_{\phi(N)} 1$).

4. Given an RSA modulus $N = pq$, find any $x \not\equiv_N \pm 1$ such that $x^2 \equiv_N 1$.

To prove the theorem, we will show:

- if there is an efficient algorithm for (1), then we can use it as a subroutine to construct an efficient algorithm for (2). This is straight-forward: if you have a subroutine factoring N into p and q, then you can call the subroutine and then compute $(p-1)(q-1)$.
- if there is an efficient algorithm for (2), then we can use it as a subroutine to construct an efficient algorithm for (3). This is also straight-forward: if you have a subroutine computing $\phi(N)$ given N, then you can compute d exactly how it is computed in the key generation algorithm.
- if there is an efficient algorithm for (3), then we can use it as a subroutine to construct an efficient algorithm for (4).
- if there is an efficient algorithm for (4), then we can use it as a subroutine to construct an efficient algorithm for (1).

Below we focus on the final two implications.

Using square roots of unity to factor N

Problem (4) of Theorem 13.12 concerns a new concept known as square roots of unity:

Definition 13.13 (Sqrt of unity)

x is a square root of unity modulo N if $x^2 \equiv_N 1$. If $x \not\equiv_N 1$ and $x \neq_N -1$, then we say that x is a non-trivial square root of unity.

Since $(\pm 1)^2 = 1$ over the integers, it is also true that $(\pm 1)^2 \equiv_N 1$. In other words, ± 1 are always square roots of unity modulo N, for any N. But some values of N have even more square roots of unity. If N is the product of distinct odd primes, then N has 4 square roots of unity: two trivial and two non-trivial ones (and you are asked to prove this fact in an exercise).

Claim 13.14

Suppose there is an efficient algorithm for computing nontrivial square roots of unity modulo$N$. Then there is an efficient algorithm for factoring N. (This is the $(4) \Rightarrow (1)$ step in Theorem 13.12.)

Proof

The reduction is rather simple. Suppose NTSRU is an algorithm that on input N returns a non-trivial square root of unity modulo N. Then we can factor N with the following algorithm:

```
FACTOR(N):
x := NTSRU(N)
return gcd(N, x + 1) and gcd(N, x − 1)
```

The algorithm is simple, but we must argue that it is correct. When x is a nontrivial square root of unity modulo N, we have the following:

$$\begin{array}{lll} x^2 \equiv_{pq} 1 & \Rightarrow pq \mid x^2 - 1 & \Rightarrow pq \mid (x+1)(x-1); \\ x \not\equiv_{pq} 1 & & \Rightarrow pq \nmid (x-1); \\ x \not\equiv_{pq} -1 & & \Rightarrow pq \nmid (x+1). \end{array}$$

The prime factorization of $(x+1)(x-1)$ contains a factor of p and a factor of q. But neither $x+1$ nor $x-1$ contain factors of both p and q. Hence $x+1$ and $x-1$ must each contain factors of exactly one of $\{p, q\}$. In other words, $\{\gcd(pq, x-1), \gcd(pq, x+1)\} = \{p, q\}$.

Finding square roots of unity

Claim 13.15:

If there is an efficient algorithm for computing $d \equiv_{\phi(N)} e^{-1}$ given N and e, then there is an efficient algorithm for computing nontrivial square roots of unity modulo N. (This is the (3) ⇒ (4) step in Theorem 13.12.)

Proof: Suppose we have an algorithm find_D that on input (N, e) returns the corresponding exponent d. Then consider the following algorithm which uses find_D as a subroutine:

```
SRU(N):
  choose e as a random n-bit prime
  d := FIND_D(N, e)
  write ed − 1 = 2^s r, with r odd
  // i.e., factor out as many 2s as possible
  w ← Z_N
  if gcd(w, N) ≠ 1: // w ∉ Z*_N
    use gcd(w, N) to factor N = pq
    compute a nontrivial square root of unity using p & q
  x := w^r % N
  if x ≡_N 1 then return 1
  for i = 0 to s:
    if x^2 ≡_N 1 then return x
    x := x^2 % N
```

There are several return statements in this algorithm, and it should be clear that all of them indeed return a square root of unity. Furthermore, the algorithm does eventually return within the main for-loop, because x takes on the sequence of values:

$$w^r, w^{2r}, w^{4r}, w^{8r}, \dots, w^{2^s r}$$

and the final value of that sequence satisfies

$$w^{2^s r} = w^{ed-1} \equiv_N w^{(ed-1)\%\phi(N)} = w^{1-1} = 1.$$

Although we don't prove it here, it is possible to show that the algorithm returns a square root of unity chosen uniformly at random from among the four possible square roots of unity. So with probability $1/2$ the output is a nontrivial square root. We can repeat this basic process n times, and eventually encounter a nontrivial square root of unity with probability $1 - 2^{-n}$. □

Exercises

13.1. Prove by induction the correctness of the EXTGCD algorithm. That is, whenever extgcd (x, y) outputs (d, a, b), we have $\gcd(x, y) = d = ax + by$. You may use the fact that the original Euclidean algorithm correctly computes the GCD.

13.2. Prove that if $g^a \equiv_n 1$ and $g^b \equiv_n 1$, then $g^{\gcd(a,b)} \equiv_n 1$.

13.3. Prove that $\gcd(2^a - 1, 2^b - 1) = 2^{\gcd(a,b)} - 1$.

13.4. Prove that $x^a \% n = x^{a\%\phi(n)} \% n$ for any $x \in \mathbb{Z}_n^*$. In other words, when working modulo n, you can reduce exponents modulo $\phi(n)$.

13.5. How many fractions a/b in lowest terms are there, where $0 < a/b < 1$ and $b \leqslant n$? For $n = 5$ the answer is 9 since the relevant fractions are:

$$\frac{1}{5}, \frac{1}{4}, \frac{1}{3}, \frac{2}{5}, \frac{1}{2}, \frac{3}{5}, \frac{2}{3}, \frac{3}{4}, \frac{4}{5}$$

Write a formula in terms of n. What is the answer for $n = 100$?

13.6. In this problem we determine the efficiency of Euclid's GCD algorithm. Since its input is a pair of numbers (x, y), let's call $x + y$ the size of the input. Let F_k denote the k th Fibonacci number, using the indexing convention $F_0 = 1; F_1 = 2$. Prove that (F_k, F_{k-1}) is the smallest-size input on which Euclid's algorithm makes k recursive calls.

Note that the size of input (F_k, F_{k-1}) is F_{k+1}, and recall that $F_{k+1} \approx \phi^{k+1}$, where $\phi \approx 1.618 \ldots$ is the golden ratio. Thus, for any inputs of size $N \in [F_k, F_{k+1})$, Euclid's algorithm will make less than $k \leqslant \log_\phi N$ recursive calls. In other words, the worst-case number of recursive calls made by Euclid's algorithm on an input of size N is $O(\log N)$, which is linear in the number of bits needed to write such an input. [8]

13.7. Consider the following symmetric-key encryption scheme with plaintext space $\mathcal{M} = \{0,1\}^\lambda$. To encrypt a message m, we "pad" m into a prime number by appending a zero and then random non-zero bytes. We then mulitply by the secret key. To decrypt, we divide off the key and then strip away the "padding."

The idea is that decrypting a ciphertext without knowledge of the secret key requires factoring the product of two large primes, which is a hard problem.

```
KeyGen:
  choose random λ-bit prime k
  return k

Dec(k, c):
  m' := c/k
  while m' not a multiple of 10:
    m' := ⌊m'/10⌋
  return m'/10

Enc(k, m ∈ {0,1}^λ):
  m' := 10 · m
  while m' not prime:
    d ← {1, ..., 9}
    m' := 10 · m' + d
  return k · m'
```

Show an attack breaking CPA-security of the scheme. That is, describe a distinguisher and compute its bias.

13.8. Explain why the RSA exponents e and d must always be odd numbers.

13.9. Why must p and q be distinct primes? Why is it a bad idea to choose $p = q$?

13.10. A simple power analysis (SPA) attack is a physical attack on a computer, where the attacker monitors precisely how much electrical current the processor consumes while performing a cryptographic algorithm. In this exercise, we will consider an SPA attack against the ModExp algorithm shown in Section 13.2.

The ModExp algorithm consists mainly of squarings and multiplications. Suppose that by monitoring a computer it is easy to tell when the processor is running a squaring vs. a multiplication step (this is a very realistic assumption). This assumption is analogous to having access to the printed output of this modified algorithm:

```
ModExp(m, e, N): // compute m^e % N
  if e = 0: return 1
  if e even:
    res := ModExp(m, e/2, N)^2 % N
    print "square"
  if e odd:
    res := ModExp(m, (e-1)/2, N)^2 · m % N
    print "square"
    print "mult"
  return res
```

Describe how the printed output of this algorithm lets the attacker completely learn the value e. Remember that in RSA it is indeed the exponent that is secret, so this attack leads to key recovery for RSA.

13.11. The Chinese Remainder Theorem states that there is always a solution for x in the following system of equations, when $\gcd(r, s) = 1$:

$$x \equiv_r u$$

$$x \equiv_s v$$

Give an example u, v, r, s, with $\gcd(r, s) \neq 1$ for which the equations have no solution. Explain why there is no solution.

13.12. Prove Claims 13.10 and 13.11.

13.13. Consider a rectangular grid of points, with width w and height h. Starting in the lowerleft of the grid, start walking diagonally northeast. When you fall off end the grid, wrap around to the opposite side (i.e., Pac-Man topology). Below is an example of the first few steps you take on a grid with $w = 3$ and $h = 5$:

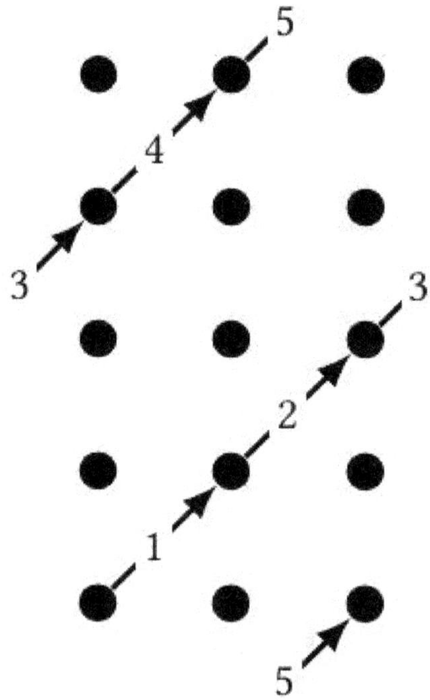

Show that if $\gcd(w, h) = 1$ then you will eventually visit every point in the grid.

13.14. Suppose $(u, v) \in \mathbb{Z}_r \times \mathbb{Z}_s$ is a CRT encoding of $x \in \mathbb{Z}_{rs}$. Prove that $x \in \mathbb{Z}_{rs}^*$ if and only if $u \in \mathbb{Z}_r^*$ and $v \in \mathbb{Z}_s^*$.

Note: this problem implies that $\phi(rs) = \phi(r)\phi(s)$ when $\gcd(r, s) = 1$. A special case of this identity is the familiar expression $\phi(pq) = (p - 1)(q - 1)$ when p and q are distinct primes.

13.15. There is a bug (or at least an oversight) in the proof that $x \mapsto x^e \% N$ and $y \mapsto y^d \% N$ are inverses. We used the fact that $x^{\phi(N)} \equiv_N 1$, but this is only necessarily true for $x \in \mathbb{Z}_N^*$. Using the Chinese Remainder Theorem, show that the RSA function and its inverse are truly inverses, even when applied to $x \notin \mathbb{Z}_N^*$.

13.16. We are supposed to choose RSA exponents e and d such that $ed \equiv_{\phi(N)} 1$. Let $N = pq$ and define the value $L = \text{lcm}(p - 1, q - 1)$. Suppose we choose e and d such that $ed \equiv_L 1$. Show that RSA still works for this choice of e and d – in other words, $x \mapsto x^e \% N$ and $y \mapsto y^d \% N$ are inverses.

⋆ 13.17. If $y^e \equiv_N x$ then we call y an " e-th root" of x. One way to think about RSA is that raising something to the d power is equivalent to computing an e-th root. Our assumption about RSA is that it's hard to compute e-th roots given only public e and N.

In this problem, show that if you are given an a-th root of x and b-th root of the same x, and $\gcd(a, b) = 1$, then you can easily compute an ab-th root of x.

More formally, given x, y, z and N where $y^a \equiv_N x$ and $z^b \equiv_N x$, show how to efficiently compute a value w such that $w^{ab} \equiv_N x$.

Compute w for the following values (after verifying that y is an a-th root and z is a b-th root of $x \bmod N$):

$$
\begin{aligned}
N &= 318753895014839414391833197387495582828703628009180678460009\\
x &= 183418622076108277295248802695684859123490073011079896375192\\
a &= 566853947472812968051456497740656934420165123016289460510 59\\
b &= 178205100585526989632998577959780764157496762062661723119813\\
y &= 185575838649944725271855413520846311652963277243867273346885\\
z &= 206975500658421641692780245070415368842607139963715728073 44
\end{aligned}
$$

13.18. Suppose Alice uses the CRT method to sign some message m in textbook RSA. In other words, she computes $m^d \% p$, then $m^d \% q$, and finally converts this CRT encoding back to $\mathbb{Z}_N$. But suppose Alice is using faulty hardware (or Eve is bombarding her hardware with electromagnetic pulses), so that she computes the wrong value $\bmod q$. The rest of the computation happens correctly, and Alice publishes m and the (incorrect) signature σ.

Show that, no matter what m is, and no matter what Alice's computational error was, Eve can factor N (upon seeing m, σ, and the public RSA information N and e).

13.19. (a) Show that given an RSA modulus N and $\phi(N)$, it is possible to factor N easily.

(b) Write a Sage function that takes as input an RSA modulus N and $\phi(N)$ and outputs the prime factors of N. Use it to factor the following 2048-bit RSA modulus. Note: take care that there are no precision issues in how you solve the problem; double-check your factorization!

```
N =1331402728893351929221084092606621744763038316523836716885470094
   2532359405869171404826691822563682852609928294472079801831701748
   6203589522309699864475593305834924296366272986403385965318945565
   0131131543468232122717489278596479945345861335532180229838481084
   4654420899190906105423447682944817251037572224219171159710630268
   5871412875870372651506536690943231166865745365588665916473610533
   0465160130696690368667341265580177443937511616112191957695784885
   8829023972483090339116614750058546968200210690725022485333287548
   6986162384052213812521451374399190908000859552743893827218449566
   1138745095472005761807
phi =1331402728893351929221084092606621744763038316523836716885470094
     2532359405869171404826691822563682852609928294472079801831701748
     6203589522309699864475593305834924296366272986403385965318945565
     0131131543468232122717489278596479945345861335532180229838481084
     4654420899190906105423447682944817251037572149322920465388672184
     6352567722273701090667853120965897796223554954190060499745678951
     6873181104980586923156308566936720693205290623996815635903820151
     3229097447493307026079314281541837265520045272019562263968355003
     7790624942596389831911789150278351345277516070178590645117315204
     2981816860178885028680
```

13.20. True or false: if $x^2 \equiv_N 1$ then $x \in \mathbb{Z}_N^*$. Prove or give a counterexample.

13.21. Discuss the computational difficulty of the following problem:

$$\text{Given an integer } N \text{, find a nonzero element of } \mathbb{Z}_N \setminus \mathbb{Z}_N^*.$$

If you can, relate its difficulty to that of other problems we've discussed (factoring N or inverting RSA).

13.22. (a) Show that it is possible to efficiently compute all four square roots of unity modulo pq, given p and q.

Hint: □

(b) Implement a Sage function that takes distinct primes p and q as input and returns the four square roots of unity modulo pq. Use it to compute the four square roots of unity modulo

$$1052954986442271985875778192663 \times 611174539744122090068393470777.$$

★ 13.23. Show that, conditioned on $w \in \mathbb{Z}_N^*$, the SqrtUnity subroutine outputs a square root of unity chosen uniformly at random from the 4 possible square roots of unity.

13.24. Suppose N is an RSA modulus, and $x^2 \equiv_N y^2$, but $x \not\equiv_N \pm y$. Show that N can be efficiently factored if such a pair x and y are known.

13.25. Why are ± 1 the only square roots of unity modulo p, when p is an odd prime?

13.26. When N is an RSA modulus, why is squaring modulo N a 4-to-1 function, but raising to the eth power modulo N is 1 -to- 1 ?

13.27. Implement a Sage function that efficiently factors an RSA modulus N, given only N, e, and d. Use your function to factor the following 2048-bit RSA modulus.

N =157713892705550064909750632475691896977526767652833932128735618711
213662561319634033137058267272367265499003291937716454788882499492
311117065951077245304317542978715216577264400048278064574204140564
709253009840166821302184014310192765595015483588878761062406993721
851190041888790873152584082212461847511180066690936944585390792304
663763886417861546718283897613617078370412411019301687497005038294
389148932398661048471814117247898148030982257697888167001010511378
647288478239379740416388270380035364271593609513220655573614212415
962670795230819103845127007912428958291134064942068225836213242131
15022256956985205924967

e =327598866483920224268285375349315001772252982661926675504591773242
501030864502336359508677092544631083799700755236766113095163469666
905258066495934057774395712118774014408282455244138409433389314036
198045263991986560198273156037233588691392913730537367184867549274
682884119866630822924707702796323546327425328705958528315517584489
590815901470874024949798420173098581333151755836650797037848765578
433873141626191257009250151327378074817106208930064676608134109788

d

601067077103742326030259629322458620311949453584045538305945217564
027461013225009980998673160144967719374426764116721861138496780008
63662583607572181659973
138476999734263775498100443567132759182144573474474014195021091272
755207803162019484487127866675422608401990888942659393419384528257
462434633738686176601555755842189986431725335031620097854962295968
= 391161090826380458969236418585963384717406704714837349503808786086
701573765714825783042297344050528898259745757741233099297952332012
749897281090378398001337057869189488734951853748327631883502135139
523664990296334020327713900408683264232664645438899178442633342438
198329983121207315436447041915897544445402505558420138506655106015
215450140256129977382476062366519087386576874886938585789874186326
69265500594424847344765

13.28. In this problem we'll see that it's bad to choose RSA prime factors p and q too close together.

(a) Let $N = pq$ be an RSA modulus. Show that if you know N and $\delta = |p - q|$ then you can efficiently factor N.

(b) Alice generated the following RSA modulus $N = pq$ and lets you know that $|p - q| < 10000$. Factor N :

N =8746775183889966636386983014298663158580106815933015043615059174066796003386547539786466399282312782570257923169219623297489482031536330137181753809691690061252491835470992308453223746188554253871769528654834328045758951778696267464598786957281497863826975719629618983312554055346571946810561484376490916124032583040840811718242154695949849811921627100521215353092540247206357819557397132393343984944658283238108128435821875872567449011840165466387184147152490937570393755858962578393279875012167558653534447045064410780348110129302828570898190301608227291397689825461431046253157005718870377953185530285942367688l

13.29. Here is a slightly better method to factor RSA moduli whose factors are too close together. As before, let $N = pq$.

(a) Define $t = (p + q)/2$. Note that when p and q are close, t is not much larger than $\sqrt{N}$. Show that:

- $t^2 - N$ is a perfect square.
- Given t, it is possible to efficiently factor N.

(b) Write a Sage function that factors RSA moduli whose prime factors are close. Use it to factor the following 2048-bit number. How close were the factors (how large was $|p - q|$)?

N =5142028686642665019867363402263438801932168640116432445587019561145533178800432898274874564602841039514635120242493292432281096240119153924118887240264031276867072558250560818906925957158283806908111316863831802823307755723858221021812095694119611257532424679718791313059869865256001103407905959879753455738422667664923566867621346538330645113374330892496212576291078256814295739349491013011352009186062113944134987354865996785413693758878400138424390261590371080437242218651167940341948122363812997863954572775598795757522541166127265961185280717854745510585405991988699867802867339166143356633723003246569630373323

Chapter 14

Diffie-Hellman Key Agreement

14.1 Cyclic Groups

Definition 14.1

Let $g \in \mathbb{Z}_n^*$. Define $\langle g \rangle_n = \{g^i \% n \mid i \in \mathbb{Z}\}$, the set of all powers of g reduced mod n. Then g is called a generator of $\langle g \rangle_n$, and $\langle g \rangle_n$ is called the cyclic group generated by g **mod** n.

If $\langle g \rangle_n = \mathbb{Z}_n^*$, then we say that g is a primitive root mod$n$.

The definition allows the generator g to be raised to a negative integer. Since $g \in \mathbb{Z}_n^*$, it is guaranteed that g has a multiplicative inverse mod$n$, which we can call g^{-1}. Then g^{-i} can be defined as $g^{-i} \stackrel{\text{def}}{=} (g^{-1})^i$. All of the usual laws of exponents hold with respect to this definition of negative exponents.

Example

Taking $n = 13$, we have:

$$\begin{aligned} \langle 1 \rangle_{13} &= \{1\} \\ \langle 2 \rangle_{13} &= \{1,2,4,8,3,6,12,11,9,5,10,7\} = \mathbb{Z}_{13}^* \\ \langle 3 \rangle_{13} &= \{1,3,9\} \end{aligned}$$

Thus 2 is a primitive root modulo 13. Each of the groups $\{1\}, \mathbb{Z}_{13}^*, \{1,3,9\}$ is a cyclic group under multiplication mod 13.

A cyclic group may have more than one generator, for example:

$$\langle 3 \rangle_{13} = \langle 9 \rangle_{13} = \{1,3,9\}$$

Similarly, there are four primitive roots modulo 13 (equivalently, $\mathbb{Z}_{13}^*$ has four different generators); they are 2, 6, 7, and 11.

Not every integer has a primitive root. For example, there is no primitive root modulo 15. However, when p is a prime, there is always a primitive root modulo p (and so $\mathbb{Z}_p^*$ is a cyclic group).

Let us write $\mathbb{G} = \langle g \rangle = \{g^i \mid i \in \mathbb{Z}\}$ to denote an unspecified cyclic group generated by g. The defining property of $\mathbb{G}$ is that each of its elements can be written as a power of g. From this we can conclude that:

- Any cyclic group is closed under multiplication. That is, take any $X, Y \in \mathbb{G}$; then it must be possible to write $X = g^x$ and $Y = g^y$ for some integers x, y. Using the multiplication operation of $\mathbb{G}$, the product is $XY = g^{x+y}$, which is also in $\mathbb{G}$.
- Any cyclic group is closed under inverses. Take any $X \in \mathbb{G}$; then it must be possible to write $X = g^x$ for some integer x. We can then see that $g^{-x} \in \mathbb{G}$ by definition, and $g^{-x}X = g^{-x+x} = g^0$ is the identity element. So X has a multiplicative inverse (g^{-x}) in $\mathbb{G}$.

These facts demonstrate that $\mathbb{G}$ is indeed a group in the terminology of abstract algebra.

Discrete Logarithms

It is typically easy to compute the value of g^x in a cyclic group, given g and x. For example, when using a cyclic group of the form $\mathbb{Z}_n^*$, we can easily compute the modular exponentiation $g^x \% n$ using repeated squaring.

The inverse operation in a cyclic group is called the discrete logarithm problem:

Definition 14.2

The discrete logarithm problem is: given $X \in \langle g \rangle$, determine a number x such that $g^x = X$.

(Discrete log) Here the exponentiation is with respect to the multiplication operation in $\mathbb{G} = \langle g \rangle$.

The discrete logarithm problem is conjectured to be hard (that is, no polynomial-time algorithm exists for the problem) in certain kinds of cyclic groups.

14.2 Diffie-Hellman Key Agreement

Key agreement refers to the problem of establishing a private channel using public communication. Suppose Alice & Bob have never spoken before and have no shared secrets. By exchanging public messages (i.e., that can be seen by any external observer), they would like to establish a secret that is known only to the two of them.

The Diffie-Hellman protocol is such a key-agreement protocol, and it was the first published instance of public-key cryptography:

Construction 14.3

Both parties agree (publicly) on a cyclic group $\mathbb{G}$ with generator g. Let $n = |\mathbb{G}|$. All exponen-(Diffie-Hellman) tiations are with respect to the group operation in $\mathbb{G}$.

1. Alice chooses $a \leftarrow \mathbb{Z}_n$. She sends $A = g^a$ to Bob.
2. Bob chooses $b \leftarrow \mathbb{Z}_n$. He sends $B = g^b$ to Alice.
3. Bob locally outputs $K := A^b$. Alice locally outputs $K := B^a$.
4.

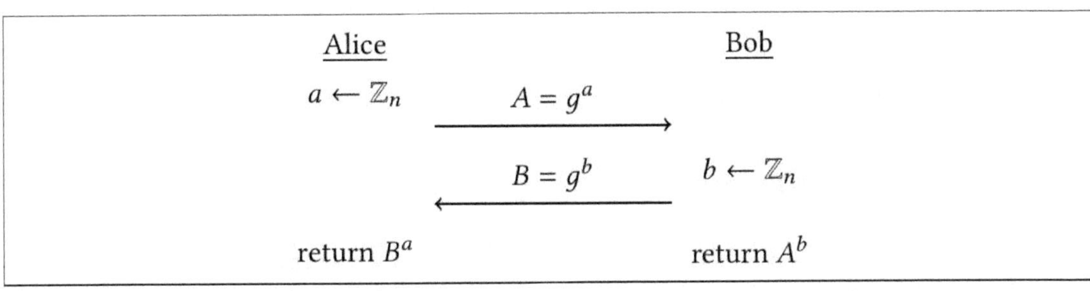

By substituting and applying standard rules of exponents, we see that both parties output a common value, namely $K = g^{ab} \in \mathbb{G}$.

Defining Security for Key Agreement

Executing a key agreement protocol leaves two artifacts behind. First, we have the collection of messages that are exchanged between the two parties. We call this collection a transcript. We envision two parties executing a key agreement protocol in the presence of an eavesdropper, and hence we imagine that the transcript is public. Second, we have the key that is output by the parties, which is private.

To define security of key agreement, we would like to require that the transcript leaks no (useful) information to the eavesdropper about the key. There are a few ways to approach the definition:

- We could require that it is hard to compute the key given the transcript. However, this turns out to be a rather weak definition. For example, it does not rule out the possibility that an eavesdropper could guess the first half of the bits of the key.

- We could require that the key is pseudorandom given the transcript. This is a better definition, and the one we use. To formalize this idea, we define two libraries. In both libraries the adversary / calling program can obtain the transcript of an execution of the key agreement protocol. In one library the adversary obtains the key that resulted from the protocol execution, while in the other library the adversary obtains a totally unrelated key (chosen uniformly from the set $\Sigma.\mathcal{K}$ of possible keys).

Definition 14.4

Let Σ be a key-agreement protocol. We write $\Sigma.\mathcal{K}$ for the keyspace of the protocol (i.e., the (KA security) set of possible keys it produces). We write $(t, K) \leftarrow$ execprot (Σ) to denote the process of executing the protocol between two honest parties, where t denotes the resulting transcript, and K is resulting key. Note that this process is randomized, and that K is presumably correlated to t.

We say that Σ is secure if $\mathcal{L}^{\Sigma}_{\text{ka-real}} \approx \mathcal{L}^{\Sigma}_{\text{ka-rand}}$, where:

$\mathcal{L}^{\Sigma}_{\text{ka-real}}$

QUERY():
  $(t, K) \leftarrow$ EXECPROT(Σ)
  return (t, K)

$\mathcal{L}^{\Sigma}_{\text{ka-rand}}$

QUERY():
  $(t, K) \leftarrow$ EXECPROT(Σ)
  $K' \leftarrow \Sigma.\mathcal{K}$
  return (t, K')

14.3 Decisional Diffie-Hellman Problem

The Diffie Hellman protocol is parameterized by the choice of cyclic group $\mathbb{G}$ (and generator g). Transcripts in the protocol consist of (g^a, g^b), where a and b are chosen uniformly. The key corresponding to such a transcript is g^{ab}. The set of possible keys is the cyclic group $\mathbb{G}$.

Let us substitute the details of the Diffie-Hellman protocol into the KA security libraries. After simplifying, we see that the security of the Diffie Hellman protocol is equivalent to the following statement:

$\mathcal{L}^{\mathbb{G}}_{\text{dh-real}}$		$\mathcal{L}^{\mathbb{G}}_{\text{dh-rand}}$
QUERY(): $a, b \leftarrow \mathbb{Z}_n$ return (g^a, g^b, g^{ab})	$\approx$	QUERY(): $a, b, c \leftarrow \mathbb{Z}_n$ return (g^a, g^b, g^c)

We have renamed the libraries to $\mathcal{L}_{\text{dh-real}}$ and $\mathcal{L}_{\text{dh-rand}}$. In $\mathcal{L}_{\text{dh-real}}$ the response to QUERY corresponds to a DHKA transcript (g^a, g^b) along with the corresponding "correct" key g^{ab}. The response in $\mathcal{L}_{\text{dh- rand}}$ corresponds to a DHKA transcript along with a completely independent random key g^c.

Definition 14.5:

The decisional Diffie-Hellman (DDH) assumption in a cyclic group $\mathbb{G}$ is that $\mathcal{L}^{\mathbb{G}}_{dh\text{-}real} \approx$ (DDH) $\mathcal{L}^{G}_{dh-rand}$ (libraries defined above).

Since we have defined the DDH assumption by simply renaming the security definition for DHKA, we immediately have:

Claim 14.6:

The DHKA protocol is a secure KA protocol if and only if the DDH assumption is true for the choice of $\mathbb{G}$ used in the protocol.

For Which Groups does the DDH Assumption Hold?

So far our only example of a cyclic group is $\mathbb{Z}_p^*$, where p is a prime. Although many textbooks describe DHKA in terms of this cyclic group, it is not a good choice because the DDH assumption is demonstrably false in $\mathbb{Z}_p^*$. To see why, we introduce a new concept:

Claim 14.7 (Euler criterion)

If p is a prime and $X = g^x \in \mathbb{Z}_p^*$, then $X^{\frac{p-1}{2}} \equiv_p (-1)^x$.

Note that $(-1)^x$ is 1 if x is even and -1 if x is odd. So, while in general it is hard to determine x given g^x, Euler's criterion says that it is possible to determine the parity of x (i.e., whether x is even or odd) given g^x.

To see how these observations lead to an attack against the Diffie-Hellman protocol, consider the following attack:

$\mathcal{A}$:
$(A, B, C) \leftarrow$ QUERY()
return $1 \overset{?}{\equiv}_p C^{\frac{p-1}{2}}$

Roughly speaking, the adversary returns true whenever C can be written as g raised to an even exponent. When linked to $\mathcal{L}_{\text{dh-real}}$, $C = g^{ab}$ where a and b are chosen uniformly. Hence ab will be even with probability 3/4. When linked to $\mathcal{L}_{\text{dh- rand}}$, $C = g^c$ for an independent random c. So c is even only with probability 1/2. Hence the adversary distinguishes the libraries with advantage 1/4.

Concretely, with this choice of group, the key g^{ab} will never be uniformly distributed. See the exercises for a slightly better attack which correlates the key to the transcript.

Quadratic Residues. Several better choices of cyclic groups have been proposed in the literature. Arguably the simplest one is based on the following definition:

Definition 14.8

A number $X \in \mathbb{Z}_n^*$ is a quadratic residue modulo n if there exists some integer Y such that $Y^2 \equiv_n X$. That is, if X can be obtained by squaring a number modn. Let $\mathbb{QR}_n^* \subseteq \mathbb{Z}_n^*$ denote the set of quadratic residues mod n.

For our purposes it is enough to know that, when p is prime, $\mathbb{QR}_p^*$ is a cyclic group with $(p-1)/2$ elements (see the exercises). When both p and $(p-1)/2$ are prime, we call p a safe prime (and call $(p-1)/2$ a Sophie Germain prime). To the best of our knowledge the DDH assumption is true in $\mathbb{QR}_p^*$ when p is a safe prime.

Exercises

14.1. Let p be an odd prime, as usual. Recall that $\mathbb{QR}_p^*$ is the set of quadratic residues mod$p$ - that is, $\mathbb{Q}_p^* = \{x \in \mathbb{Z}_p^* \mid \exists y : x \equiv_p y^2\}$. Show that if g is a primitive root of $\mathbb{Z}_p^*$ then $\langle g^2 \rangle = \mathbb{QR}_p^*$.

Note: This means that $g^a \in \mathbb{QR}_p^*$ if and only if a is even - and in particular, the choice of generator g doesn't matter.

14.2. Suppose $N = pq$ where p and q are distinct primes. Show that $|\mathbb{QR}_N^*| = |\mathbb{QR}_p^*| \cdot |\mathbb{QR}_q^*|$.

14.3. Suppose you are given $X \in \langle g \rangle$. You are allowed to choose any $X' \neq X$ and learn the discrete log of X' (with respect to base g). Show that you can use this ability to learn the discrete log of X.

14.4. Let $\langle g \rangle$ be a cyclic group with n elements and generator g. Show that for all integers a, it is true that $g^a = g^{a \% n}$.

Note: As a result, $\langle g \rangle$ is isomorphic to the additive group $\mathbb{Z}_n$.

14.5. Let g be a primitive root of $\mathbb{Z}_n^*$. Recall that $\mathbb{Z}_n^*$ has $\phi(n)$ elements. Show that g^a is a primitive root of $\mathbb{Z}_n^*$ if and only if $\gcd(a, \phi(n)) = 1$.

Note: It follows that, for every n, there are either 0 or $\phi(\phi(n))$ primitive roots mod$n$.

14.6. Let $\langle g \rangle$ be a cyclic group with n elements. Show that for all $x, y \in \langle g \rangle$, it is true that $x^n = y^n$.

14.7. (a) Prove the following variant of Lemma 4.10: Suppose you fix a value $x \in \mathbb{Z}_N$. Then when sampling $q = \sqrt{2N}$ values $r_1, \dots, r_q$ uniformly from $\mathbb{Z}_N$, with probability at least 0.6 there exist $i \neq j$ with $r_i \equiv_N r_j + x$.

(b) Let g be a primitive root of $\mathbb{Z}_p^*$ (for some prime p). Consider the problem of computing the discrete log of $X \in \mathbb{Z}_p^*$ with respect to g - that is, finding x such that $X \equiv_p g^x$. Argue that if one can find integers r and s such that $g^r \equiv_p X \cdot g^s$ then one can compute the discrete log of X.

(c) Combine the above two observations to describe a $O(\sqrt{p})$-time algorithm for the discrete logarithm problem in $\mathbb{Z}_p^*$.

14.8. In an execution of DHKA, the eavesdropper observes the following values:

$$p = 461733370363 \quad A = 114088419126$$
$$g = 2 \quad B = 276312808197$$

What will be Alice & Bob's shared key?

14.9. Explain what is wrong in the following argument:

In Diffie-Hellman key agreement, Alice sends $A = g^a$ and Bob sends $B = g^b$. Their shared key is g^{ab}. To break the scheme, the eavesdropper can simply compute $A \cdot B = (g^a)(g^b) = g^{ab}$.

14.10. Let $\mathbb{G}$ be a cyclic group with n elements and generator g. Consider the following algorithm:

$$\begin{array}{l}\underline{\text{RAND}(A, B, C):}\\ r, s, t \leftarrow \mathbb{Z}_n\\ A' := A^t g^r\\ B' := B g^s\\ C' := C^t B^r A^{st} g^{rs}\\ \text{return } (A', B', C')\end{array}$$

Let $DH = \{(g^a, g^b, g^{ab}) \in \mathbb{G}^3 \mid a, b, \in \mathbb{Z}_n\}$.

(a) Suppose $(A, B, C) \in DH$. Show that the output distribution of Rand(A, B, C) is the uniform distribution over DH

(b) Suppose $(A, B, C) \notin DH$. Show that the output distribution of rand(A, B, C) is the uniform distribution over $\mathbb{G}^3$.

(c) Consider the problem of determining whether a given triple (A, B, C) is in the set DH. Suppose you have an algorithm $\mathcal{A}$ that solves this problem on average slightly better than chance. That is:

$$\Pr[\mathcal{A}(A, B, C) = 1] > 0.51 \text{ when } (A, B, C) \text{ chosen uniformly in } DH$$
$$\Pr[\mathcal{A}(A, B, C) = 0] > 0.51 \text{ when } (A, B, C) \text{ chosen uniformly in } \mathbb{G}^3$$

The algorithm $\mathcal{A}$ does not seem very useful if you have a particular triple (A, B, C) and you really want to know whether it is in DH. You might have one of the triples for which $\mathcal{A}$ gives the wrong answer, and there's no real way to know.

Show how to construct a randomized algorithm $\mathcal{A}'$ such that: for every $(A, B, C) \in \mathbb{G}^3$:

$$\Pr\left[\mathcal{A}'(A, B, C) = [(A, B, C) \stackrel{?}{\in} DH]\right] > 0.99$$

Here the input A, B, C is fixed and the probability is over the internal randomness in $\mathcal{A}'$. So on every possible input, $\mathcal{A}'$ gives a very reliable answer.

Chapter-15

Public-Key Encryption

So far, the encryption schemes that we've seen are symmetric-key schemes. The same key is used to encrypt and decrypt. In this chapter we introduce public-key (sometimes called asymmetric) encryption schemes, which use different keys for encryption and decryption. The idea is that the encryption key can be made public, so that anyone can send an encryption to the owner of that key, even if the two users have never spoken before and have no shared secrets. The decryption key is private, so that only the designated owner can decrypt.

We modify the syntax of an encryption scheme in the following way. A public-key encryption scheme consists of the following three algorithms:

KeyGen: Outputs a pair (pk, sk) where pk is a public key and sk is a private/secret key.

Enc: Takes the public key pk and a plaintext m as input, and outputs a ciphertext c.

Dec: Takes the secret key sk and a ciphertext c as input, and outputs a plaintext m.

We modify the correctness condition similarly. A public-key encryption scheme satisfies correctness if, for all $m \in \mathcal{M}$ and all $(pk, sk) \leftarrow \text{KeyGen}$, we have $\text{Dec}(sk, \text{Enc}(pk, m)) = m$ (with probability 1 over the randomness of Enc).

15.1 Security Definitions

We now modify the definition of CPA security to fit the setting of public-key encryption. As before, the adversary calls a challenge subroutine with two plaintexts - the difference between the two libraries is which plaintext is actually encrypted. Of course, the encryption operation now takes the public key.

Then the biggest change is that we would like to make the public key public. In other words, the calling program should have a way to learn the public key (otherwise the library cannot model a situation where the public key is known to the adversary). To do this, we simply add another subroutine that returns the public key.

Definition 15.1

Let Σ be a public-key encryption scheme. Then Σ is secure against chosen-plaintext at-

tacks (CPA secure) if $\mathcal{L}^{\Sigma}_{pk-cpa-L} \approx \mathcal{L}^{\Sigma}_{pk-cpa-R}$, *where:*

$\mathcal{L}^{\Sigma}_{\text{pk-cpa-L}}$
$(pk, sk) \leftarrow \Sigma.\text{KeyGen}$
GETPK():
return pk
CHALLENGE($m_L, m_R \in \Sigma.\mathcal{M}$):
return $\Sigma.\text{Enc}(pk, m_L)$

$\mathcal{L}^{\Sigma}_{\text{pk-cpa-R}}$
$(pk, sk) \leftarrow \Sigma.\text{KeyGen}$
GETPK():
return pk
CHALLENGE($m_L, m_R \in \Sigma.\mathcal{M}$):
return $\Sigma.\text{Enc}(pk, m_R)$

to-do: *Re-iterate how deterministic encryption still can't be CPA-secure in the public-key setting.*

Pseudorandom Ciphertexts

We can modify/adapt the definition of pseudorandom ciphertexts to public-key encryption in a similar way:

Definition 15.2

Let Σ be a public-key encryption scheme. Then Σ has pseudorandom ciphertexts in the presence of chosen-plaintext attacks (CPA$ security) if $\mathcal{L}^{\Sigma}_{\text{pk-cpa\$-real}} \approx \mathcal{L}^{\Sigma}_{\text{pk-cpa\$-rand}}$, where:

$\mathcal{L}^{\Sigma}_{\text{pk-cpa\$-real}}$
$(pk, sk) \leftarrow \Sigma.\text{KeyGen}$
GETPK():
returnpk
cHALLENGE($m \in \Sigma.\mathcal{M}$):
return$\Sigma.\text{Enc}(pk, m)$

$\mathcal{L}^{\Sigma}_{\text{pk-cpa\$-rand}}$
$(pk, sk) \leftarrow \Sigma.\text{KeyGen}$
GETPK():   **return** pk
CHALLENGE($m \in \Sigma.\mathcal{M}$): $c \leftarrow \Sigma.\mathcal{C}$ **return** c

As in the symmetric-key setting, CPA$ security (for public-key encryption) implies CPA security:

Claim 15.3

Let Σ be a public-key encryption scheme. If Σ has CPA $ security, then Σ has CPA security.

The proof is extremely similar to the proof of the analogous statement for symmetrickey encryption (Theorem 7.3), and is left as an exercise.

15.2 One-Time Security Implies Many-Time Security

So far, everything about public-key encryption has been directly analogous to what we've seen about symmetric-key encryption. We now discuss a peculiar property that is different between the two settings.

In symmetric-key encryption, we saw examples of encryption schemes that are secure when the adversary sees only one ciphertext, but insecure when the adversary sees more ciphertexts. One-time pad is the standard example of such an encryption scheme.

Surprisingly, if a public-key encryption scheme is secure when the adversary sees just one ciphertext, then it is also secure for many ciphertexts! In short, there is no public-key one-time pad that is weaker than full-fledged public-key encryption - there is public-key encryption or nothing.

To show this property formally, we first adapt the definition of one-time secrecy (Definition 2.6) to the public-key setting. There is one small but important technical subtlety: in Definition 2.6 the encryption key is chosen at the last possible moment in the body of challenge. This ensures that the key is local to this scope, and therefore each value of the key is only used to encrypt one plaintext.

In the public-key setting, however, it turns out to be important to allow the adversary to see the public key before deciding which plaintexts to encrypt. (This concern is not present in the symmetric-key setting precisely because there is nothing public upon which the adversary's choice of plaintexts can depend.) For that reason, in the public-key setting we must sample the keys at initialization time so that the adversary can obtain the public key via GETPK. To ensure that the key is used to encrypt only one plaintext, we add a counter and a guard condition to challenge, so that it only responds once with a ciphertext.

Definition 15.4:

Let Σ be a public-key encryption scheme. Then Σ has one-time secrecy if $\mathcal{L}^{\Sigma}_{\text{pk-ots-L}} \approx \mathcal{L}^{\Sigma}_{\text{pk-ots-R}}$, *where:*

$\mathcal{L}^{\Sigma}_{\text{pk-ots-L}}$

$(pk, sk) \leftarrow \Sigma.\text{KeyGen}$
$count := 0$

GETPK():
  return pk

CHALLENGE($m_L, m_R \in \Sigma.\mathcal{M}$):
  $count := count + 1$
  if $count > 1$: return null
  return $\Sigma.\text{Enc}(pk, m_L)$

$\mathcal{L}^{\Sigma}_{\text{pk-ots-R}}$

$(pk, sk) \leftarrow \Sigma.\text{KeyGen}$
$count := 0$

GETPK():
  return pk

CHALLENGE($m_L, m_R \in \Sigma.\mathcal{M}$):
  $count := count + 1$
  if $count > 1$: return null
  return $\Sigma.\text{Enc}(pk, m_R)$

Claim 15.5

Let Σ be a public-key encryption scheme. If Σ has one-time secrecy, then Σ is CPA-secure.

Proof:

Suppose $\mathcal{L}^{\Sigma}_{\text{pk-ots-L}} \approx \mathcal{L}^{\Sigma}_{\text{pk-ots-R}}$. Our goal is to show that $\mathcal{L}^{\Sigma}_{\text{pk-cpa-L}} \approx \mathcal{L}^{\Sigma}_{\text{pk-cpa-R}}$. The proof centers around the following hybrid library $\mathcal{L}_{\text{hyb-}h}$, which is designed to be linked to either

$\mathcal{L}_{\text{pk-ots-L}}$ or $\mathcal{L}_{\text{pk-ots-R}}$:

$\mathcal{L}_{\text{hyb-}h}$

$count = 0$
$pk := \text{GETPK}()$

$\text{CHALLENGE}(m_L, m_R \in \Sigma.\mathcal{M})$:
  $count := count + 1$
  if $count < h$:
    return $\Sigma.\mathsf{Enc}(pk, m_R)$
  elsif $count = h$:
    return $\text{CHALLENGE}'(m_L, m_R)$
  else:
    return $\Sigma.\mathsf{Enc}(pk, m_L)$

Here the value h is an unspecified value that will be a hard-coded constant, and challenge' (called by the "elsif" branch) and getpk refer to the subroutine in $\mathcal{L}_{\text{pk-ots-}\star}$. Note that $\mathcal{L}_{\text{hyb-}h}$ is designed so that it only makes one call to challenge' - in particular, only when its own challenge subroutine is called for the hth time.

We now make a few observations:

In both libraries, every call to challenge encrypts the left plaintext. In particular, the _rst call to challenge in Lhyb-1 triggers the "elsif" branch, so the challenge is routed to Lpk-ots-L, which encrypts the left plaintext. In all other calls to challenge, the "else" branch is triggered and the left plaintext is encrypted explicitly.

$$\mathcal{L}_{\text{hyb-1}} \diamond \mathcal{L}_{\text{pk-ots-L}} \equiv \mathcal{L}_{\text{pk-cpa-L}}:$$

for all h. In both of these libraries, the first h calls to challenge encrypt the right plaintext, and all subsequent calls encrypt the left plaintext.

$$\mathcal{L}_{\text{hyb-}h} \diamond \mathcal{L}_{\text{pk-ots-R}} \equiv \mathcal{L}_{\text{hyb-}(h+1)} \diamond \mathcal{L}_{\text{pk-ots-L}},$$

for all h This simply follows from the fact that Lpk-ots-≈Lpk-ots-R.

$$\mathcal{L}_{\text{hyb-}h} \diamond \mathcal{L}_{\text{pk-ots-L}} \approx \mathcal{L}_{\text{hyb-}h} \diamond \mathcal{L}_{\text{pk-ots-R}},$$

, where q is the number of times the calling program calls challenge. In particular, every call to challenge encrypts the right plaintext.

$$\mathcal{L}_{\text{hyb-}q} \diamond \mathcal{L}_{\text{pk-ots-R}} \equiv \mathcal{L}_{\text{pk-cpa-R}}$$

Putting everything together, we have that:

$$\begin{aligned}
\mathcal{L}_{\text{pk-cpa-L}} &\equiv \mathcal{L}_{\text{hyb-1}} \diamond \mathcal{L}_{\text{pk-ots-L}} \approx \mathcal{L}_{\text{hyb-1}} \diamond \mathcal{L}_{\text{pk-ots-R}} \\
&\equiv \mathcal{L}_{\text{hyb-2}} \diamond \mathcal{L}_{\text{pk-ots-L}} \approx \mathcal{L}_{\text{hyb-2}} \diamond \mathcal{L}_{\text{pk-ots-R}} \\
&\vdots \\
&\equiv \mathcal{L}_{\text{hyb-}q} \diamond \mathcal{L}_{\text{pk-ots-L}} \approx \mathcal{L}_{\text{hyb-}q} \diamond \mathcal{L}_{\text{pk-ots-R}} \\
&\equiv \mathcal{L}_{\text{pk-cpa-R}}
\end{aligned}$$

and so $\mathcal{L}_{\text{pk-cpa-L}} \approx \mathcal{L}_{\text{pk-cpa-R}}$.

The reason this proof goes through for public-key encryption but not symmetric-key encryption is that anyone can encrypt in a public-key scheme. In a symmetric-key scheme, it is not possible to generate encryptions without the key. But in a public-key scheme, the encryption key is public.

In more detail, the $\mathcal{L}_{\text{hyb-}h}$ library can indeed obtain pk from $\mathcal{L}_{\text{pk-ots-}\star}$. It therefore has enough information to perform the encryptions for all calls to challenge. Indeed, you can think of $\mathcal{L}_{\text{hyb-}0}$ as doing everything that $\mathcal{L}_{\text{pk-cpa-L}}$ does, even though it doesn't know the secret key. We let $\mathcal{L}_{\text{hyb-}h}$ designate the hth call to challenge as a special one to be handled by $\mathcal{L}_{\text{pk-ots-}\star}$. This allows us to change the hth encryption from using m_L to m_R.

15.3 ElGamal Encryption

ElGamal encryption is a public-key encryption scheme that is based on DHKA.

Construction 15.6 The public parameters are a choice of cyclic group $\mathbb{G}$ with n elements and generator g.

(ElGamal)

$$\begin{array}{llll}
 & \text{KeyGen:} & \text{Enc}(A, M \in \mathbb{G}): & \\
\mathcal{M} = \mathbb{G} & sk := a \leftarrow \mathbb{Z}_n & b \leftarrow \mathbb{Z}_n & \text{Dec}(a, (B, X)): \\
C = \mathbb{G}^2 & pk := A := g^a & B := g^b & \text{return} X (B^a)^{-1} \\
 & \text{return}(pk, sk) & \text{return}(B, M \cdot A^b) &
\end{array}$$

The scheme satisfies correctness, since for all M :

$$\begin{aligned}
\text{Dec}(sk, \text{Enc}(pk, M)) &= \text{Dec}\big(sk, (g^b, M \cdot A^b)\big) \\
&= (M \cdot A^b)((g^b)^a)^{-1} \\
&= M \cdot (g^{ab})(g^{ab})^{-1} = M.
\end{aligned}$$

Security

Imagine an adversary who is interested in attacking an ElGamal scheme. This adversary sees the public key $A = g^a$ and a ciphertext (g^b, Mg^{ab}) go by. Intuitively, the Decisional Diffie-Hellman assumption says that the value g^{ab} looks random, even to someone who has seen g^a and g^b. Thus, the message M is masked with a pseudorandom group element - as we've seen before, this is a lot like masking the message with a random pad as in one-time pad. The only change here is that instead of the xor operation, we are using the group operation in $\mathbb{G}$.

More formally, we can prove the security of ElGamal under the DDH assumption:

Claim 15.7:

If the DDH assumption in group $\mathbb{G}$ is true, then ElGamal in group $\mathbb{G}$ is CPA \$-secure.

Proof

It suffices to show that ElGamal has pseudorandom ciphertexts when the calling program sees only a single ciphertext. In other words, we will show that $\mathcal{L}_{\text{pk-ots \$-real}} \approx \mathcal{L}_{\text{pk-ots \$-rand}}$, where these libraries are the $\mathcal{L}_{\text{pk-cpa\$-}\star}$ libraries from Definition 15.2 but with the singleciphertext restriction used in Definition 15.4. It is left as an exercise to show that $\mathcal{L}_{\text{pk-ots\$-real}} \approx \mathcal{L}_{\text{pk-ots \$-rand}}$ implies CPA\$ security (which in turn implies CPA security); the proof is very similar to that of Claim 15.5.

The sequence of hybrid libraries is given below:

The starting point is the $\mathcal{L}_{\text{pk-ots\$-real}}$ library, shown here with the details of ElGamal filled in.

$\mathcal{L}_{\text{pk-ots\$-real}}$

$a \leftarrow \mathbb{Z}_n$
$A := g^a$
$count = 0$
 	
GETPK():
  return A
 	
QUERY($M \in \mathbb{G}$):
  $count : count + 1$
  if $count > 1$: return null
  $b \leftarrow \mathbb{Z}_n$
  $B := g^b$
  $X := M \cdot A^b$
  return (B, X)

The main body of query computes some intermediate values B and A^b. But since those lines are only reachable one time, it does not change anything to precompute them at initialization time.

```
a ← ℤn;  b ← ℤn
A := g^a;  B := g^b;  C := A^b
count = 0

GETPK():
  return A

QUERY(M ∈ 𝔾):
  count : count + 1
  if count > 1: return null
  X := M · C
  return (B, X)
```

We can factor out the generation of A; B;C in terms of the Ldh-real library from the Decisional Di_e-Hellman security de_nition (De_nition 14.5).

```
(A, B, C) ← DHQUERY()            ◇   ℒdh-real
count = 0                            DHQUERY():
                                       a, b ← ℤn
GETPK():                               return (g^a, g^b, g^ab)
  return A

QUERY(M ∈ 𝔾):
  count : count + 1
  if count > 1: return null
  X := M · C
  return (B, X)
```

Applying the security of DDH, we can replace $\mathcal{L}_{\text{dh-real}}$ with $\mathcal{L}_{\text{dh-rand}}$.

```
(A, B, C) ← DHQUERY()            ◇   ℒdh-rand
count = 0                            DHQUERY():
                                       a, b, c ← ℤn
GETPK():                               return (g^a, g^b, g^c)
  return A

QUERY(M ∈ 𝔾):
  count : count + 1
  if count > 1: return null
  X := M · C
  return (B, X)
```

The call to dHQUERY has been inlined.

```
a, b, c ← Z_n
A := g^a; B := g^b; C := g^c
count = 0

GETPK():
  return A

QUERY(M ∈ G):
  count : count + 1
  if count > 1: return null
  X := M · C
  return (B, X)
```

As before, since the main body of query is only reachable once, we can move the choice of B and C into that subroutine instead of at initialization time.

```
a ← Z_n
A := g^a
count = 0

GETPK():
  return A

QUERY(M ∈ G):
  count : count + 1
  if count > 1: return null
  b, c ← Z_n
  B := g^b;  C := g^c
  X := M · C
  return (B, X)
```

When b is sampled uniformly from $\mathbb{Z}_n$, the expression $B = g^b$ is a uniformly distributed element of $\mathbb{G}$. Also recall that when C is a uniformly distributed element of $\mathbb{G}$, then $M \cdot C$ is uniformly distributed - this is analogous to the one-time pad property (see Exercise 2.5). Applying this change gives the library to the left.

```
ℒ_pk-ots$-rand

a ← Z_n
A := g^a
count = 0

GETPK():
  return A

QUERY(M ∈ G):
  count : count + 1
  if count > 1: return null
  b, x ← Z_n
  B := g^b;  X := g^x
  return (B, X)
```

In the final hybrid, the response to query is a pair of uniformly distributed group elements (B, X). Hence that library is exactly $\mathcal{L}_{\text{pk-ots\$-rand}}$, as desired.

15.4 Hybrid Encryption

As a rule, public-key encryption schemes are much more computationally expensive than symmetric-key schemes. Taking ElGamal as a representative example, computing g^b in a cryptographically secure cyclic group is considerably more expensive than one evaluation of AES. As the plaintext data increases in length, the difference in cost between public-key and symmetric-key techniques only gets worse.

A clever way to minimize the cost of public-key cryptography is to use a method called hybrid encryption. The idea is to use the expensive public-key scheme to encrypt a temporary key for a symmetric-key scheme. Then use the temporary key to (cheaply) encrypt the large plaintext data.

To decrypt, one can use the decryption key of the public-key scheme to obtain the temporary key. Then the temporary key can be used to decrypt the main payload.

Construction 15.8 (Hybrid Enc)

Let Σ_{pub} be a public-key encryption scheme, and let Σ_{sym} be a symmetric-key encryption scheme, where $\Sigma_{sym} \cdot \mathcal{K} \subseteq \Sigma_{pub} \cdot \mathcal{M}$ - that is, the public-key scheme is capable of encrypting keys of the symmetric-key scheme.

Then we define Σ_{hyb} to be the following construction:

$\mathcal{M} = \Sigma_{sym}.\mathcal{M}$
$\mathcal{C} = \Sigma_{pub}.\mathcal{C} \times \Sigma_{sym}.\mathcal{C}$

KeyGen:
$(pk, sk) \leftarrow \Sigma_{\text{pub}}.\text{KeyGen}$
return (pk, sk)

Enc(pk, m):
$tk \leftarrow \Sigma_{\text{sym}}.\text{KeyGen}$
$c_{\text{pub}} \leftarrow \Sigma_{\text{pub}}.\text{Enc}(pk, tk)$
$c_{\text{sym}} \leftarrow \Sigma_{\text{sym}}.\text{Enc}(tk, m)$
return $(c_{\text{pub}}, c_{\text{sym}})$

Dec$(sk, (c_{\text{pub}}, c_{\text{sym}}))$:
$tk := \Sigma_{\text{pub}}.\text{Dec}(sk, c_{\text{pub}})$
return $\Sigma_{\text{sym}}.\text{Dec}(tk, c_{\text{sym}})$

Importantly, the message space of the hybrid encryption scheme is the message space of the symmetric-key scheme (think of this as involving very long plaintexts), but encryption and decryption involves expensive public-key operations only on a small temporary key (think of this as a very short string).

The correctness of the scheme can be verified via:

$$\begin{aligned}
\text{Dec}(sk, \text{Enc}(pk, m)) &= \text{Dec}\Big(sk, (\Sigma_{\text{pub}} \cdot \text{Enc}(pk, tk), \Sigma_{\text{sym}} \cdot \text{Enc}(tk, m))\Big) \\
&= \Sigma_{\text{sym}} \cdot \text{Dec}\big(\Sigma_{\text{pub}} \cdot \text{Dec}\big(sk, \Sigma_{\text{pub}} \cdot \text{Enc}(pk, tk)\big), \Sigma_{\text{sym}} \cdot \text{Enc}(tk, m)\big) \\
&= \Sigma_{\text{sym}} \cdot \text{Dec}\big(tk, \Sigma_{\text{sym}} \cdot \text{Enc}(tk, m)\big) \\
&= m
\end{aligned}$$

To show that hybrid encryption is a valid way to encrypt data, we prove that it provides CPA security, when its two components have appropriate security properties:

Claim 15.9

If Σ_{sym} is a one-time-secret symmetric-key encryption scheme and Σ_{pub} is a CPA-secure publickey encryption scheme, then the hybrid scheme Σ_{hyb} (Construction 15.8) is also a CPA-secure public-key encryption scheme.

Note that Σ_{sym} does not even need to be CPA-secure. Intuitively, one-time secrecy suffices because each temporary key tk is used only once to encrypt just a single plaintext.

Proof: As usual, our goal is to show that $\mathcal{L}^{\Sigma_{\text{hyb}}}_{\text{pk-cpa-L}} \approx \mathcal{L}^{\Sigma_{\text{hyb}}}_{\text{pk-cpa-R}}$, which we do in a standard sequence of hybrids:

The starting point is $\mathcal{L}_{\text{pk-cpa-L}}$, shown here with the details of Σ_{hyb} filled in.

$\mathcal{L}^{\Sigma_{\text{hyb}}}_{\text{pk-cpa-L}}$
$(pk, sk) \leftarrow \Sigma_{\text{pub}}.\text{KeyGen}$
GETPK():
return pk
CHALLENGE(m_L, m_R):
$tk \leftarrow \Sigma_{\text{sym}}.\text{KeyGen}$
$c_{\text{pub}} \leftarrow \Sigma_{\text{pub}}.\text{Enc}(pk, tk)$
$c_{\text{sym}} \leftarrow \Sigma_{\text{sym}}.\text{Enc}(tk, m_L)$
return $(c_{\text{pub}}, c_{\text{sym}})$

Our only goal is to somehow replace m_L with m_R. Since m_L is only used as a plaintext for Σ_{sym}, it is tempting to simply apply the one-time-secrecy property of Σ_{sym} to argue that m_L can be replaced with m_R. Unfortunately, this cannot work because the key used for that ciphertext is tk, which is used elsewhere. In particular, it is used as an argument to Σ_{pub}.Enc.

However, using tk as the plaintext argument to Σ_{pub}. Enc should hide tk to the calling program, if Σ_{pub} is CPA-secure. That is, the Σ_{pub}-encryption of tk should look like a Σ_{pub} encryption of some unrelated dummy value. More formally, we can factor out the call to Σ_{pub}. Enc in terms of the $\mathcal{L}_{\text{pk-cpa-L}}$ library, as follows:

```
CHALLENGE(m_L, m_R):
  tk  ← Σ_sym.KeyGen
  tk' ← Σ_sym.KeyGen
  c_pub ← CHALLENGE'(tk, tk')
  c_sym ← Σ_sym.Enc(tk, m_L)
  return (c_pub, c_sym)
```

$\diamond$

```
L^{Σ_pub}_{pk-cpa-L}
(pk, sk) ← Σ_pub.KeyGen

GETPK():
  return pk

CHALLENGE'(tk_L, tk_R):
  return Σ_pub.Enc(pk, tk_L)
```

Here we have changed the variable names of the arguments of challenge' to avoid unnecessary confusion. Note also that challenge now chooses two temporary keys - one which is actually used to encrypt m_L and one which is not used anywhere. This is because syntactically we must have two arguments to pass into challenge'.

Now imagine replacing $\mathcal{L}_{\text{pk-cpa-L}}$ with $\mathcal{L}_{\text{pk-cpa-R}}$ and then inlining subroutine calls. The result is:

```
(pk, sk) ← Σ_pub.KeyGen

GETPK():
  return pk

CHALLENGE(m_L, m_R):
  tk  ← Σ_sym.KeyGen
  tk' ← Σ_sym.KeyGen
  c_pub ← Σ_pub.Enc(pk, tk')
  c_sym ← Σ_sym.Enc(tk, m_L)
  return (c_pub, c_sym)
```

At this point, it does now work to factor out the call to Σ_{sym}. Enc in terms of the $\mathcal{L}_{\text{ots-L}}$ library. This is because the key tk is not used anywhere else in the library. The result of factoring out in this way is:

```
(pk, sk) ← Σpub.KeyGen

GETPK():
  return pk

CHALLENGE(mL, mR):
  tk' ← Σsym.KeyGen
  cpub ← Σpub.Enc(pk, tk')
  csym ← CHALLENGE'(mL, mR)
  return (cpub, csym)
```

$\diamond$

```
L_ots-L^Σsym

CHALLENGE'(mL, mR):
  tk ← Σsym.KeyGen
  return Σsym.Enc(tk, mL)
```

At this point, we can replace $\mathcal{L}_{\text{ots-L}}$ with $\mathcal{L}_{\text{ots-R}}$. After this change the Σ_{sym}-ciphertext encrypts m_R instead of m_L. This is the "half-way point" of the proof, and the rest of the steps are a mirror image of what has come before. In summary: we inline $\mathcal{L}_{\text{ots-R}}$, then we apply CPA security to replace the Σ_{pub}-encryption of tk' with tk. The result is exactly $\mathcal{L}_{\text{pk-cpa-R}}$, as desired. □

Exercises

15.1. Prove Claim 15.3.

15.2. Show that a 2 -message key-agreement protocol exists if and only if CPA-secure public-key encryption exists.

In other words, show how to construct a CPA-secure encryption scheme from any 2 message KA protocol, and vice-versa. Prove the security of your constructions.

15.3. (a) Suppose you are given an ElGamal encryption of an unknown plaintext $M \in \mathbb{G}$. Show how to construct a different ciphertext that also decrypts to the same M.

(b) Suppose you are given two ElGamal encryptions, of unknown plaintexts $M_1, M_2 \in \mathbb{G}$. Show how to construct a ciphertext that decrypts to their product $M_1 \cdot M_2$.

15.4. Suppose you obtain two ElGamal ciphertexts $(B_1, C_1), (B_2, C_2)$ that encrypt unknown plaintexts M_1 and M_2. Suppose you also know the public key A and cyclic group generator g.

(a) What information can you infer about M_1 and M_2 if you observe that $B_1 = B_2$?

(b) What information can you infer about M_1 and M_2 if you observe that $B_1 = g \cdot B_2$?

(c) What information can you infer about M_1 and M_2 if you observe that $B_1 = (B_2)^2$?

Index of Security Definitions

One-time uniform ciphertexts for symmetric-key encryption (Definition 2.5):

$\mathcal{L}^{\Sigma}_{\text{ots\$-real}}$	$\mathcal{L}^{\Sigma}_{\text{ots\$-rand}}$
$\text{CTXT}(m \in \Sigma.\mathcal{M})$: $\quad k \leftarrow \Sigma.\mathsf{KeyGen}$ $\quad c \leftarrow \Sigma.\mathsf{Enc}(k, m)$ $\quad$ return c	$\text{CTXT}(m \in \Sigma.\mathcal{M})$: $\quad c \leftarrow \Sigma.\mathcal{C}$ $\quad$ return c

One-time secrecy for symmetric-key encryption (Definition 2.6):

$\mathcal{L}^{\Sigma}_{\text{ots-L}}$	$\mathcal{L}^{\Sigma}_{\text{ots-R}}$
$\text{EAVESDROP}(m_L, m_R \in \Sigma.\mathcal{M})$: $\quad k \leftarrow \Sigma.\mathsf{KeyGen}$ $\quad c \leftarrow \Sigma.\mathsf{Enc}(k, m_L)$ $\quad$ return c	$\text{EAVESDROP}(m_L, m_R \in \Sigma.\mathcal{M})$: $\quad k \leftarrow \Sigma.\mathsf{KeyGen}$ $\quad c \leftarrow \Sigma.\mathsf{Enc}(k, m_R)$ $\quad$ return c

t-out-of- n secret sharing (Definition 3.3):

$\mathcal{L}^{\Sigma}_{\text{tsss-L}}$	$\mathcal{L}^{\Sigma}_{\text{tsss-R}}$
$\text{SHARE}(m_L, m_R \in \Sigma.\mathcal{M}, U)$: $\quad$ if $\lvert U \rvert \geqslant \Sigma.t$: return $\mathtt{err}$ $\quad s \leftarrow \Sigma.\mathsf{Share}(m_L)$ $\quad$ return $\{s_i \mid i \in U\}$	$\text{SHARE}(m_L, m_R \in \Sigma.\mathcal{M}, U)$: $\quad$ if $\lvert U \rvert \geqslant \Sigma.t$: return $\mathtt{err}$ $\quad s \leftarrow \Sigma.\mathsf{Share}(m_R)$ $\quad$ return $\{s_i \mid i \in U\}$

Pseudorandom generator (Definition 5.1):

$\mathcal{L}^{G}_{\text{prg-real}}$	$\mathcal{L}^{G}_{\text{prg-rand}}$
$\text{QUERY}()$: $\quad s \leftarrow \{\mathtt{0},\mathtt{1}\}^{\lambda}$ $\quad$ return $G(s)$	$\text{QUERY}()$: $\quad r \leftarrow \{\mathtt{0},\mathtt{1}\}^{\lambda+\ell}$ $\quad$ return r

Pseudorandom function (Definition 6.1):

$\mathcal{L}^{F}_{\text{prf-real}}$

$k \leftarrow \{0,1\}^{\lambda}$

<u>LOOKUP($x \in \{0,1\}^{in}$):</u>
  return $F(k, x)$

$\mathcal{L}^{F}_{\text{prf-rand}}$

T := empty assoc. array

<u>LOOKUP($x \in \{0,1\}^{in}$):</u>
  if $T[x]$ undefined:
    $T[x] \leftarrow \{0,1\}^{out}$
  return $T[x]$

Pseudorandom permutation (Definition 6.6):

$\mathcal{L}^{F}_{\text{prp-real}}$

$k \leftarrow \{0,1\}^{\lambda}$

<u>LOOKUP($x \in \{0,1\}^{blen}$):</u>
  return $F(k, x)$

$\mathcal{L}^{F}_{\text{prp-rand}}$

T := empty assoc. array

<u>LOOKUP($x \in \{0,1\}^{blen}$):</u>
  if $T[x]$ undefined:
    $T[x] \leftarrow \{0,1\}^{blen} \setminus T.\text{values}$
  return $T[x]$

Strong pseudorandom permutation (Definition 6.13):

$\mathcal{L}^{F}_{\text{sprp-real}}$

$k \leftarrow \{0,1\}^{\lambda}$

<u>LOOKUP($x \in \{0,1\}^{blen}$):</u>
  return $F(k, x)$

<u>INVLOOKUP($y \in \{0,1\}^{blen}$):</u>
  return $F^{-1}(k, y)$

$\mathcal{L}^{F}_{\text{sprp-rand}}$

T, T_{inv} := empty assoc. arrays

<u>LOOKUP($x \in \{0,1\}^{blen}$):</u>
  if $T[x]$ undefined:
    $y \leftarrow \{0,1\}^{blen} \setminus T.\text{values}$
    $T[x] := y; \quad T_{inv}[y] := x$
  return $T[x]$

<u>INVLOOKUP($y \in \{0,1\}^{blen}$):</u>
  if $T_{inv}[y]$ undefined:
    $x \leftarrow \{0,1\}^{blen} \setminus T_{inv}.\text{values}$
    $T_{inv}[y] := x; \quad T[x] := y$
  return $T_{inv}[y]$

CPA security for symmetric-key encryption (Definition 7.1, Section 8.2):

$\mathcal{L}^{\Sigma}_{\text{cpa-L}}$

```
k ← Σ.KeyGen

EAVESDROP(m_L, m_R ∈ Σ.M):
  if |m_L| ≠ |m_R| return err
  c := Σ.Enc(k, m_L)
  return c
```

$\mathcal{L}^{\Sigma}_{\text{cpa-R}}$

```
k ← Σ.KeyGen

EAVESDROP(m_L, m_R ∈ Σ.M):
  if |m_L| ≠ |m_R| return err
  c := Σ.Enc(k, m_R)
  return c
```

CPA$ security for symmetric-key encryption (Definition 7.2, Section 8.2):

$\mathcal{L}^{\Sigma}_{\text{cpa\$-real}}$

```
k ← Σ.KeyGen

CHALLENGE(m ∈ Σ.M):
  c := Σ.Enc(k, m)
  return c
```

$\mathcal{L}^{\Sigma}_{\text{cpa\$-rand}}$

```
CHALLENGE(m ∈ Σ.M):
  c ← Σ.C(|m|)
  return c
```

CCA security for symmetric-key encryption (Definition 9.1):

$\mathcal{L}^{\Sigma}_{\text{cca-L}}$

```
k ← Σ.KeyGen
S := ∅

EAVESDROP(m_L, m_R ∈ Σ.M):
  if |m_L| ≠ |m_R| return err
  c := Σ.Enc(k, m_L)
  S := S ∪ {c}
  return c

DECRYPT(c ∈ Σ.C):
  if c ∈ S return err
  return Σ.Dec(k, c)
```

$\mathcal{L}^{\Sigma}_{\text{cca-R}}$

```
k ← Σ.KeyGen
S := ∅

EAVESDROP(m_L, m_R ∈ Σ.M):
  if |m_L| ≠ |m_R| return err
  c := Σ.Enc(k, m_R)
  S := S ∪ {c}
  return c

DECRYPT(c ∈ Σ.C):
  if c ∈ S return err
  return Σ.Dec(k, c)
```

CCA$ security for symmetric-key encryption (Definition 9.2):

$\mathcal{L}^{\Sigma}_{\text{cca\$-real}}$	$\mathcal{L}^{\Sigma}_{\text{cca\$-rand}}$
$k \leftarrow \Sigma.\text{KeyGen}$ $\mathcal{S} := \emptyset$ $\text{CTXT}(m \in \Sigma.\mathcal{M})$: $\quad c := \Sigma.\text{Enc}(k, m)$ $\quad \mathcal{S} := \mathcal{S} \cup \{c\}$ $\quad$ return c $\text{DECRYPT}(c \in \Sigma.\mathcal{C})$: $\quad$ if $c \in \mathcal{S}$ return `err` $\quad$ return $\Sigma.\text{Dec}(k, c)$	$k \leftarrow \Sigma.\text{KeyGen}$ $\mathcal{S} := \emptyset$ $\text{CTXT}(m \in \Sigma.\mathcal{M})$: $\quad c \leftarrow \Sigma.\mathcal{C}(\lvert m \rvert)$ $\quad \mathcal{S} := \mathcal{S} \cup \{c\}$ $\quad$ return c $\text{DECRYPT}(c \in \Sigma.\mathcal{C})$: $\quad$ if $c \in \mathcal{S}$ return `err` $\quad$ return $\Sigma.\text{Dec}(k, c)$

MAC (Definition 10.2):

$\mathcal{L}^{\Sigma}_{\text{mac-real}}$	$\mathcal{L}^{\Sigma}_{\text{mac-fake}}$
$k \leftarrow \Sigma.\text{KeyGen}$ $\text{GETTAG}(m \in \Sigma.\mathcal{M})$: $\quad$ return $\Sigma.\text{MAC}(k, m)$ $\text{CHECKTAG}(m \in \Sigma.\mathcal{M}, t)$: $\quad$ return $t \stackrel{?}{=} \Sigma.\text{MAC}(k, m)$	$k \leftarrow \Sigma.\text{KeyGen}$ $\mathcal{T} := \emptyset$ $\text{GETTAG}(m \in \Sigma.\mathcal{M})$: $\quad t := \Sigma.\text{MAC}(k, m)$ $\quad \mathcal{T} := \mathcal{T} \cup \{(m, t)\}$ $\quad$ return t $\text{CHECKTAG}(m \in \Sigma.\mathcal{M}, t)$: $\quad$ return $(m, t) \stackrel{?}{\in} \mathcal{T}$

Collision resistance (Definition 11.1):

$\mathcal{L}^{\mathcal{H}}_{\text{cr-real}}$	$\mathcal{L}^{\mathcal{H}}_{\text{cr-fake}}$
$s \leftarrow \{0,1\}^{\lambda}$ $\text{GETSALT}()$: $\quad$ return s $\text{TEST}(x, x' \in \{0,1\}^*)$: $\quad$ if $x \neq x'$ and $H(s, x) = H(s, x')$: return `true` $\quad$ return `false`	$s \leftarrow \{0,1\}^{\lambda}$ $\text{GETSALT}()$: $\quad$ return s $\text{TEST}(x, x' \in \{0,1\}^*)$: $\quad$ return `false`

Digital signatures (Definition 13.6):

$\mathcal{L}^{\Sigma}_{\text{sig-real}}$

```
(vk, sk) ← Σ.KeyGen

GETVK():
  return vk

GETSIG(m):
  return Σ.Sign(sk, m)

VERSIG(m, σ):
  return Σ.Ver(vk, m, σ)
```

$\mathcal{L}^{\Sigma}_{\text{sig-fake}}$

```
(vk, sk) ← Σ.KeyGen
S := ∅

GETVK():
  return vk

GETSIG(m):
  σ := Σ.Sign(sk, m)
  S := S ∪ {(m, σ)}
  return σ

VERSIG(m, σ):
  return (m, σ) ∈? S
```

Key agreement (Definition 14.4):

$\mathcal{L}^{\Sigma}_{\text{ka-real}}$

```
QUERY():
  (t, K) ← EXECPROT(Σ)
  return (t, K)
```

$\mathcal{L}^{\Sigma}_{\text{ka-rand}}$

```
QUERY():
  (t, K) ← EXECPROT(Σ)
  K' ← Σ.K
  return (t, K')
```

Decisional Diffie-Hellman assumption (Definition 14.5):

$\mathcal{L}^{\mathbb{G}}_{\text{dh-real}}$

```
QUERY():
  a, b ← Z_n
  return (g^a, g^b, g^ab)
```

$\mathcal{L}^{\mathbb{G}}_{\text{dh-rand}}$

```
QUERY():
  a, b, c ← Z_n
  return (g^a, g^b, g^c)
```

CPA security for public-key encryption (Definition 15.1):

$\mathcal{L}^{\Sigma}_{\text{pk-cpa-L}}$

```
(pk, sk) ← Σ.KeyGen

GETPK():
  return pk

CHALLENGE(m_L, m_R ∈ Σ.M):
  return Σ.Enc(pk, m_L)
```

$\mathcal{L}^{\Sigma}_{\text{pk-cpa-R}}$

```
(pk, sk) ← Σ.KeyGen

GETPK():
  return pk

CHALLENGE(m_L, m_R ∈ Σ.M):
  return Σ.Enc(pk, m_R)
```

CPA$ security for public-key encryption (Definition 15.2):

$\mathcal{L}^{\Sigma}_{\text{pk-cpa\$-real}}$
$(pk, sk) \leftarrow \Sigma.\text{KeyGen}$
GETPK():
return pk
CHALLENGE($m \in \Sigma.\mathcal{M}$):
return $\Sigma.\text{Enc}(pk, m)$

$\mathcal{L}^{\Sigma}_{\text{pk-cpa\$-rand}}$
$(pk, sk) \leftarrow \Sigma.\text{KeyGen}$
GETPK():
return pk
CHALLENGE($m \in \Sigma.\mathcal{M}$):
$c \leftarrow \Sigma.\mathcal{C}$
return c

One-time secrecy for public-key encryption (Definition 15.4):

$\mathcal{L}^{\Sigma}_{\text{pk-ots-L}}$
$(pk, sk) \leftarrow \Sigma.\text{KeyGen}$
$count := 0$
GETPK():
return pk
CHALLENGE($m_L, m_R \in \Sigma.\mathcal{M}$):
$count := count + 1$
if $count > 1$: return null
return $\Sigma.\text{Enc}(pk, m_L)$

$\mathcal{L}^{\Sigma}_{\text{pk-ots-R}}$
$(pk, sk) \leftarrow \Sigma.\text{KeyGen}$
$count := 0$
GETPK():
return pk
CHALLENGE($m_L, m_R \in \Sigma.\mathcal{M}$):
$count := count + 1$
if $count > 1$: return null
return $\Sigma.\text{Enc}(pk, m_R)$

Index